When I tried to break the old blade off, I broke the whole utility blade.

—*Hiromu Arakawa, 2007*

Born in Hokkaido (northern Japan), Hiromu Arakawa first attracted national attention in 1999 with her award-winning manga *Stray Dog*. Her series *Fullmetal Alchemist* debuted in 2001 in Square Enix's monthly manga anthology *Shonen Gangan*.

FULLMETAL ALCHEMIST
VOL. 17

Story and Art by Hiromu Arakawa

Translation/Akira Watanabe
English Adaptation/Jake Forbes
Touch-up Art & Lettering/Wayne Truman
Design/Florian Fangohr
Editor/Annette Roman

Editor in Chief, Books/Alvin Lu
Editor in Chief, Magazines/Marc Weidenbaum
VP of Publishing Licensing/Rika Inouye
VP of Sales/Gonzalo Ferreyra
Sr. VP of Marketing/Liza Coppola
Publisher/Hyoe Narita

Hagane no RenkinJutsushi vol. 17 © 2007 Hiromu Arakawa/SQUARE ENIX.
First published in Japan in 2007 by SQUARE ENIX CO., LTD. English translation
rights arranged with SQUARE ENIX CO., LTD. and VIZ Media, LLC. The stories,
characters and incidents mentioned in this publication are entirely fictional.

No portion of this book may be reproduced or transmitted in any form or by
any means without written permission from the copyright holders.

Printed in the U.S.A.

Published by VIZ Media, LLC
P.O. Box 77010
San Francisco, CA 94107

10 9 8 7 6 5 4 3 2 1
First printing, October 2008

PARENTAL ADVISORY
FULLMETAL ALCHEMIST is rated T for Teen and
is recommended for ages 13 and up. Contains mildly
strong language, tobacco/alcohol use and fantasy
violence.
ratings.viz.com

www.viz.com

store.viz.com

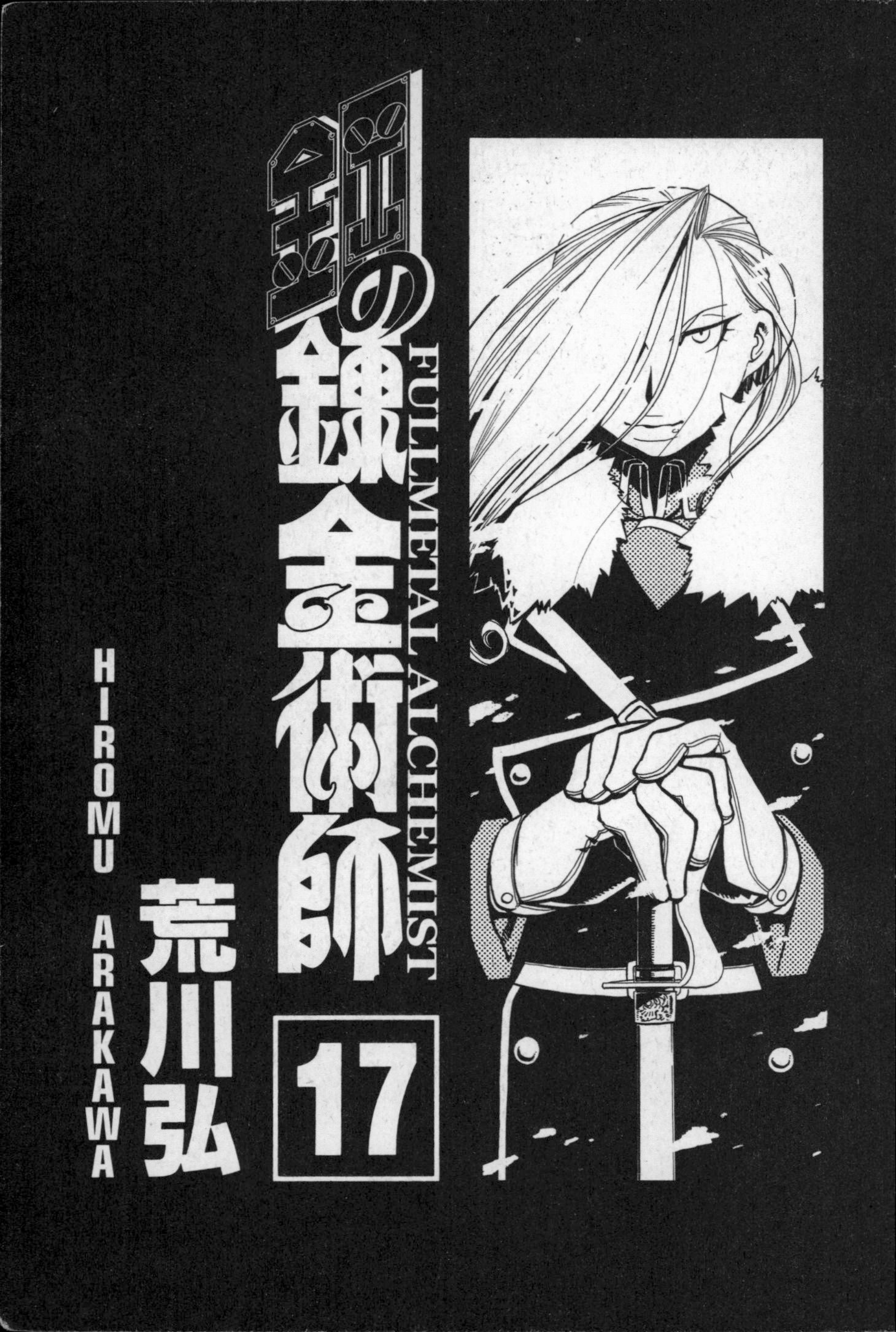

鋼の錬金術師

FULLMETAL ALCHEMIST

17

荒川弘

HIROMU ARAKAWA

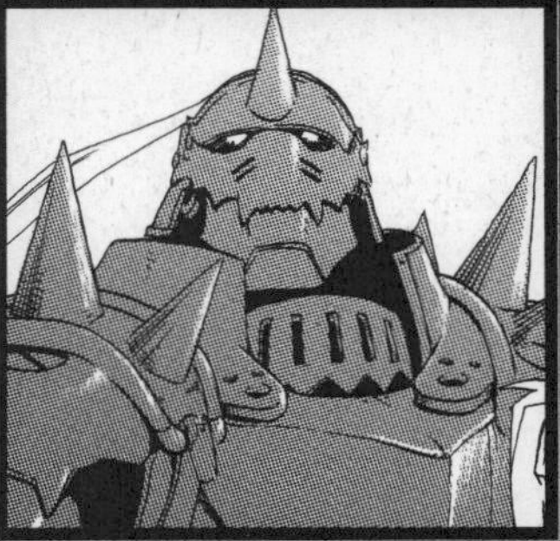

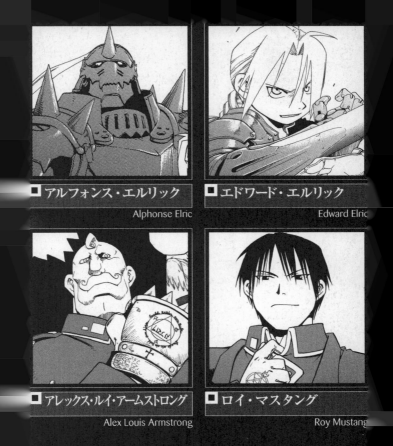

□アルフォンス・エルリック

Alphonse Elric

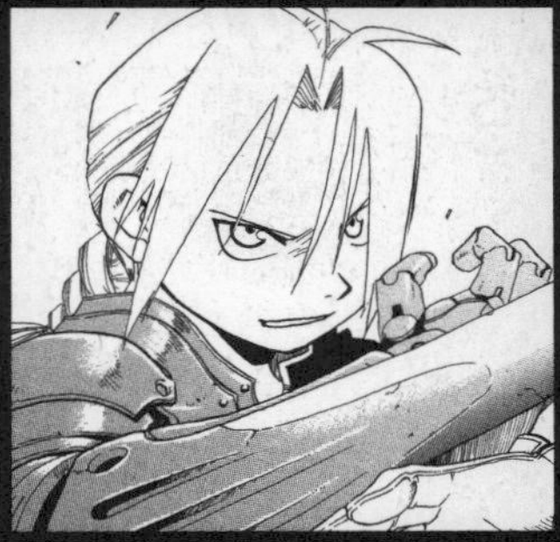

□エドワード・エルリック

Edward Elric

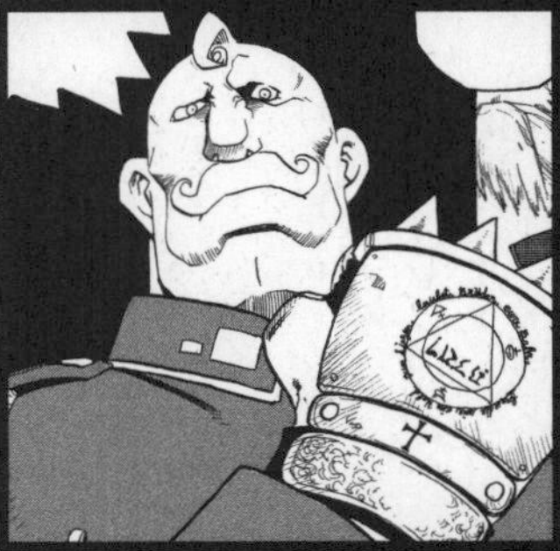

□アレックス・ルイ・アームストロング

Alex Louis Armstrong

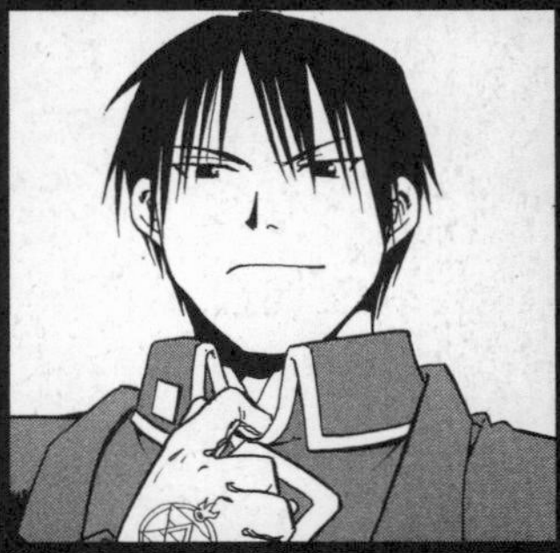

□ロイ・マスタング

Roy Mustang

UTLINE

LMETAL ALCHEMIST

forbidden alchemical ritual, the Elric Brothers attempted to bring their other back to life. But the ritual went wrong, consuming Edward Elric's l honse Elric's entire body. At the cost of his arm, Edward was able to gra her's soul into a suit of armor. Equipped with mechanical "auto-mail" to his missing limbs, Edward became a state alchemist, serving the military aming the world with his brother in search of the Philosopher's Stone, ndary substance with the power to restore what they have lost.

ects that the answers they seek might lie with the unique alchemy nded by the young girl May, from Xing, who travels with Scar. Tipped of y was spotted headed north, the Elric brothers set off for Briggs—the an military's northernmost outpost. But as Ed and Al quickly discover, t ng less forgiving than Briggs's weather is the regiment of hardened

鋼の錬金術師
FULLMETAL ALCHEMIST

CHARACTERS
FULLMETAL ALCHEMIST

□ ウィンリィ・ロックベル

Winry Rockbell

□ スカー

Scar

□ リザ・ホークアイ

Riza Hawkeye

□ キング・ブラッドレイ

King Bradley

□ ゾルフ・J・キンブリー

□ メイ・チャン

CONTENTS

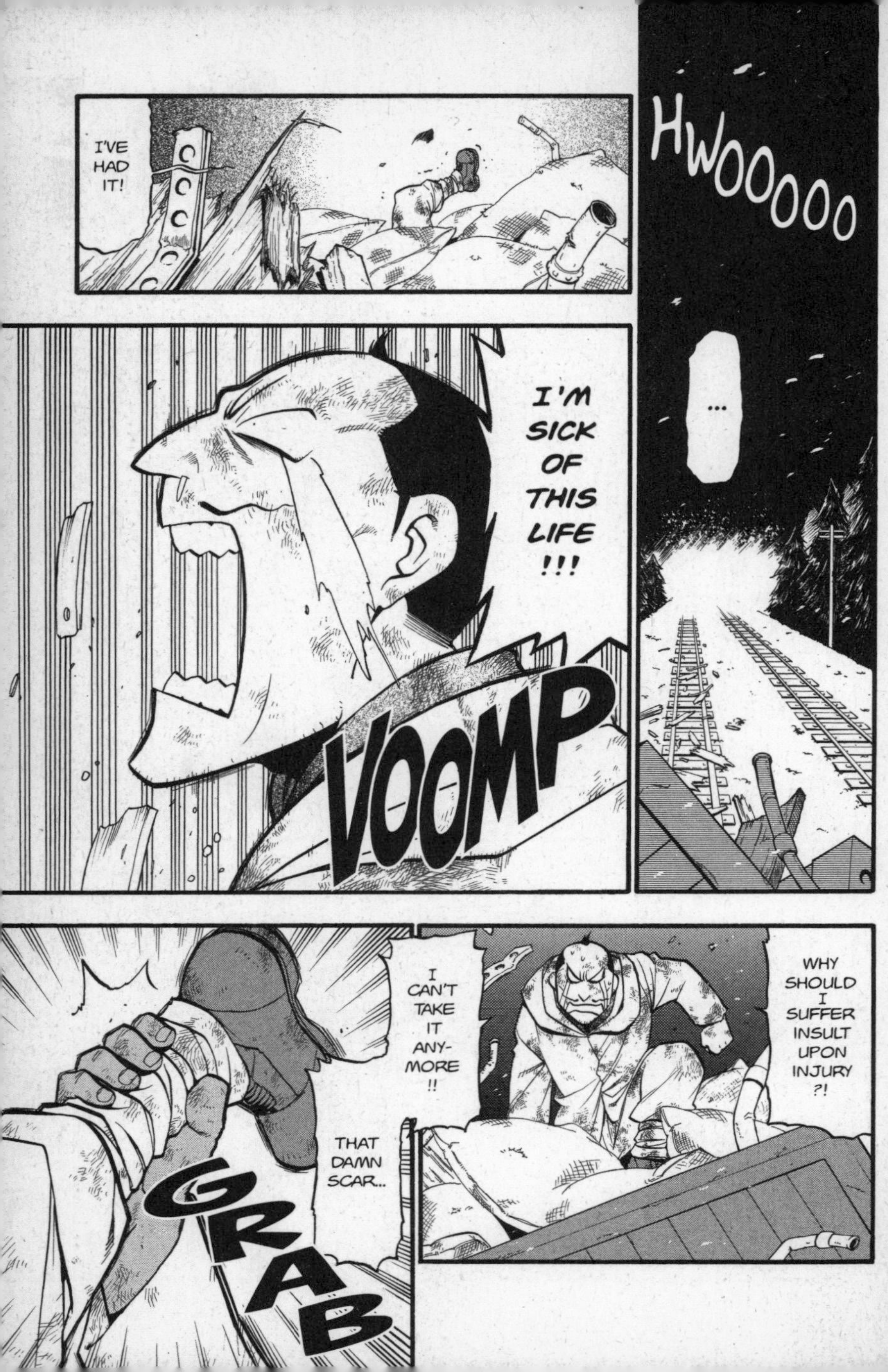
HWOOOOOO
...
I'VE HAD IT!
I'M SICK OF THIS LIFE!!!
VOOMP
WHY SHOULD I SUFFER INSULT UPON INJURY?!
I CAN'T TAKE IT ANYMORE!!
THAT DAMN SCAR...
GRAB

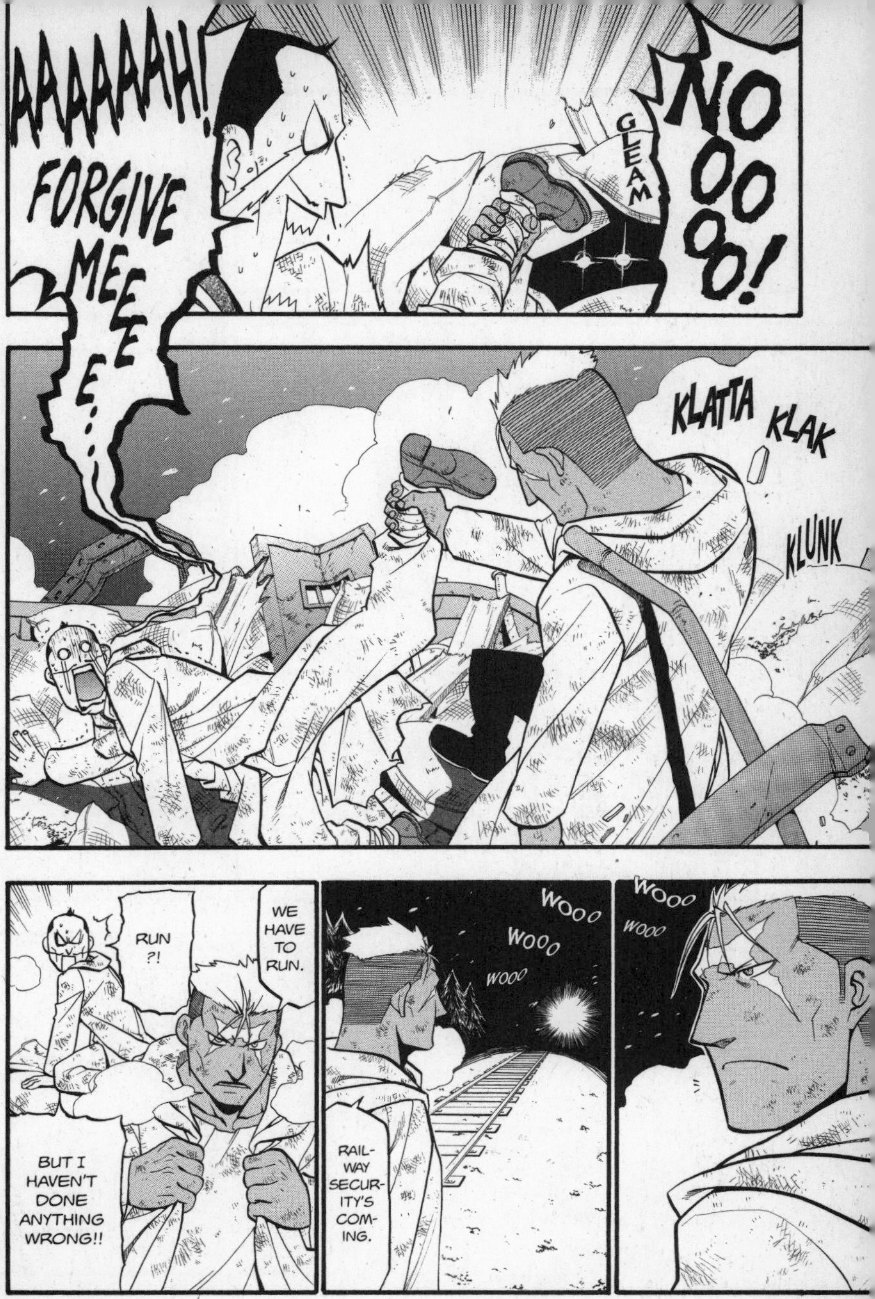
NOOOOOO!
GLEAM
AAAAAAH!
FORGIVE MEEEEE...
KLATTA KLAK
KLUNK
WOOO WOOO
WOOO WOOO WOOO
RAIL-WAY SECUR-ITY'S COM-ING.
WE HAVE TO RUN.
RUN ?!
BUT I HAVEN'T DONE ANYTHING WRONG!!

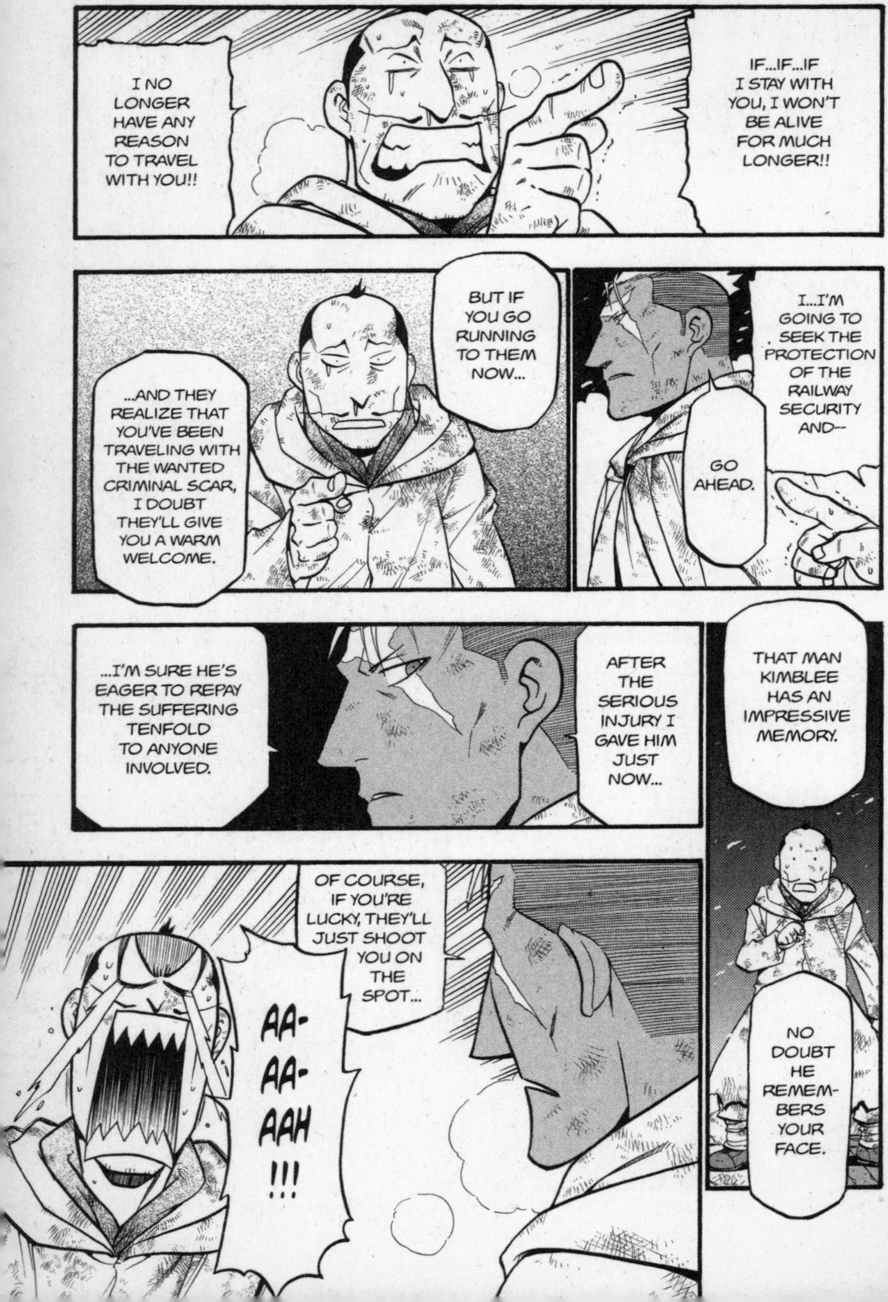
IF...IF...IF I STAY WITH YOU, I WON'T BE ALIVE FOR MUCH LONGER!!
I NO LONGER HAVE ANY REASON TO TRAVEL WITH YOU!!
I...I'M GOING TO SEEK THE PROTECTION OF THE RAILWAY SECURITY AND--
GO AHEAD.
BUT IF YOU GO RUNNING TO THEM NOW...
...AND THEY REALIZE THAT YOU'VE BEEN TRAVELING WITH THE WANTED CRIMINAL SCAR, I DOUBT THEY'LL GIVE YOU A WARM WELCOME.
THAT MAN KIMBLEE HAS AN IMPRESSIVE MEMORY.
NO DOUBT HE REMEM-BERS YOUR FACE.
AFTER THE SERIOUS INJURY I GAVE HIM JUST NOW...
...I'M SURE HE'S EAGER TO REPAY THE SUFFERING TENFOLD TO ANYONE INVOLVED.
OF COURSE, IF YOU'RE LUCKY, THEY'LL JUST SHOOT YOU ON THE SPOT...
AA-AA-AAH!!!

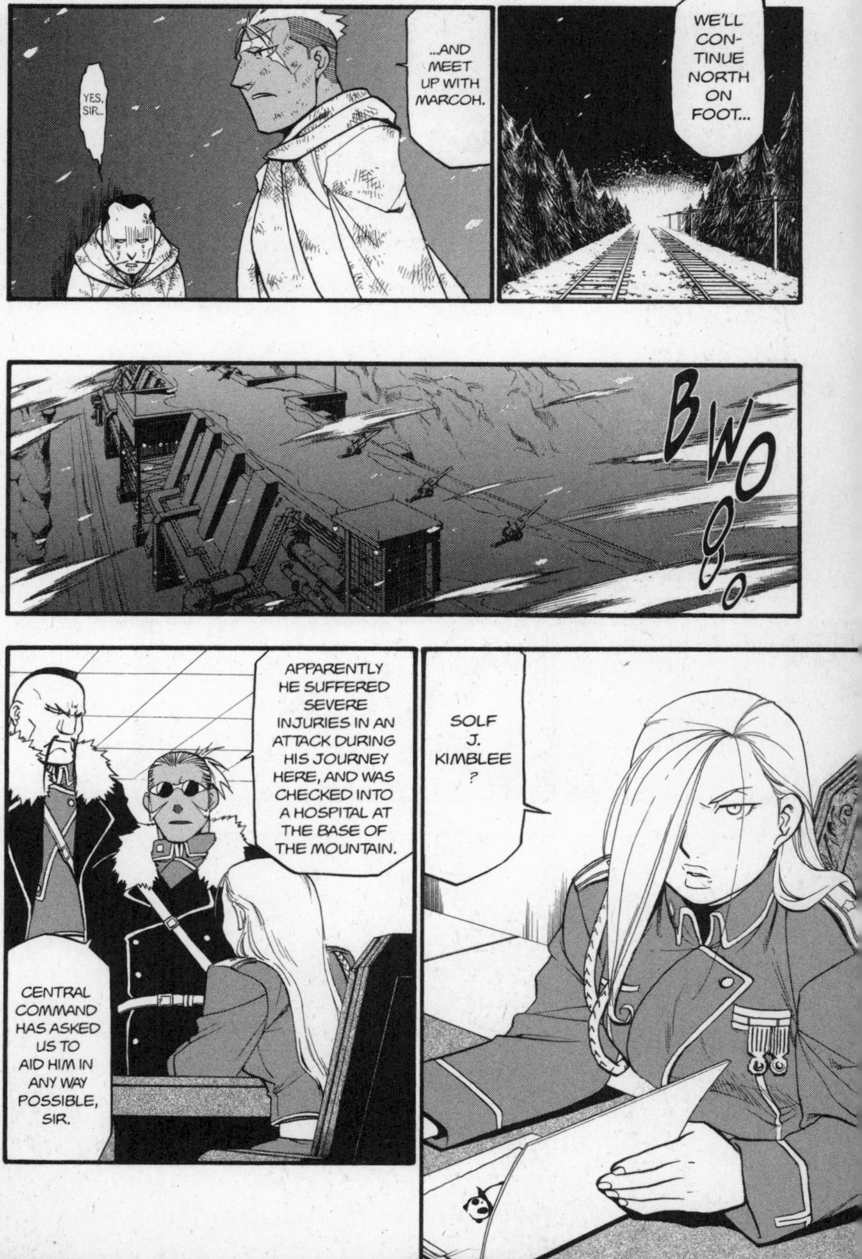
WE'LL CON- TINUE NORTH ON FOOT...
...AND MEET UP WITH MARCOH.
YES, SIR...
BWOOOO
SOLF J. KIMBLEE ?
APPARENTLY HE SUFFERED SEVERE INJURIES IN AN ATTACK DURING HIS JOURNEY HERE, AND WAS CHECKED INTO A HOSPITAL AT THE BASE OF THE MOUNTAIN.
CENTRAL COMMAND HAS ASKED US TO AID HIM IN ANY WAY POSSIBLE, SIR.

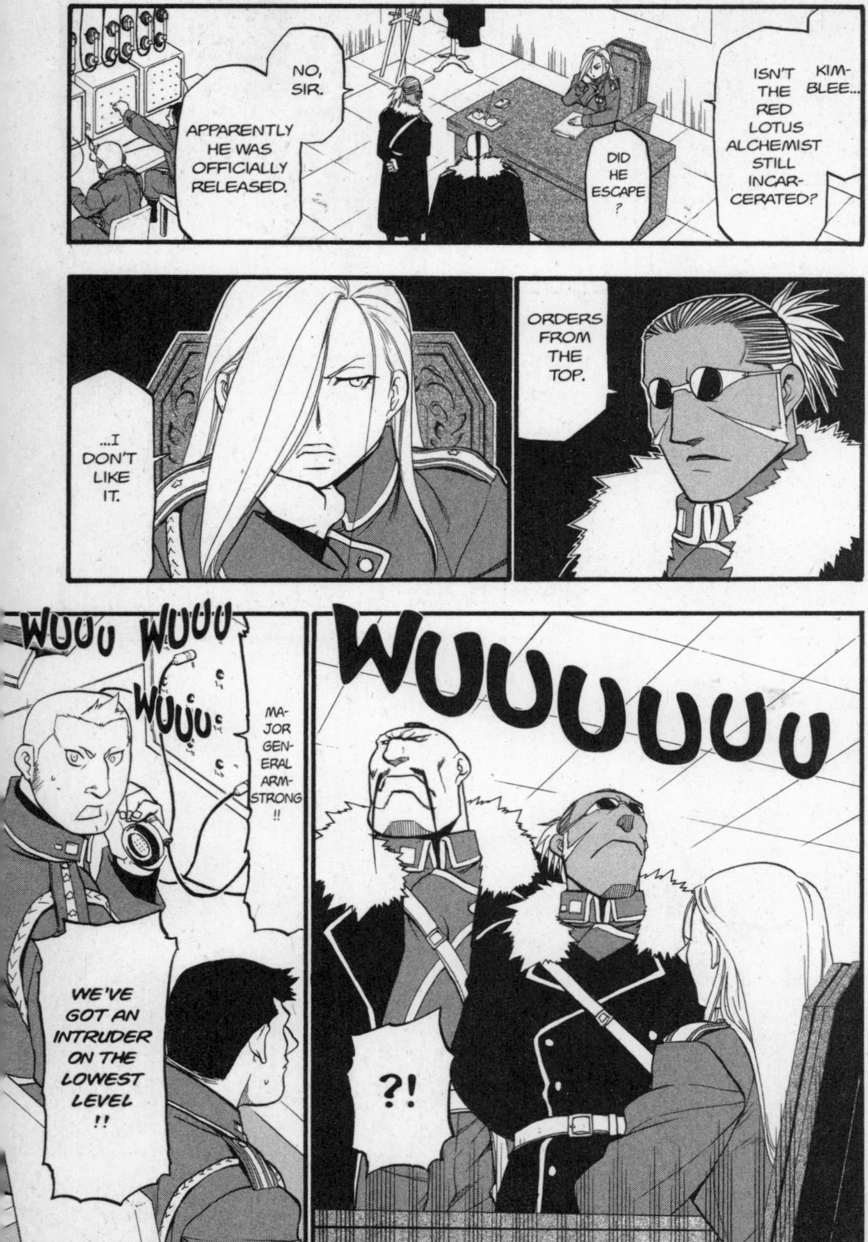
KIMBLEE...
ISN'T THE RED LOTUS ALCHEMIST STILL INCARCERATED?
DID HE ESCAPE?
NO, SIR.
APPARENTLY HE WAS OFFICIALLY RELEASED.
ORDERS FROM THE TOP.
...I DON'T LIKE IT.
WUUUUUUU
?!
WUUU WUUU
WUUU
MAJOR GENERAL ARMSTRONG!!
WE'VE GOT AN INTRUDER ON THE LOWEST LEVEL!!

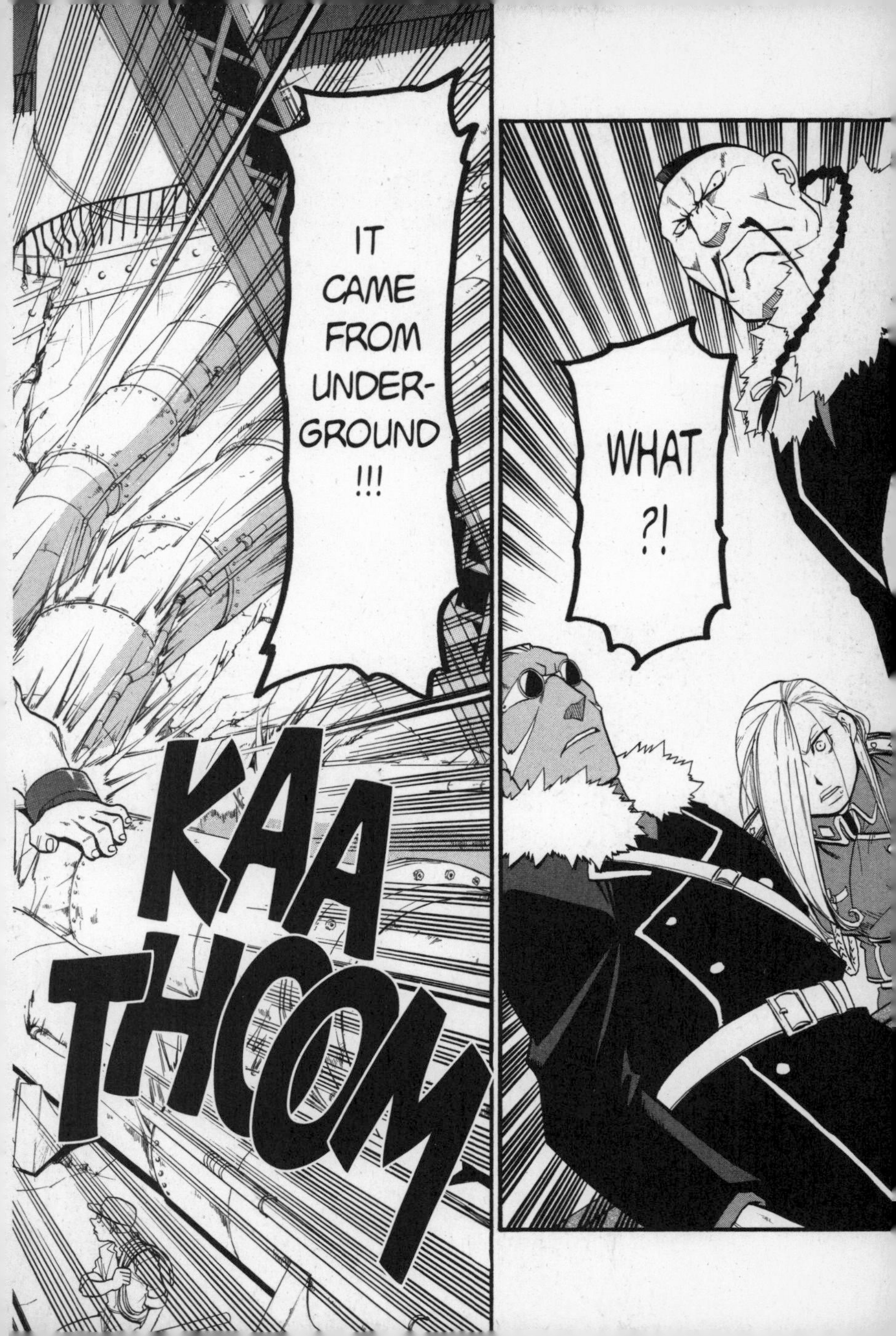
WHAT ?!
IT CAME FROM UNDER-GROUND !!!
KAA THOOM

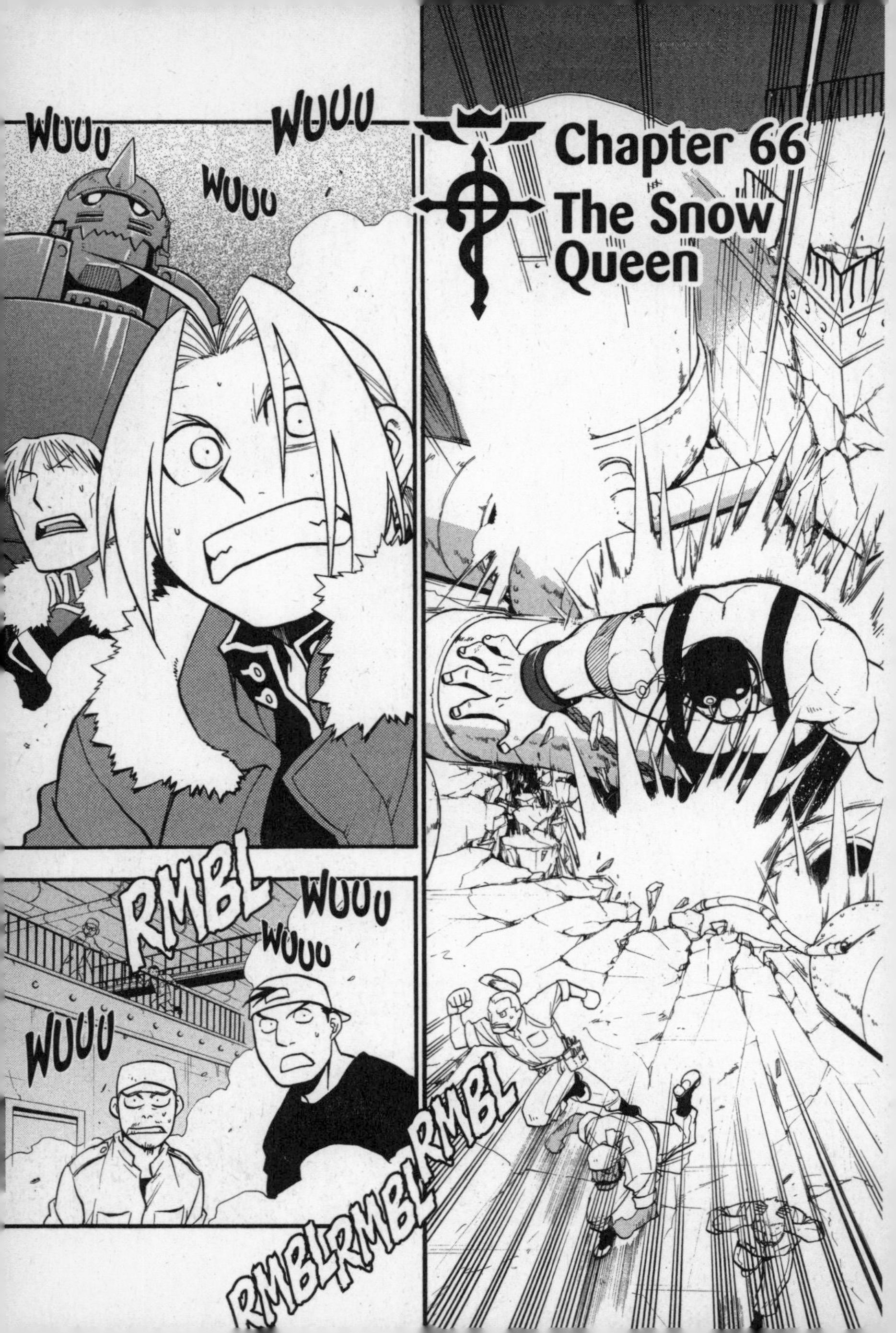
Chapter 66
The Snow Queen
RMBLRMBLRMBL
WUUU
WUUU
WUUU
WUUU
WUUU
RMBL
WUUU

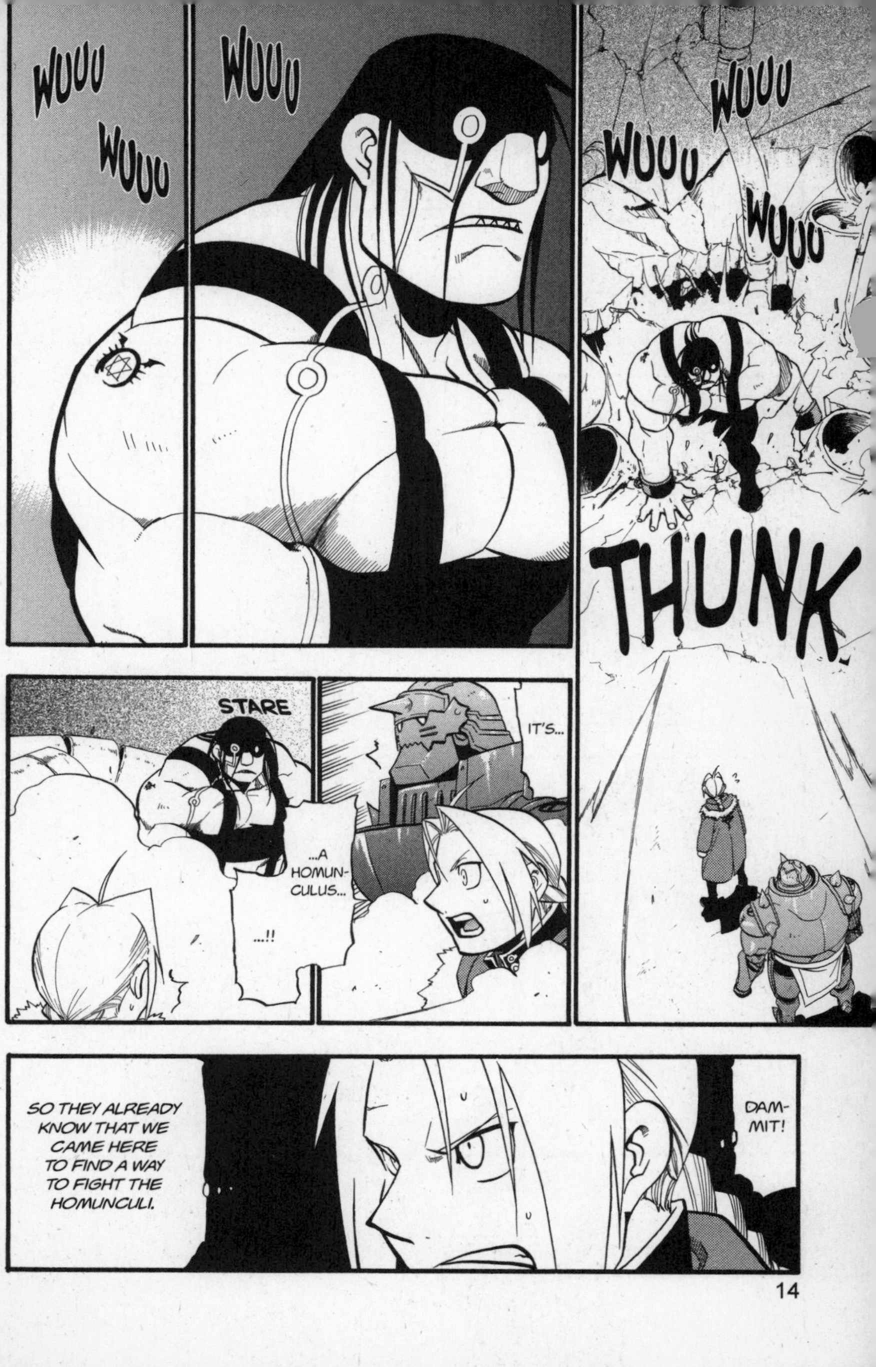
WUUU
WUUU
WUUU
THUNK
WUUU
WUUU
WUUU
IT'S...
...A HOMUN-CULUS...
...!!
STARE
DAM-MIT!
SO THEY ALREADY KNOW THAT WE CAME HERE TO FIND A WAY TO FIGHT THE HOMUNCULI.

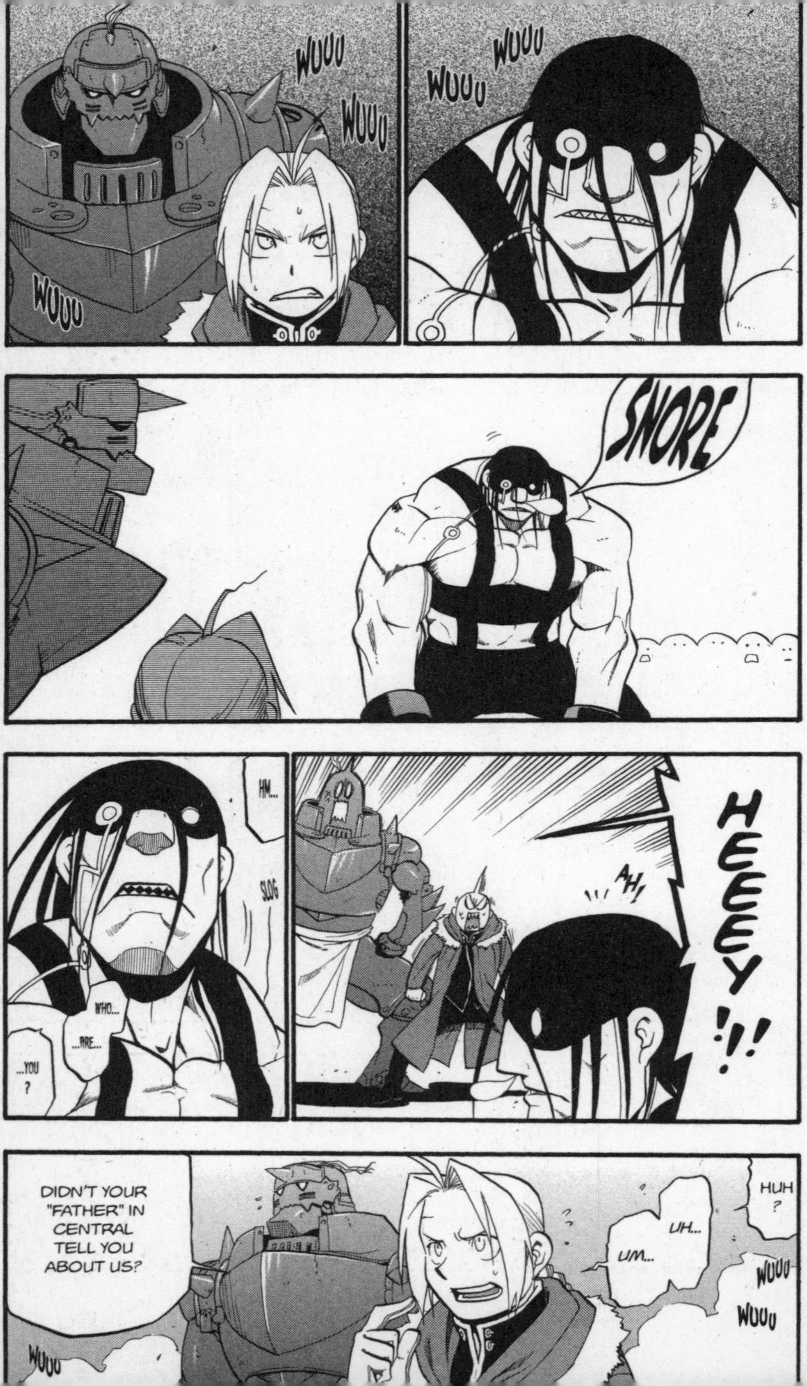
WUUU
WUUU
WUUU
WUUU
WUUU
SNORE
HEEEY!!!
AH!
HM...
SLOG
WHO...
...ARE...
...YOU ?
HUH ?
UH...
UM...
WUUU
WUUU
DIDN'T YOUR "FATHER" IN CENTRAL TELL YOU ABOUT US?
WUUU

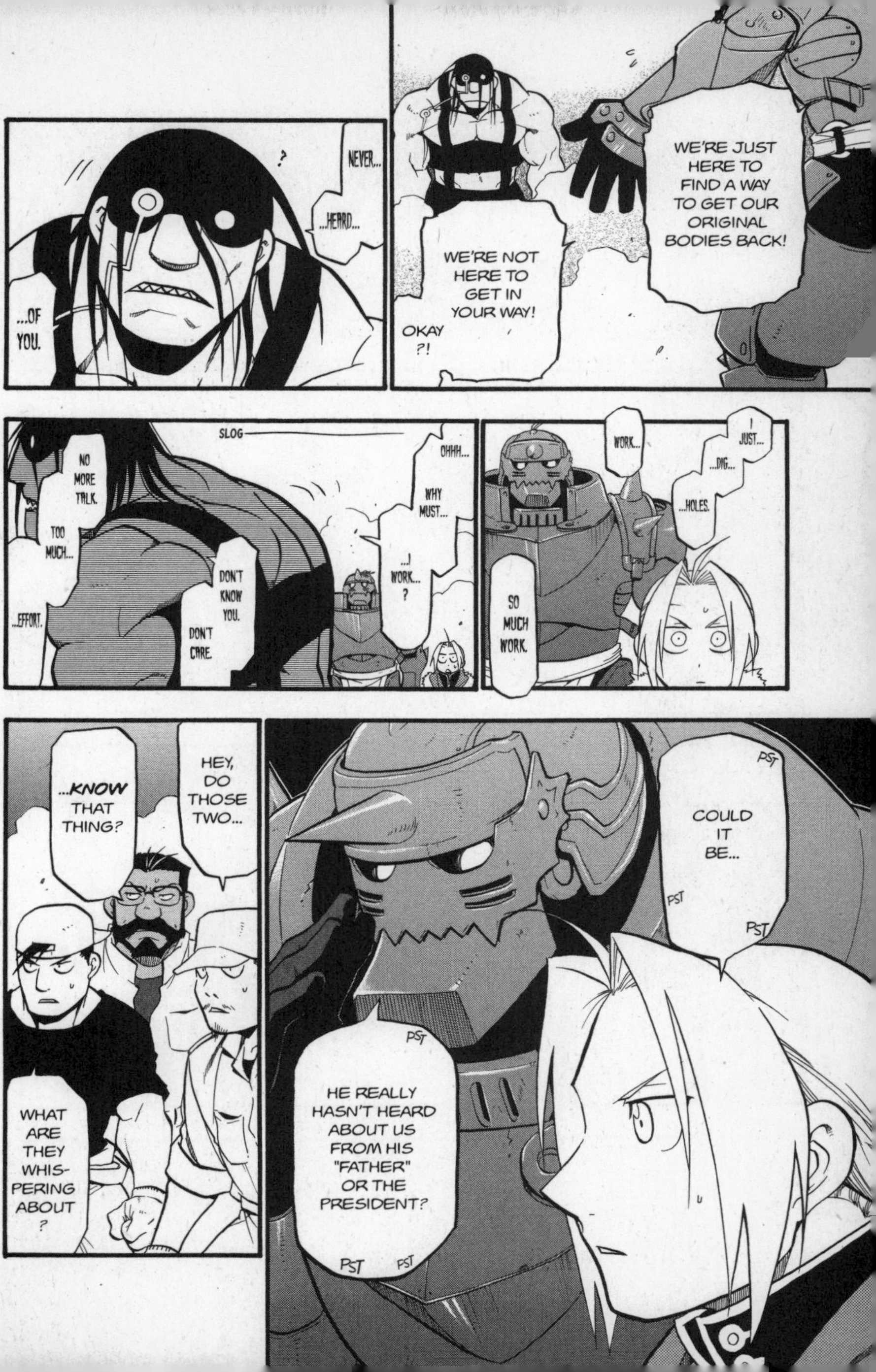
WE'RE JUST HERE TO FIND A WAY TO GET OUR ORIGINAL BODIES BACK!
WE'RE NOT HERE TO GET IN YOUR WAY!
OKAY ?!
?
NEVER...
...HEARD...
...OF YOU.
I JUST...
...DIG...
...HOLES.
WORK...
SO MUCH WORK.
OHHH...
WHY MUST...
...I WORK...?
SLOG
DON'T KNOW YOU.
DON'T CARE.
NO MORE TALK.
TOO MUCH...
...EFFORT.
PST
COULD IT BE...
PST
PST
PST
HE REALLY HASN'T HEARD ABOUT US FROM HIS "FATHER" OR THE PRESIDENT?
PST PST
HEY, DO THOSE TWO...
...KNOW THAT THING?
WHAT ARE THEY WHISPERING ABOUT ?

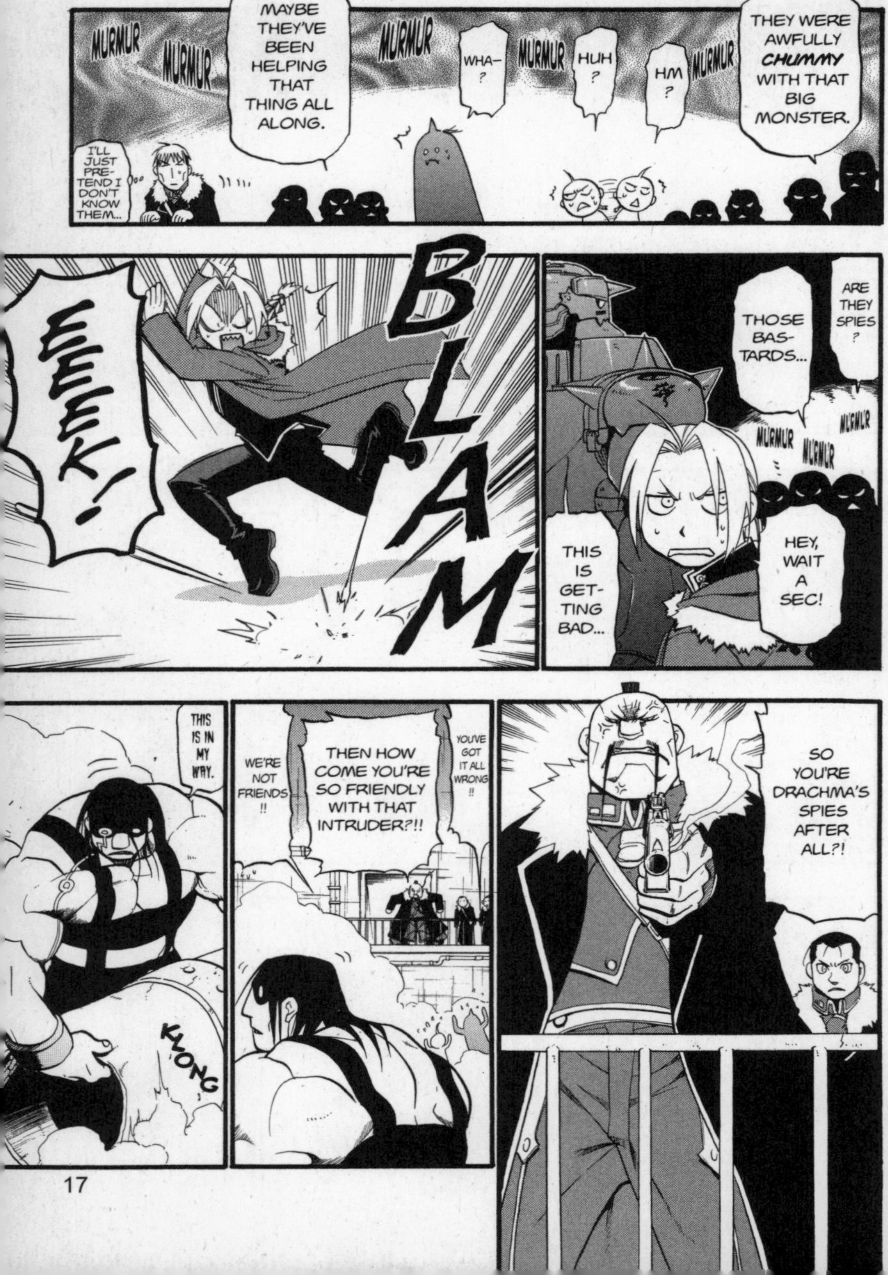
THEY WERE AWFULLY CHUMMY WITH THAT BIG MONSTER.
MURMUR
HM?
MURMUR
HUH?
MURMUR
WHA-?
MURMUR
MAYBE THEY'VE BEEN HELPING THAT THING ALL ALONG.
MURMUR
MURMUR
I'LL JUST PRETEND I DON'T KNOW THEM...
ARE THEY SPIES?
THOSE BASTARDS...
MURMUR
MURMUR
MURMUR
HEY, WAIT A SEC!
THIS IS GETTING BAD...
BLAM
EEEEEK!!
SO YOU'RE DRACHMA'S SPIES AFTER ALL?!
YOU'VE GOT IT ALL WRONG!!
THEN HOW COME YOU'RE SO FRIENDLY WITH THAT INTRUDER?!!
WE'RE NOT FRIENDS!!
THIS IS IN MY WAY.
KLONG

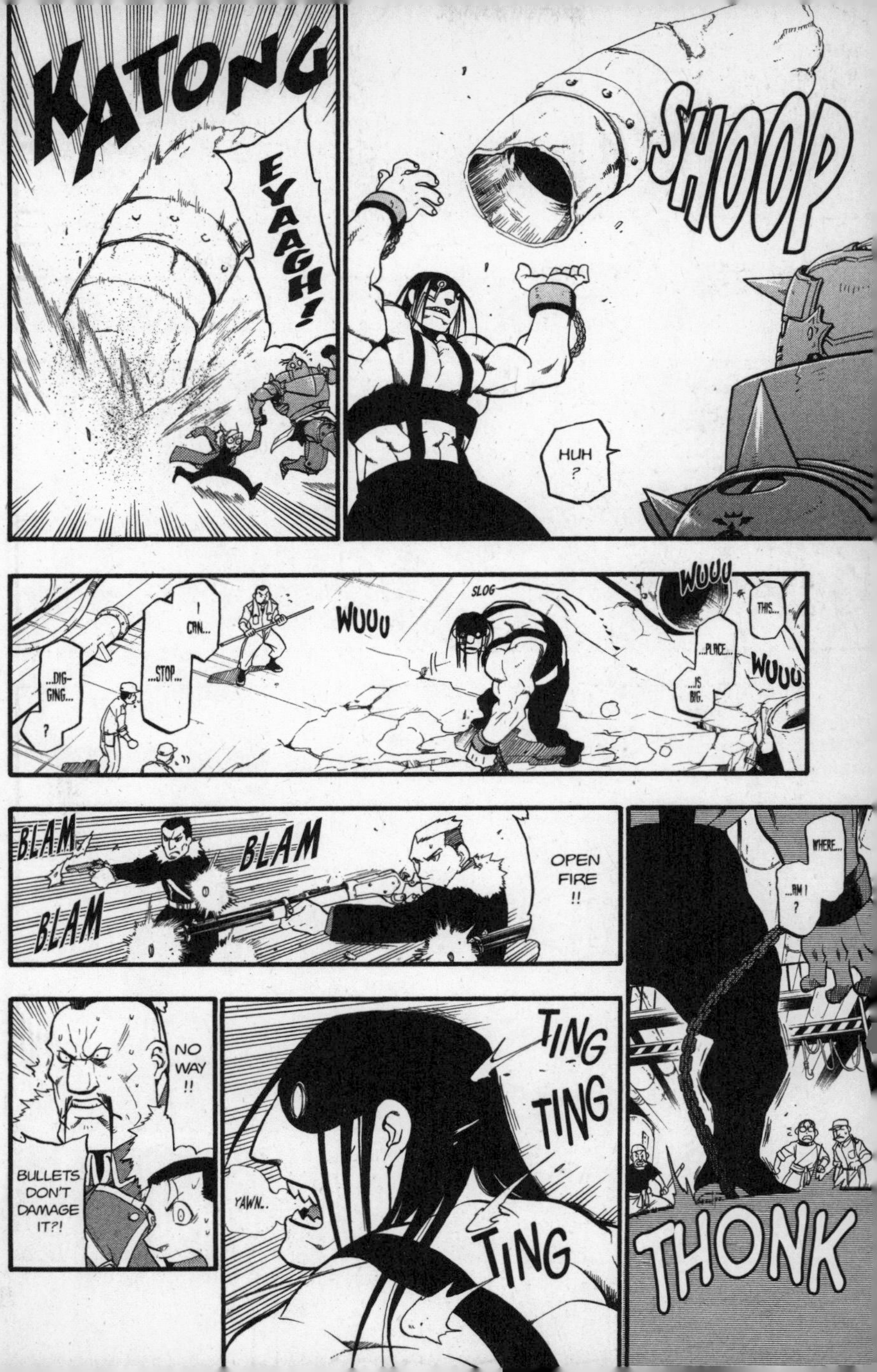
SHOOP
HUH?
KATONG
EYAAGH!
WUUU
THIS...
...PLACE...
...IS BIG.
WUUU
SLOG
WUUU
I CAN...
...STOP...
...DIG-GING...?
WHERE...
...AM I?
THONK
OPEN FIRE!!
BLAM
BLAM
BLAM
TING
TING
TING
YAWN...
NO WAY!!
BULLETS DON'T DAMAGE IT?!

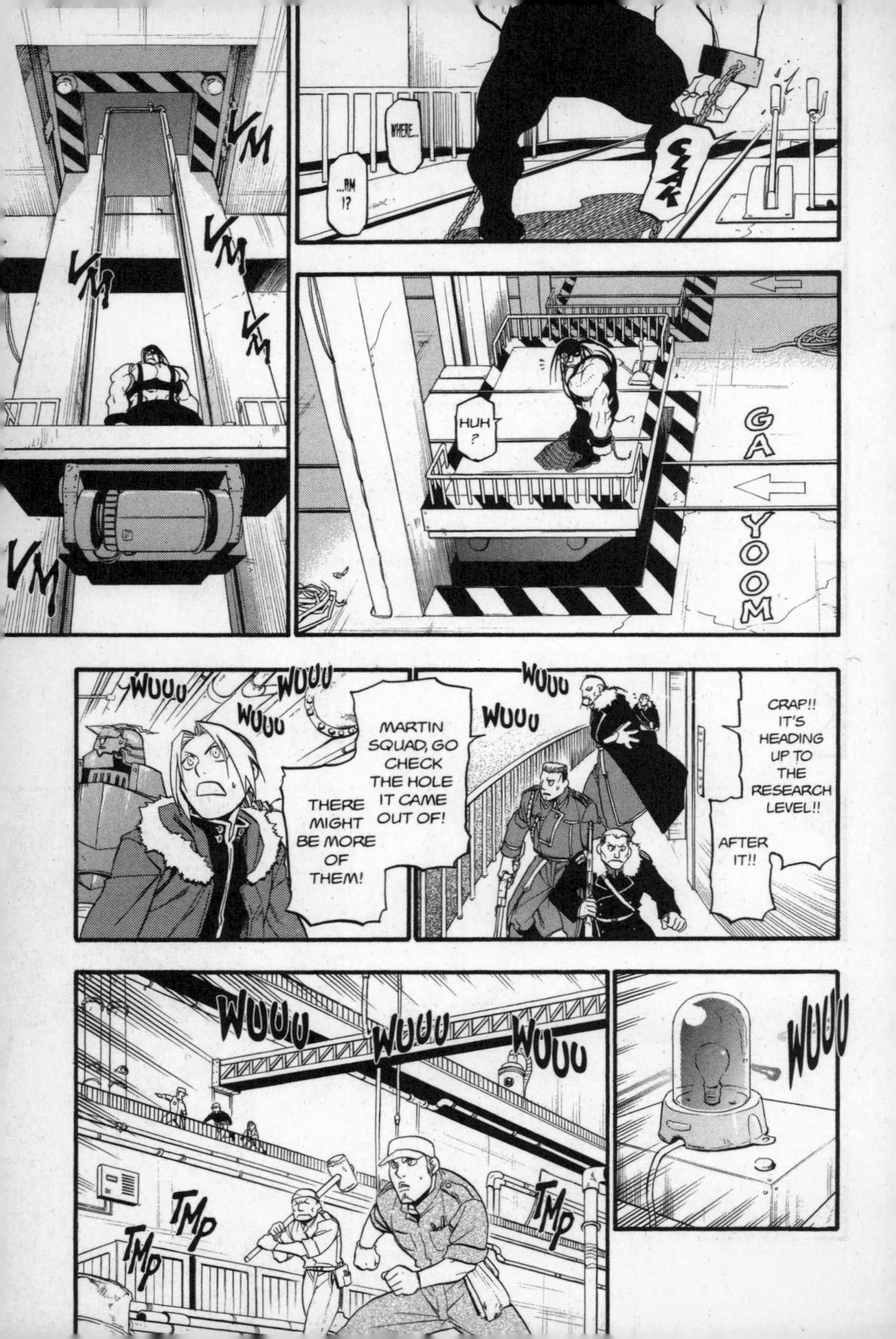
WHERE...
...AM I?
CLAK
HUH?
GA
YOOM
VM
VM
VM
VM
VM
WUUU
WUUU
CRAP!! IT'S HEADING UP TO THE RESEARCH LEVEL!!
AFTER IT!!
WUUU
WUUU
WUUU
MARTIN SQUAD, GO CHECK THE HOLE IT CAME OUT OF!
THERE MIGHT BE MORE OF THEM!
WUUU
WUUU
WUUU
WUUU
TMP
TMP
TMP

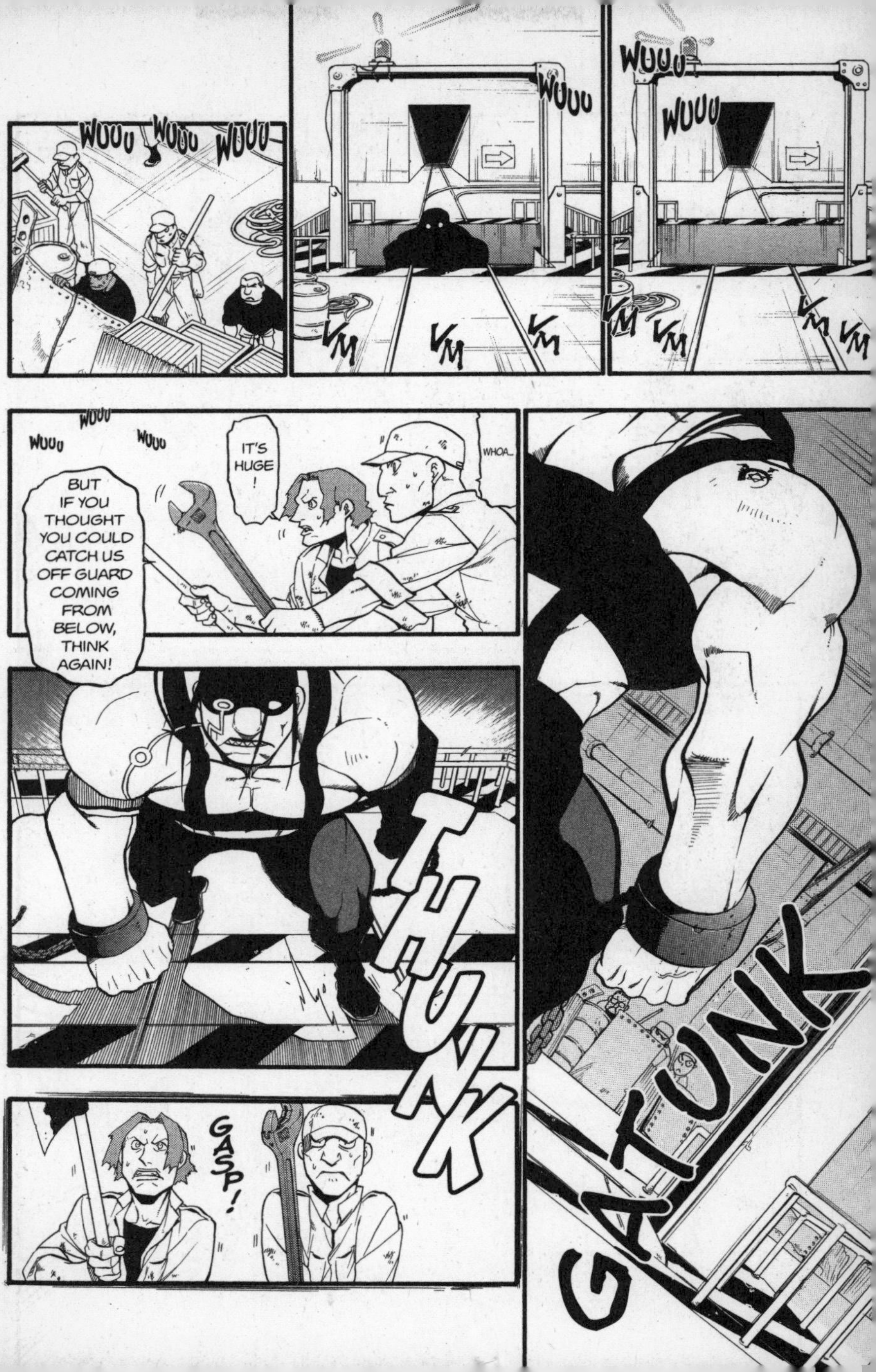
WUUU
WUUU
VM
VM
VM
VM
WUUU
VM
VM
VM
WUUU
WUUU
WUUU
GATUNK
WUUU
WUUU
WUUU
WHOA...
IT'S HUGE!
BUT IF YOU THOUGHT YOU COULD CATCH US OFF GUARD COMING FROM BELOW, THINK AGAIN!
THUNK
GASP!

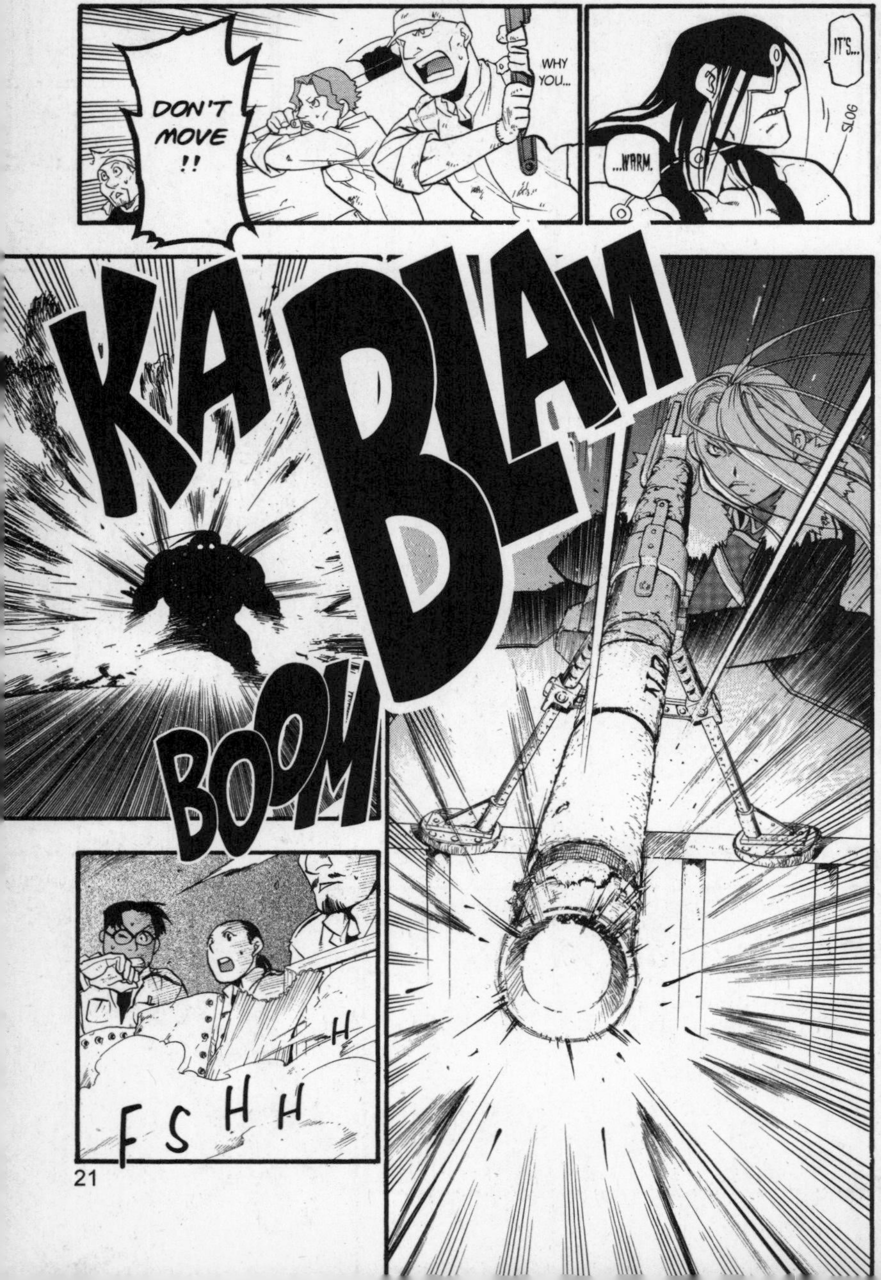
IT'S...
...WARM.
SLOG
WHY YOU...
DON'T MOVE !!
KABLAM
BOOM
FSHHH

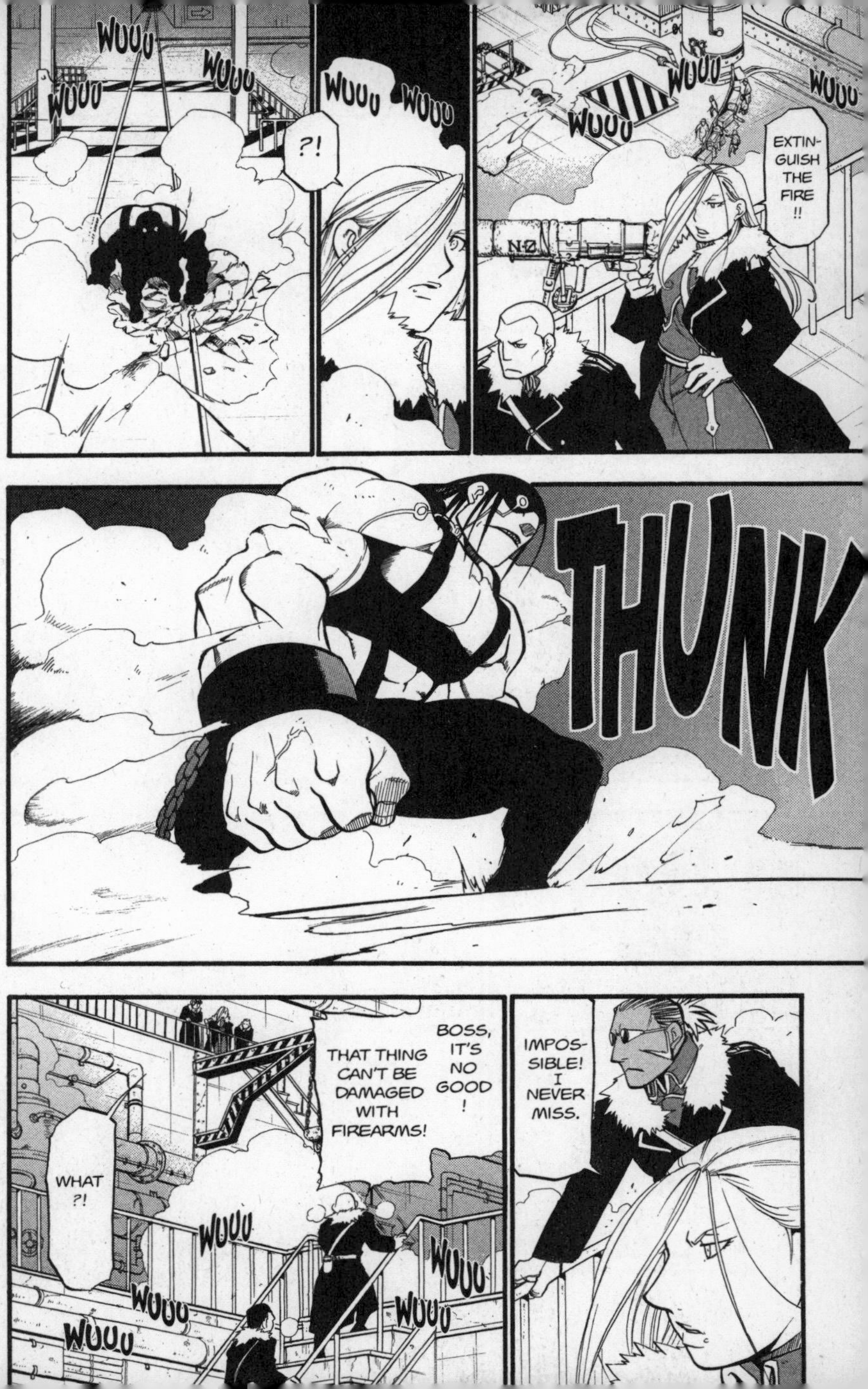
WUUU
WUUU
WUUU
EXTIN-GUISH THE FIRE !!
WUUU
WUUU
?!
WUUU
WUUU
WUUU
THUNK
IMPOS-SIBLE! I NEVER MISS.
BOSS, IT'S NO GOOD !
THAT THING CAN'T BE DAMAGED WITH FIREARMS!
WHAT ?!
WUUU
WUUU
WUUU
WUUU
WUUU

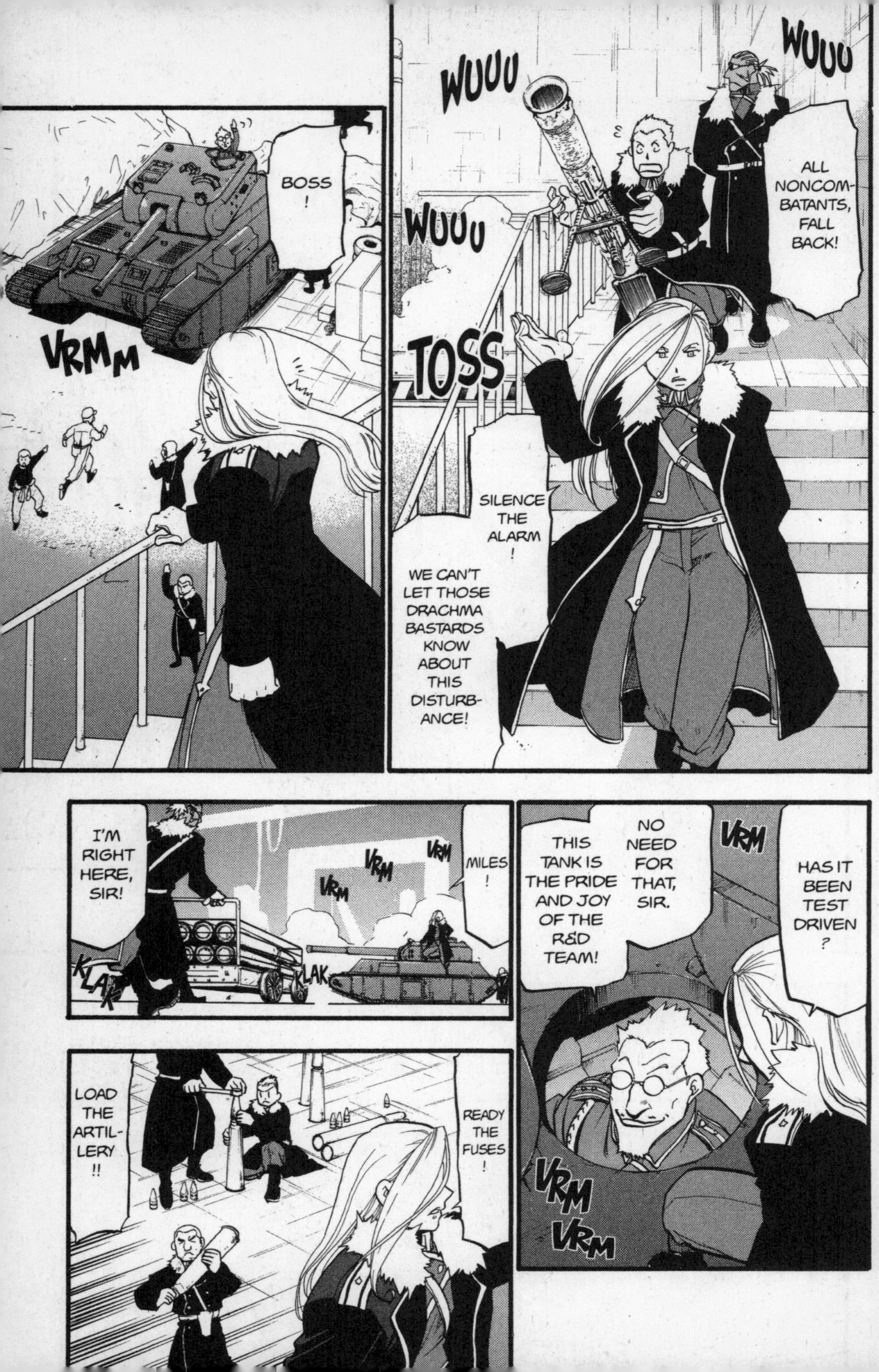
WUUU
ALL NONCOMBATANTS, FALL BACK!
WUUU
WUUU
TOSS
SILENCE THE ALARM!
WE CAN'T LET THOSE DRACHMA BASTARDS KNOW ABOUT THIS DISTURBANCE!
BOSS!
VRMM
HAS IT BEEN TEST DRIVEN?
VRM
NO NEED FOR THAT, SIR.
THIS TANK IS THE PRIDE AND JOY OF THE R&D TEAM!
VRM
VRM
MILES!
VRM
VRM
VRM
I'M RIGHT HERE, SIR!
KLAK
KLAK
READY THE FUSES!
LOAD THE ARTILLERY!!

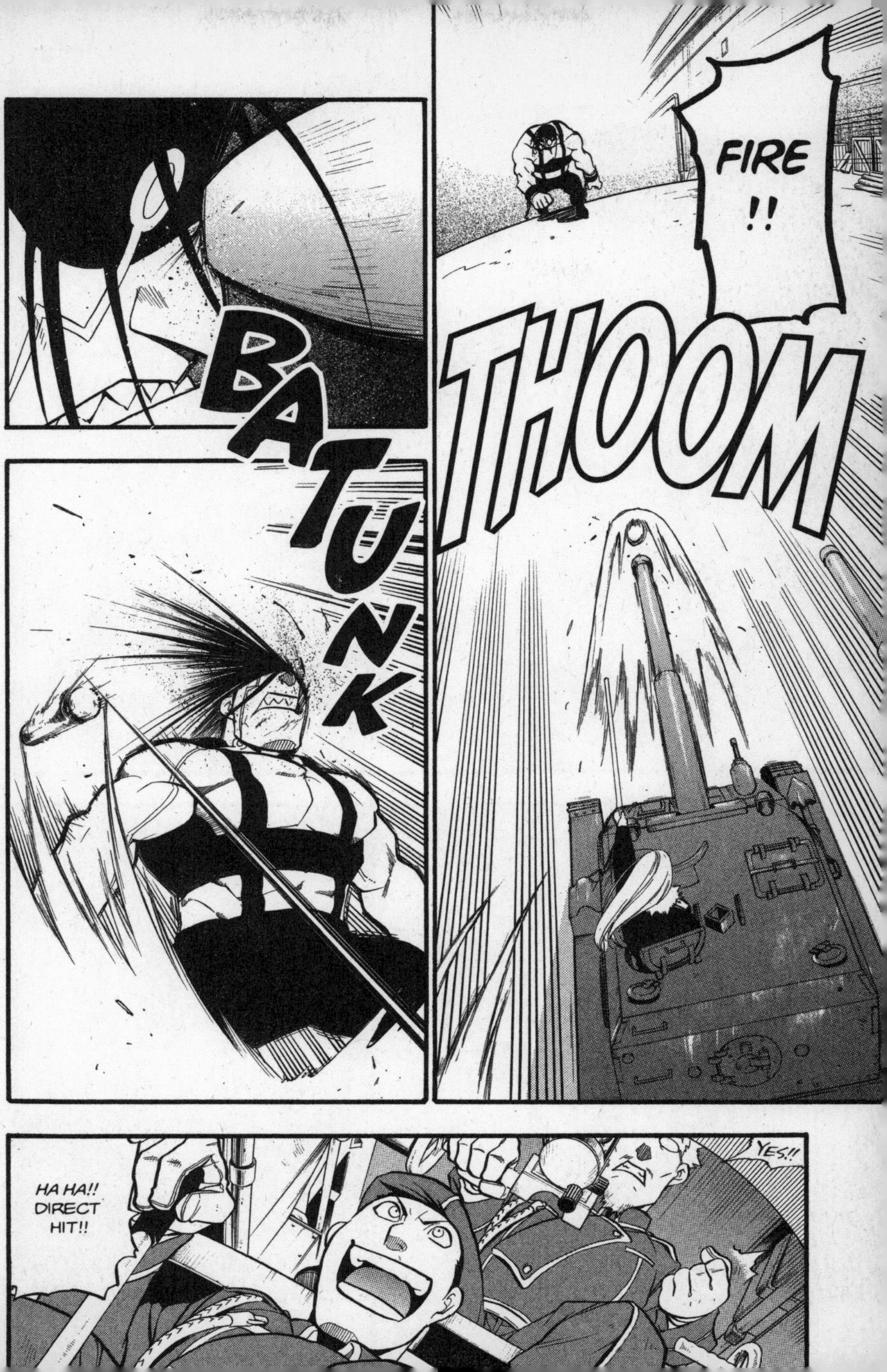
FIRE!!
THOOM
BATUNK
YES!!
HA HA!! DIRECT HIT!!

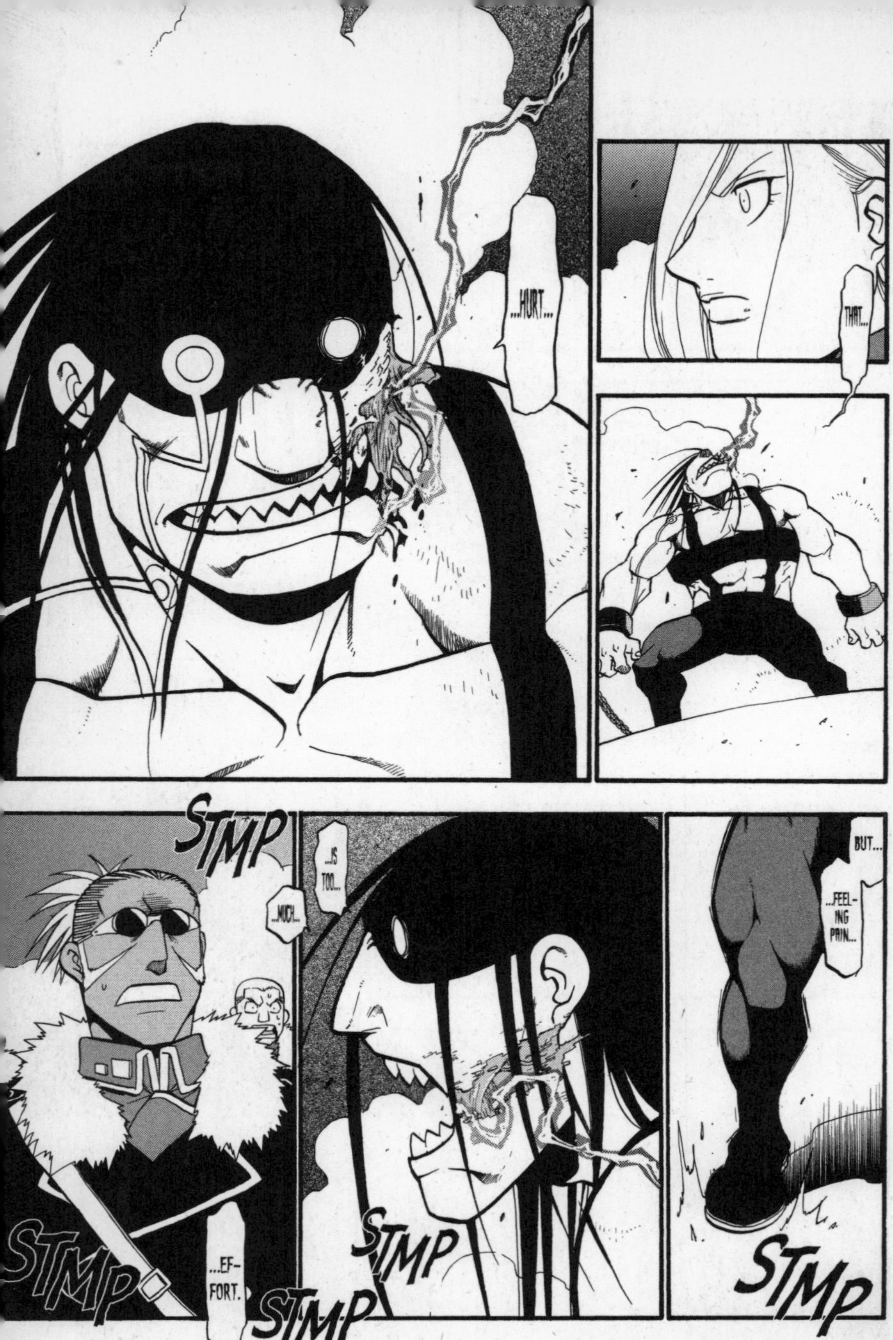
THAT...
...HURT...
BUT...
...FEEL-ING PAIN...
STMP
...IS TOO...
...MUCH...
STMP
STMP
...EF-FORT.
STMP
STMP

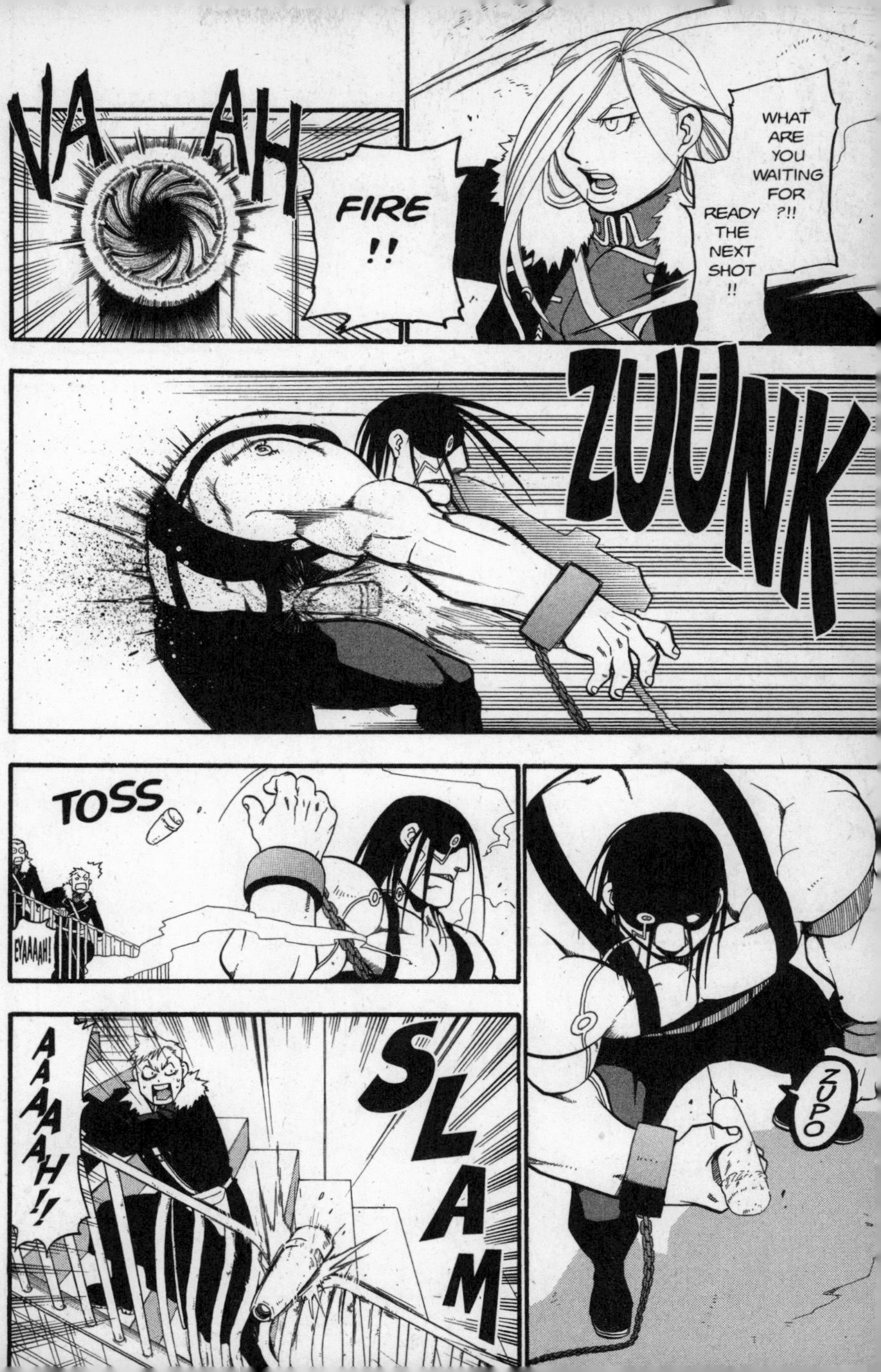
WHAT ARE YOU WAITING FOR ?!!
READY THE NEXT SHOT !!
FIRE !!
VA AH
ZUUNK
ZUPO
TOSS
EYAAAAH!
SLAM
AAAAAH!!

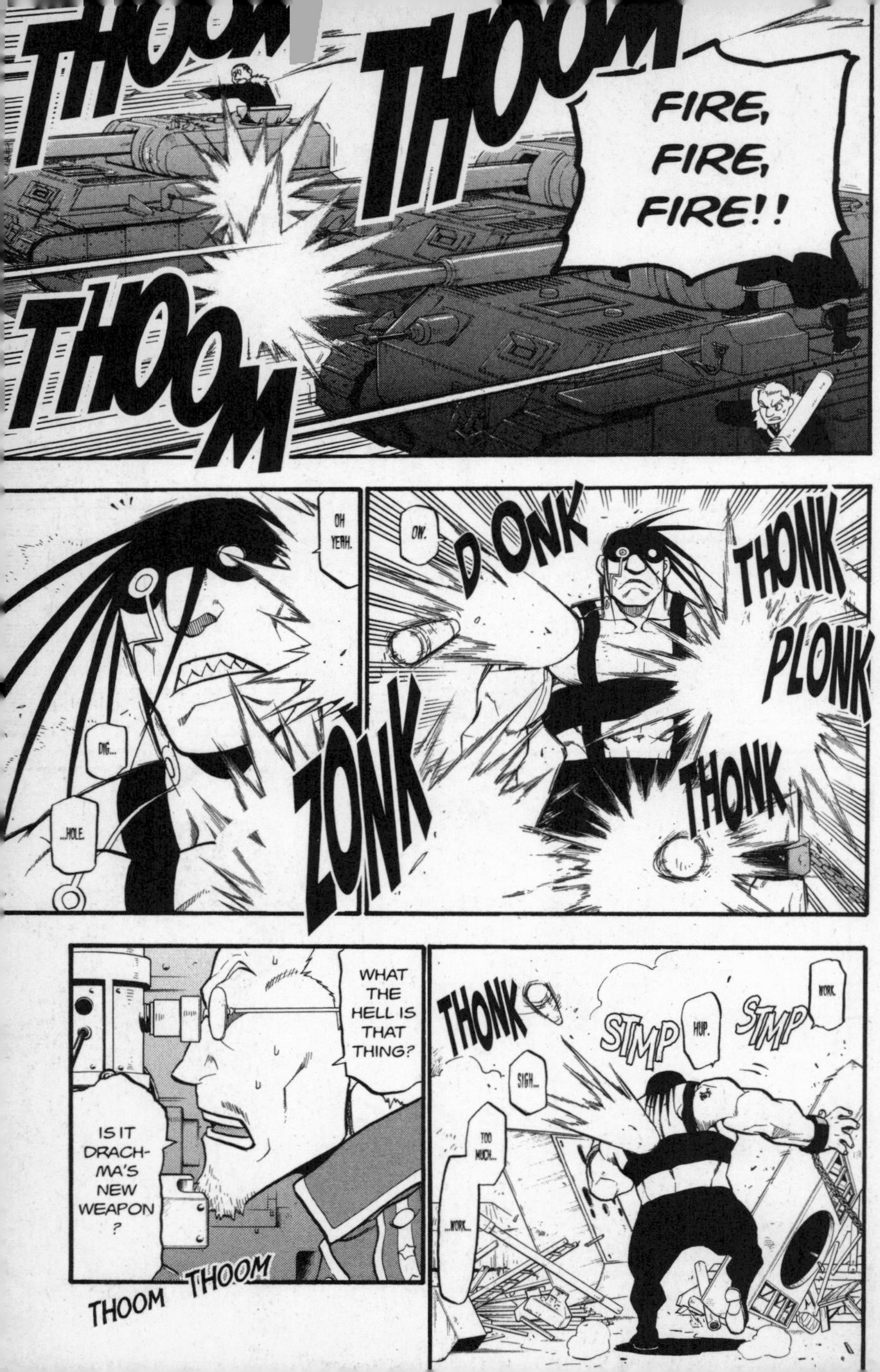
FIRE, FIRE, FIRE!!
THOOM
THOOM
THOOM
OW.
DONK
THONK
PLONK
THONK
ZONK
OH YEAH.
DIG...
...HOLE.
WORK.
STMP
HUP.
STMP
THONK
SIGH...
TOO MUCH...
...WORK...
WHAT THE HELL IS THAT THING?
IS IT DRACHMA'S NEW WEAPON?
THOOM
THOOM

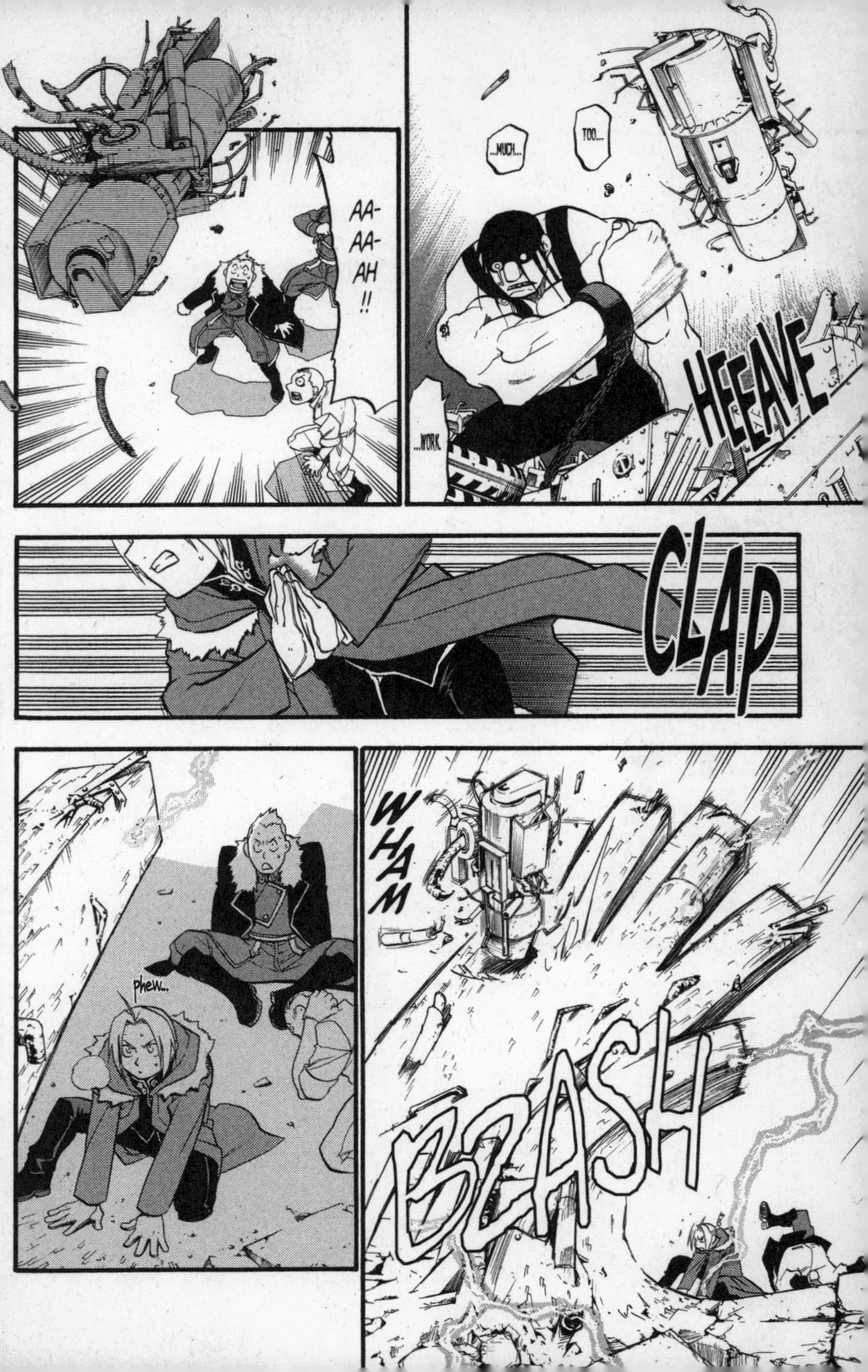
TOO...
...MUCH...
...WORK.
HEEAVE
AA-AA-AH!!
CLAP
WHAM
BRASH
phew...

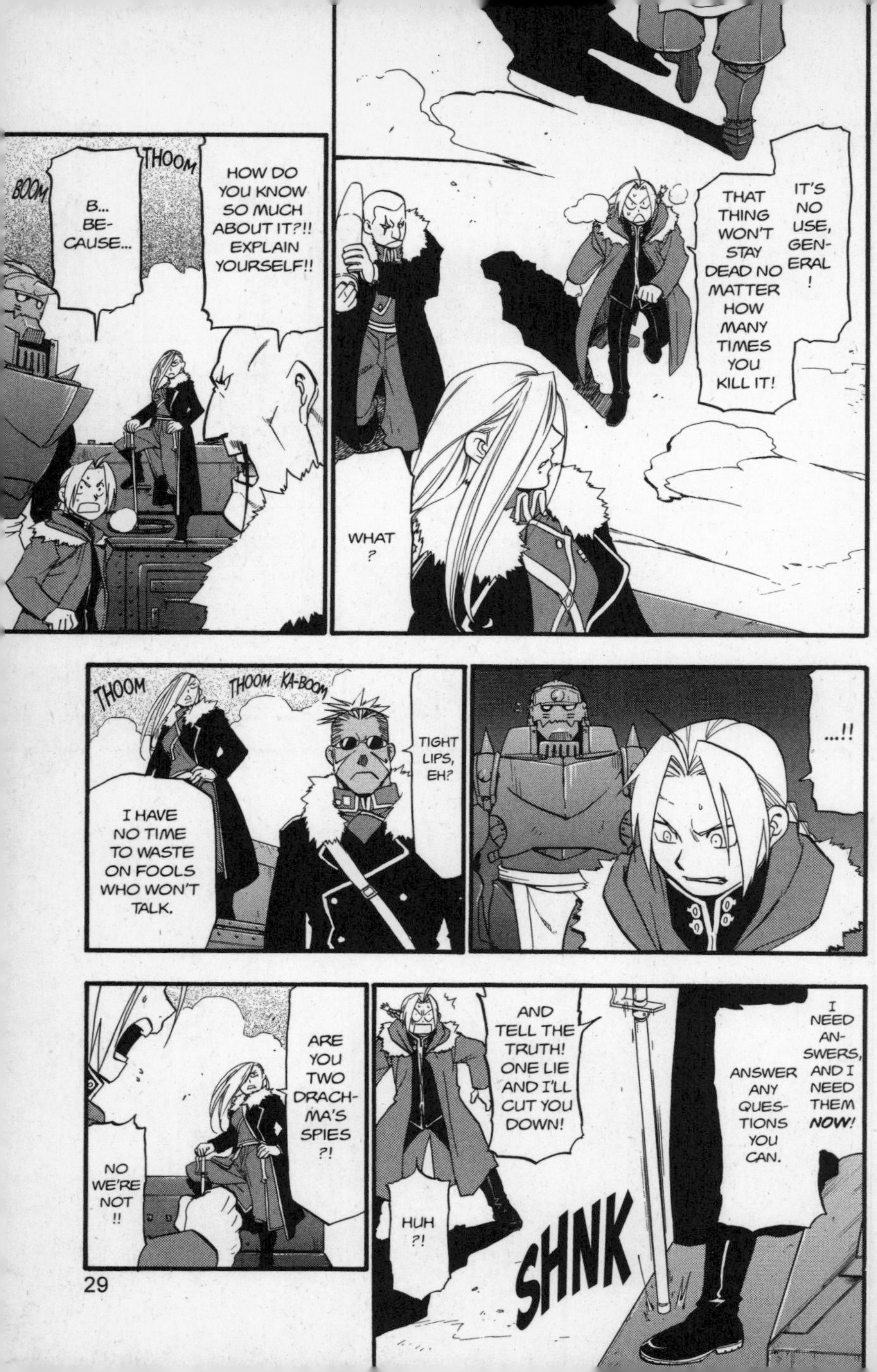
IT'S NO USE, GEN-ERAL!
THAT THING WON'T STAY DEAD NO MATTER HOW MANY TIMES YOU KILL IT!
WHAT?
HOW DO YOU KNOW SO MUCH ABOUT IT?!! EXPLAIN YOURSELF!!
THOOM
BOOM
B... BE-CAUSE...
...!!
TIGHT LIPS, EH?
THOOM
THOOM KA-BOOM
I HAVE NO TIME TO WASTE ON FOOLS WHO WON'T TALK.
I NEED AN-SWERS, AND I NEED THEM *NOW*!
ANSWER ANY QUES-TIONS YOU CAN.
SHNK
AND TELL THE TRUTH! ONE LIE AND I'LL CUT YOU DOWN!
HUH?!
ARE YOU TWO DRACH-MA'S SPIES?!
NO WE'RE NOT!!

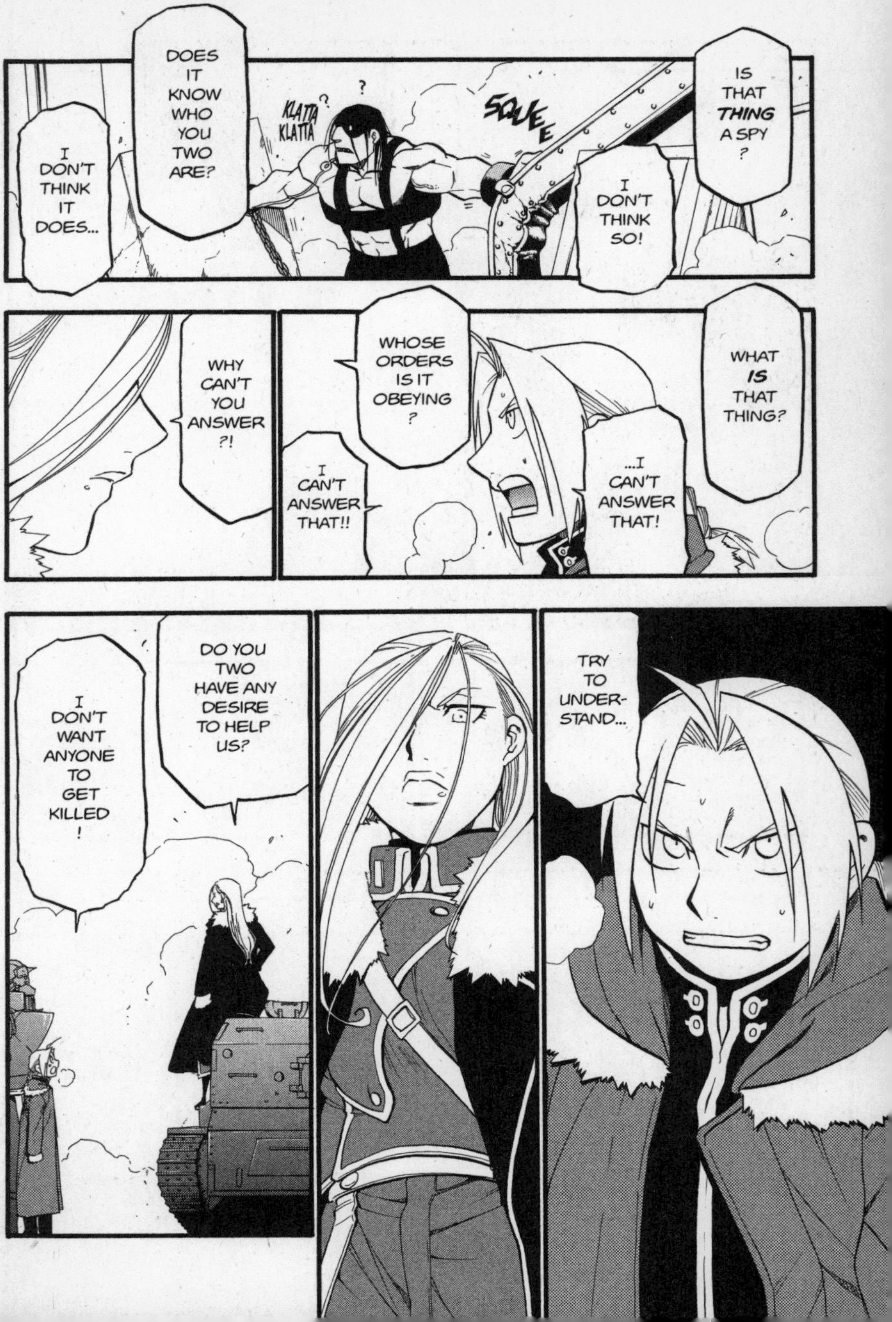
IS THAT THING A SPY?
I DON'T THINK SO!
SQUEE
KLATTA KLATTA
DOES IT KNOW WHO YOU TWO ARE?
I DON'T THINK IT DOES...
WHAT IS THAT THING?
...I CAN'T ANSWER THAT!
WHOSE ORDERS IS IT OBEYING?
I CAN'T ANSWER THAT!!
WHY CAN'T YOU ANSWER?!
TRY TO UNDER-STAND...
DO YOU TWO HAVE ANY DESIRE TO HELP US?
I DON'T WANT ANYONE TO GET KILLED!

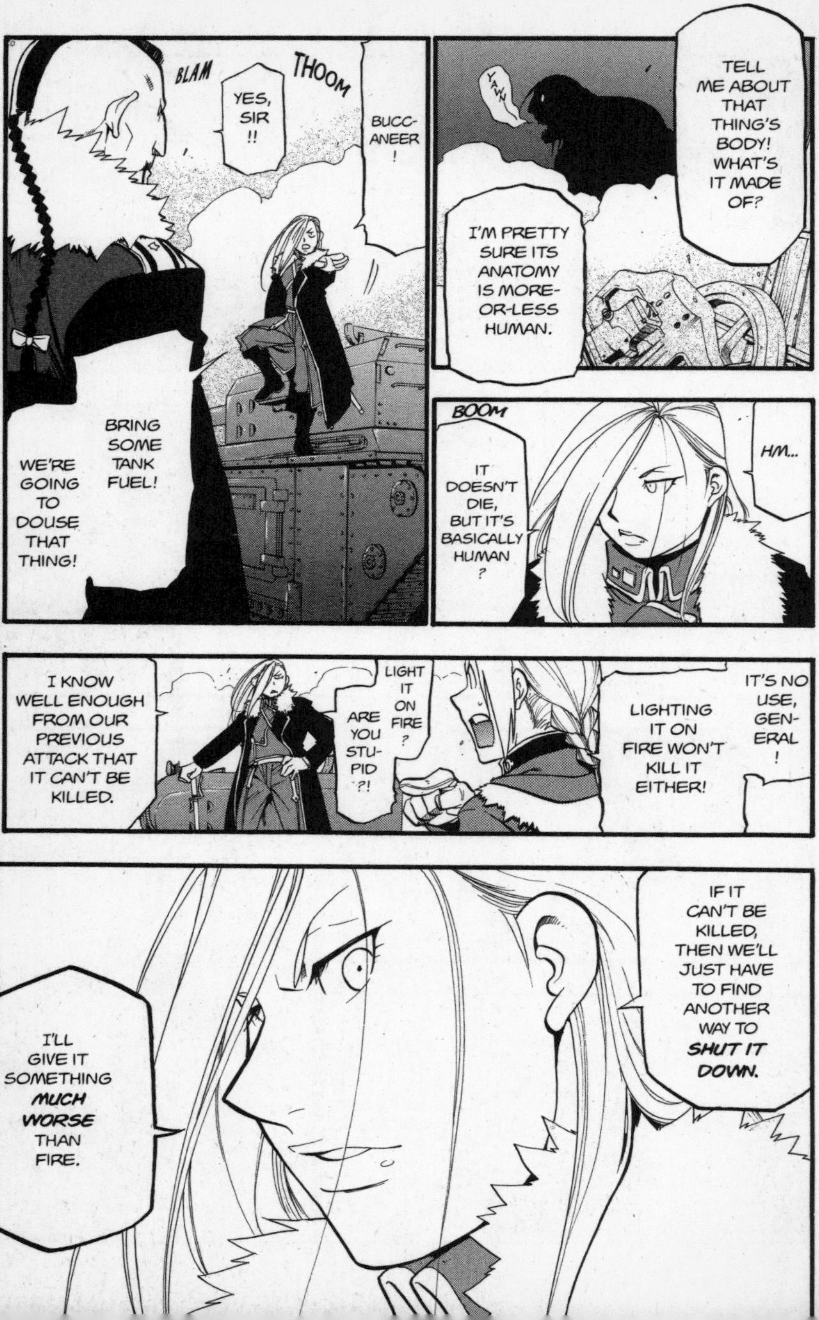
TELL ME ABOUT THAT THING'S BODY! WHAT'S IT MADE OF?
YAWN
I'M PRETTY SURE ITS ANATOMY IS MORE-OR-LESS HUMAN.
HM...
BOOM
IT DOESN'T DIE, BUT IT'S BASICALLY HUMAN?
BLAM
THOOM
BUCCANEER!
YES, SIR!!
BRING SOME TANK FUEL!
WE'RE GOING TO DOUSE THAT THING!
IT'S NO USE, GENERAL!
LIGHTING IT ON FIRE WON'T KILL IT EITHER!
LIGHT IT ON FIRE?
ARE YOU STUPID?!
I KNOW WELL ENOUGH FROM OUR PREVIOUS ATTACK THAT IT CAN'T BE KILLED.
IF IT CAN'T BE KILLED, THEN WE'LL JUST HAVE TO FIND ANOTHER WAY TO **SHUT IT DOWN.**
I'LL GIVE IT SOMETHING **MUCH WORSE** THAN FIRE.

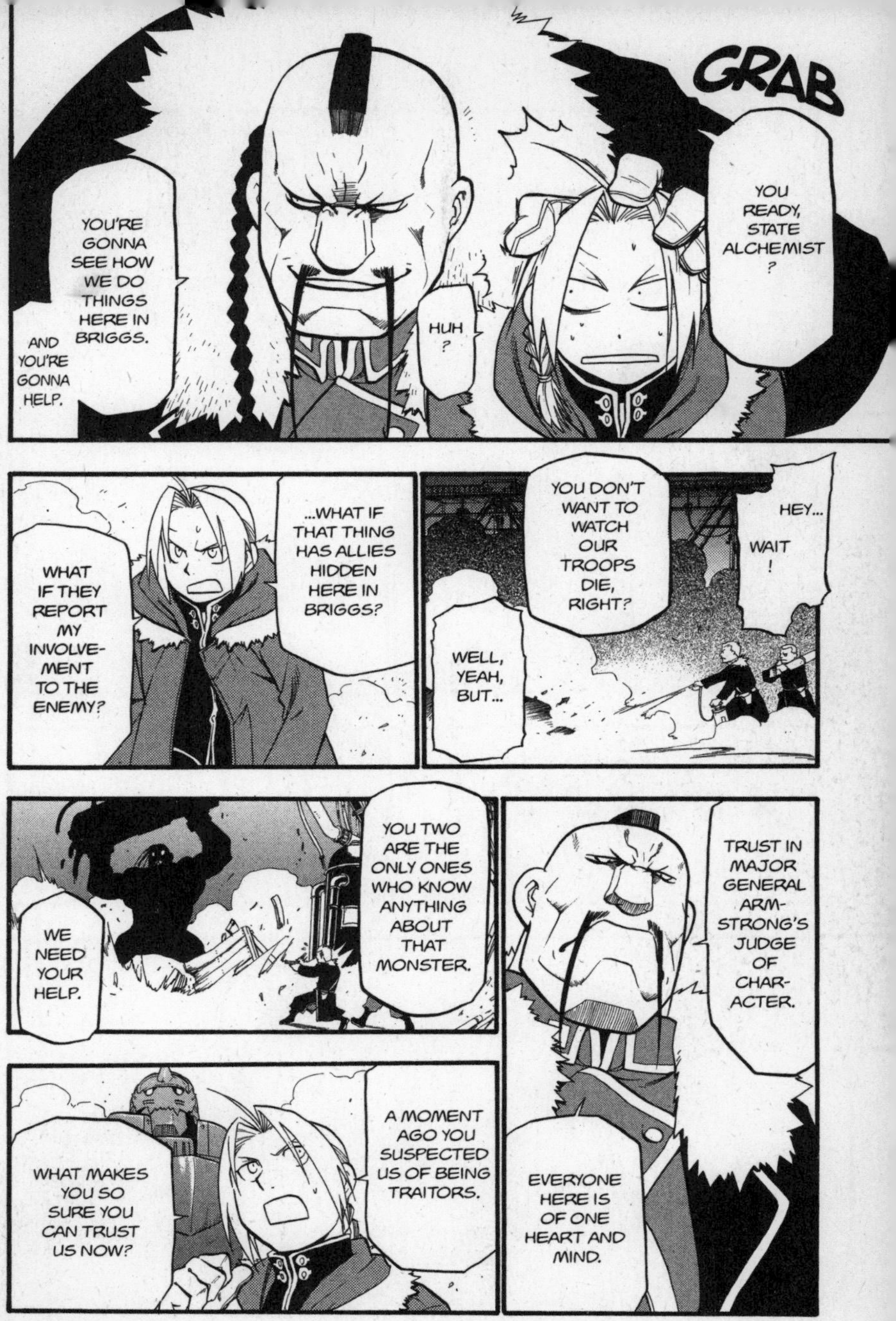
GRAB
YOU READY, STATE ALCHEMIST?
HUH?
YOU'RE GONNA SEE HOW WE DO THINGS HERE IN BRIGGS.
AND YOU'RE GONNA HELP.
HEY... WAIT!
YOU DON'T WANT TO WATCH OUR TROOPS DIE, RIGHT?
WELL, YEAH, BUT...
...WHAT IF THAT THING HAS ALLIES HIDDEN HERE IN BRIGGS?
WHAT IF THEY REPORT MY INVOLVEMENT TO THE ENEMY?
TRUST IN MAJOR GENERAL ARMSTRONG'S JUDGE OF CHARACTER.
EVERYONE HERE IS OF ONE HEART AND MIND.
YOU TWO ARE THE ONLY ONES WHO KNOW ANYTHING ABOUT THAT MONSTER.
WE NEED YOUR HELP.
A MOMENT AGO YOU SUSPECTED US OF BEING TRAITORS.
WHAT MAKES YOU SO SURE YOU CAN TRUST US NOW?

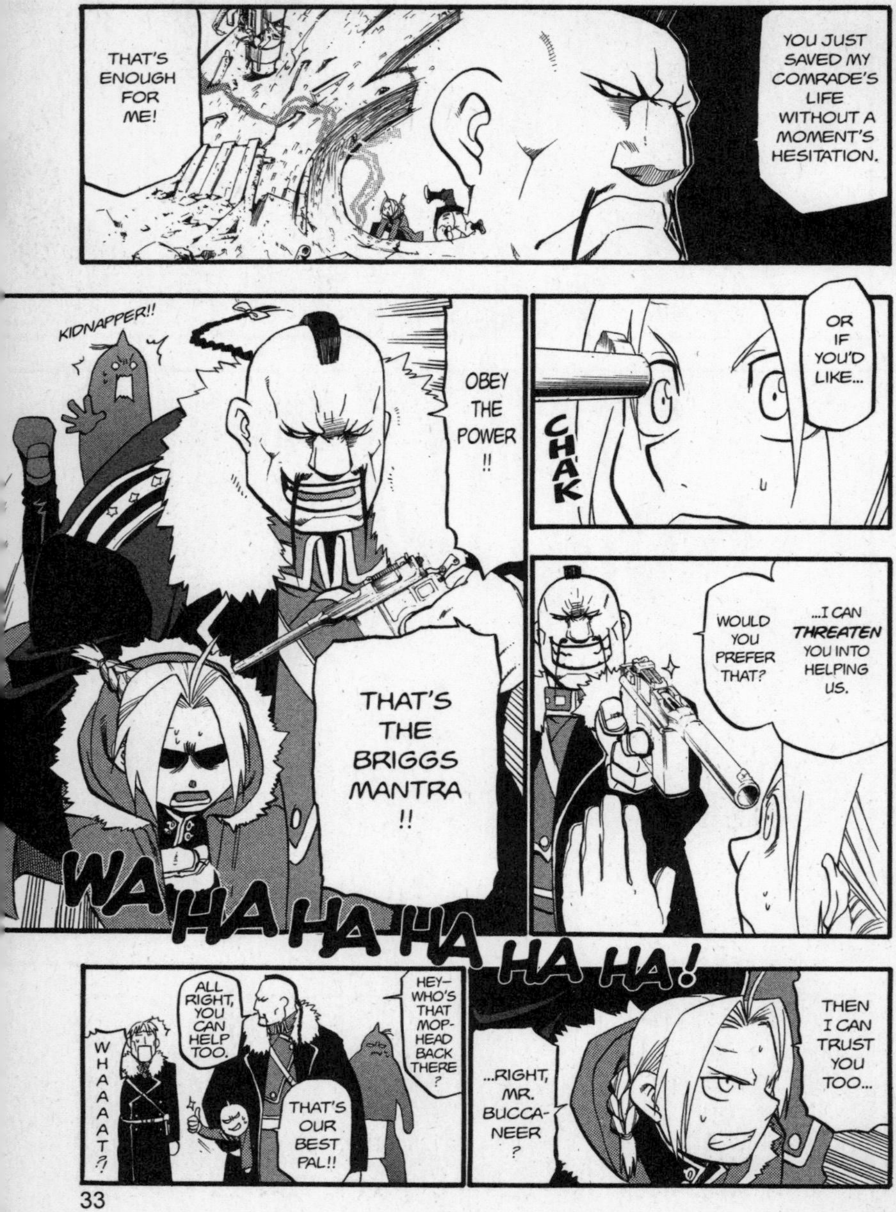

YOU JUST SAVED MY COMRADE'S LIFE WITHOUT A MOMENT'S HESITATION.
THAT'S ENOUGH FOR ME!
OR IF YOU'D LIKE...
CHAK
...I CAN THREATEN YOU INTO HELPING US.
WOULD YOU PREFER THAT?
OBEY THE POWER !!
THAT'S THE BRIGGS MANTRA !!
KIDNAPPER!!
WA HA HA HA HA HA HA!
THEN I CAN TRUST YOU TOO...
...RIGHT, MR. BUCCANEER?
HEY— WHO'S THAT MOP-HEAD BACK THERE?
THAT'S OUR BEST PAL!!
ALL RIGHT, YOU CAN HELP TOO.
WHAAAAAT?!

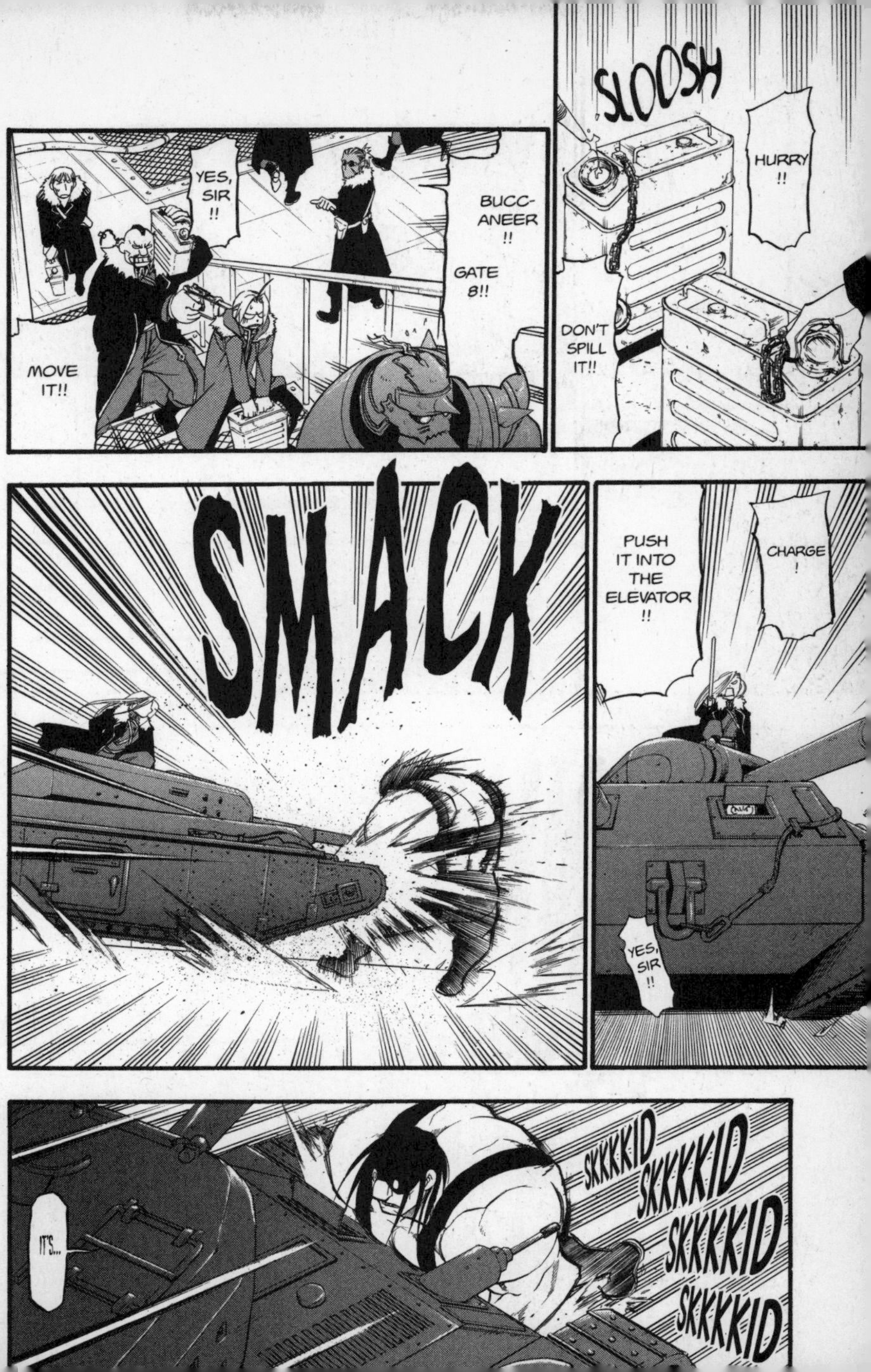
SLOOSH
HURRY!!
DON'T SPILL IT!!
BUCCANEER!!
GATE 8!!
YES, SIR!!
MOVE IT!!
CHARGE!
PUSH IT INTO THE ELEVATOR!!
YES, SIR!!
SMACK
SKKKID
SKKKID
SKKKID
SKKKID
IT'S...

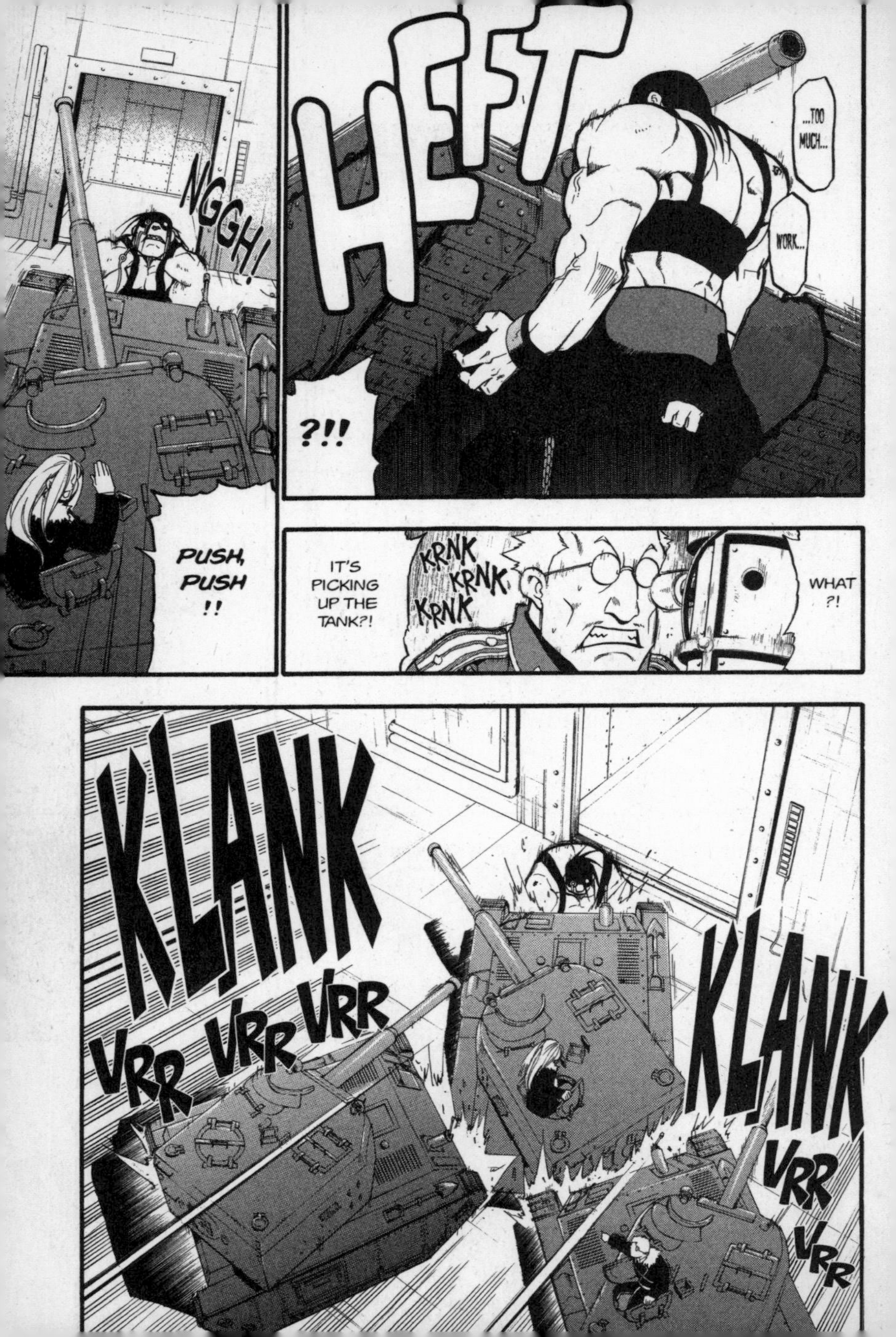

...TOO MUCH...
WORK...
HEFT
?!!
WHAT ?!
KRNK KRNK KRNK
IT'S PICKING UP THE TANK?!
NGGH!
PUSH, PUSH !!
KLANK
VRR VRR
KLANK
VRR VRR VRR

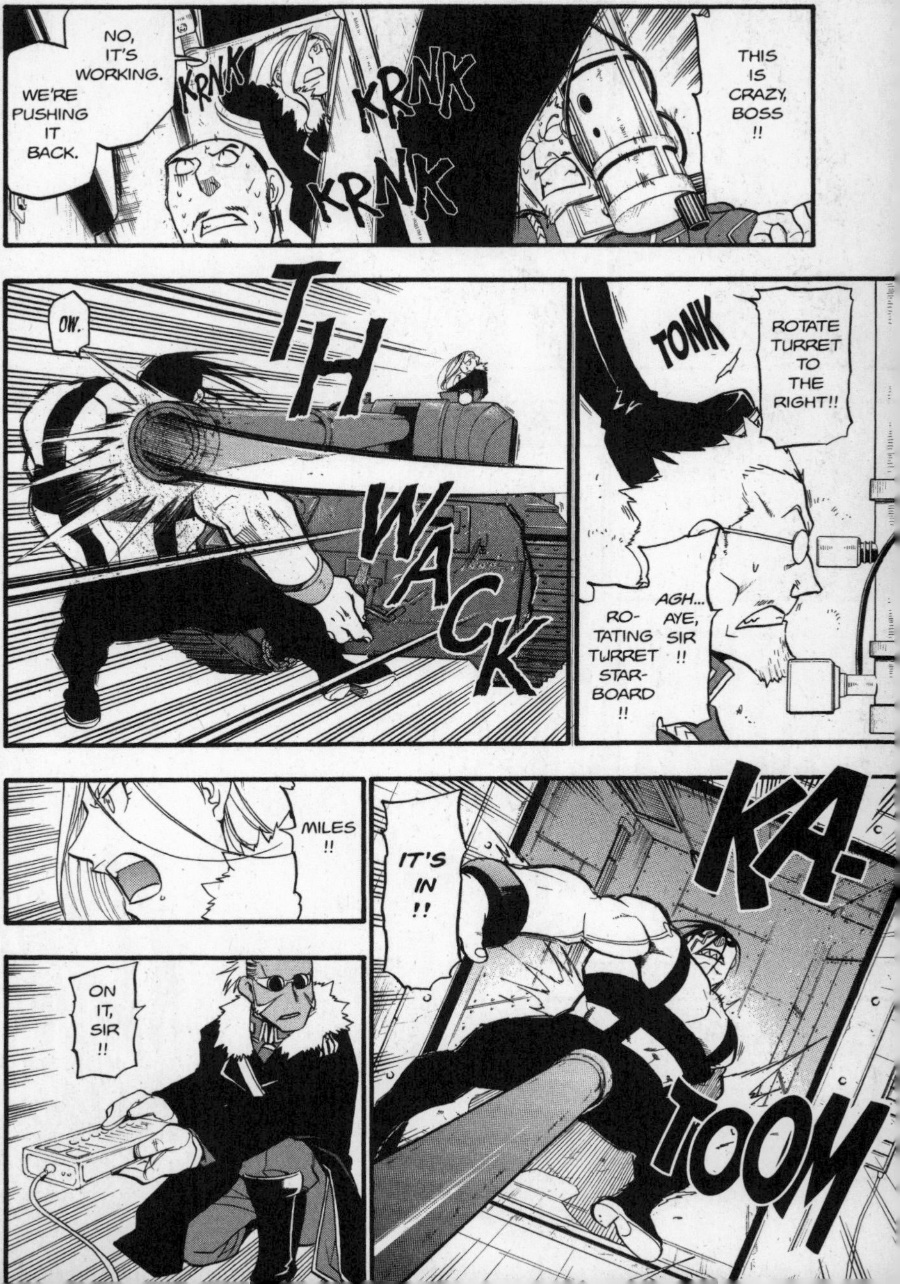
THIS IS CRAZY, BOSS!!
KRNK KRNK KRNK
NO, IT'S WORKING. WE'RE PUSHING IT BACK.
ROTATE TURRET TO THE RIGHT!!
TONK
AGH... AYE, SIR!!
RO-TATING TURRET STAR-BOARD!!
THWACK
OW.
KA-
IT'S IN!!
TOOM
MILES!!
ON IT, SIR!!

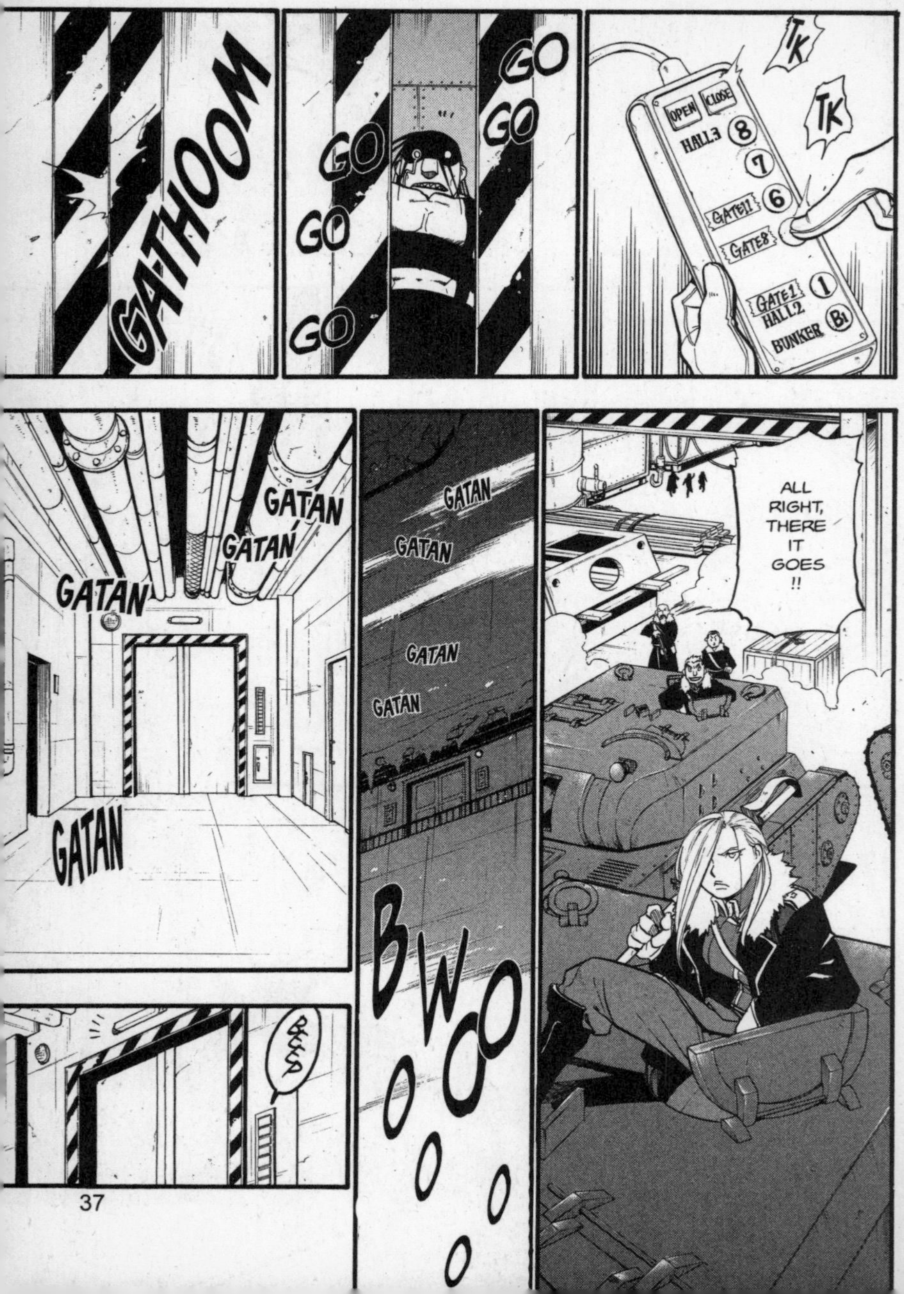
TK
TK
OPEN
CLOSE
HALL 3
8
7
GATE 11
6
GATE 8
GATE 1
HALL 2
1
BUNKER
B1
GO
GO
GO
GO
GO
GO
GATHOOM
ALL RIGHT, THERE IT GOES!!
GATAN
GATAN
GATAN
GATAN
BWOOOOOOOO
GATAN
GATAN
GATAN
GATAN

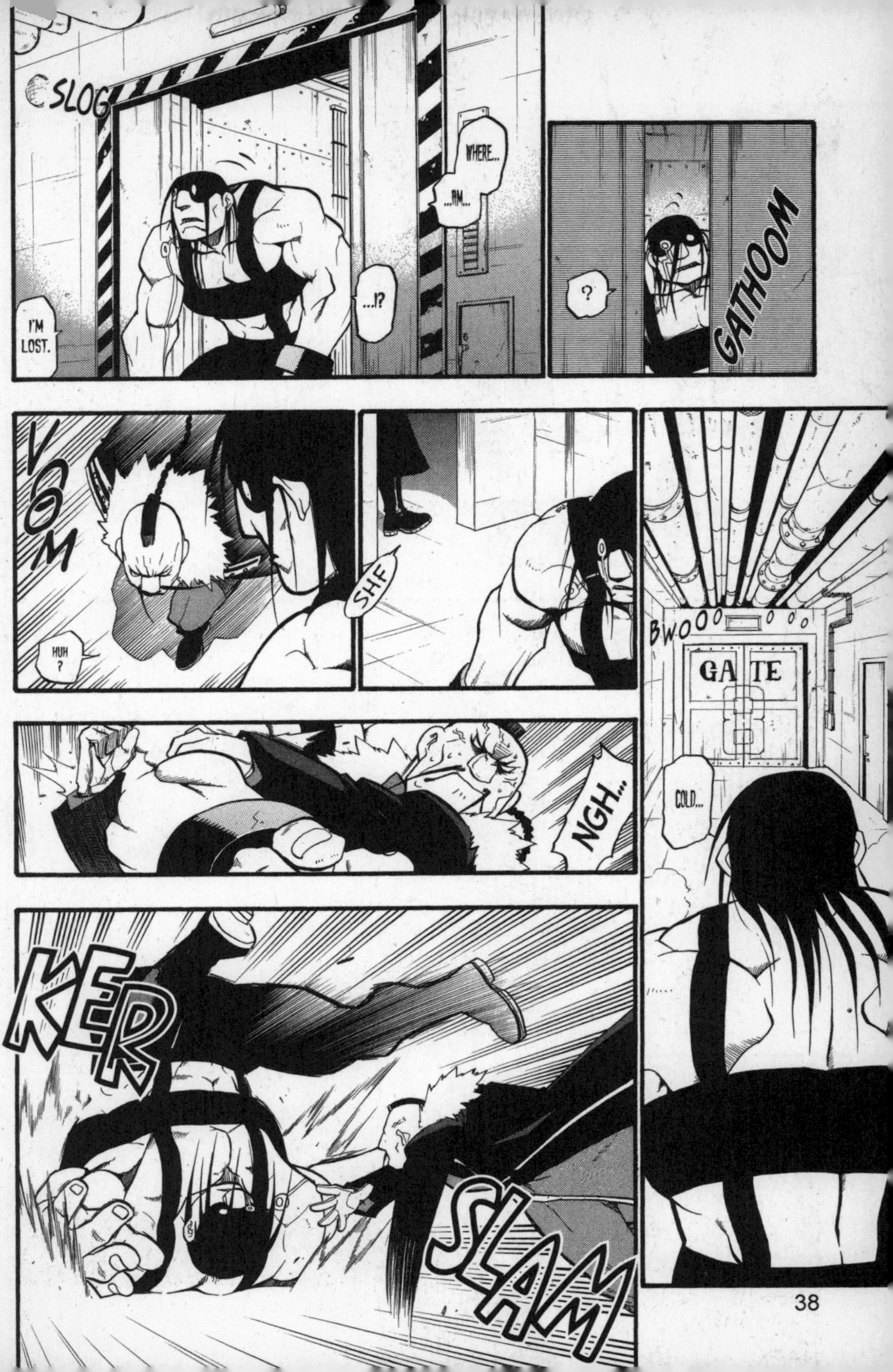

?
GATHOOM
WHERE...
...AM...
...I?
SLOG
I'M LOST.
BWOOOOOOO
GATE
COLD...
SHF
VOOM
HUH ?
NGH...
KER
SLAM

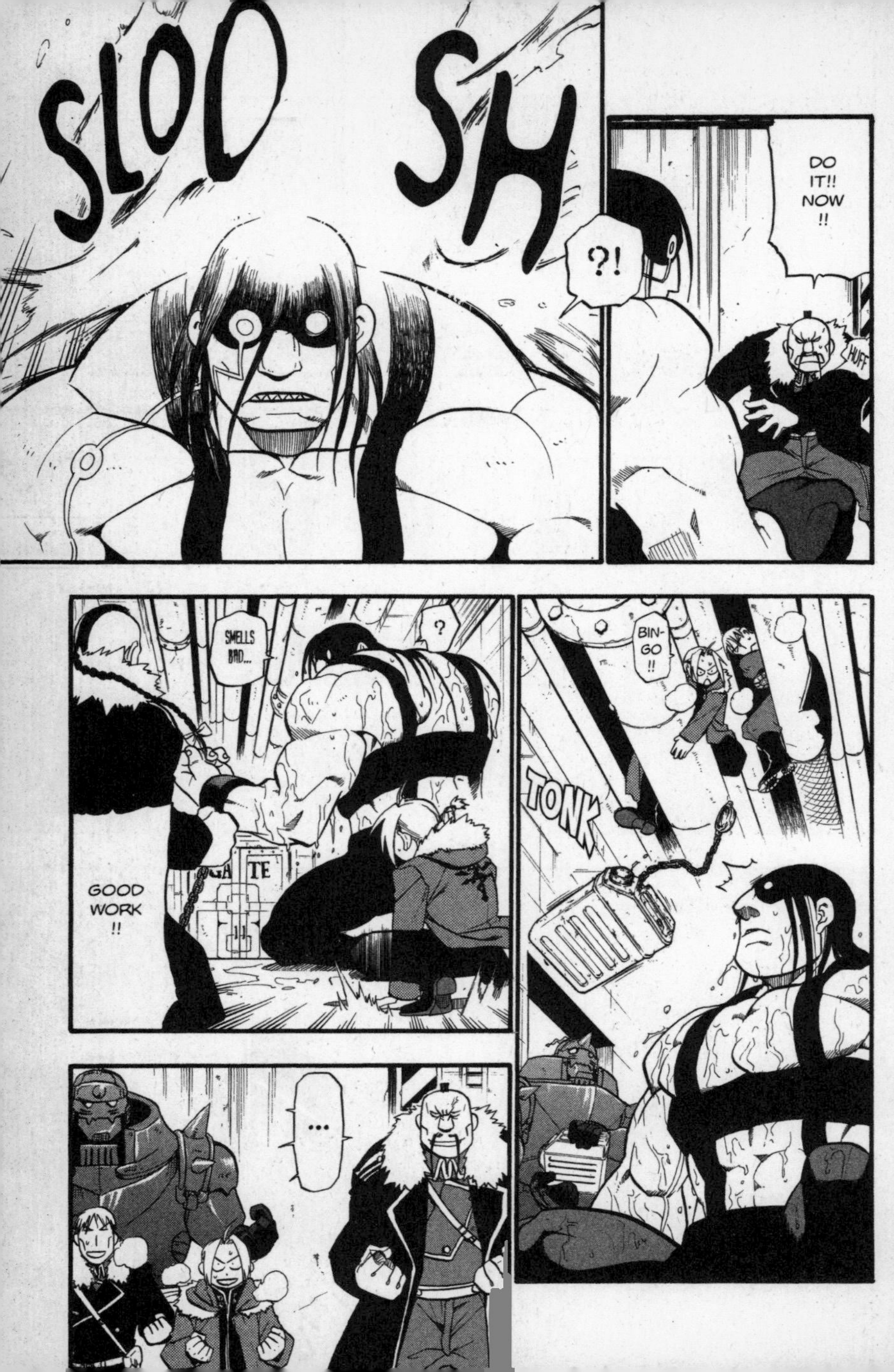
DO IT!! NOW !!
HUFF
?!
SLOOSH
BIN-GO !!
TONK
?
SMELLS BAD...
GOOD WORK !!
...

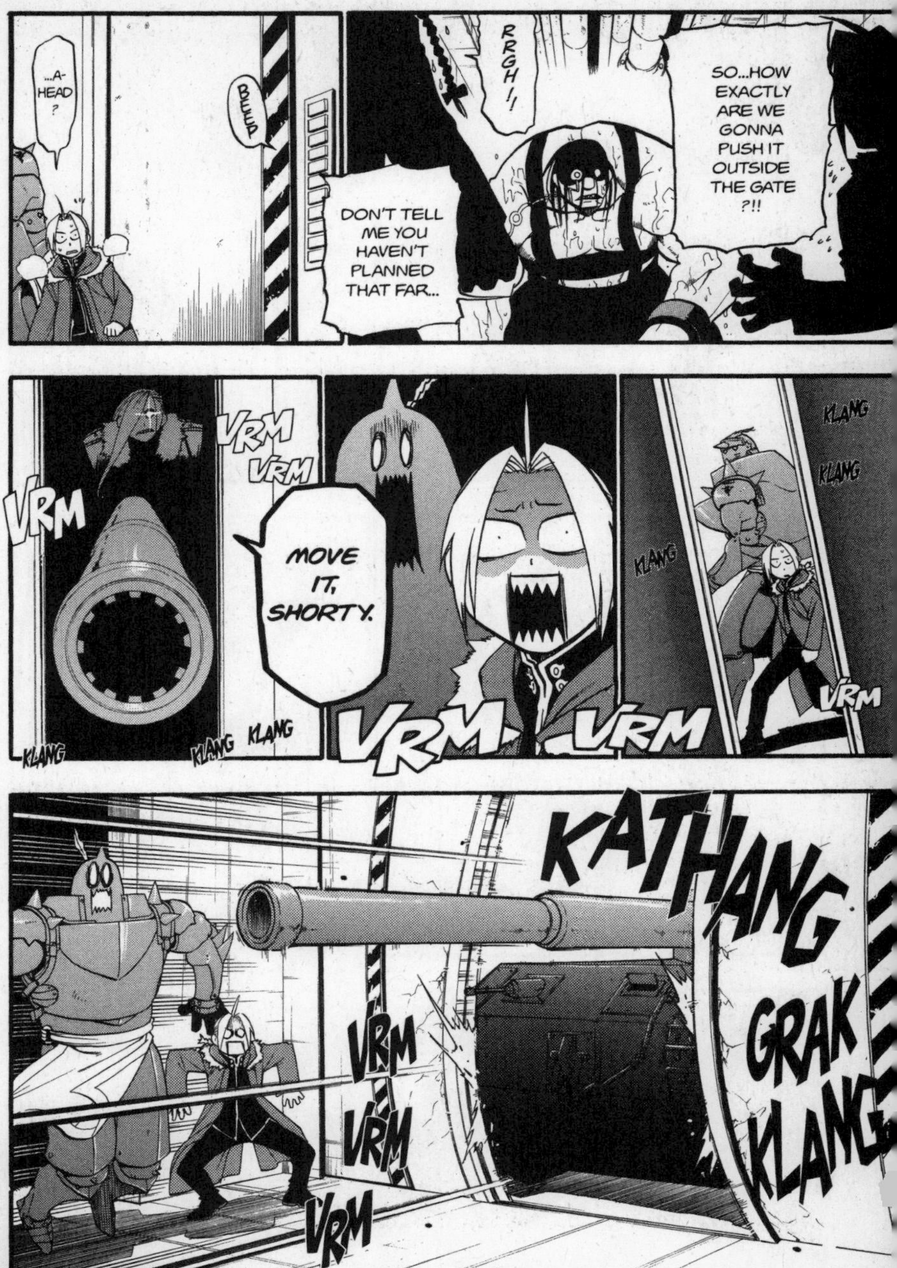

RRGH!!
SO...HOW EXACTLY ARE WE GONNA PUSH IT OUTSIDE THE GATE?!!
DON'T TELL ME YOU HAVEN'T PLANNED THAT FAR...
BEEP
...A-HEAD?
KLANG
KLANG
KLANG
VRM
MOVE IT, SHORTY.
VRM
VRM
VRM
VRM
VRM
KLANG KLANG
KLANG
KATHANG
GRAK
KLANG
VRM
VRM
VRM

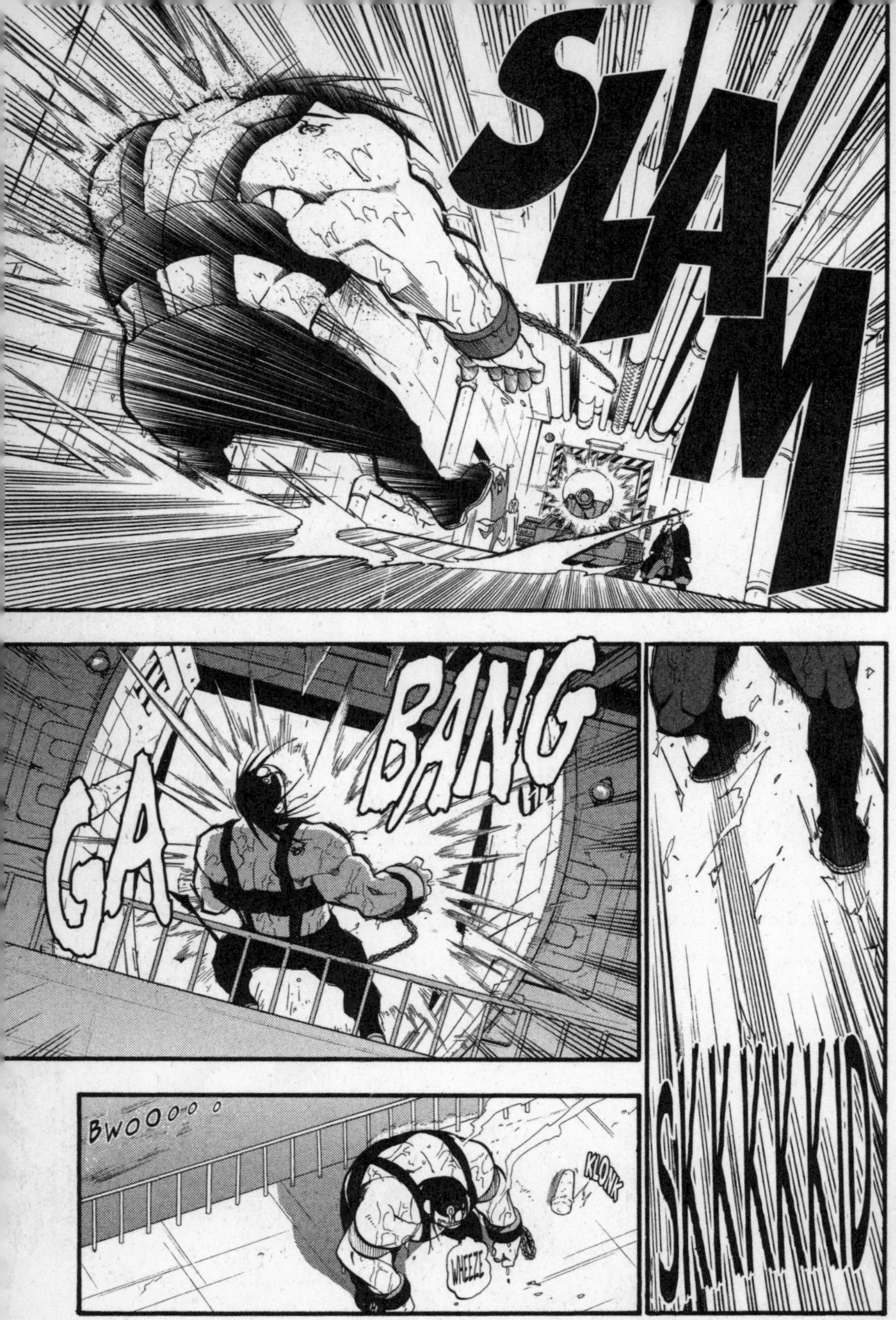
SLAM
SKKKKID
BANG
GA
KLONK
WHEEZE
BWOOOO o

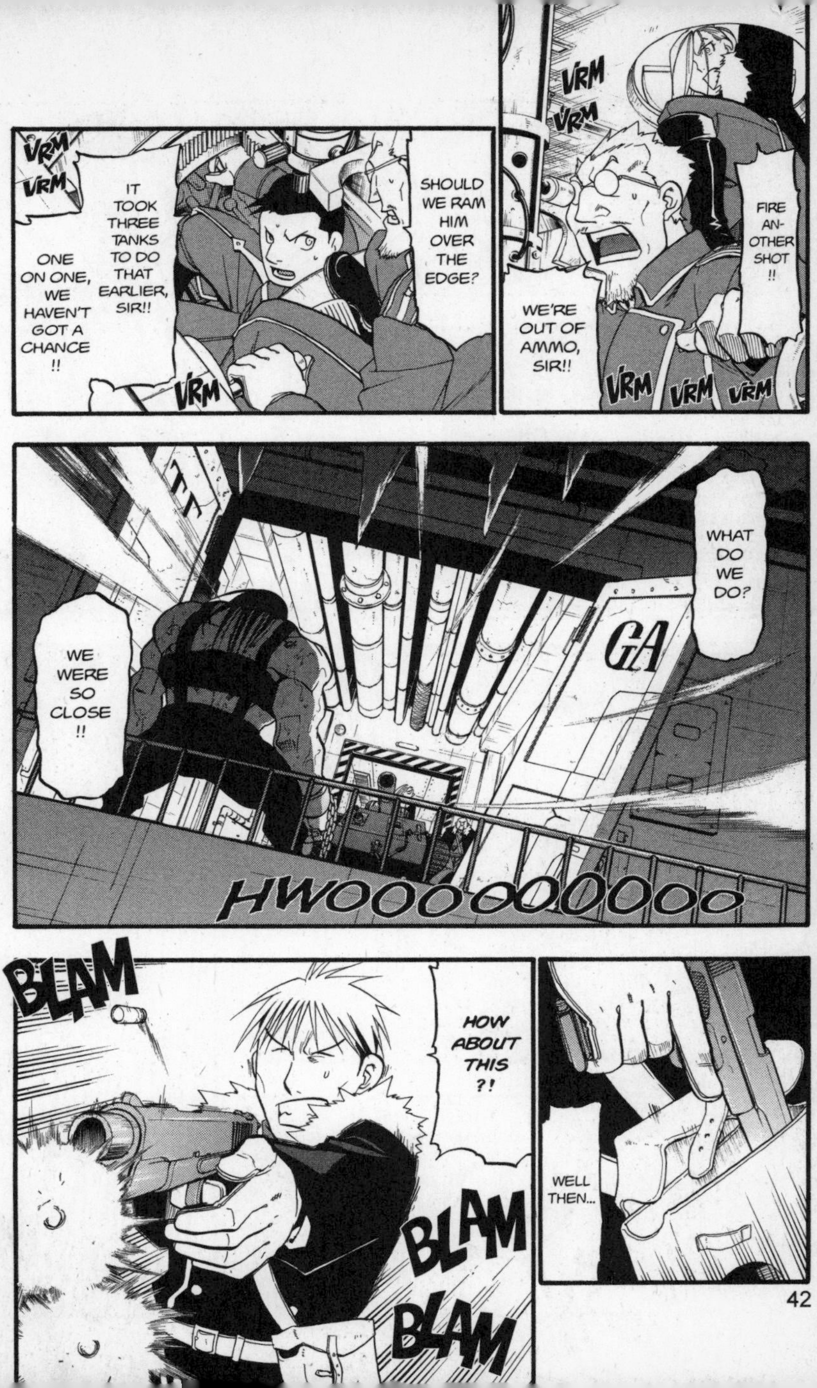
VRM
VRM
FIRE AN-OTHER SHOT!!
WE'RE OUT OF AMMO, SIR!!
VRM VRM VRM
VRM
VRM
SHOULD WE RAM HIM OVER THE EDGE?
IT TOOK THREE TANKS TO DO THAT EARLIER, SIR!!
ONE ON ONE, WE HAVEN'T GOT A CHANCE!!
VRM
WHAT DO WE DO?
GA
WE WERE SO CLOSE!!
HWOOOOOOOOOO
WELL THEN...
BLAM
HOW ABOUT THIS?!
BLAM
BLAM

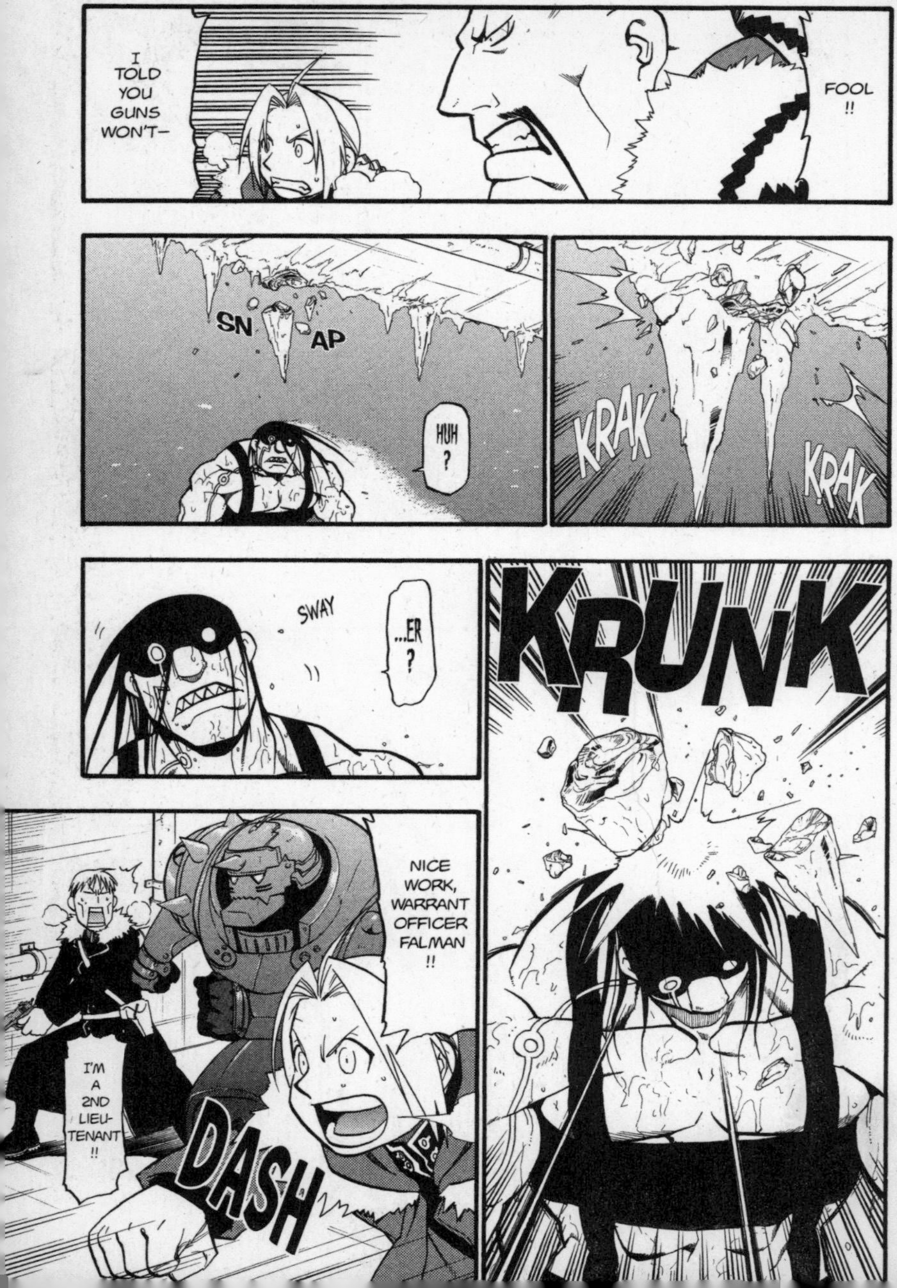
FOOL !!
I TOLD YOU GUNS WON'T—
KRAK
KRAK
SN AP
HUH ?
KRUNK
...ER ?
SWAY
NICE WORK, WARRANT OFFICER FALMAN !!
I'M A 2ND LIEU-TENANT !!
DASH

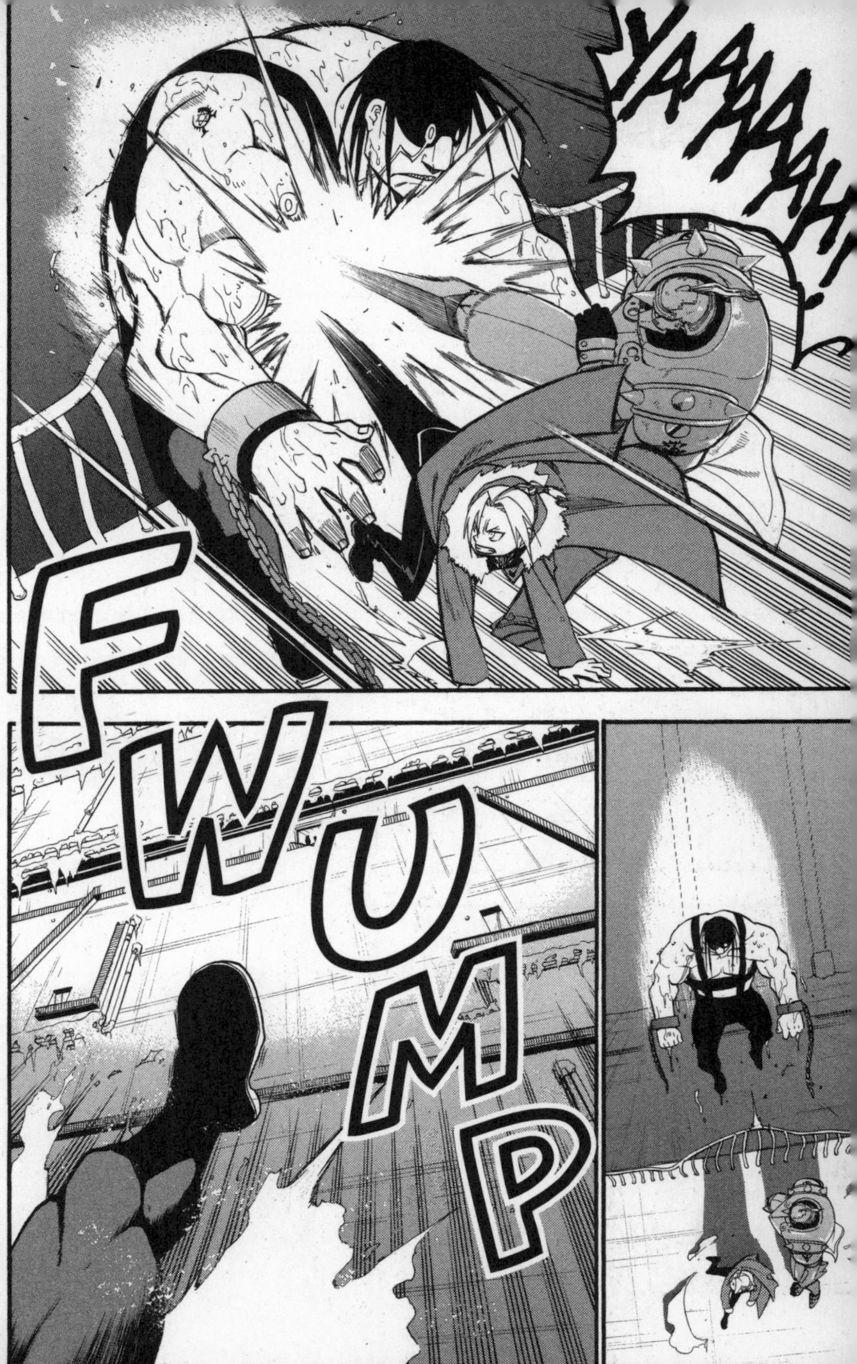
YAAAAAH!!
FWUMP

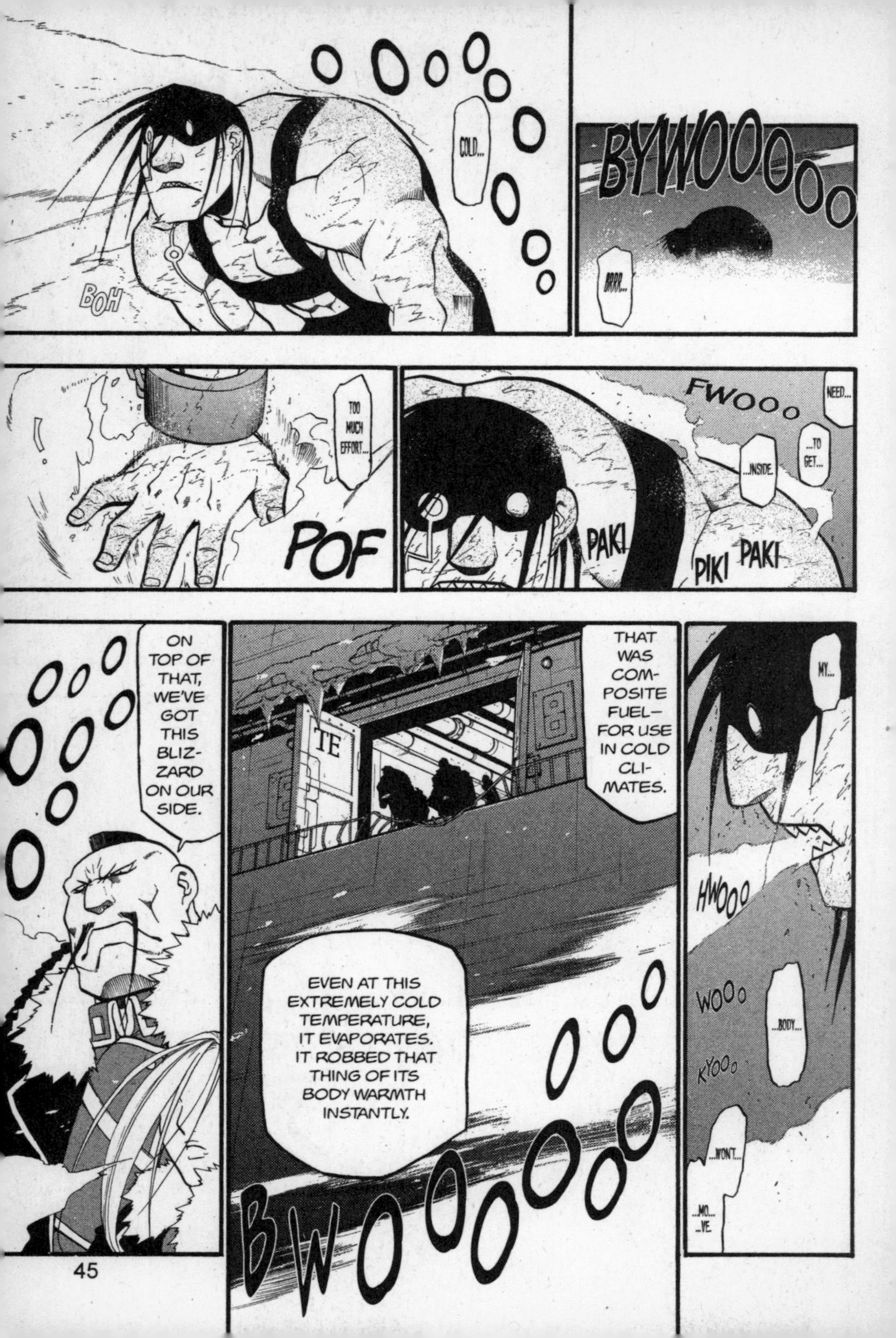
BYWOOOOOO
BRRR...
OOOOOOOOOOO
COLD...
BOH
FWOOO
NEED...
...TO GET...
...INSIDE.
PAKI
PIKI PAKI
TOO MUCH EFFORT...
POF
MY...
HWOOO
WOOO
...BODY...
KYOOO
...WON'T...
...MO... ...VE.
THAT WAS COMPOSITE FUEL—FOR USE IN COLD CLIMATES.
EVEN AT THIS EXTREMELY COLD TEMPERATURE, IT EVAPORATES. IT ROBBED THAT THING OF ITS BODY WARMTH INSTANTLY.
BWOOOOOOOOOOO
ON TOP OF THAT, WE'VE GOT THIS BLIZZARD ON OUR SIDE.
OOOOOOOOOO

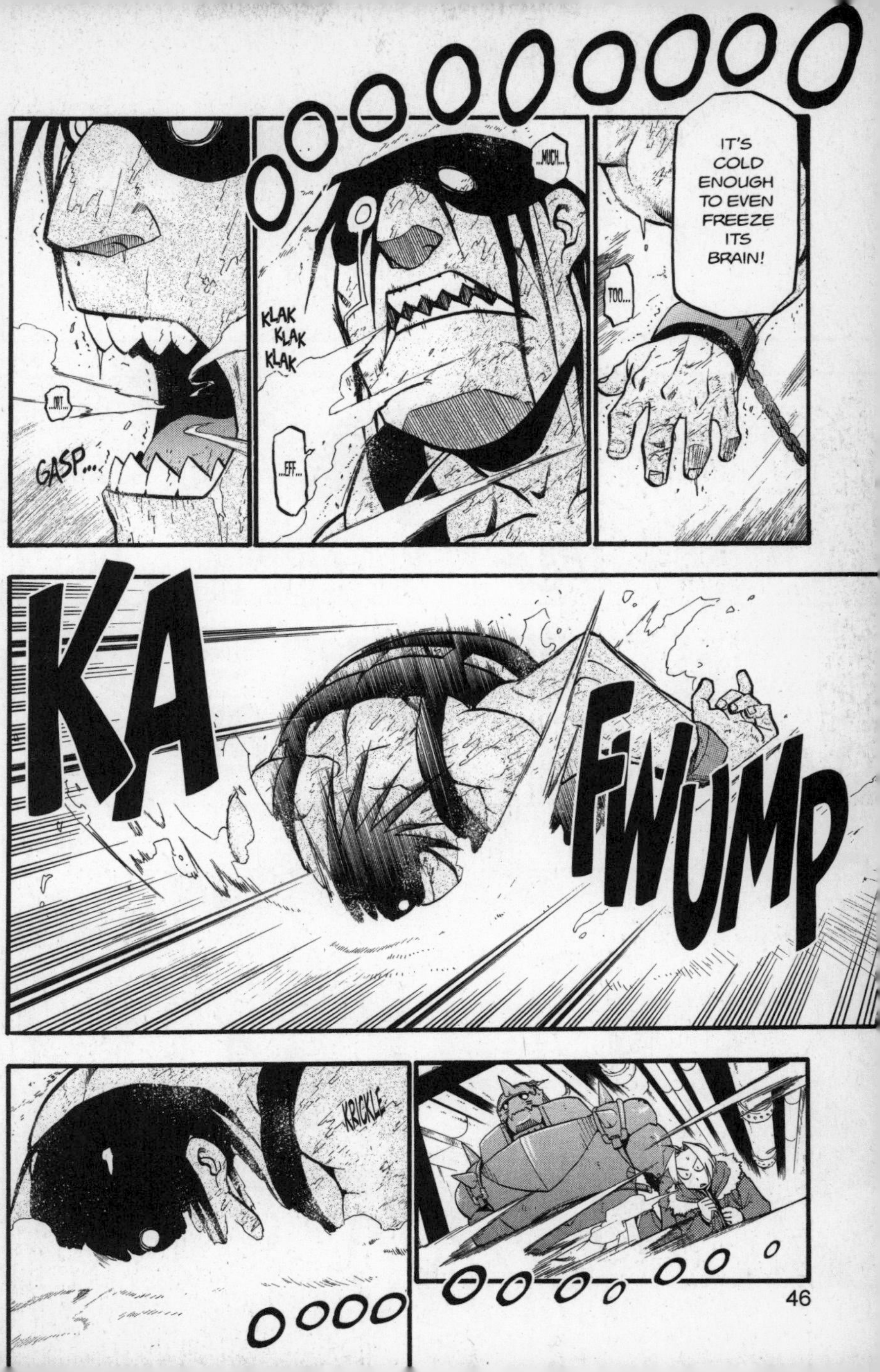
OOOOOOOOOOO
IT'S COLD ENOUGH TO EVEN FREEZE ITS BRAIN!
TOO...
...MUCH...
KLAK KLAK KLAK
...EFF...
...ORT...
GASP...
KA
FWUMP
OOOOOOOO
KRICKLE
OOOO

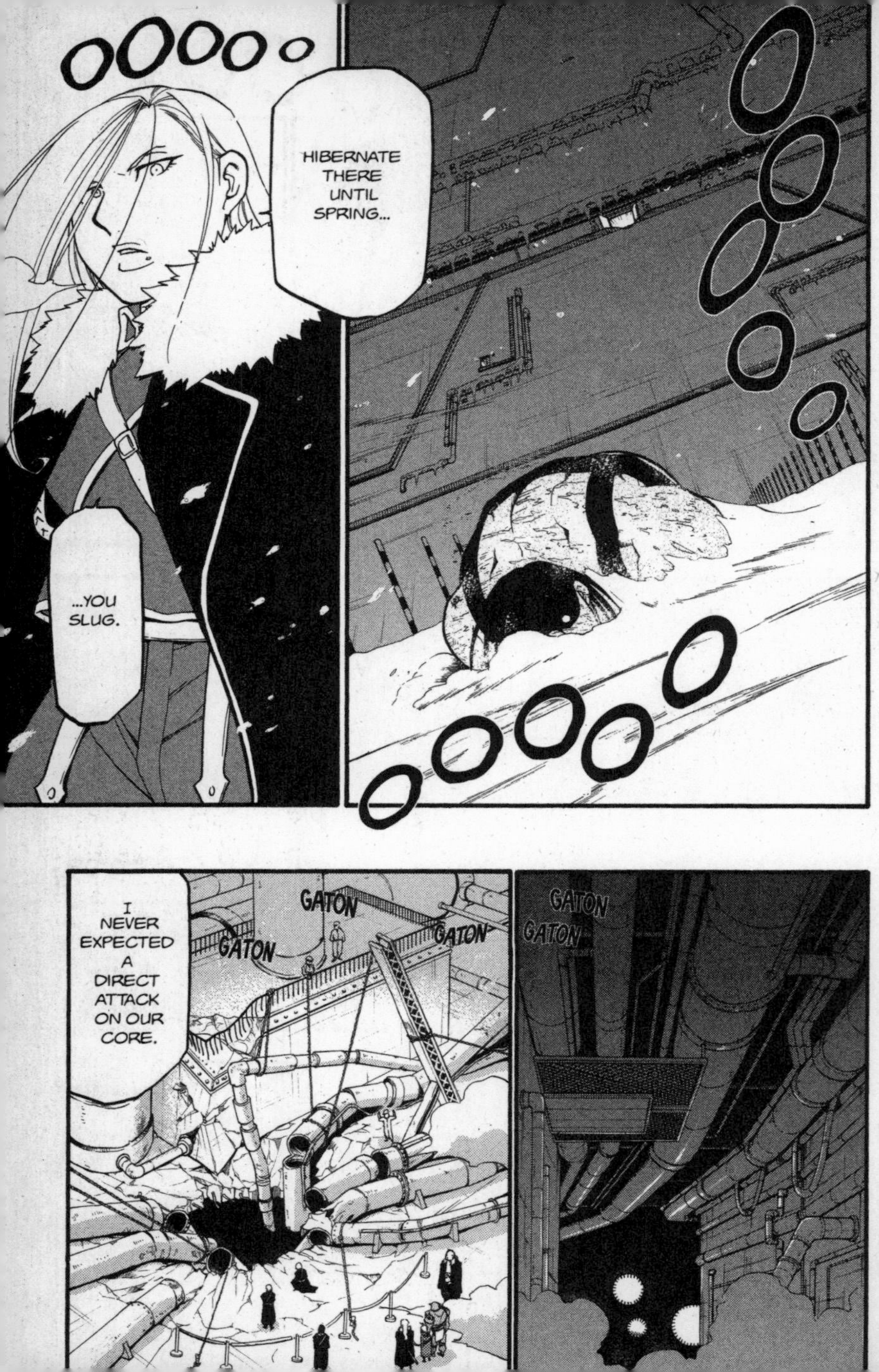
OOOOOOOOOO
OOOOOO
OOOOO
HIBERNATE THERE UNTIL SPRING...
...YOU SLUG.
GATON
GATON
I NEVER EXPECTED A DIRECT ATTACK ON OUR CORE.
GATON
GATON
GATON

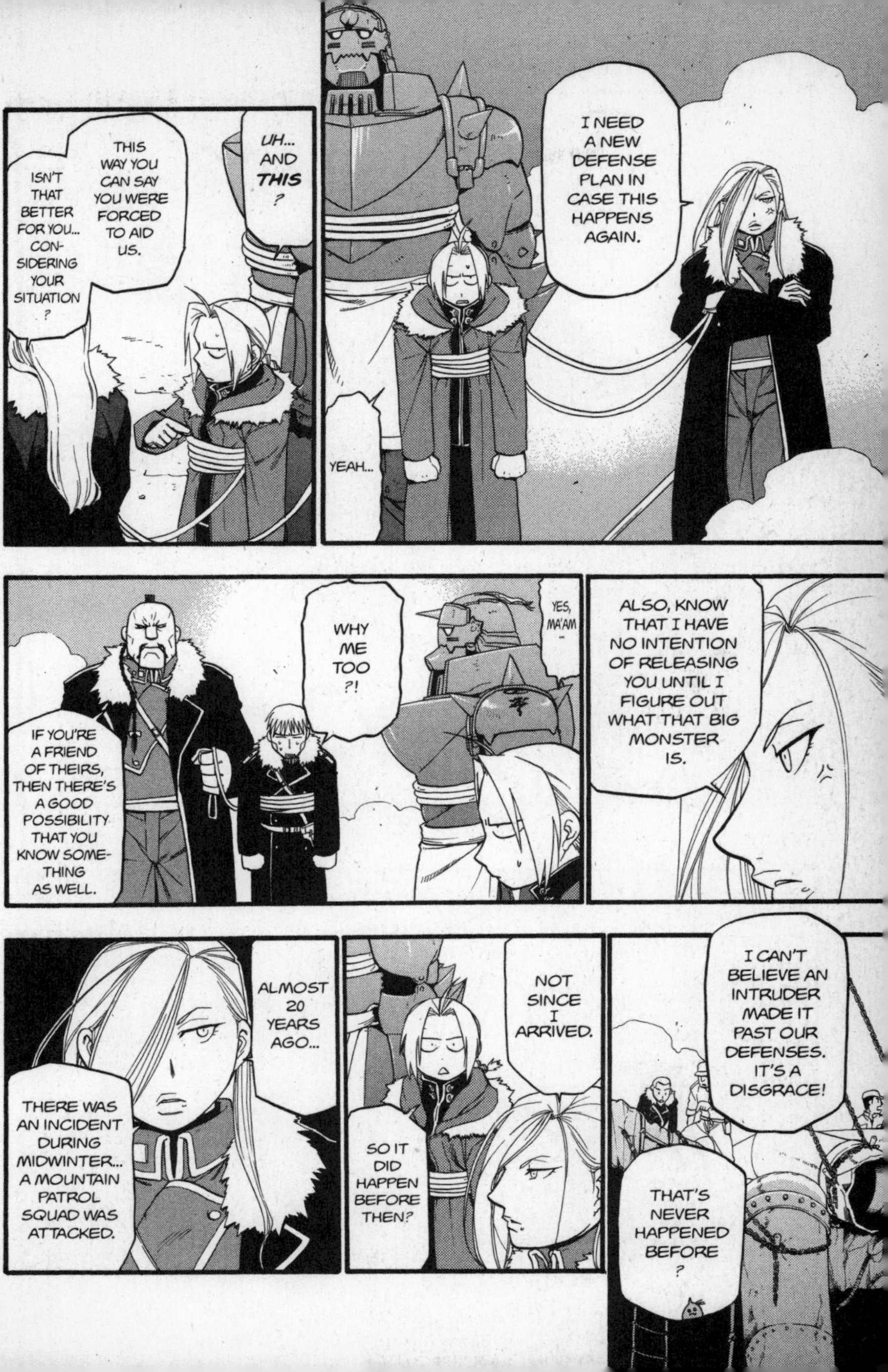
I NEED A NEW DEFENSE PLAN IN CASE THIS HAPPENS AGAIN.
YEAH...
UH... AND *THIS*?
THIS WAY YOU CAN SAY YOU WERE FORCED TO AID US.
ISN'T THAT BETTER FOR YOU... CONSIDERING YOUR SITUATION?
ALSO, KNOW THAT I HAVE NO INTENTION OF RELEASING YOU UNTIL I FIGURE OUT WHAT THAT BIG MONSTER IS.
YES, MA'AM...
WHY ME TOO?!
IF YOU'RE A FRIEND OF THEIRS, THEN THERE'S A GOOD POSSIBILITY THAT YOU KNOW SOMETHING AS WELL.
I CAN'T BELIEVE AN INTRUDER MADE IT PAST OUR DEFENSES. IT'S A DISGRACE!
THAT'S NEVER HAPPENED BEFORE?
NOT SINCE I ARRIVED.
SO IT DID HAPPEN BEFORE THEN?
ALMOST 20 YEARS AGO...
THERE WAS AN INCIDENT DURING MIDWINTER... A MOUNTAIN PATROL SQUAD WAS ATTACKED.

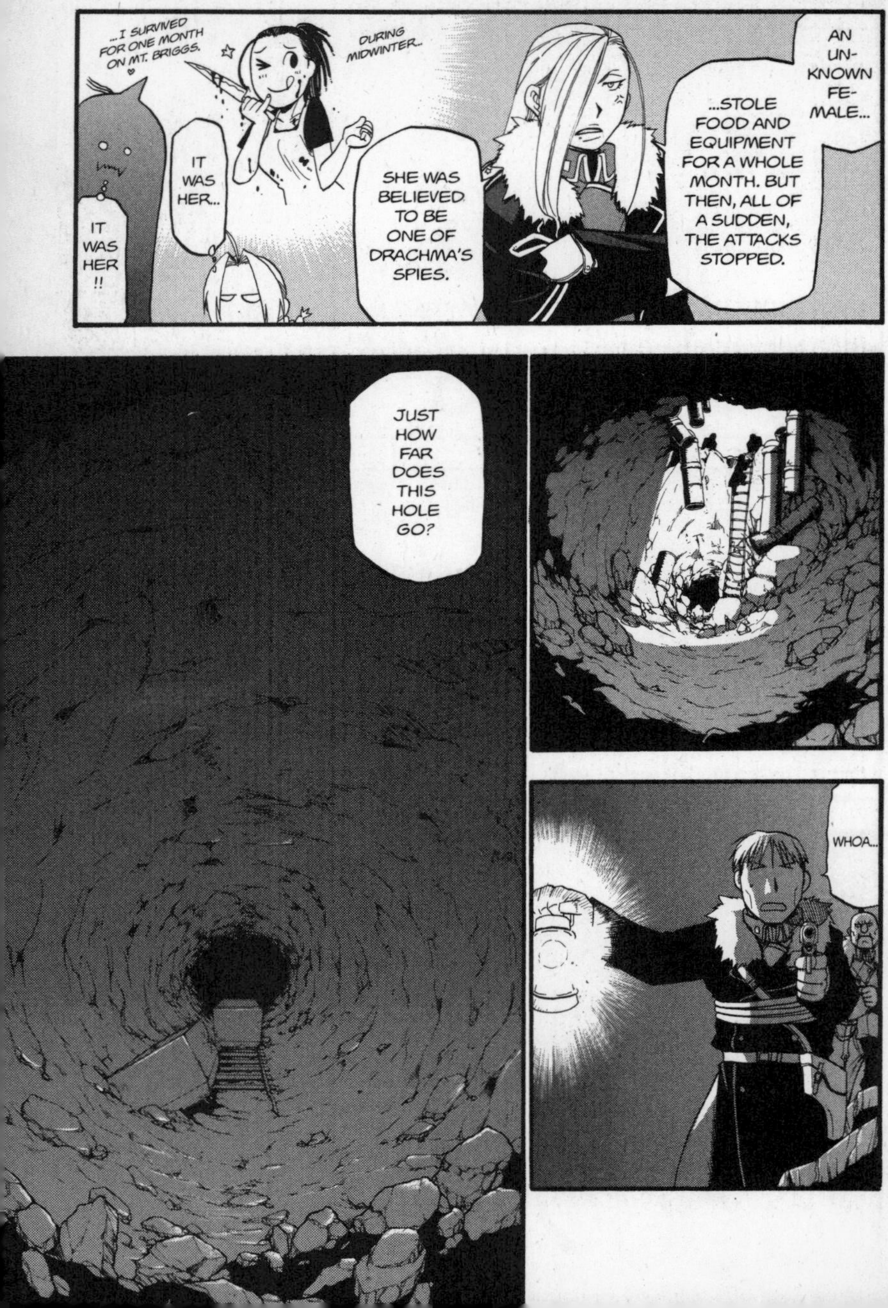
AN UNKNOWN FEMALE...
...STOLE FOOD AND EQUIPMENT FOR A WHOLE MONTH. BUT THEN, ALL OF A SUDDEN, THE ATTACKS STOPPED.
SHE WAS BELIEVED TO BE ONE OF DRACHMA'S SPIES.
DURING MIDWINTER...
...I SURVIVED FOR ONE MONTH ON MT. BRIGGS.
IT WAS HER...
IT WAS HER!!
WHOA...
JUST HOW FAR DOES THIS HOLE GO?

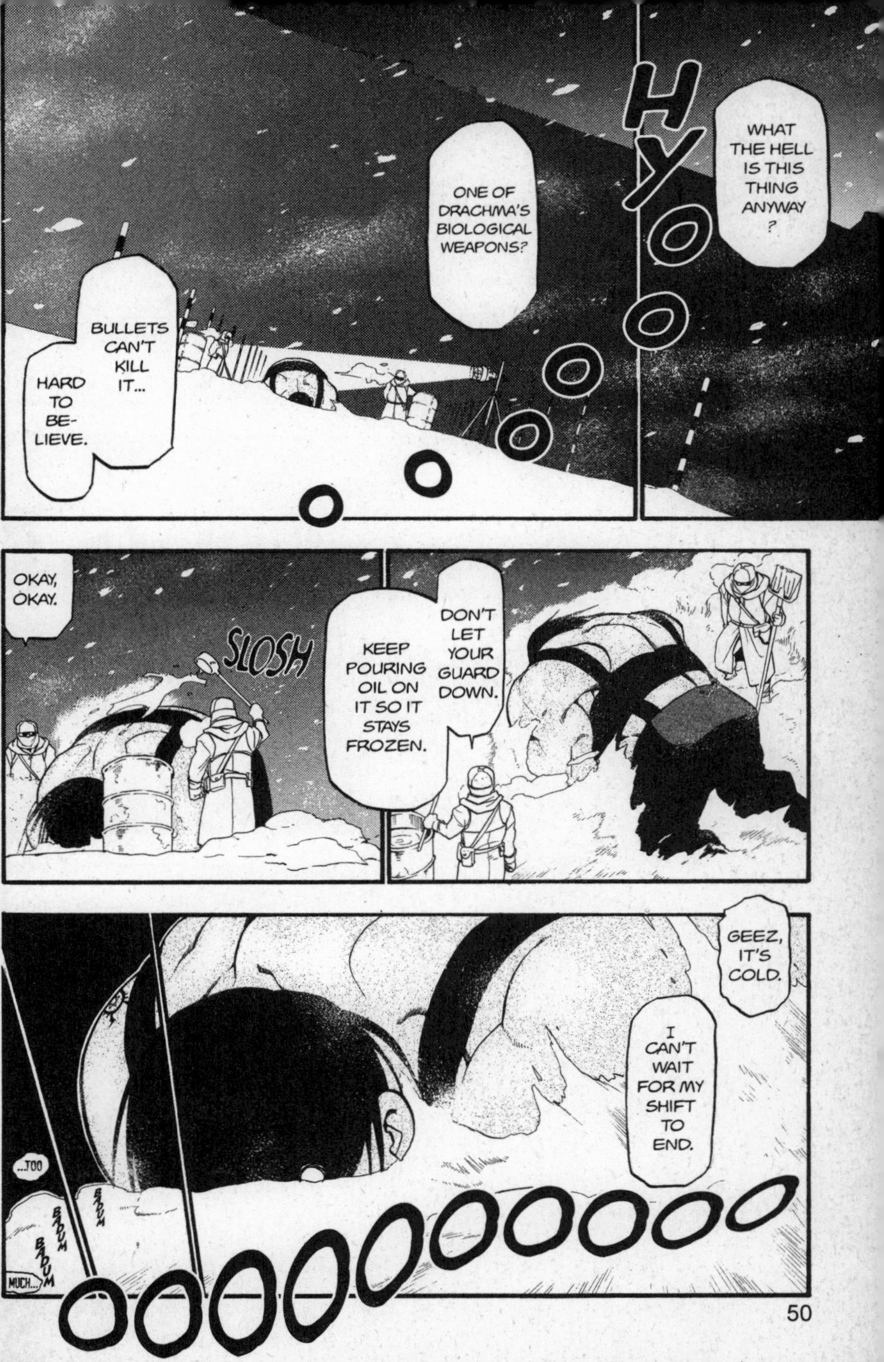
HYOOOOOO
WHAT THE HELL IS THIS THING ANYWAY?
ONE OF DRACHMA'S BIOLOGICAL WEAPONS?
BULLETS CAN'T KILL IT...
HARD TO BE-LIEVE.
DON'T LET YOUR GUARD DOWN.
KEEP POURING OIL ON IT SO IT STAYS FROZEN.
OKAY, OKAY.
SLOSH
GEEZ, IT'S COLD.
I CAN'T WAIT FOR MY SHIFT TO END.
...TOO
BADUM
BADUM
MUCH...
OOOOOOOOOOOOOO

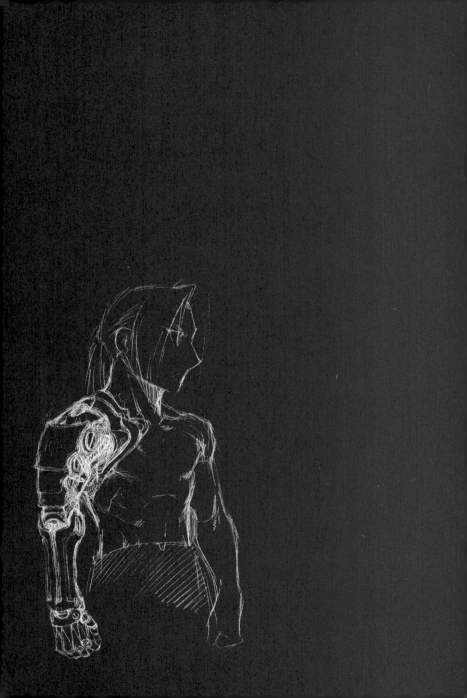

FULLMETAL
ALCHEMIST

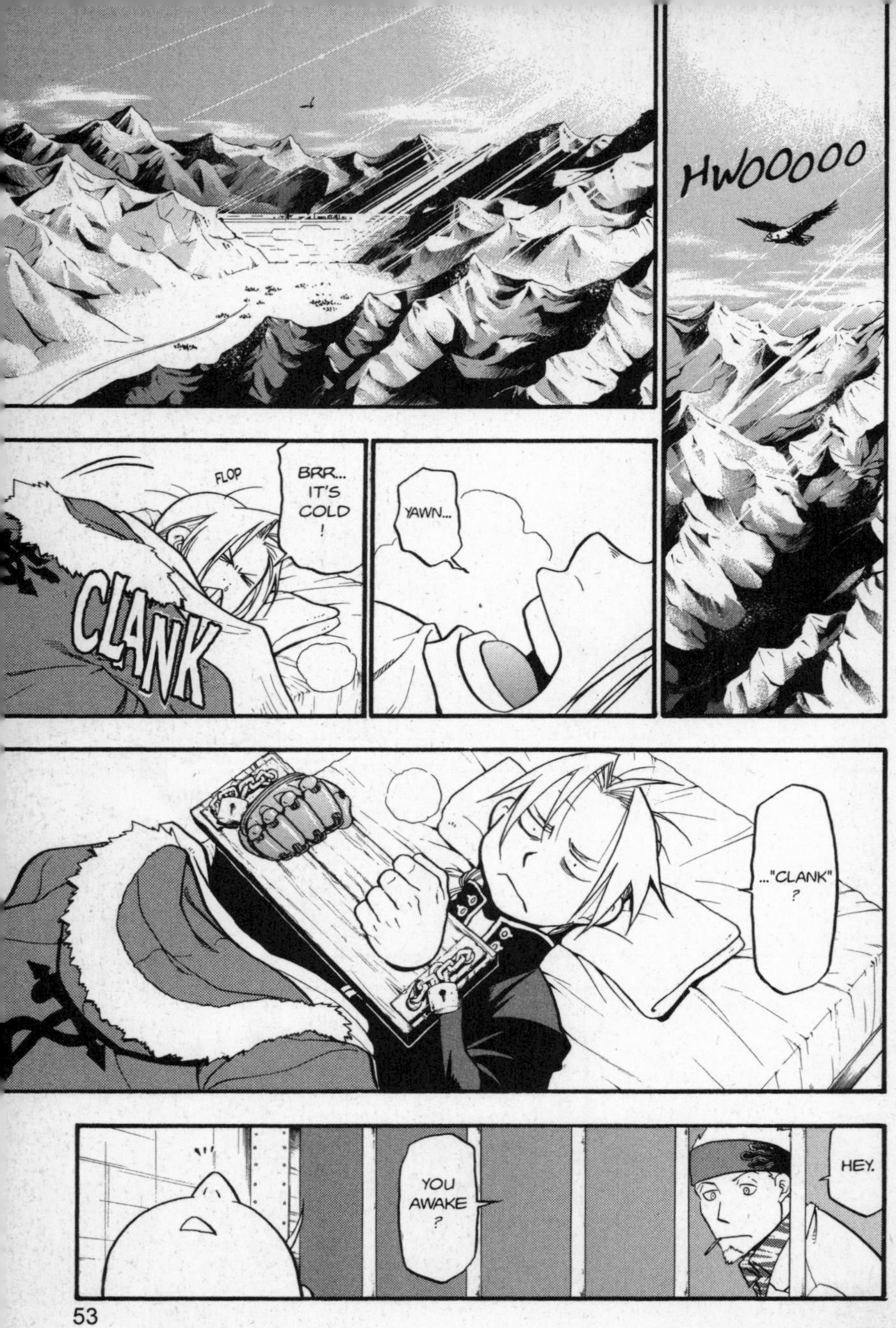
HWOOOOO
YAWN...
BRR... IT'S COLD!
FLOP
CLANK
..."CLANK"?
HEY.
YOU AWAKE?

Chapter 67
Burgeoning Borders

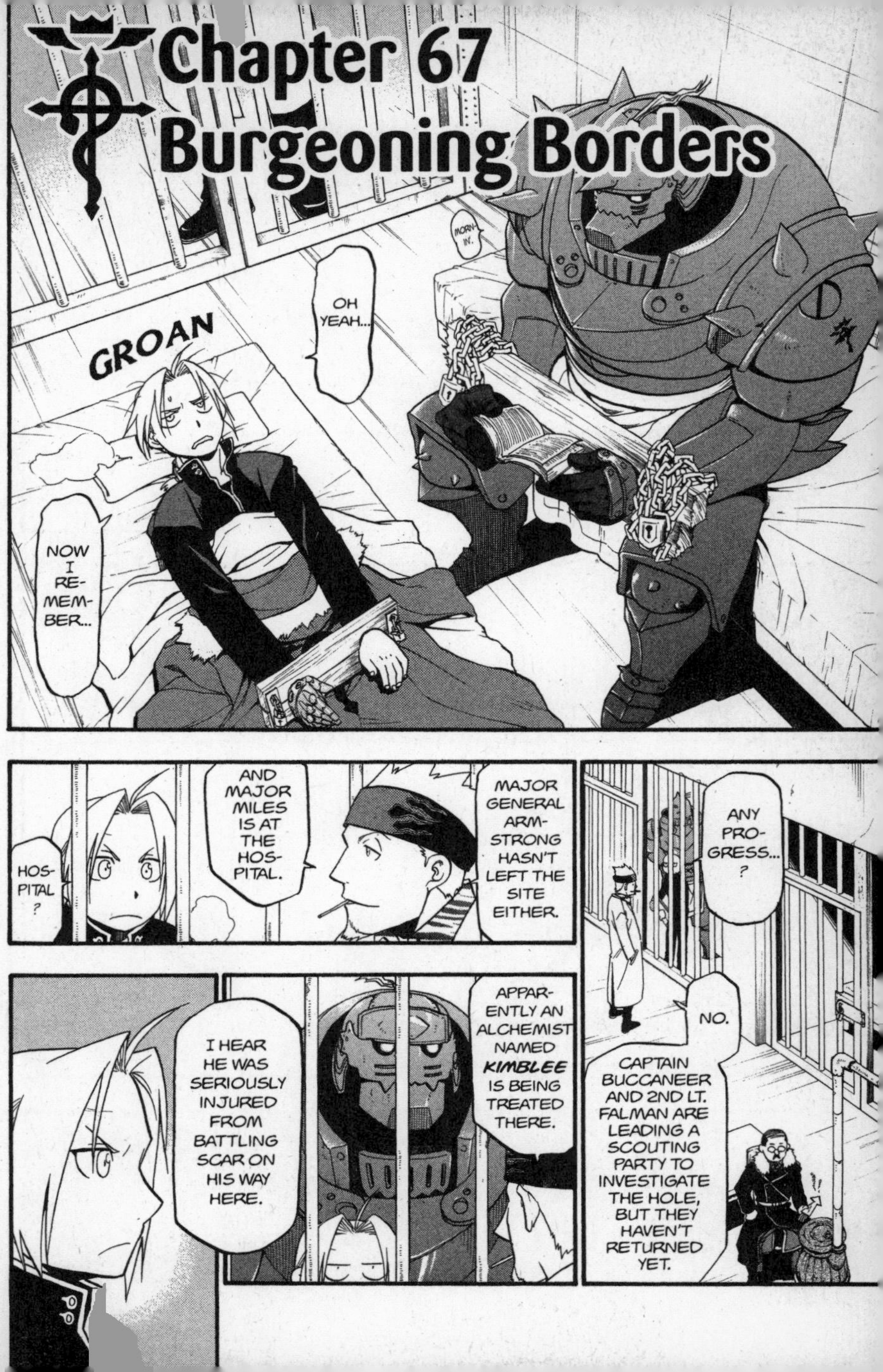
MORN-IN'.
OH YEAH...
GROAN
NOW I RE-MEM-BER...
ANY PRO-GRESS...?
NO.
CAPTAIN BUCCANEER AND 2ND LT. FALMAN ARE LEADING A SCOUTING PARTY TO INVESTIGATE THE HOLE, BUT THEY HAVEN'T RETURNED YET.
MAJOR GENERAL ARM-STRONG HASN'T LEFT THE SITE EITHER.
AND MAJOR MILES IS AT THE HOS-PITAL.
HOS-PITAL?
APPAR-ENTLY AN ALCHEMIST NAMED KIMBLEE IS BEING TREATED THERE.
I HEAR HE WAS SERIOUSLY INJURED FROM BATTLING SCAR ON HIS WAY HERE.

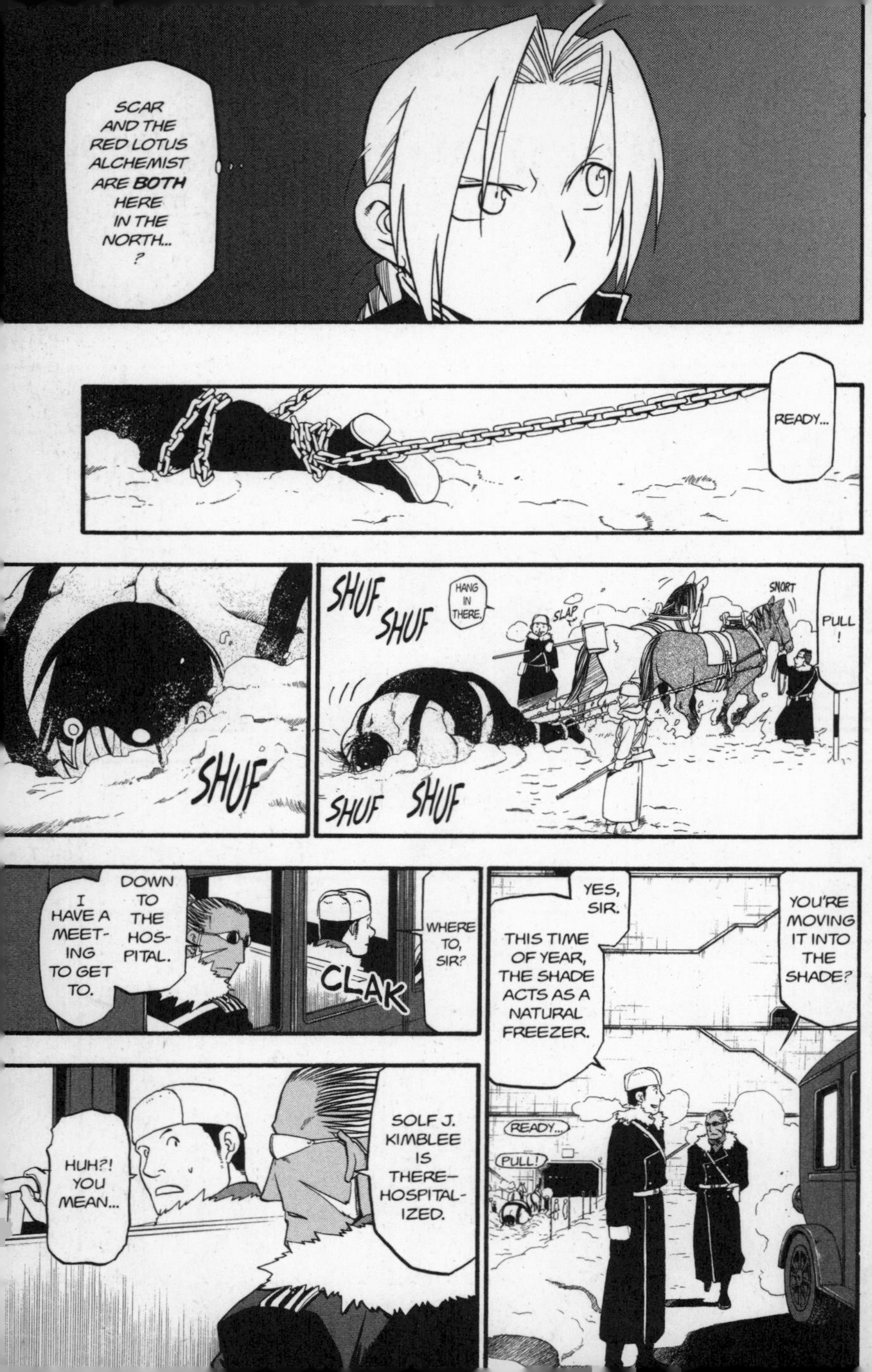
SCAR AND THE RED LOTUS ALCHEMIST ARE BOTH HERE IN THE NORTH... ?
READY...
PULL !
SNORT
SLAP
HANG IN THERE.
SHUF SHUF
SHUF SHUF
SHUF
YOU'RE MOVING IT INTO THE SHADE?
YES, SIR.
THIS TIME OF YEAR, THE SHADE ACTS AS A NATURAL FREEZER.
READY...
PULL!
WHERE TO, SIR?
CLAK
DOWN TO THE HOSPITAL.
I HAVE A MEETING TO GET TO.
SOLF J. KIMBLEE IS THERE—HOSPITALIZED.
HUH?! YOU MEAN...

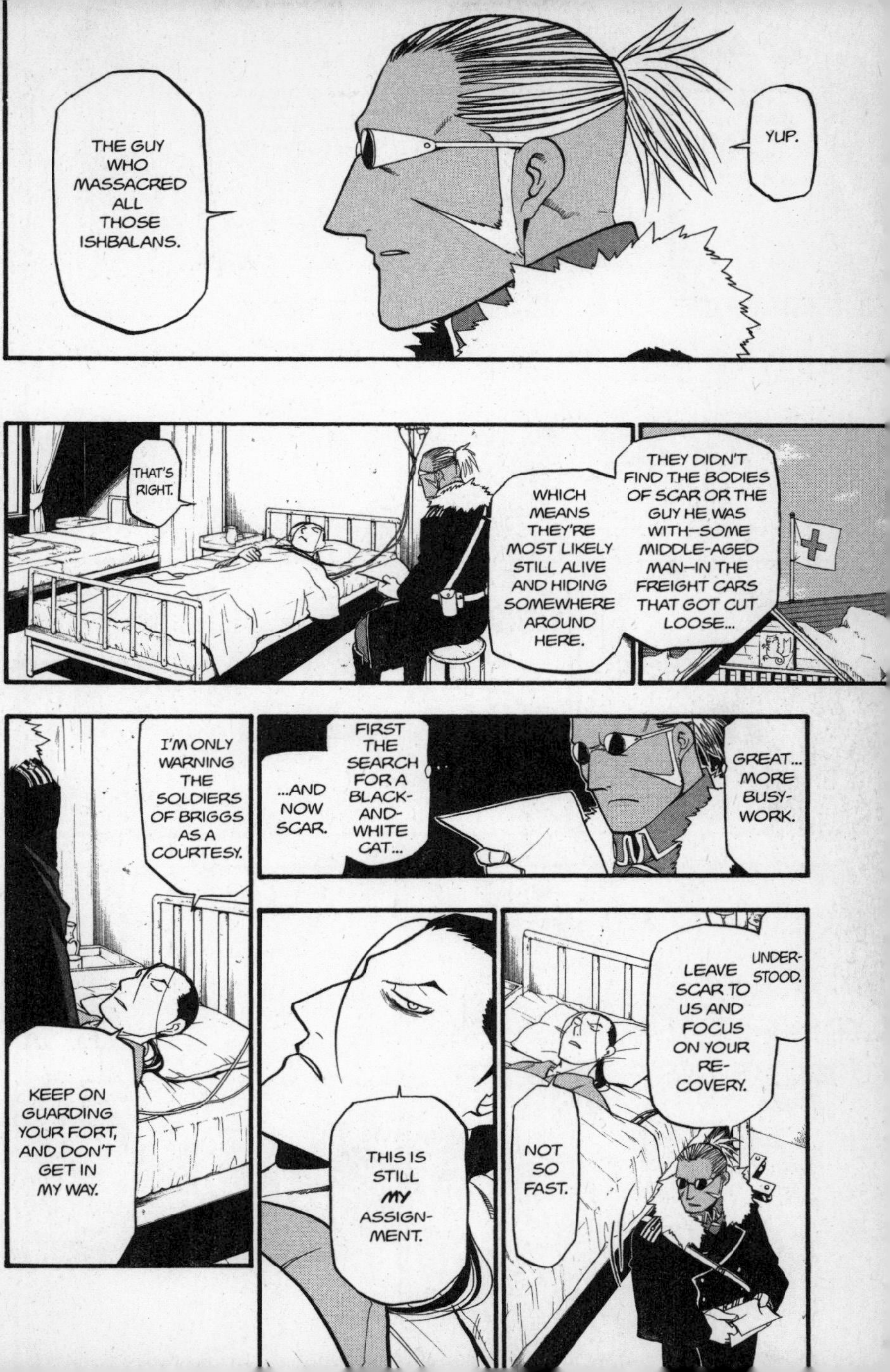
YUP.
THE GUY WHO MASSACRED ALL THOSE ISHBALANS.
THEY DIDN'T FIND THE BODIES OF SCAR OR THE GUY HE WAS WITH—SOME MIDDLE-AGED MAN—IN THE FREIGHT CARS THAT GOT CUT LOOSE...
WHICH MEANS THEY'RE MOST LIKELY STILL ALIVE AND HIDING SOMEWHERE AROUND HERE.
THAT'S RIGHT.
GREAT... MORE BUSY-WORK.
FIRST THE SEARCH FOR A BLACK-AND-WHITE CAT...
...AND NOW SCAR.
UNDER-STOOD.
LEAVE SCAR TO US AND FOCUS ON YOUR RE-COVERY.
NOT SO FAST.
THIS IS STILL *MY* ASSIGN-MENT.
I'M ONLY WARNING THE SOLDIERS OF BRIGGS AS A COURTESY.
KEEP ON GUARDING YOUR FORT, AND DON'T GET IN MY WAY.

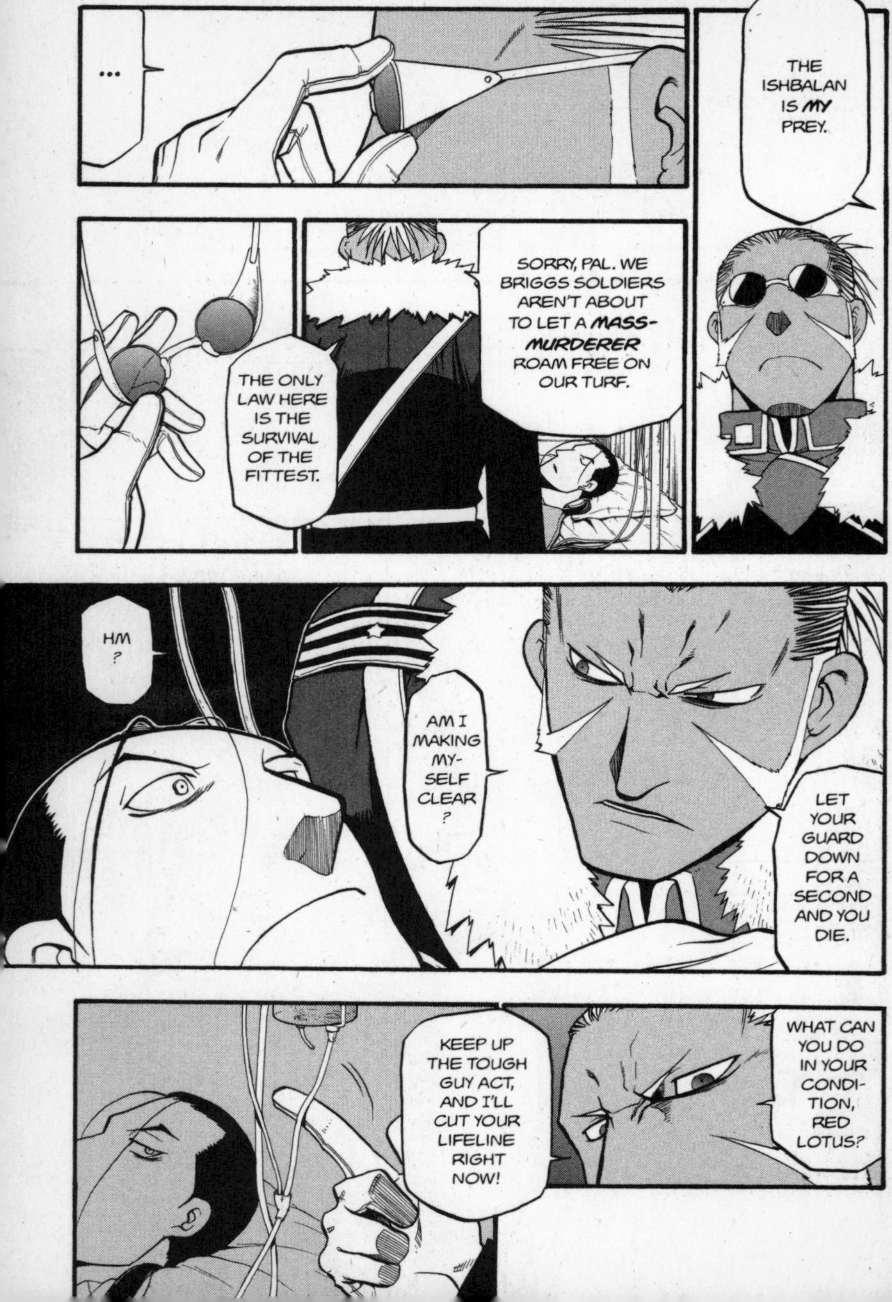
THE ISHBALAN IS MY PREY.
...
SORRY, PAL. WE BRIGGS SOLDIERS AREN'T ABOUT TO LET A MASS-MURDERER ROAM FREE ON OUR TURF.
THE ONLY LAW HERE IS THE SURVIVAL OF THE FITTEST.
LET YOUR GUARD DOWN FOR A SECOND AND YOU DIE.
AM I MAKING MY-SELF CLEAR?
HM?
WHAT CAN YOU DO IN YOUR CONDI-TION, RED LOTUS?
KEEP UP THE TOUGH GUY ACT, AND I'LL CUT YOUR LIFELINE RIGHT NOW!

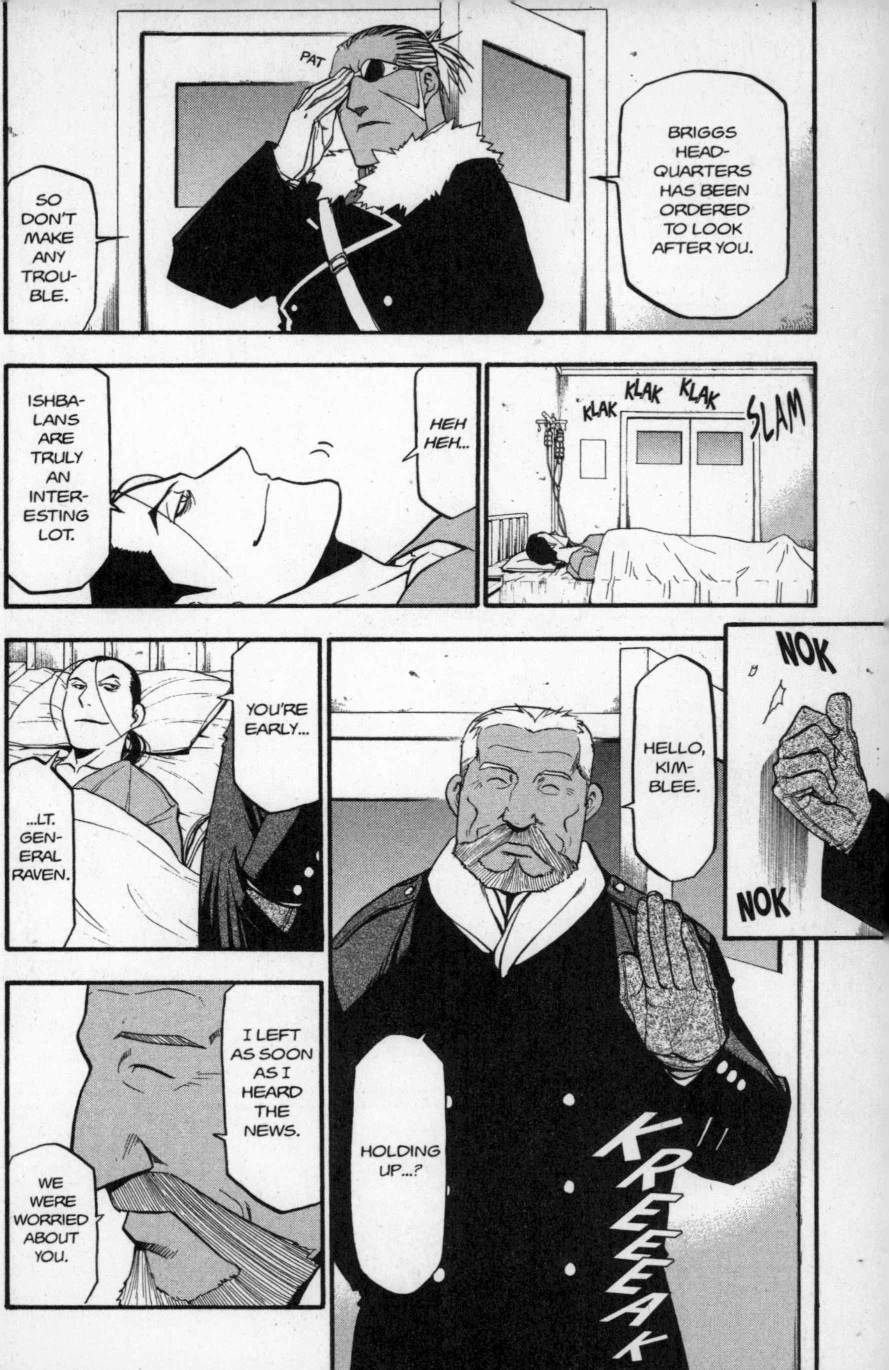
PAT
BRIGGS HEAD-QUARTERS HAS BEEN ORDERED TO LOOK AFTER YOU.
SO DON'T MAKE ANY TROU-BLE.
KLAK
KLAK
KLAK
SLAM
HEH HEH...
ISHBA-LANS ARE TRULY AN INTER-ESTING LOT.
NOK
NOK
KREEEAK
HELLO, KIM-BLEE.
HOLDING UP...?
YOU'RE EARLY...
...LT. GEN-ERAL RAVEN.
I LEFT AS SOON AS I HEARD THE NEWS.
WE WERE WORRIED ABOUT YOU.

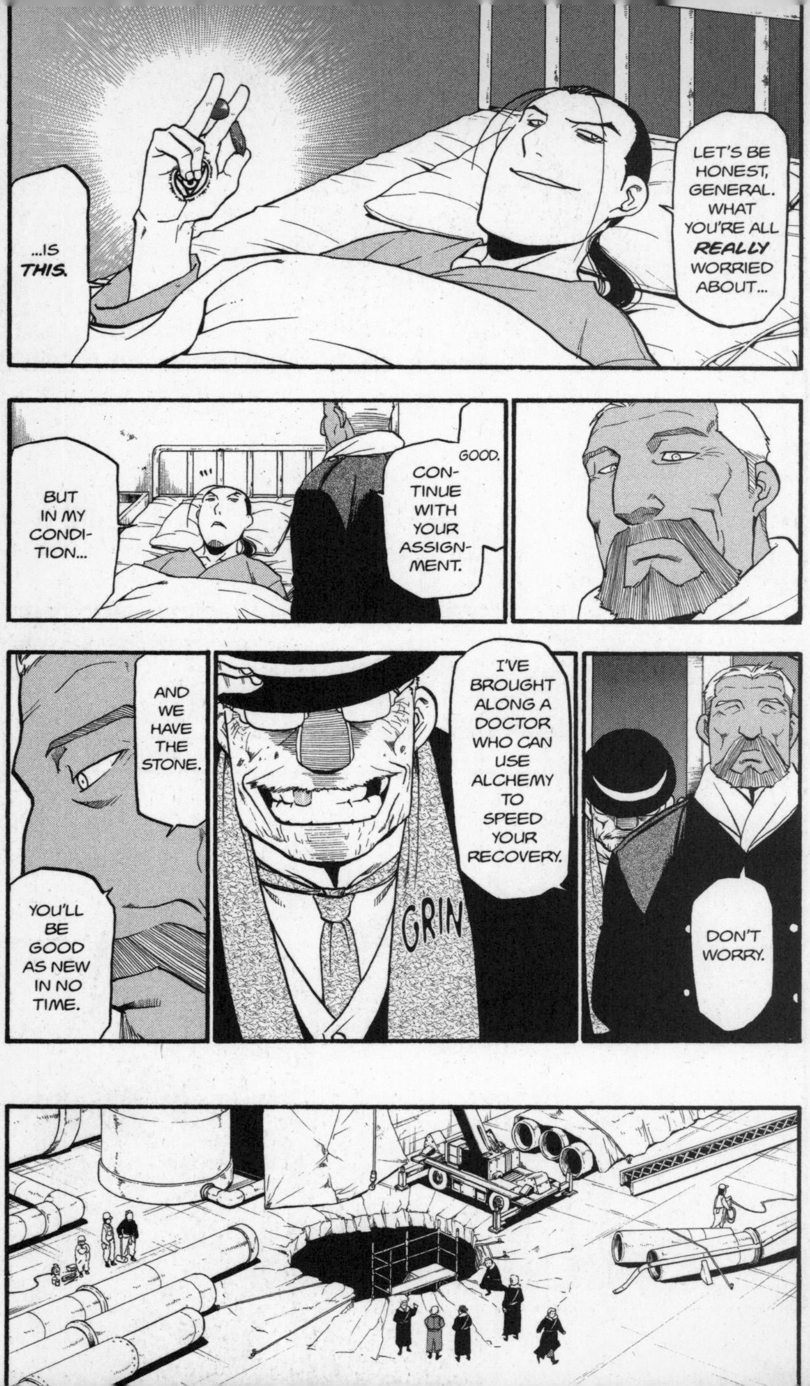
LET'S BE HONEST, GENERAL. WHAT YOU'RE ALL *REALLY* WORRIED ABOUT...
...IS *THIS.*
GOOD.
CONTINUE WITH YOUR ASSIGNMENT.
BUT IN MY CONDITION...
DON'T WORRY.
I'VE BROUGHT ALONG A DOCTOR WHO CAN USE ALCHEMY TO SPEED YOUR RECOVERY.
GRIN
AND WE HAVE THE STONE.
YOU'LL BE GOOD AS NEW IN NO TIME.

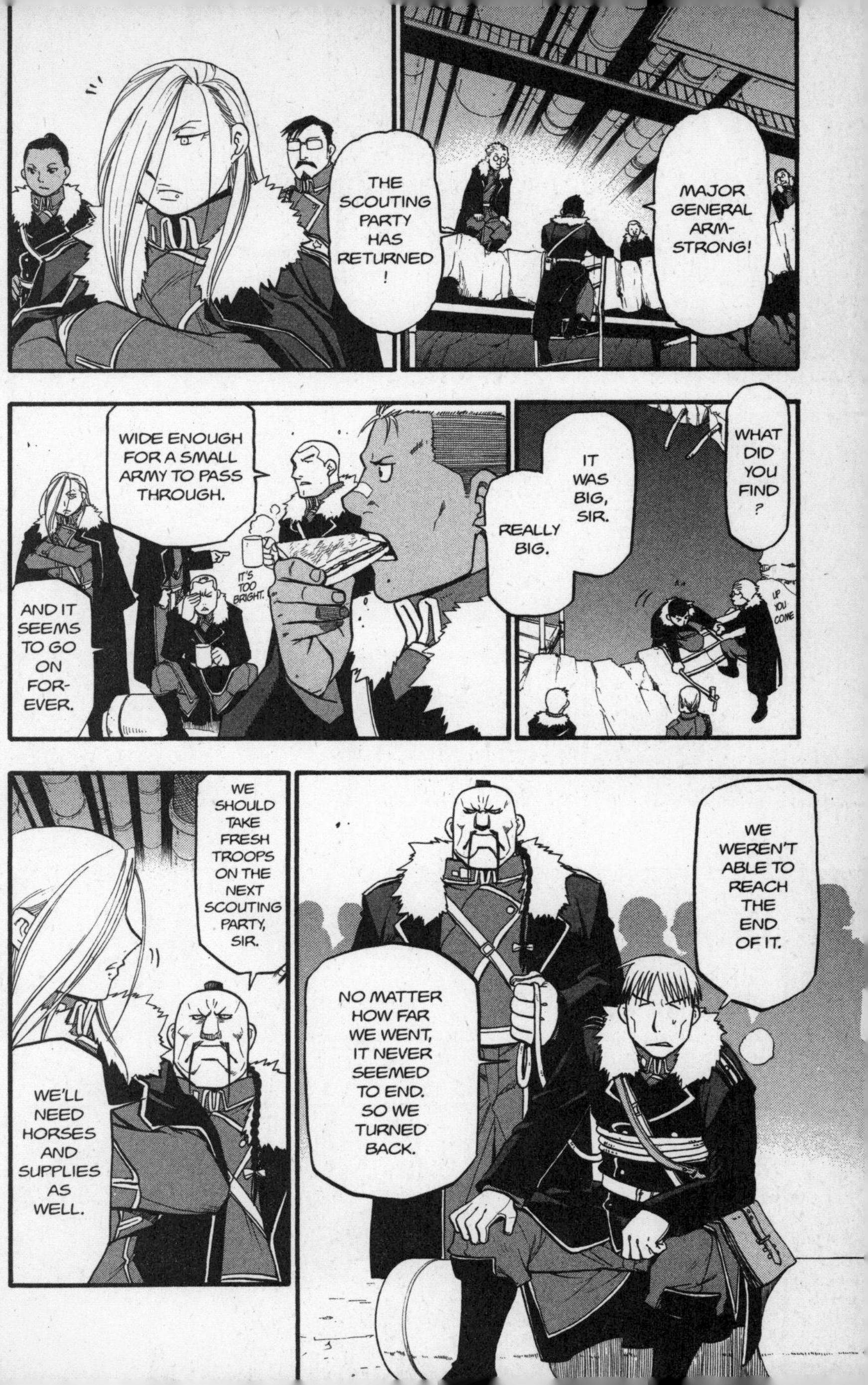
MAJOR GENERAL ARM-STRONG!
THE SCOUTING PARTY HAS RETURNED!
WHAT DID YOU FIND?
UP YOU COME
IT WAS BIG, SIR.
REALLY BIG.
WIDE ENOUGH FOR A SMALL ARMY TO PASS THROUGH.
IT'S TOO BRIGHT.
AND IT SEEMS TO GO ON FOR-EVER.
WE WEREN'T ABLE TO REACH THE END OF IT.
NO MATTER HOW FAR WE WENT, IT NEVER SEEMED TO END. SO WE TURNED BACK.
WE SHOULD TAKE FRESH TROOPS ON THE NEXT SCOUTING PARTY, SIR.
WE'LL NEED HORSES AND SUPPLIES AS WELL.

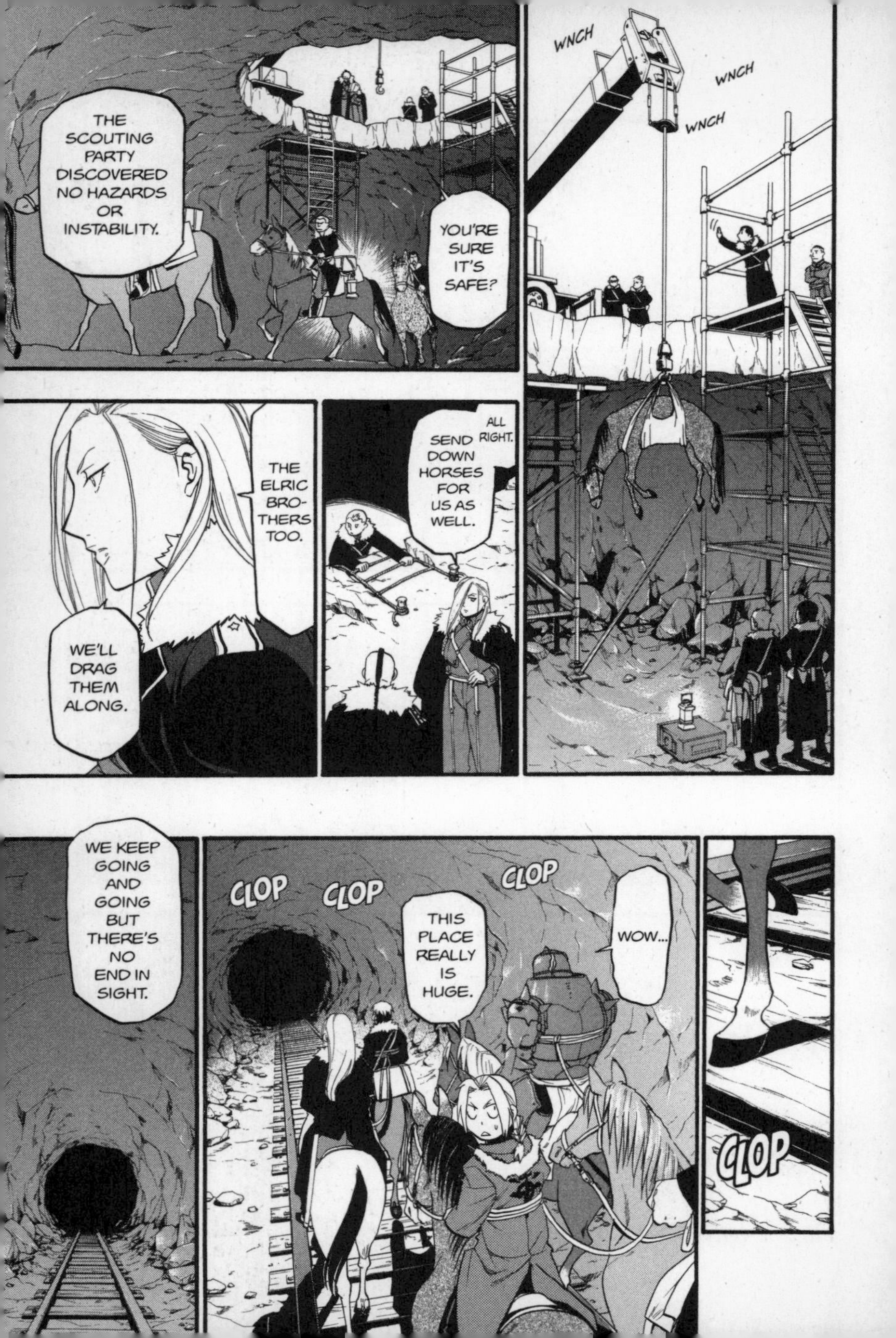
WNCH
WNCH
WNCH
YOU'RE SURE IT'S SAFE?
THE SCOUTING PARTY DISCOVERED NO HAZARDS OR INSTABILITY.
ALL RIGHT.
SEND DOWN HORSES FOR US AS WELL.
THE ELRIC BRO-THERS TOO.
WE'LL DRAG THEM ALONG.
CLOP
CLOP
WOW...
THIS PLACE REALLY IS HUGE.
CLOP
CLOP
WE KEEP GOING AND GOING BUT THERE'S NO END IN SIGHT.

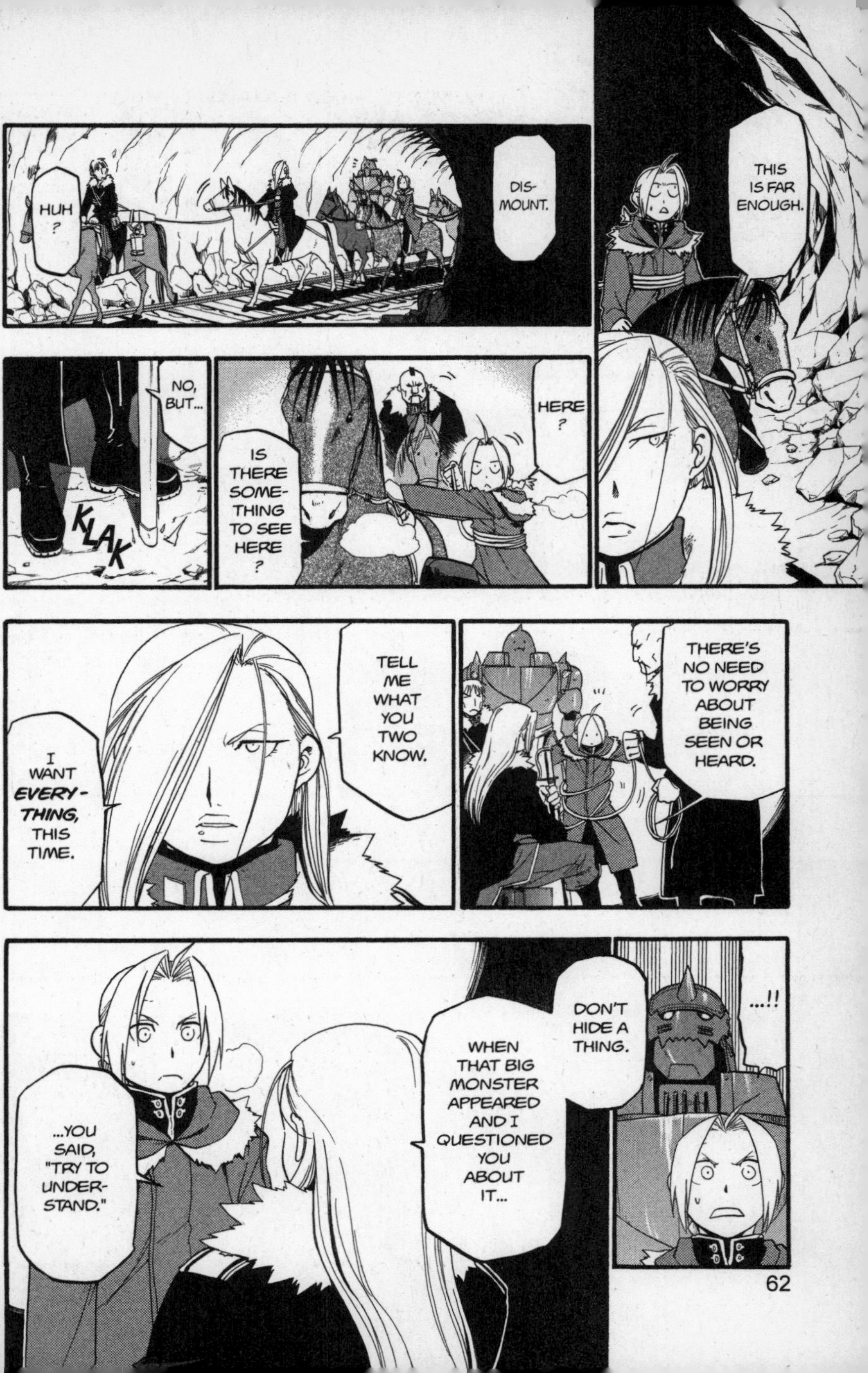
THIS IS FAR ENOUGH.
DIS-MOUNT.
HUH?
HERE?
IS THERE SOMETHING TO SEE HERE?
NO, BUT...
KLAK
THERE'S NO NEED TO WORRY ABOUT BEING SEEN OR HEARD.
TELL ME WHAT YOU TWO KNOW.
I WANT EVERYTHING, THIS TIME.
...!!
DON'T HIDE A THING.
WHEN THAT BIG MONSTER APPEARED AND I QUESTIONED YOU ABOUT IT...
...YOU SAID, "TRY TO UNDERSTAND."

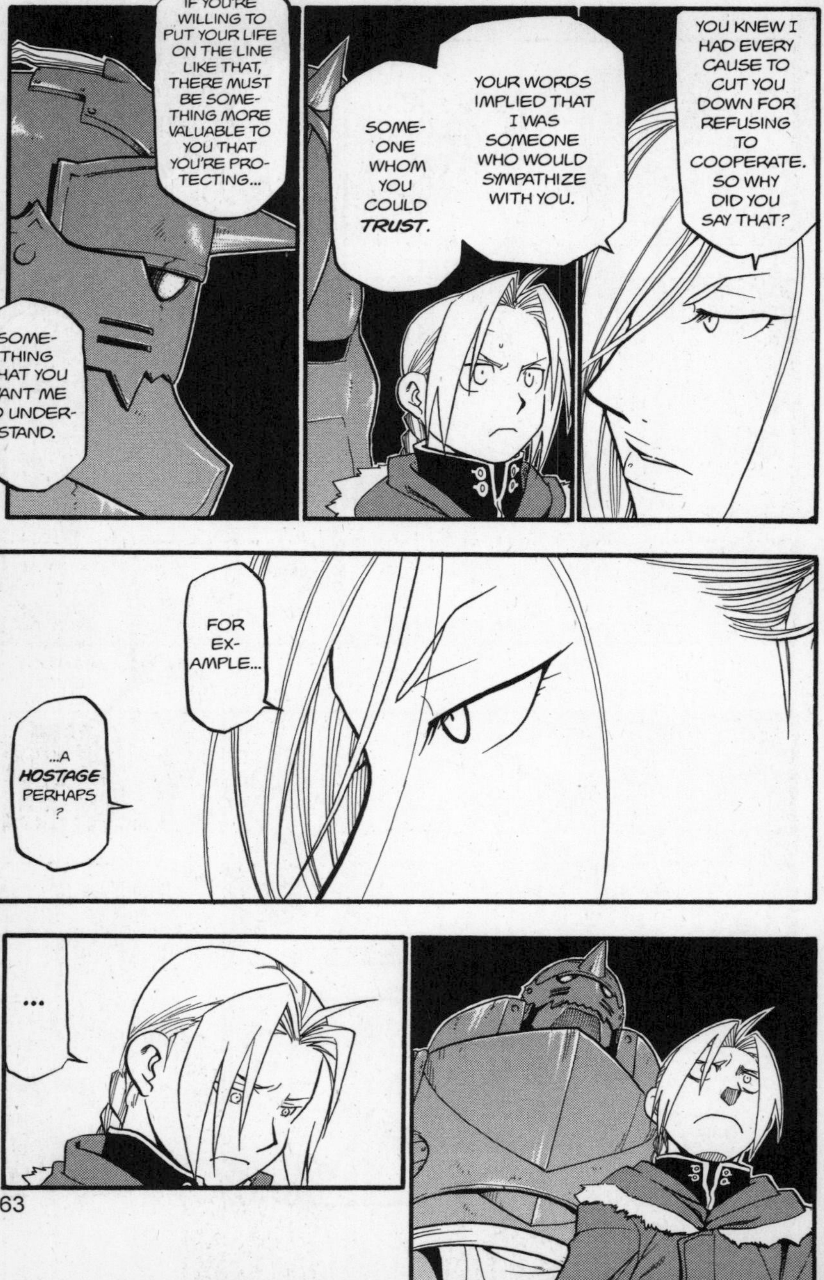
YOU KNEW I HAD EVERY CAUSE TO CUT YOU DOWN FOR REFUSING TO COOPERATE. SO WHY DID YOU SAY THAT?
YOUR WORDS IMPLIED THAT I WAS SOMEONE WHO WOULD SYMPATHIZE WITH YOU.
SOME-ONE WHOM YOU COULD **TRUST**.
IF YOU'RE WILLING TO PUT YOUR LIFE ON THE LINE LIKE THAT, THERE MUST BE SOME-THING MORE VALUABLE TO YOU THAT YOU'RE PRO-TECTING...
SOME-THING THAT YOU WANT ME TO UNDER-STAND.
FOR EX-AMPLE...
...A **HOSTAGE** PERHAPS?
...

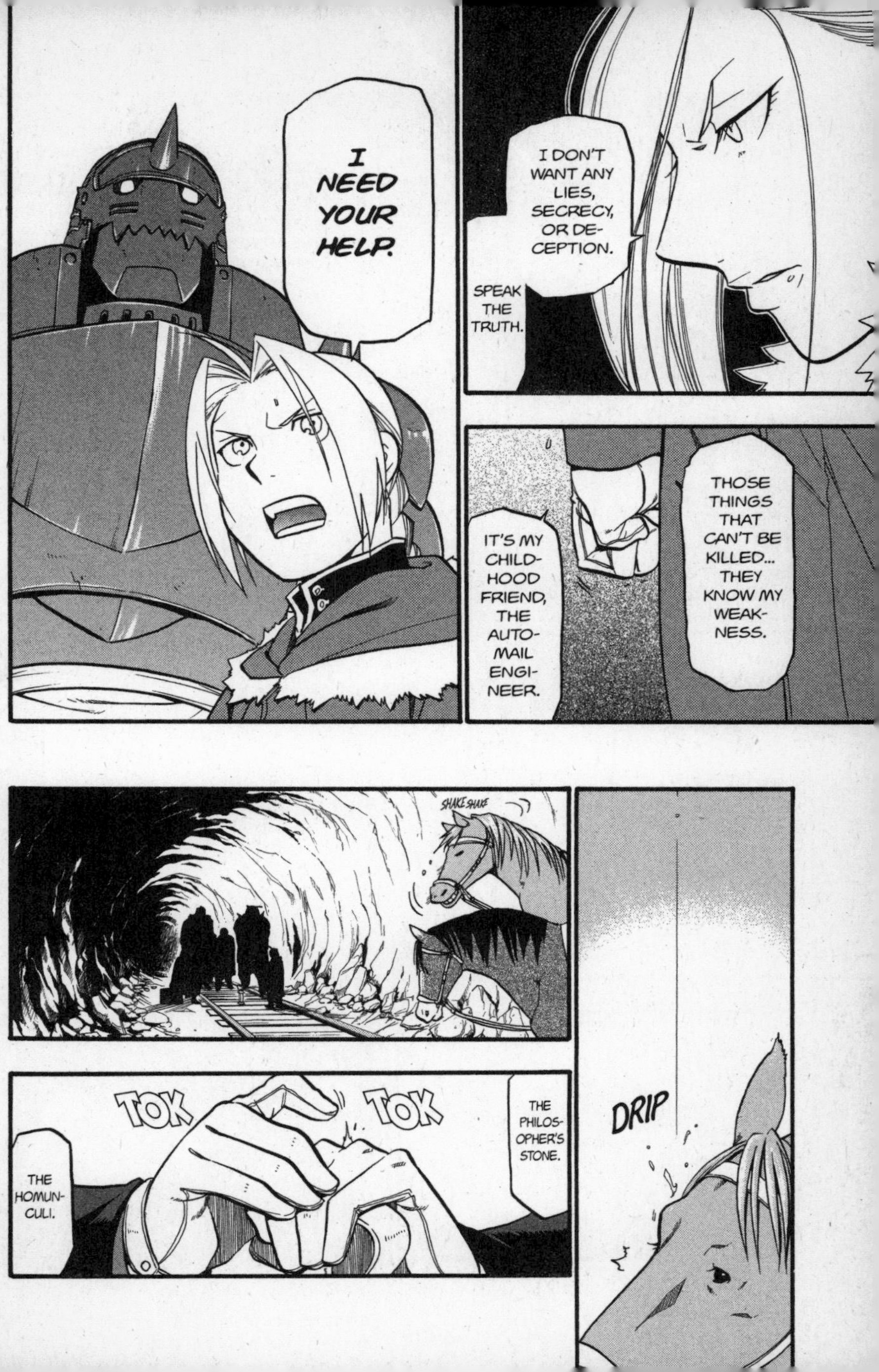
I DON'T WANT ANY LIES, SECRECY, OR DE-CEPTION.
SPEAK THE TRUTH.
THOSE THINGS THAT CAN'T BE KILLED... THEY KNOW MY WEAK-NESS.
IT'S MY CHILD-HOOD FRIEND, THE AUTO-MAIL ENGI-NEER.
I NEED YOUR HELP.
DRIP
SHAKE SHAKE
TOK TOK
THE PHILOS-OPHER'S STONE.
THE HOMUN-CULI.

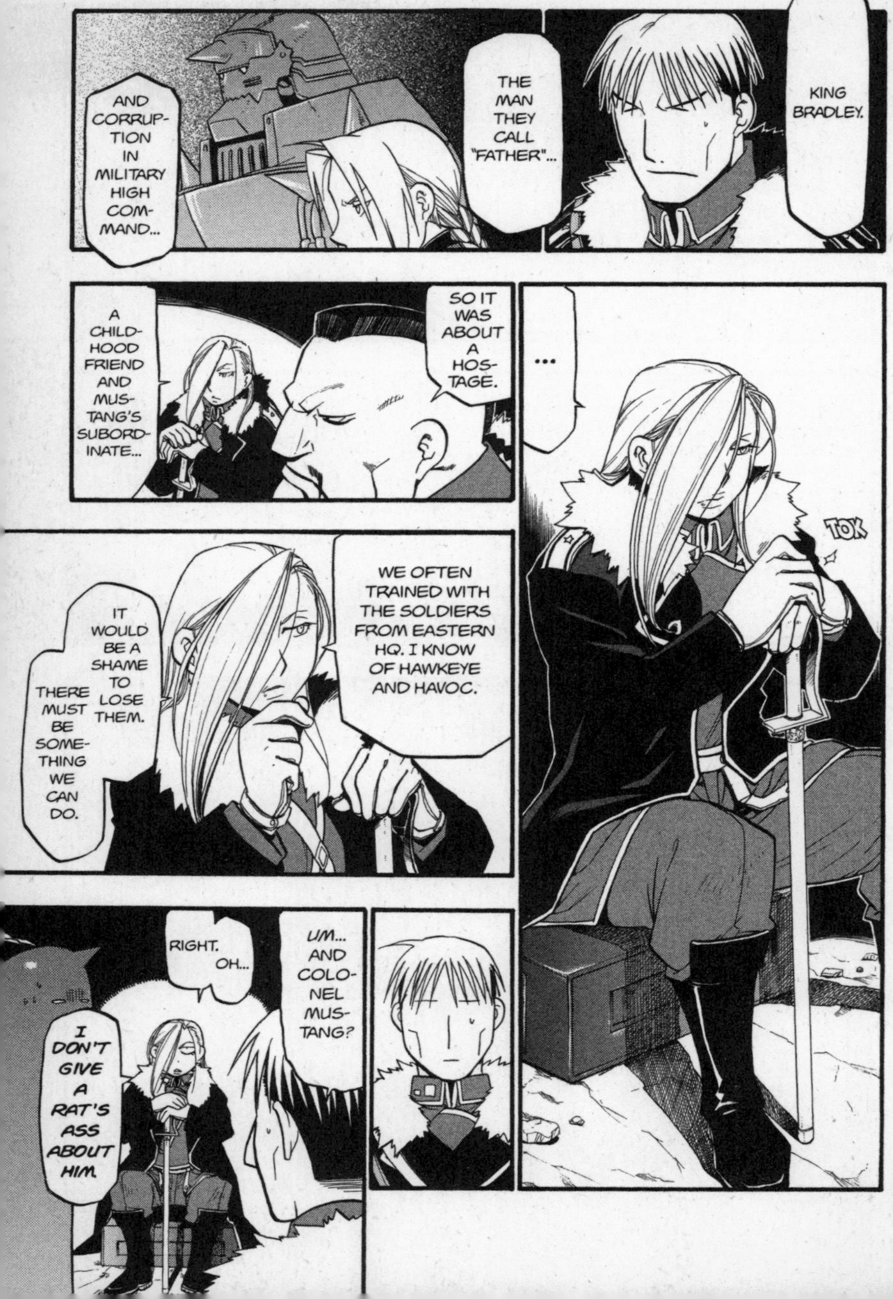
KING BRADLEY.
THE MAN THEY CALL "FATHER"...
AND CORRUPTION IN MILITARY HIGH COMMAND...
...
TOK
SO IT WAS ABOUT A HOSTAGE.
A CHILDHOOD FRIEND AND MUSTANG'S SUBORDINATE...
WE OFTEN TRAINED WITH THE SOLDIERS FROM EASTERN HQ. I KNOW OF HAWKEYE AND HAVOC.
IT WOULD BE A SHAME TO LOSE THEM.
THERE MUST BE SOMETHING WE CAN DO.
UM... AND COLONEL MUSTANG?
RIGHT. OH...
I DON'T GIVE A RAT'S ASS ABOUT HIM.

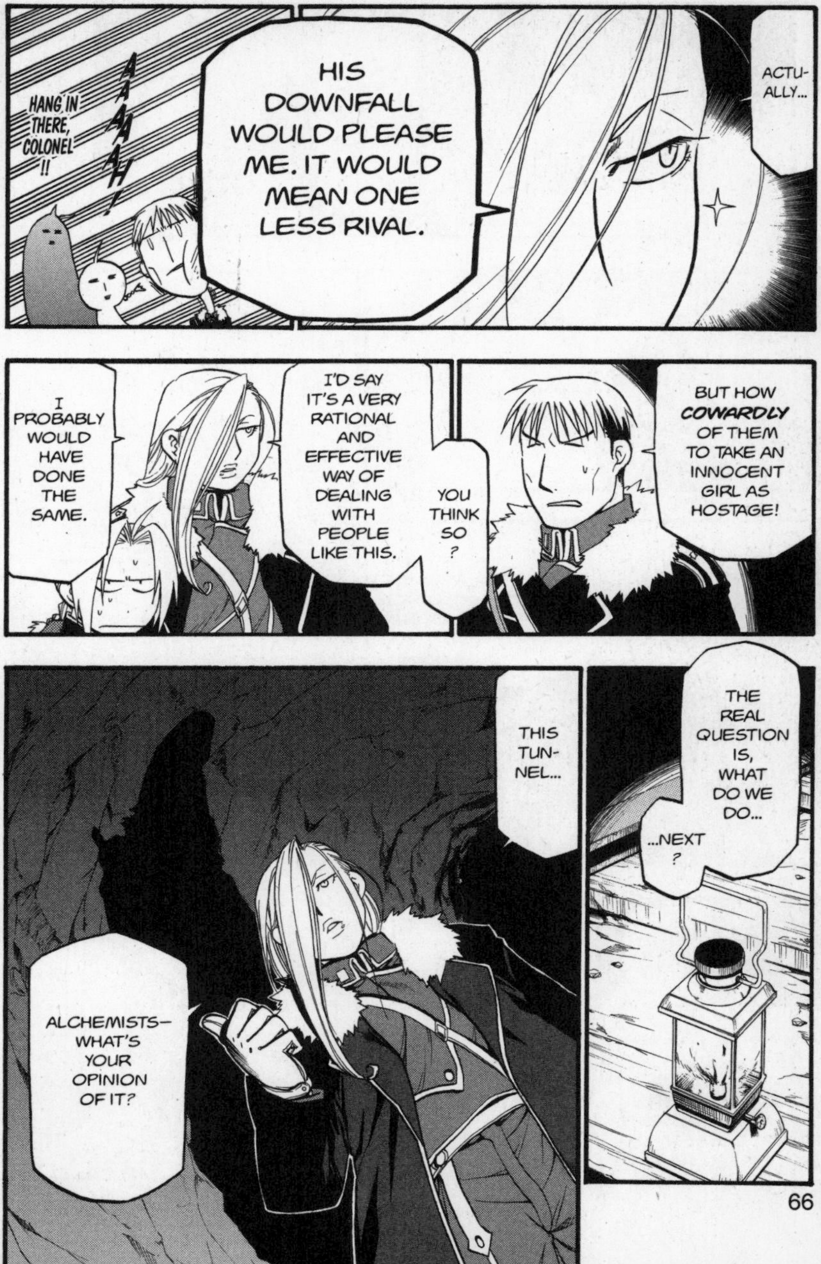

ACTU-ALLY...
HIS DOWNFALL WOULD PLEASE ME. IT WOULD MEAN ONE LESS RIVAL.
AAAAAH!
HANG IN THERE, COLONEL!!
BUT HOW COWARDLY OF THEM TO TAKE AN INNOCENT GIRL AS HOSTAGE!
YOU THINK SO?
I'D SAY IT'S A VERY RATIONAL AND EFFECTIVE WAY OF DEALING WITH PEOPLE LIKE THIS.
I PROBABLY WOULD HAVE DONE THE SAME.
THE REAL QUESTION IS, WHAT DO WE DO...
...NEXT?
THIS TUN-NEL...
ALCHEMISTS—WHAT'S YOUR OPINION OF IT?

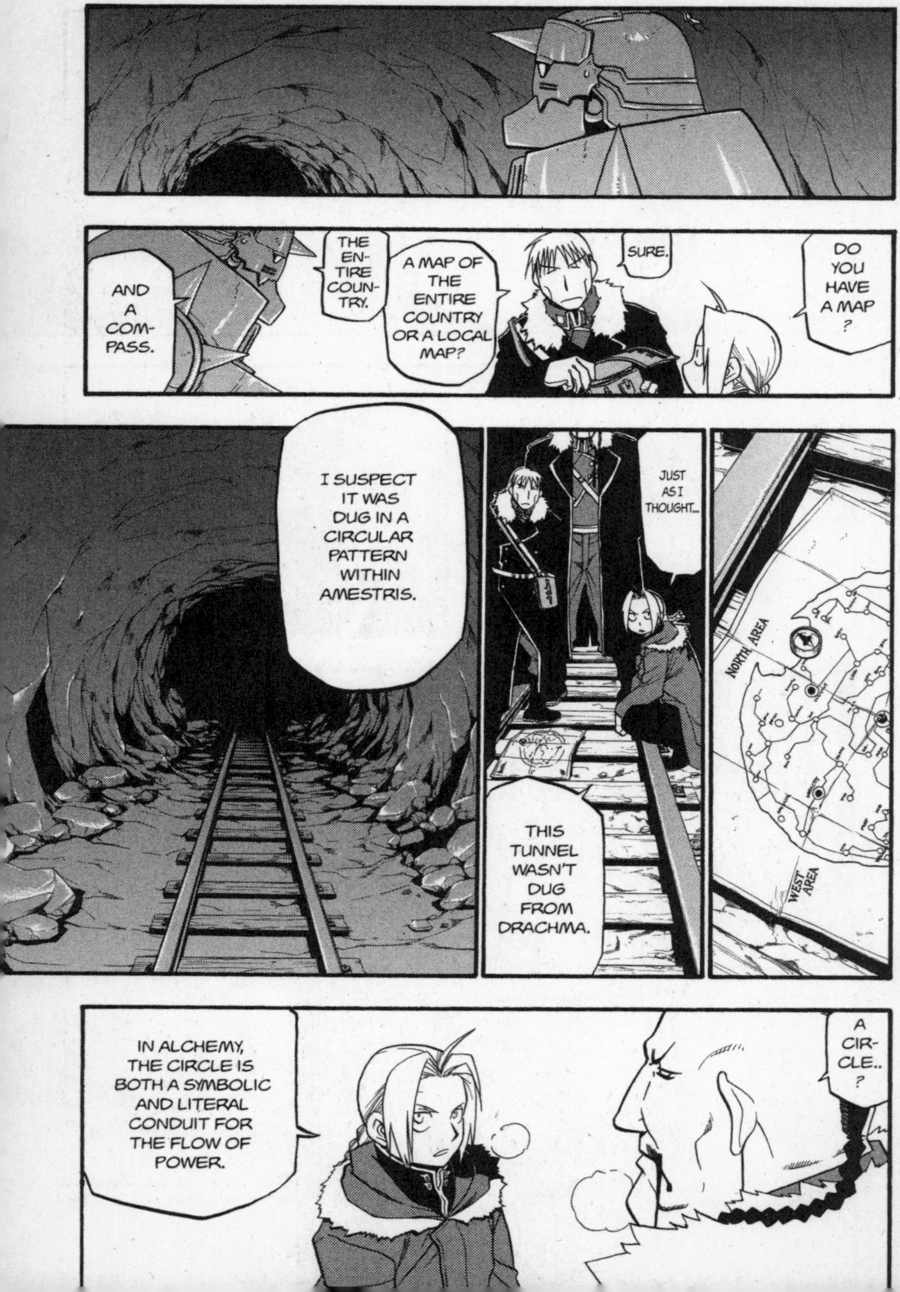
DO YOU HAVE A MAP?
SURE.
A MAP OF THE ENTIRE COUNTRY OR A LOCAL MAP?
THE ENTIRE COUNTRY.
AND A COMPASS.
NORTH AREA
WEST AREA
JUST AS I THOUGHT...
THIS TUNNEL WASN'T DUG FROM DRACHMA.
I SUSPECT IT WAS DUG IN A CIRCULAR PATTERN WITHIN AMESTRIS.
A CIRCLE..?
IN ALCHEMY, THE CIRCLE IS BOTH A SYMBOLIC AND LITERAL CONDUIT FOR THE FLOW OF POWER.

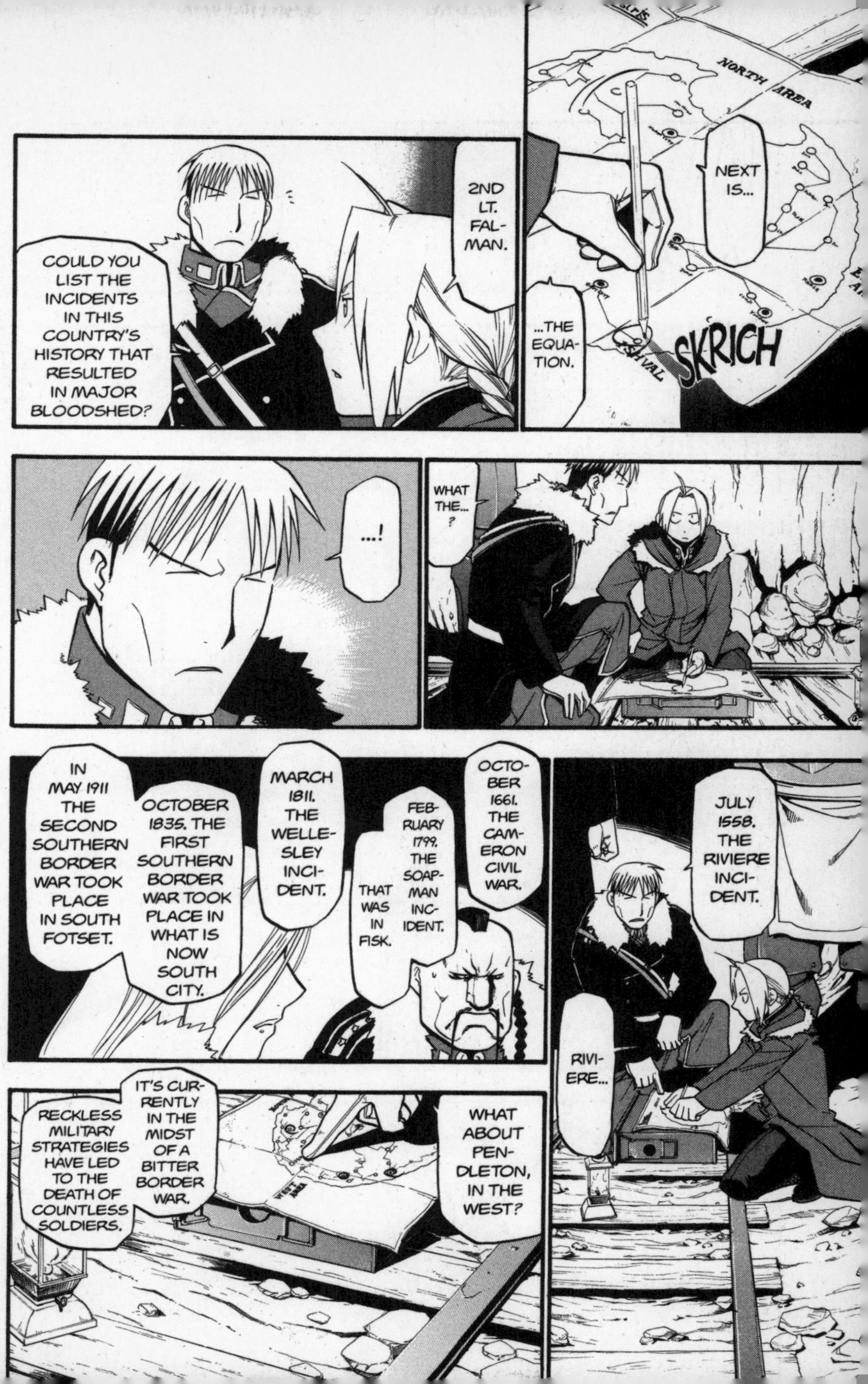
NORTH AREA
NEXT IS...
...THE EQUATION.
ISHVAL
SKRICH
2ND LT. FALMAN.
COULD YOU LIST THE INCIDENTS IN THIS COUNTRY'S HISTORY THAT RESULTED IN MAJOR BLOODSHED?
WHAT THE...?
...!
JULY 1558. THE RIVIERE INCIDENT.
RIVIERE...
OCTOBER 1661. THE CAMERON CIVIL WAR.
FEBRUARY 1799. THE SOAPMAN INCIDENT.
THAT WAS IN FISK.
MARCH 1811. THE WELLESLEY INCIDENT.
OCTOBER 1835. THE FIRST SOUTHERN BORDER WAR TOOK PLACE IN WHAT IS NOW SOUTH CITY.
IN MAY 1911 THE SECOND SOUTHERN BORDER WAR TOOK PLACE IN SOUTH FOTSET.
WHAT ABOUT PENDLETON, IN THE WEST?
IT'S CURRENTLY IN THE MIDST OF A BITTER BORDER WAR.
RECKLESS MILITARY STRATEGIES HAVE LED TO THE DEATH OF COUNTLESS SOLDIERS.
WEST AREA

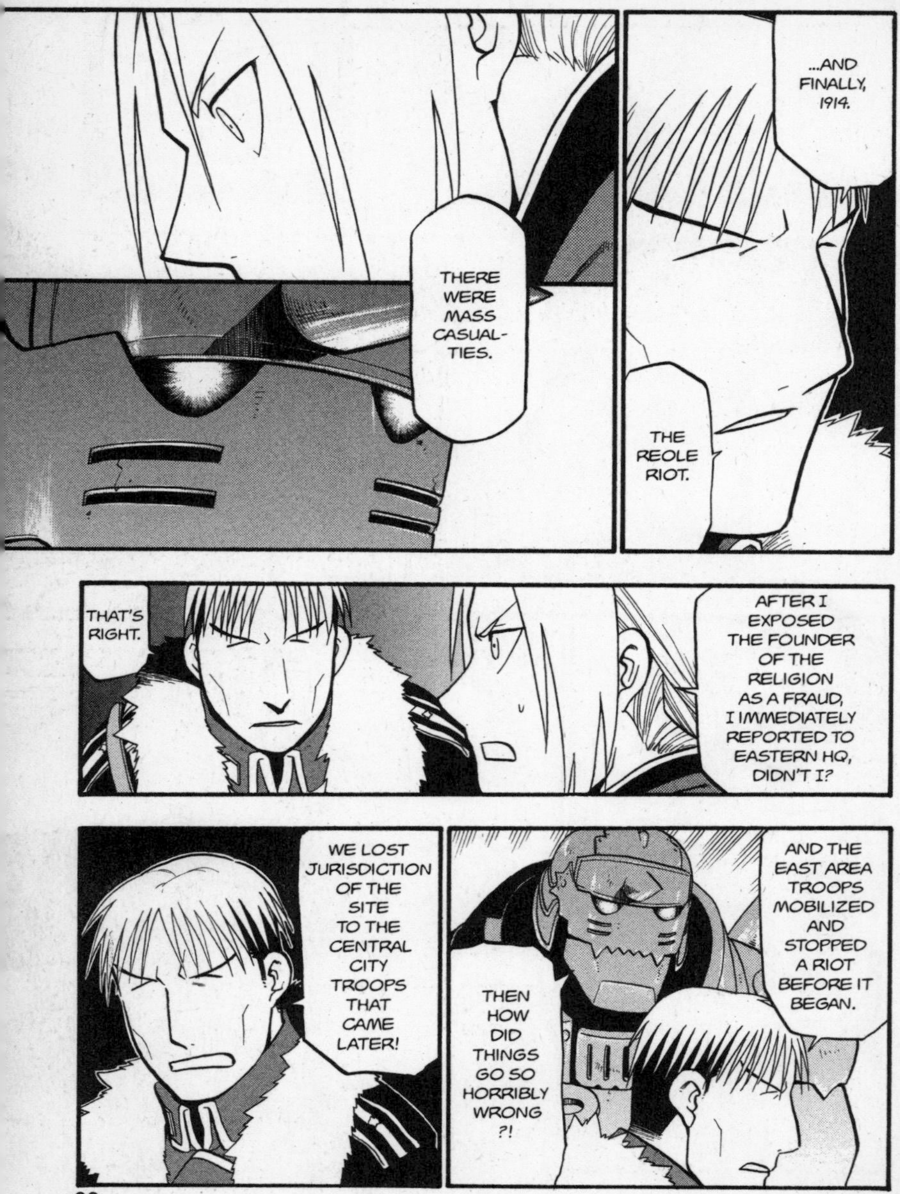
...AND FINALLY, 1914.
THE REOLE RIOT.
THERE WERE MASS CASUALTIES.
AFTER I EXPOSED THE FOUNDER OF THE RELIGION AS A FRAUD, I IMMEDIATELY REPORTED TO EASTERN HQ, DIDN'T I?
THAT'S RIGHT.
AND THE EAST AREA TROOPS MOBILIZED AND STOPPED A RIOT BEFORE IT BEGAN.
THEN HOW DID THINGS GO SO HORRIBLY WRONG?!
WE LOST JURISDICTION OF THE SITE TO THE CENTRAL CITY TROOPS THAT CAME LATER!

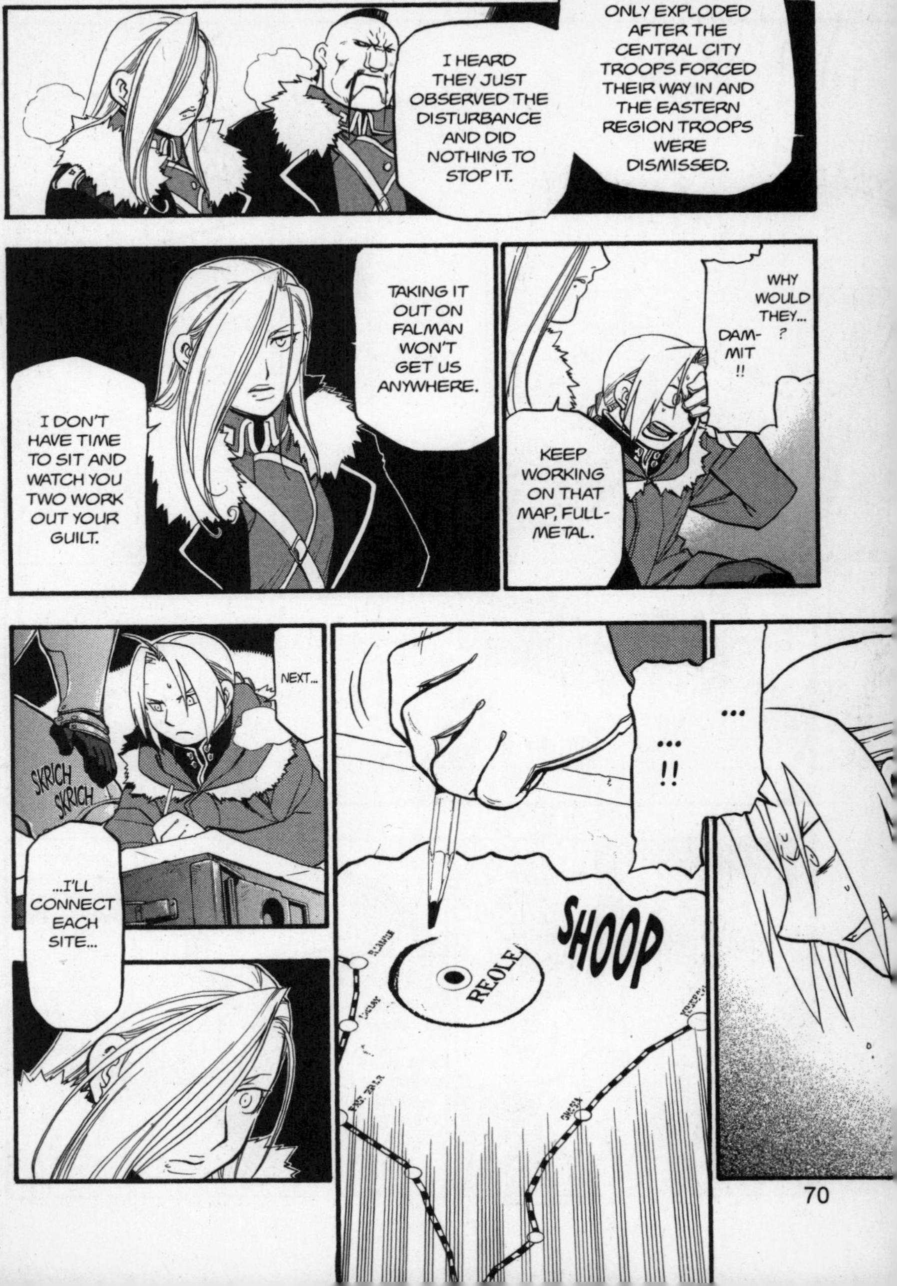

THE SITUATION ONLY EXPLODED AFTER THE CENTRAL CITY TROOPS FORCED THEIR WAY IN AND THE EASTERN REGION TROOPS WERE DISMISSED.
I HEARD THEY JUST OBSERVED THE DISTURBANCE AND DID NOTHING TO STOP IT.
WHY WOULD THEY...?
DAM-MIT!!
KEEP WORKING ON THAT MAP, FULL-METAL.
TAKING IT OUT ON FALMAN WON'T GET US ANYWHERE.
I DON'T HAVE TIME TO SIT AND WATCH YOU TWO WORK OUT YOUR GUILT.
...
...!!
SHOOP
REOLE
NEXT...
SKRICH SKRICH
...I'LL CONNECT EACH SITE...

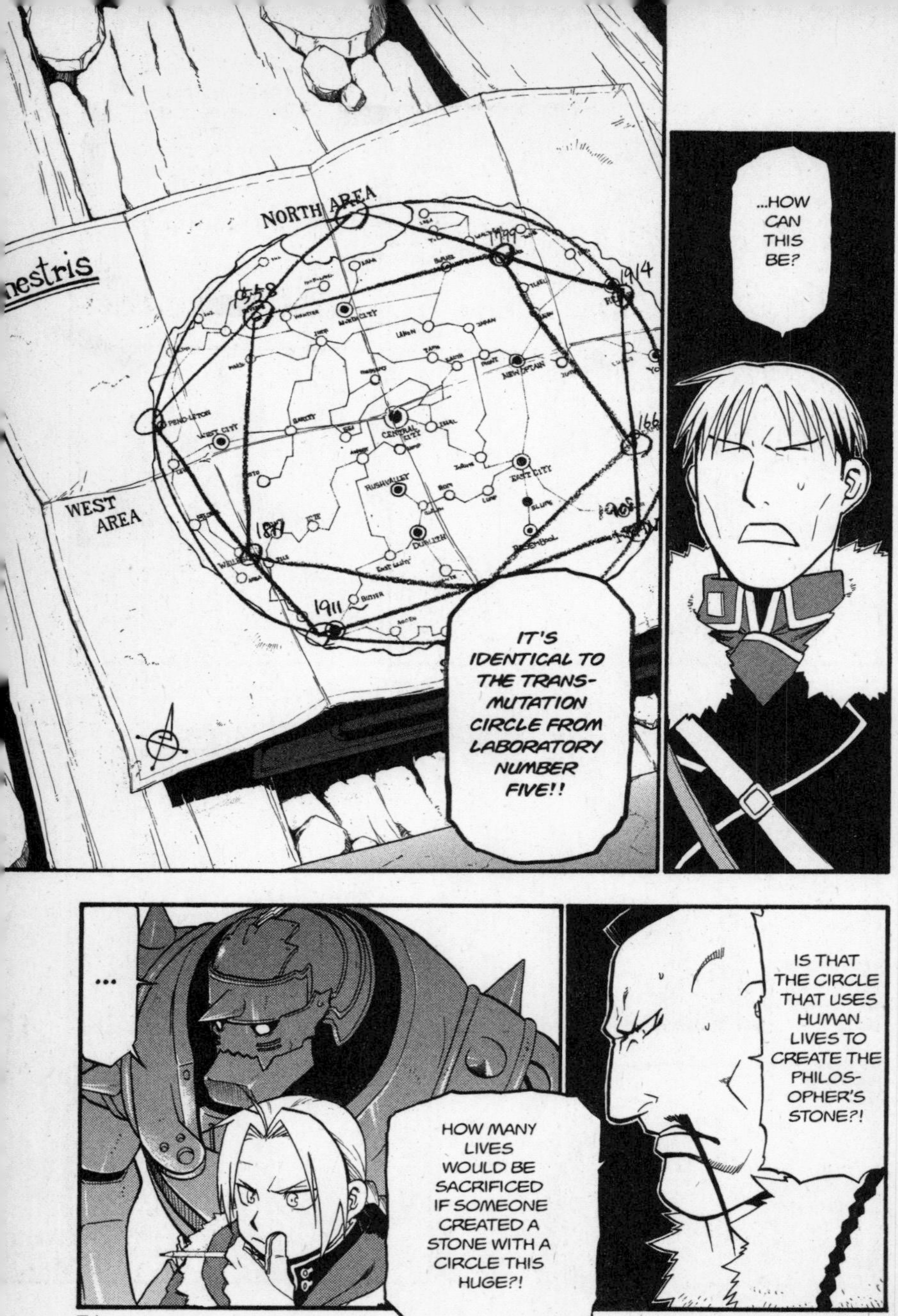
...HOW CAN THIS BE?
NORTH AREA
nestris
WEST AREA
1799
1914
1911
IT'S IDENTICAL TO THE TRANS-MUTATION CIRCLE FROM LABORATORY NUMBER FIVE!!
IS THAT THE CIRCLE THAT USES HUMAN LIVES TO CREATE THE PHILOS-OPHER'S STONE?!
HOW MANY LIVES WOULD BE SACRIFICED IF SOMEONE CREATED A STONE WITH A CIRCLE THIS HUGE?!
...

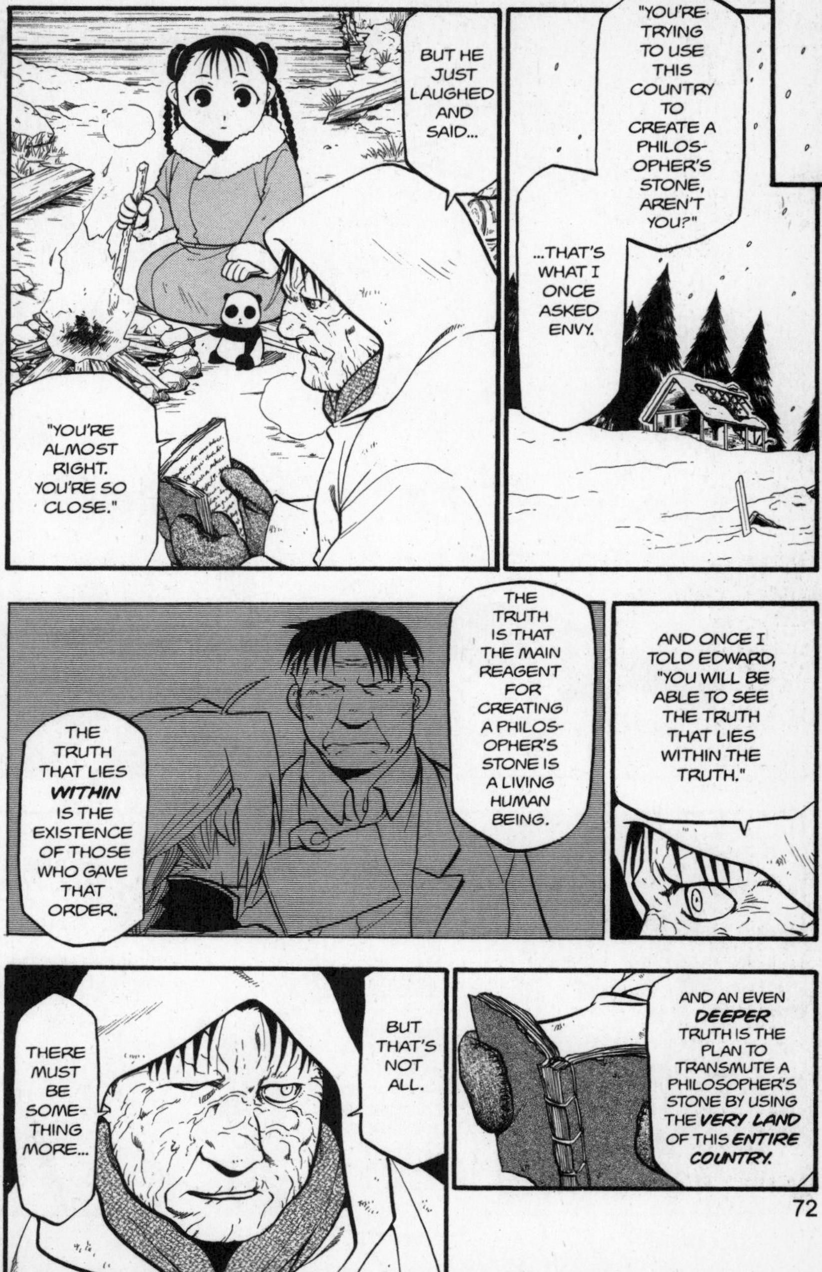
"YOU'RE TRYING TO USE THIS COUNTRY TO CREATE A PHILOSOPHER'S STONE, AREN'T YOU?"
...THAT'S WHAT I ONCE ASKED ENVY.
BUT HE JUST LAUGHED AND SAID...
"YOU'RE ALMOST RIGHT. YOU'RE SO CLOSE."
AND ONCE I TOLD EDWARD, "YOU WILL BE ABLE TO SEE THE TRUTH THAT LIES WITHIN THE TRUTH."
THE TRUTH IS THAT THE MAIN REAGENT FOR CREATING A PHILOSOPHER'S STONE IS A LIVING HUMAN BEING.
THE TRUTH THAT LIES ***WITHIN*** IS THE EXISTENCE OF THOSE WHO GAVE THAT ORDER.
AND AN EVEN ***DEEPER*** TRUTH IS THE PLAN TO TRANSMUTE A PHILOSOPHER'S STONE BY USING THE ***VERY LAND*** OF THIS ***ENTIRE COUNTRY.***
BUT THAT'S NOT ALL.
THERE MUST BE SOMETHING MORE...

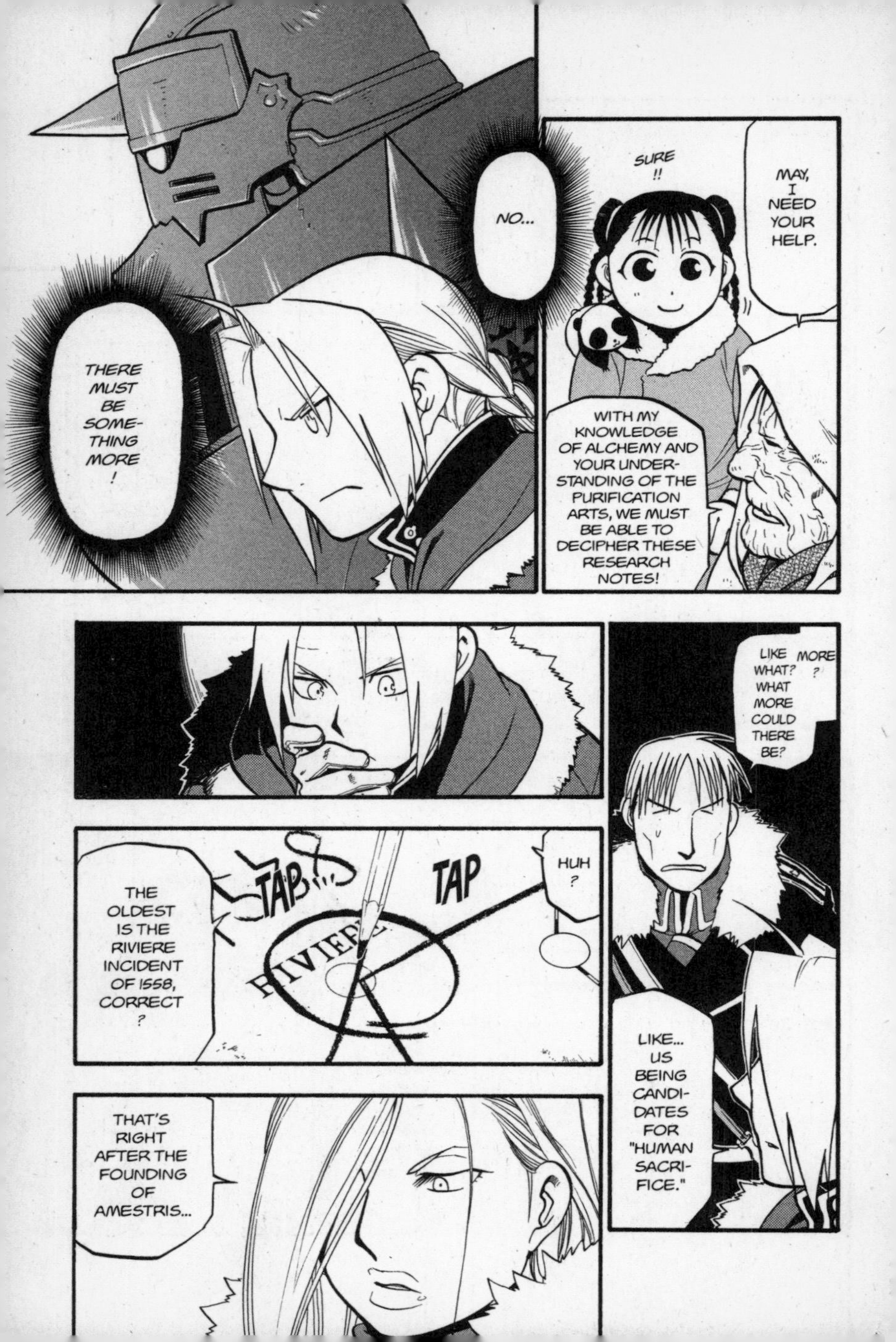
MAY, I NEED YOUR HELP.
SURE!!
WITH MY KNOWLEDGE OF ALCHEMY AND YOUR UNDERSTANDING OF THE PURIFICATION ARTS, WE MUST BE ABLE TO DECIPHER THESE RESEARCH NOTES!
NO...
THERE MUST BE SOMETHING MORE!
MORE?
LIKE WHAT? WHAT MORE COULD THERE BE?
LIKE... US BEING CANDIDATES FOR "HUMAN SACRIFICE."
HUH?
TAP
TAP
THE OLDEST IS THE RIVIERE INCIDENT OF 1558, CORRECT?
THAT'S RIGHT AFTER THE FOUNDING OF AMESTRIS...

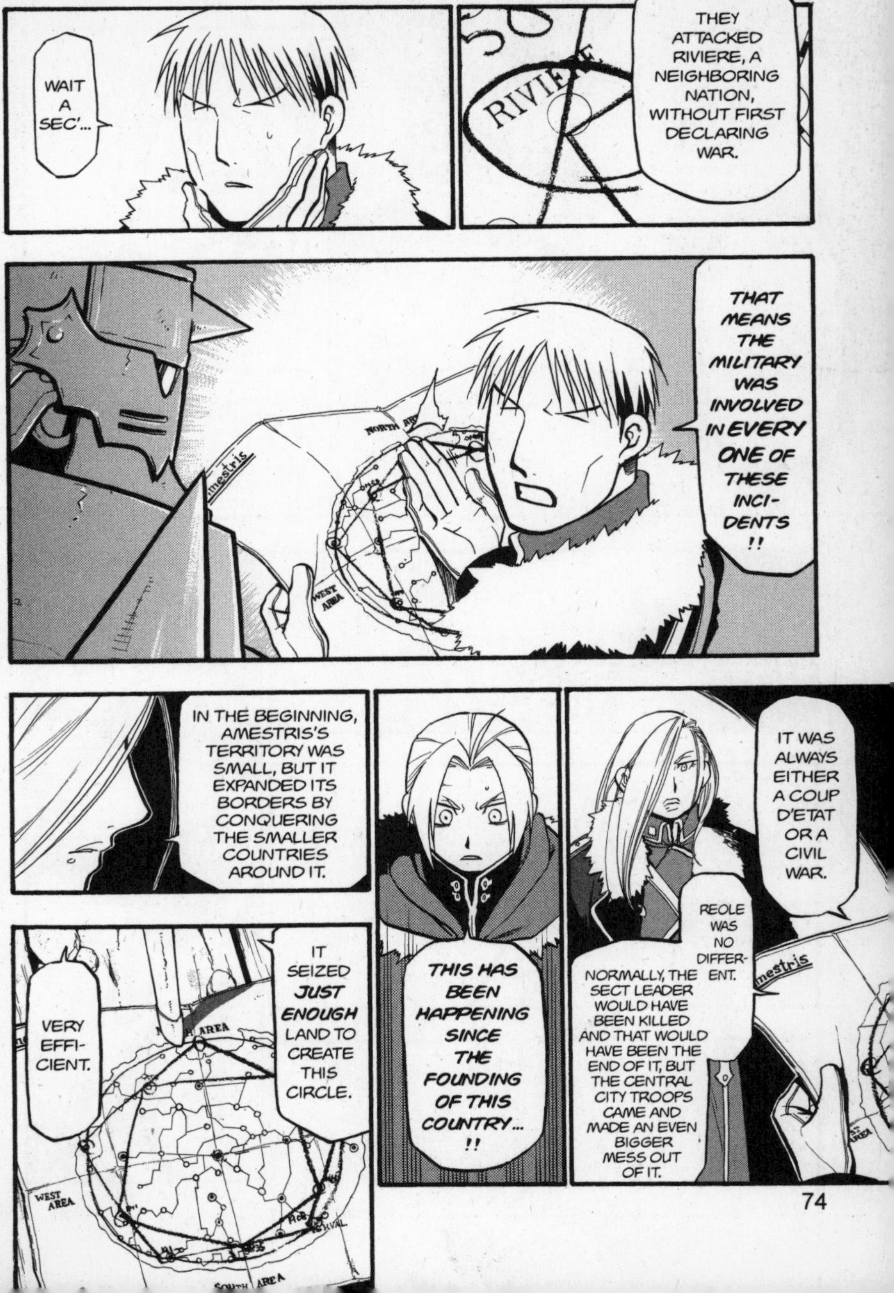
THEY ATTACKED RIVIERE, A NEIGHBORING NATION, WITHOUT FIRST DECLARING WAR.
WAIT A SEC'...
THAT MEANS THE MILITARY WAS INVOLVED IN EVERY ONE OF THESE INCI-DENTS !!
IT WAS ALWAYS EITHER A COUP D'ETAT OR A CIVIL WAR.
REOLE WAS NO DIFFER-ENT.
NORMALLY, THE SECT LEADER WOULD HAVE BEEN KILLED AND THAT WOULD HAVE BEEN THE END OF IT, BUT THE CENTRAL CITY TROOPS CAME AND MADE AN EVEN BIGGER MESS OUT OF IT.
THIS HAS BEEN HAPPENING SINCE THE FOUNDING OF THIS COUNTRY... !!
IN THE BEGINNING, AMESTRIS'S TERRITORY WAS SMALL, BUT IT EXPANDED ITS BORDERS BY CONQUERING THE SMALLER COUNTRIES AROUND IT.
IT SEIZED JUST ENOUGH LAND TO CREATE THIS CIRCLE.
VERY EFFI-CIENT.
WEST AREA
SOUTH AREA

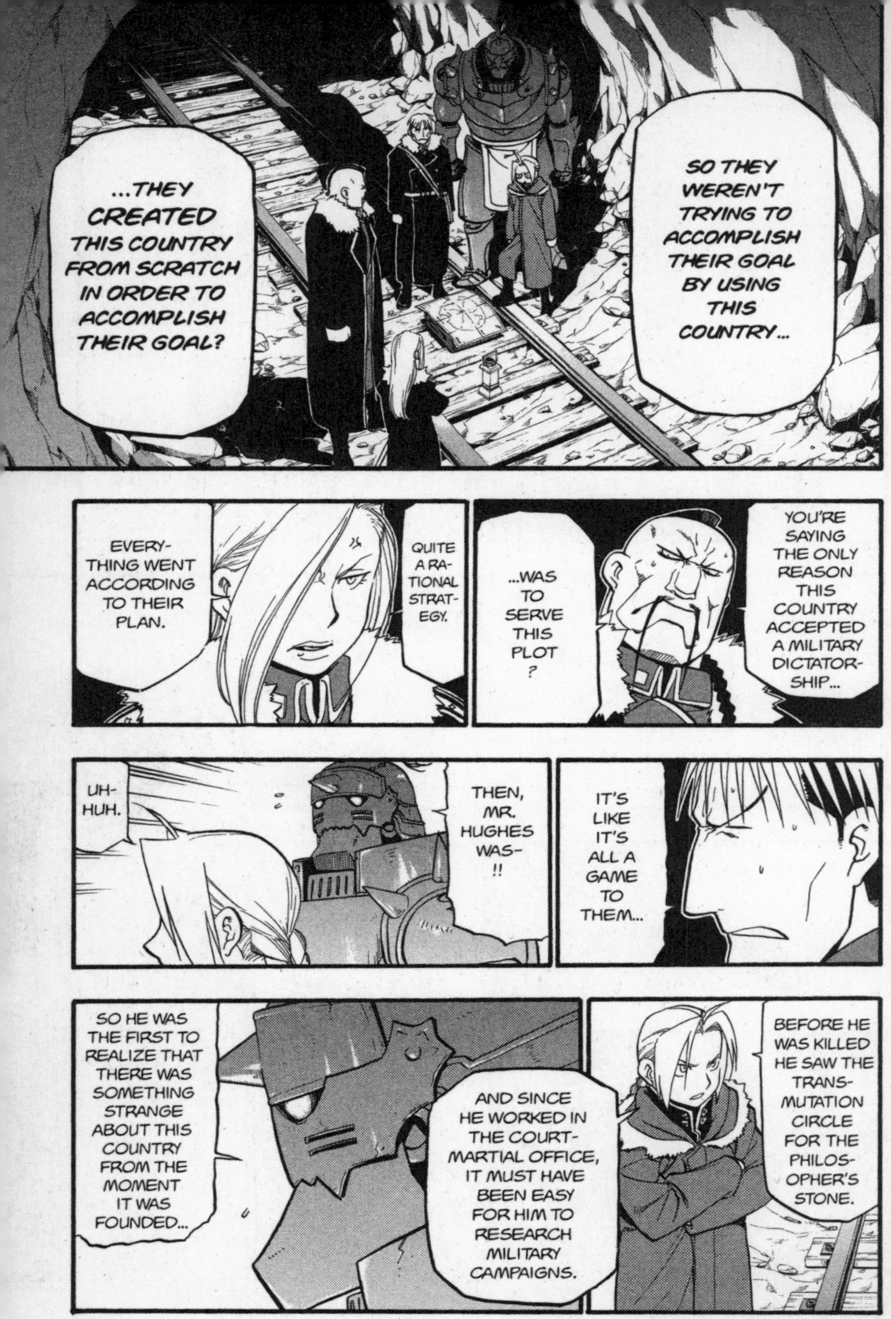
SO THEY WEREN'T TRYING TO ACCOMPLISH THEIR GOAL BY USING THIS COUNTRY...
...THEY CREATED THIS COUNTRY FROM SCRATCH IN ORDER TO ACCOMPLISH THEIR GOAL?
YOU'RE SAYING THE ONLY REASON THIS COUNTRY ACCEPTED A MILITARY DICTATORSHIP...
...WAS TO SERVE THIS PLOT ?
QUITE A RATIONAL STRATEGY.
EVERYTHING WENT ACCORDING TO THEIR PLAN.
IT'S LIKE IT'S ALL A GAME TO THEM...
THEN, MR. HUGHES WAS-!!
UH-HUH.
BEFORE HE WAS KILLED HE SAW THE TRANSMUTATION CIRCLE FOR THE PHILOSOPHER'S STONE.
AND SINCE HE WORKED IN THE COURT-MARTIAL OFFICE, IT MUST HAVE BEEN EASY FOR HIM TO RESEARCH MILITARY CAMPAIGNS.
SO HE WAS THE FIRST TO REALIZE THAT THERE WAS SOMETHING STRANGE ABOUT THIS COUNTRY FROM THE MOMENT IT WAS FOUNDED...

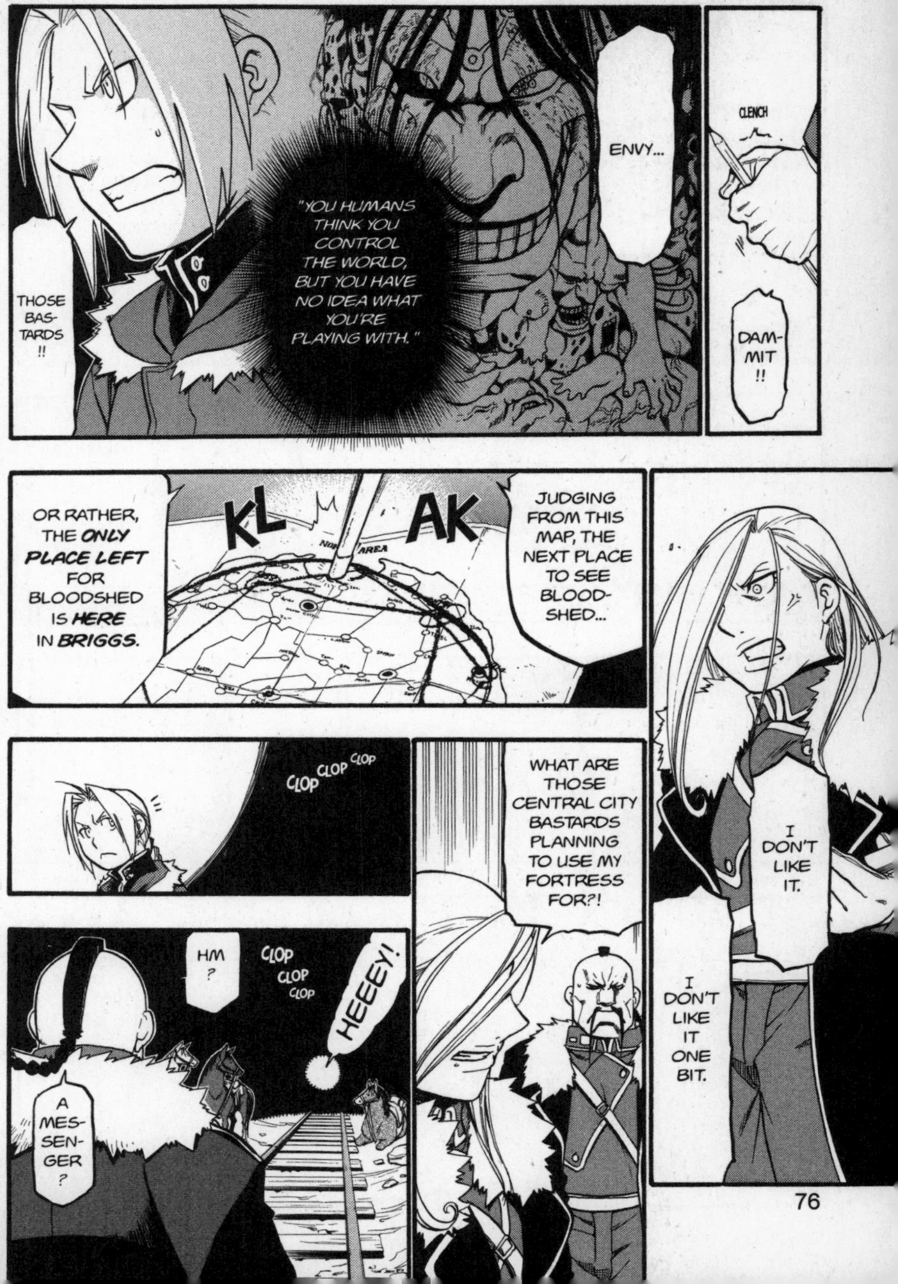
CLENCH
DAM-MIT !!
ENVY...
"YOU HUMANS THINK YOU CONTROL THE WORLD, BUT YOU HAVE NO IDEA WHAT YOU'RE PLAYING WITH."
THOSE BAS-TARDS !!
JUDGING FROM THIS MAP, THE NEXT PLACE TO SEE BLOOD-SHED...
KLAK
NORTH AREA
OR RATHER, THE ONLY PLACE LEFT FOR BLOODSHED IS HERE IN BRIGGS.
WHAT ARE THOSE CENTRAL CITY BASTARDS PLANNING TO USE MY FORTRESS FOR?!
I DON'T LIKE IT.
I DON'T LIKE IT ONE BIT.
CLOP CLOP CLOP
HEEEY!
CLOP CLOP CLOP
HM ?
A MES-SEN-GER ?

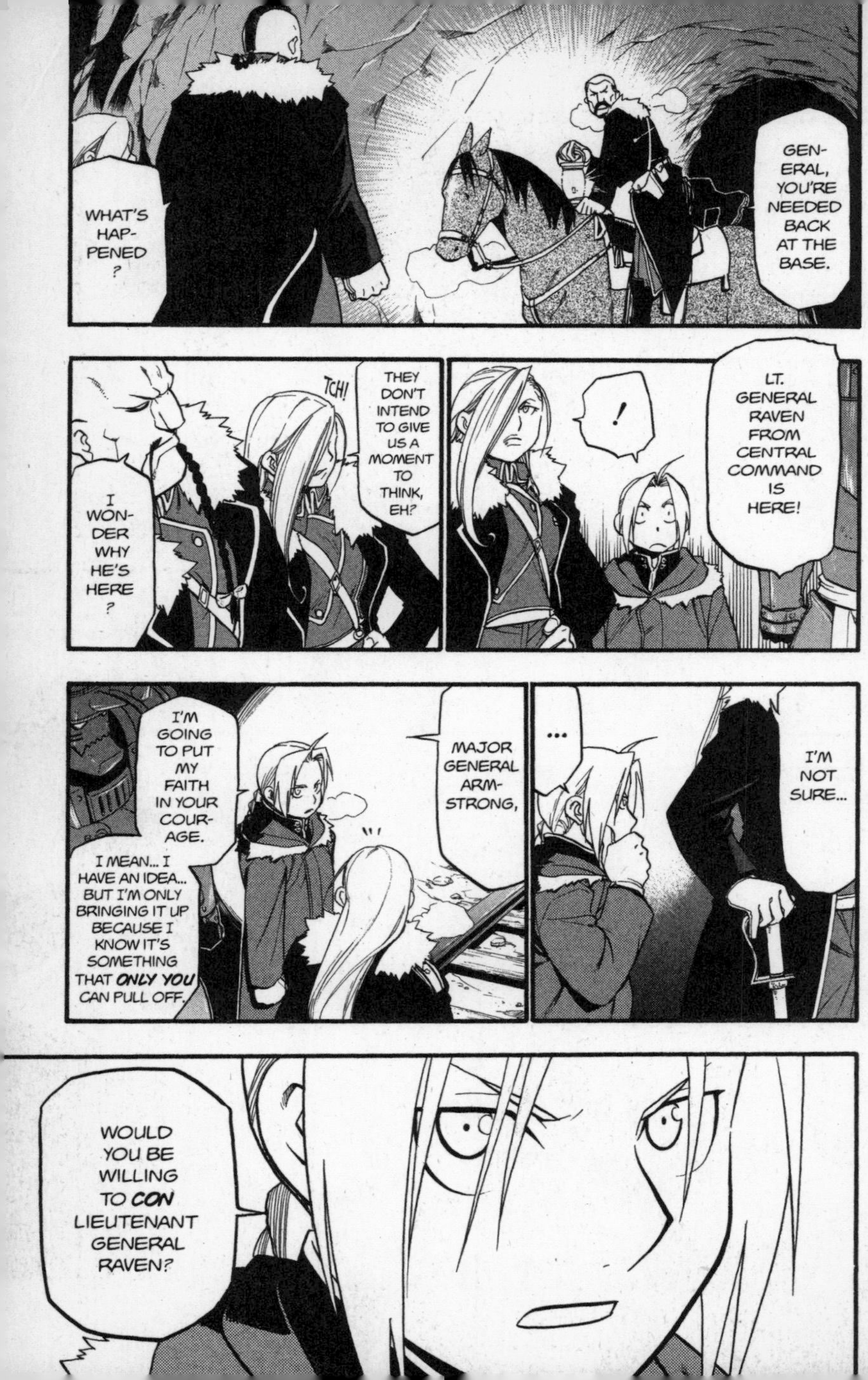
GENERAL, YOU'RE NEEDED BACK AT THE BASE.
WHAT'S HAPPENED?
LT. GENERAL RAVEN FROM CENTRAL COMMAND IS HERE!
!
TCH!
THEY DON'T INTEND TO GIVE US A MOMENT TO THINK, EH?
I WONDER WHY HE'S HERE?
I'M NOT SURE...
...
MAJOR GENERAL ARMSTRONG,
I'M GOING TO PUT MY FAITH IN YOUR COURAGE.
I MEAN... I HAVE AN IDEA... BUT I'M ONLY BRINGING IT UP BECAUSE I KNOW IT'S SOMETHING THAT **ONLY YOU** CAN PULL OFF.
WOULD YOU BE WILLING TO **CON** LIEUTENANT GENERAL RAVEN?

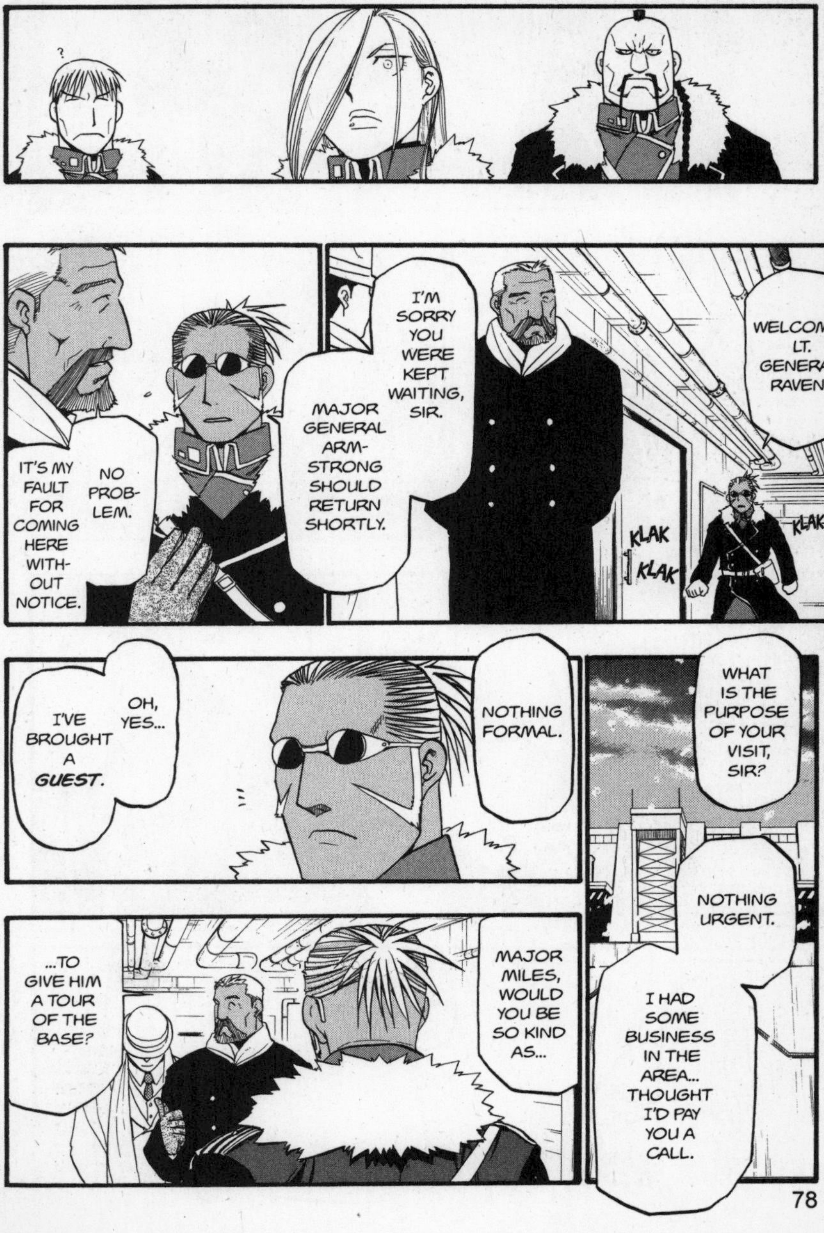
?
WELCOME, LT. GENERAL RAVEN.
KLAK
KLAK
KLAK
I'M SORRY YOU WERE KEPT WAITING, SIR.
MAJOR GENERAL ARM-STRONG SHOULD RETURN SHORTLY.
NO PROB-LEM.
IT'S MY FAULT FOR COMING HERE WITH-OUT NOTICE.
WHAT IS THE PURPOSE OF YOUR VISIT, SIR?
NOTHING URGENT.
I HAD SOME BUSINESS IN THE AREA... THOUGHT I'D PAY YOU A CALL.
NOTHING FORMAL.
OH, YES...
I'VE BROUGHT A ***GUEST***.
MAJOR MILES, WOULD YOU BE SO KIND AS...
...TO GIVE HIM A TOUR OF THE BASE?

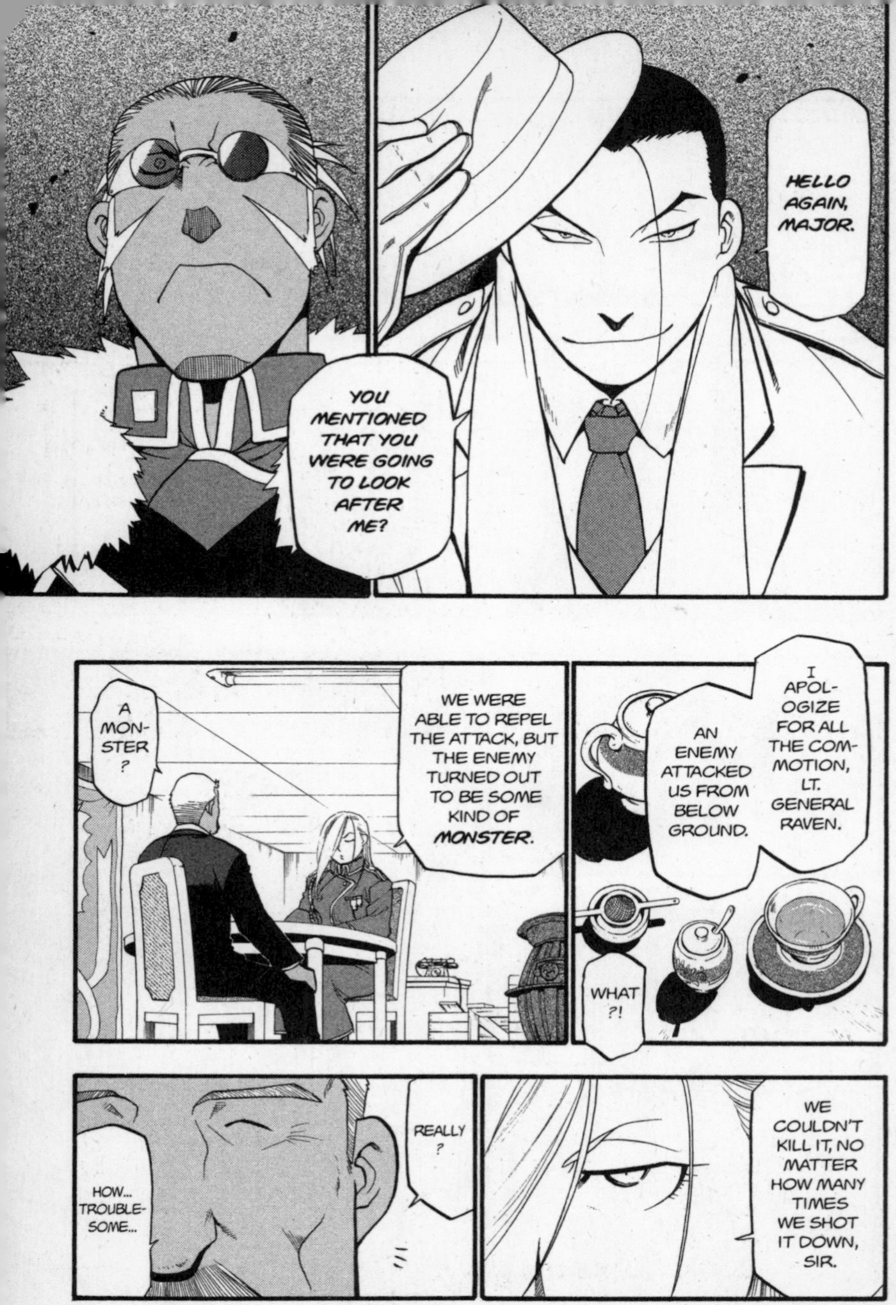
HELLO AGAIN, MAJOR.
YOU MENTIONED THAT YOU WERE GOING TO LOOK AFTER ME?
I APOLOGIZE FOR ALL THE COMMOTION, LT. GENERAL RAVEN.
AN ENEMY ATTACKED US FROM BELOW GROUND.
WHAT?!
WE WERE ABLE TO REPEL THE ATTACK, BUT THE ENEMY TURNED OUT TO BE SOME KIND OF MONSTER.
A MONSTER?
WE COULDN'T KILL IT, NO MATTER HOW MANY TIMES WE SHOT IT DOWN, SIR.
REALLY?
HOW... TROUBLESOME...

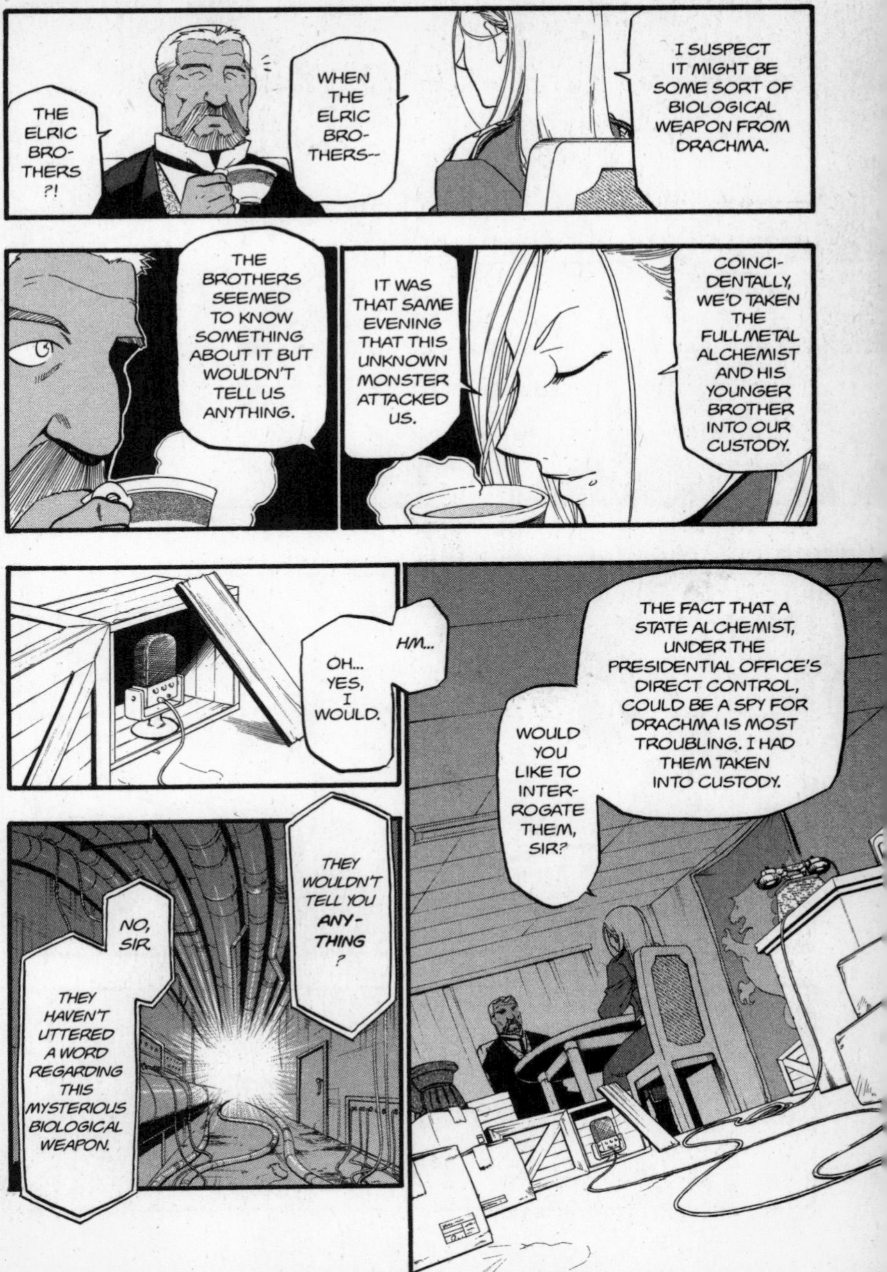
I SUSPECT IT MIGHT BE SOME SORT OF BIOLOGICAL WEAPON FROM DRACHMA.
WHEN THE ELRIC BROTHERS--
THE ELRIC BROTHERS?!
COINCIDENTALLY, WE'D TAKEN THE FULLMETAL ALCHEMIST AND HIS YOUNGER BROTHER INTO OUR CUSTODY.
IT WAS THAT SAME EVENING THAT THIS UNKNOWN MONSTER ATTACKED US.
THE BROTHERS SEEMED TO KNOW SOMETHING ABOUT IT BUT WOULDN'T TELL US ANYTHING.
THE FACT THAT A STATE ALCHEMIST, UNDER THE PRESIDENTIAL OFFICE'S DIRECT CONTROL, COULD BE A SPY FOR DRACHMA IS MOST TROUBLING. I HAD THEM TAKEN INTO CUSTODY.
WOULD YOU LIKE TO INTERROGATE THEM, SIR?
HM...
OH... YES, I WOULD.
THEY WOULDN'T TELL YOU ANYTHING?
NO, SIR.
THEY HAVEN'T UTTERED A WORD REGARDING THIS MYSTERIOUS BIOLOGICAL WEAPON.

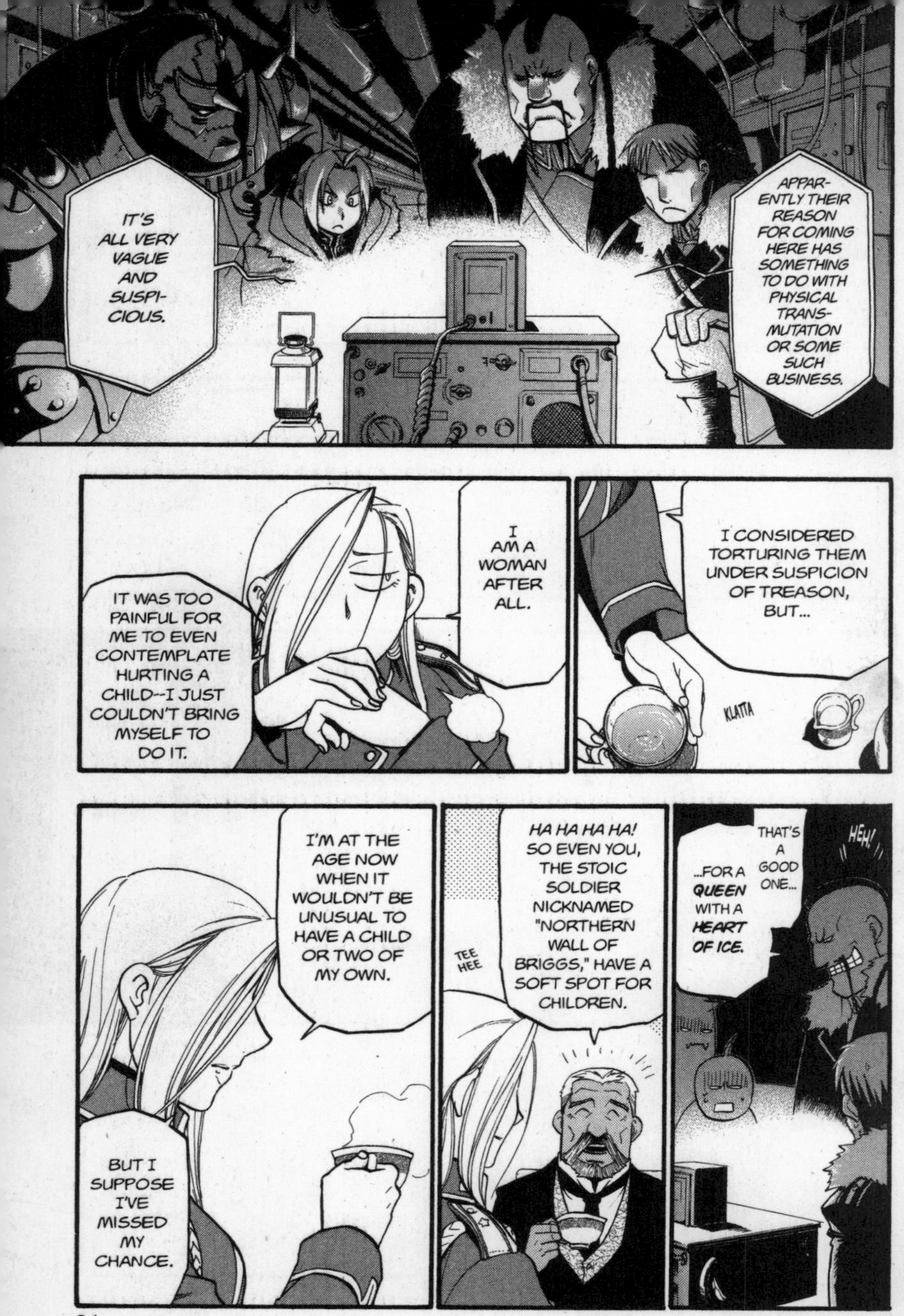
APPARENTLY THEIR REASON FOR COMING HERE HAS SOMETHING TO DO WITH PHYSICAL TRANSMUTATION OR SOME SUCH BUSINESS.
IT'S ALL VERY VAGUE AND SUSPICIOUS.
I CONSIDERED TORTURING THEM UNDER SUSPICION OF TREASON, BUT...
KLATTA
I AM A WOMAN AFTER ALL.
IT WAS TOO PAINFUL FOR ME TO EVEN CONTEMPLATE HURTING A CHILD--I JUST COULDN'T BRING MYSELF TO DO IT.
HEH!
THAT'S A GOOD ONE...
...FOR A QUEEN WITH A HEART OF ICE.
HA HA HA HA! SO EVEN YOU, THE STOIC SOLDIER NICKNAMED "NORTHERN WALL OF BRIGGS," HAVE A SOFT SPOT FOR CHILDREN.
TEE HEE
I'M AT THE AGE NOW WHEN IT WOULDN'T BE UNUSUAL TO HAVE A CHILD OR TWO OF MY OWN.
BUT I SUPPOSE I'VE MISSED MY CHANCE.

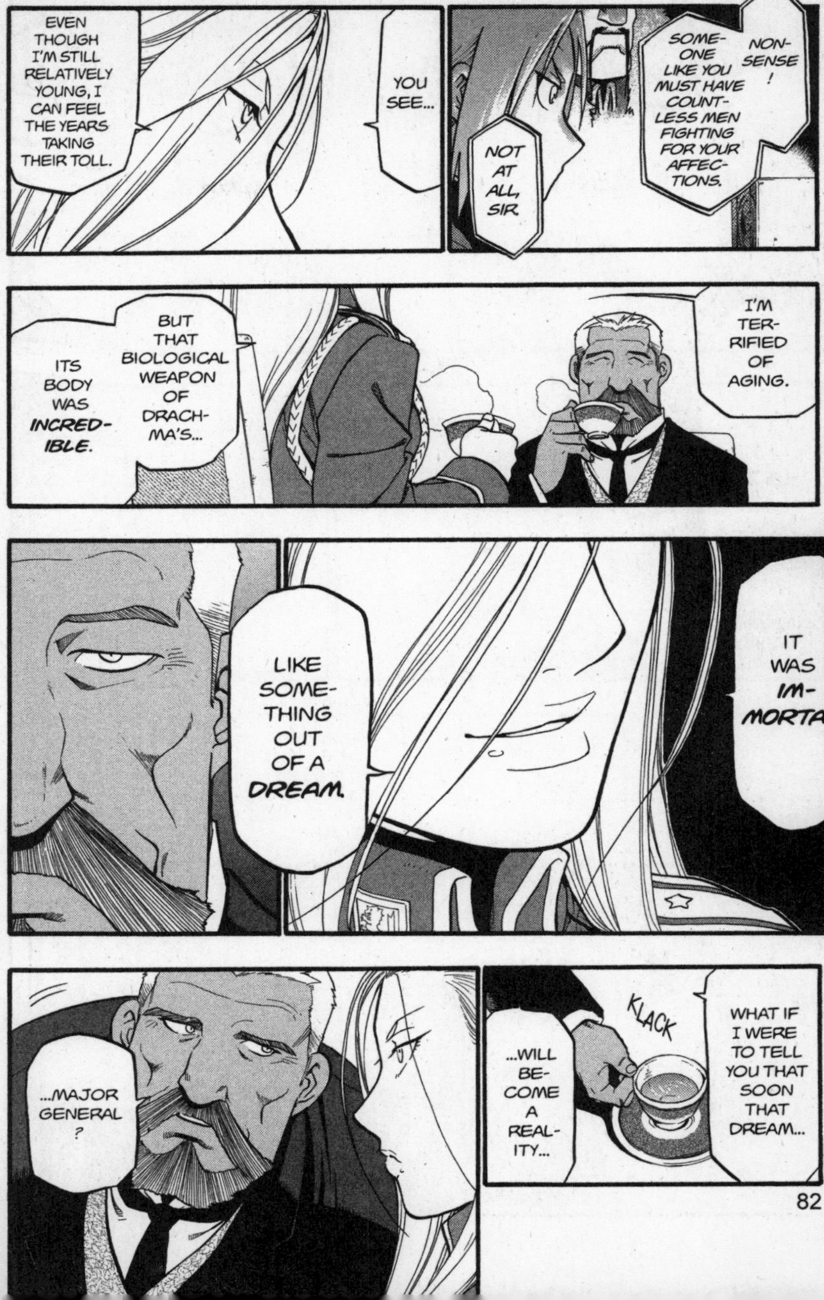
NONSENSE!
SOMEONE LIKE YOU MUST HAVE COUNTLESS MEN FIGHTING FOR YOUR AFFECTIONS.
NOT AT ALL, SIR.
YOU SEE...
EVEN THOUGH I'M STILL RELATIVELY YOUNG, I CAN FEEL THE YEARS TAKING THEIR TOLL.
I'M TERRIFIED OF AGING.
BUT THAT BIOLOGICAL WEAPON OF DRACHMA'S...
ITS BODY WAS ***INCREDIBLE***.
IT WAS ***IMMORTAL***.
LIKE SOMETHING OUT OF A ***DREAM***.
WHAT IF I WERE TO TELL YOU THAT SOON THAT DREAM...
KLACK
...WILL BECOME A REALITY...
...MAJOR GENERAL?

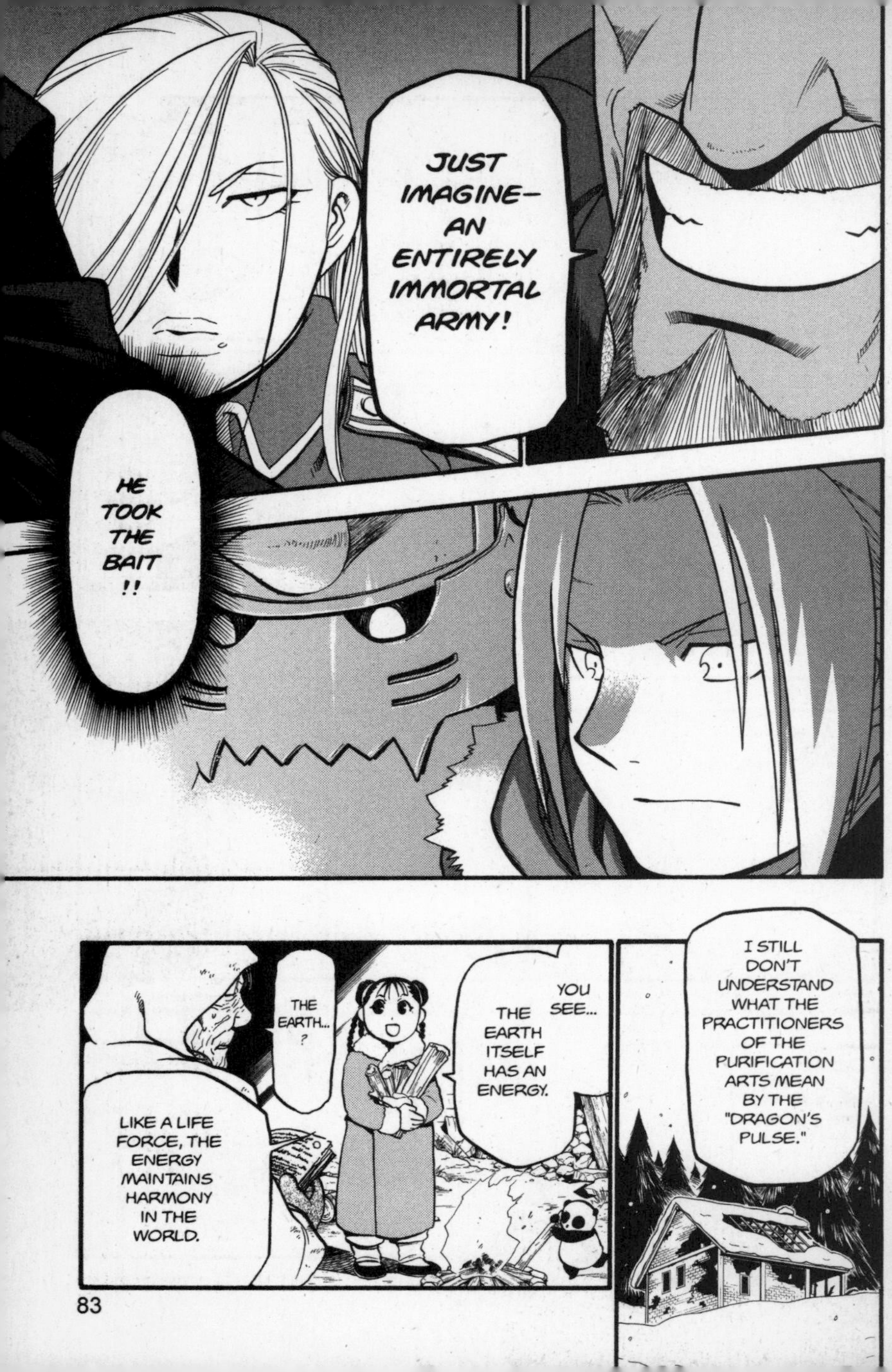
JUST IMAGINE—AN ENTIRELY IMMORTAL ARMY!
HE TOOK THE BAIT!!
I STILL DON'T UNDERSTAND WHAT THE PRACTITIONERS OF THE PURIFICATION ARTS MEAN BY THE "DRAGON'S PULSE."
YOU SEE... THE EARTH ITSELF HAS AN ENERGY.
THE EARTH...?
LIKE A LIFE FORCE, THE ENERGY MAINTAINS HARMONY IN THE WORLD.

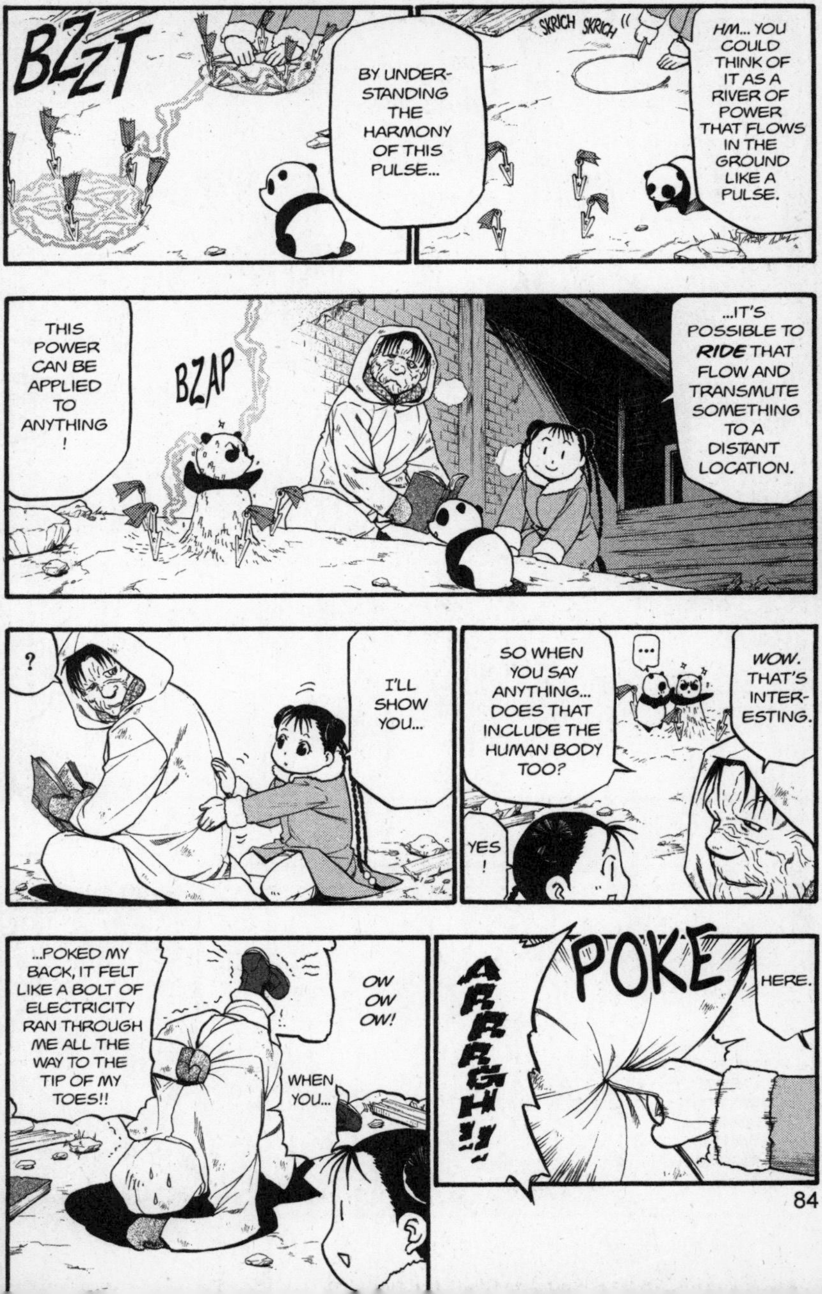
SKRICH SKRICH
HM... YOU COULD THINK OF IT AS A RIVER OF POWER THAT FLOWS IN THE GROUND LIKE A PULSE.
BY UNDER-STANDING THE HARMONY OF THIS PULSE...
BZZT
...IT'S POSSIBLE TO *RIDE* THAT FLOW AND TRANSMUTE SOMETHING TO A DISTANT LOCATION.
BZAP
THIS POWER CAN BE APPLIED TO ANYTHING!
WOW. THAT'S INTER-ESTING.
...
SO WHEN YOU SAY ANYTHING... DOES THAT INCLUDE THE HUMAN BODY TOO?
YES!
I'LL SHOW YOU...
?
HERE.
POKE
ARRRGH!!
OW OW OW!
WHEN YOU...
...POKED MY BACK, IT FELT LIKE A BOLT OF ELECTRICITY RAN THROUGH ME ALL THE WAY TO THE TIP OF MY TOES!!

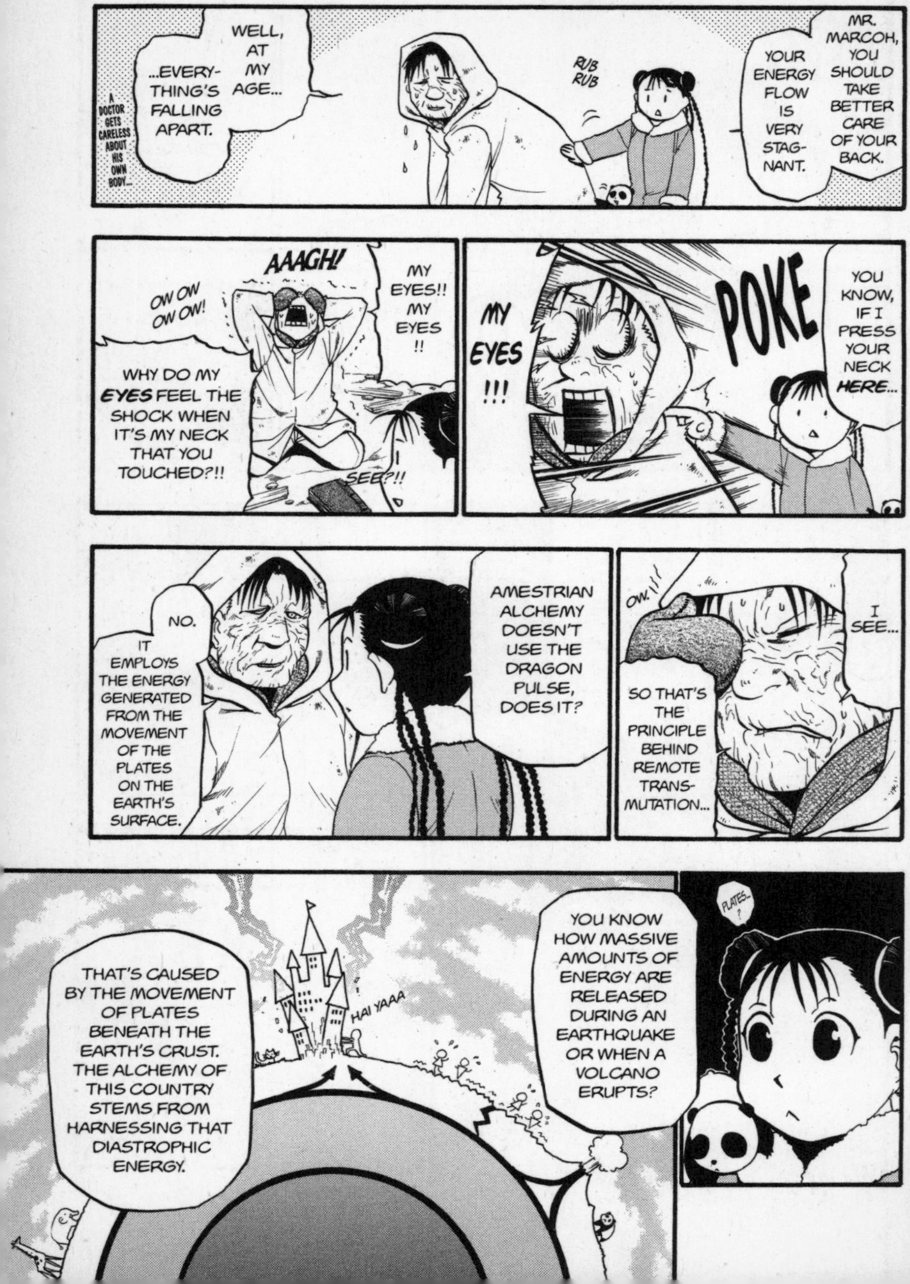
MR. MARCOH, YOU SHOULD TAKE BETTER CARE OF YOUR BACK.
YOUR ENERGY FLOW IS VERY STAG-NANT.
RUB RUB
WELL, AT MY AGE...
...EVERY-THING'S FALLING APART.
A DOCTOR GETS CARELESS ABOUT HIS OWN BODY...
YOU KNOW, IF I PRESS YOUR NECK HERE...
POKE
MY EYES !!!
MY EYES!! MY EYES !!
AAAGH!
OW OW OW OW!
WHY DO MY EYES FEEL THE SHOCK WHEN IT'S MY NECK THAT YOU TOUCHED?!!
I SEE?!!
I SEE...
OW...
SO THAT'S THE PRINCIPLE BEHIND REMOTE TRANS-MUTATION...
AMESTRIAN ALCHEMY DOESN'T USE THE DRAGON PULSE, DOES IT?
NO.
IT EMPLOYS THE ENERGY GENERATED FROM THE MOVEMENT OF THE PLATES ON THE EARTH'S SURFACE.
PLATES...?
YOU KNOW HOW MASSIVE AMOUNTS OF ENERGY ARE RELEASED DURING AN EARTHQUAKE OR WHEN A VOLCANO ERUPTS?
THAT'S CAUSED BY THE MOVEMENT OF PLATES BENEATH THE EARTH'S CRUST. THE ALCHEMY OF THIS COUNTRY STEMS FROM HARNESSING THAT DIASTROPHIC ENERGY.
HAI YAAA

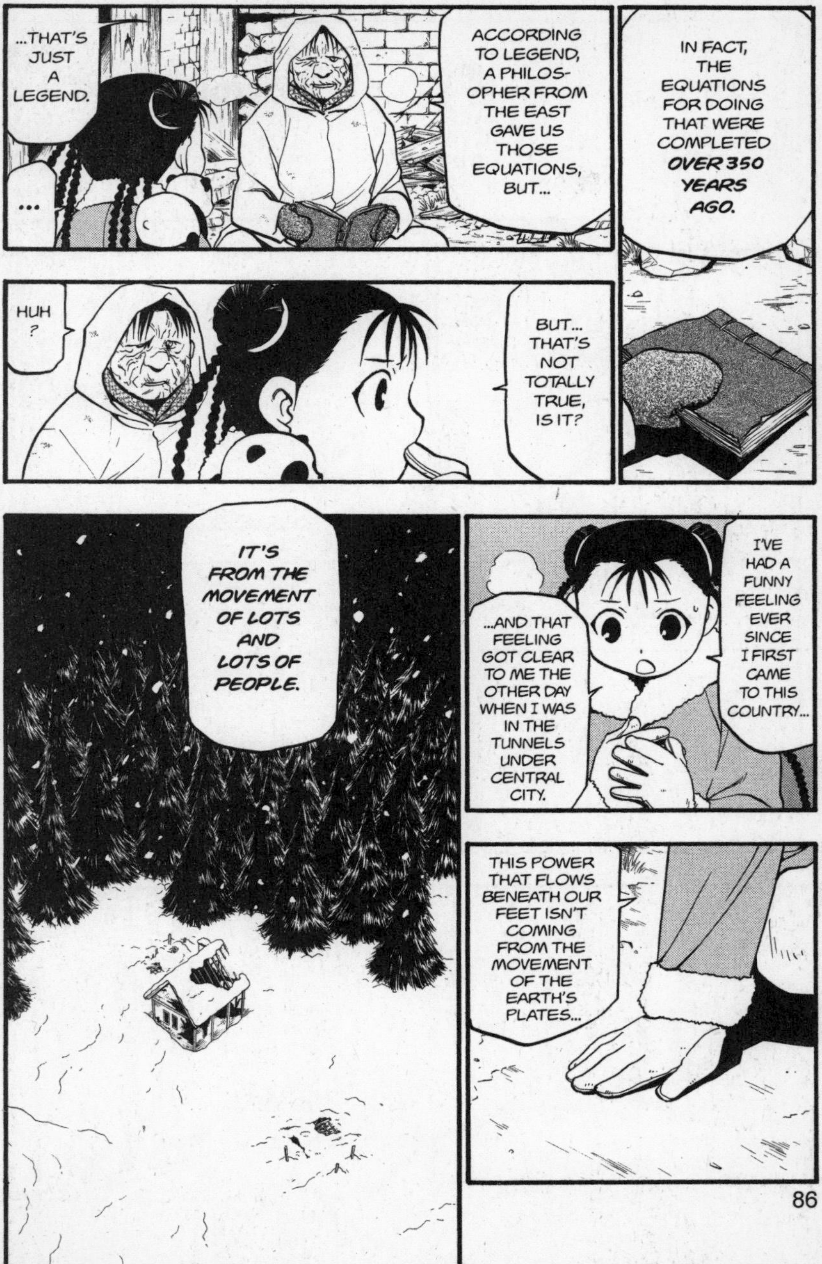
IN FACT, THE EQUATIONS FOR DOING THAT WERE COMPLETED ***OVER 350 YEARS AGO.***
ACCORDING TO LEGEND, A PHILOS-OPHER FROM THE EAST GAVE US THOSE EQUATIONS, BUT...
...THAT'S JUST A LEGEND.
...
BUT... THAT'S NOT TOTALLY TRUE, IS IT?
HUH ?
I'VE HAD A FUNNY FEELING EVER SINCE I FIRST CAME TO THIS COUNTRY...
...AND THAT FEELING GOT CLEAR TO ME THE OTHER DAY WHEN I WAS IN THE TUNNELS UNDER CENTRAL CITY.
THIS POWER THAT FLOWS BENEATH OUR FEET ISN'T COMING FROM THE MOVEMENT OF THE EARTH'S PLATES...
IT'S FROM THE MOVEMENT OF LOTS AND LOTS OF PEOPLE.

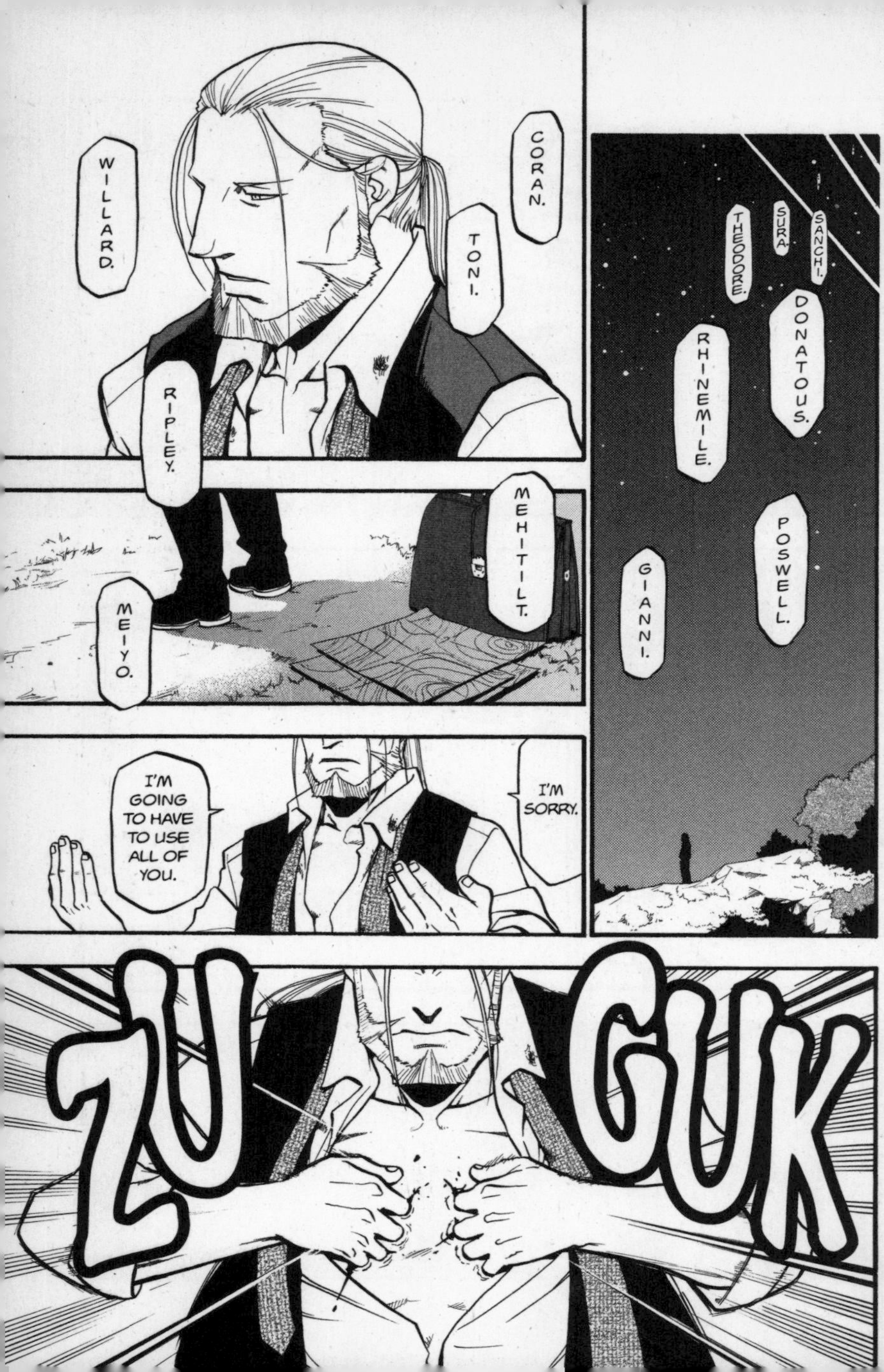
SANCHI.
SURA.
THEODORE.
DONATOUS.
RHINEMILE.
POSWELL.
GIANNI.
CORAN.
TONI.
WILLARD.
RIPLEY.
MEHITILT.
MEIYO.
I'M SORRY.
I'M GOING TO HAVE TO USE ALL OF YOU.
ZU GUK

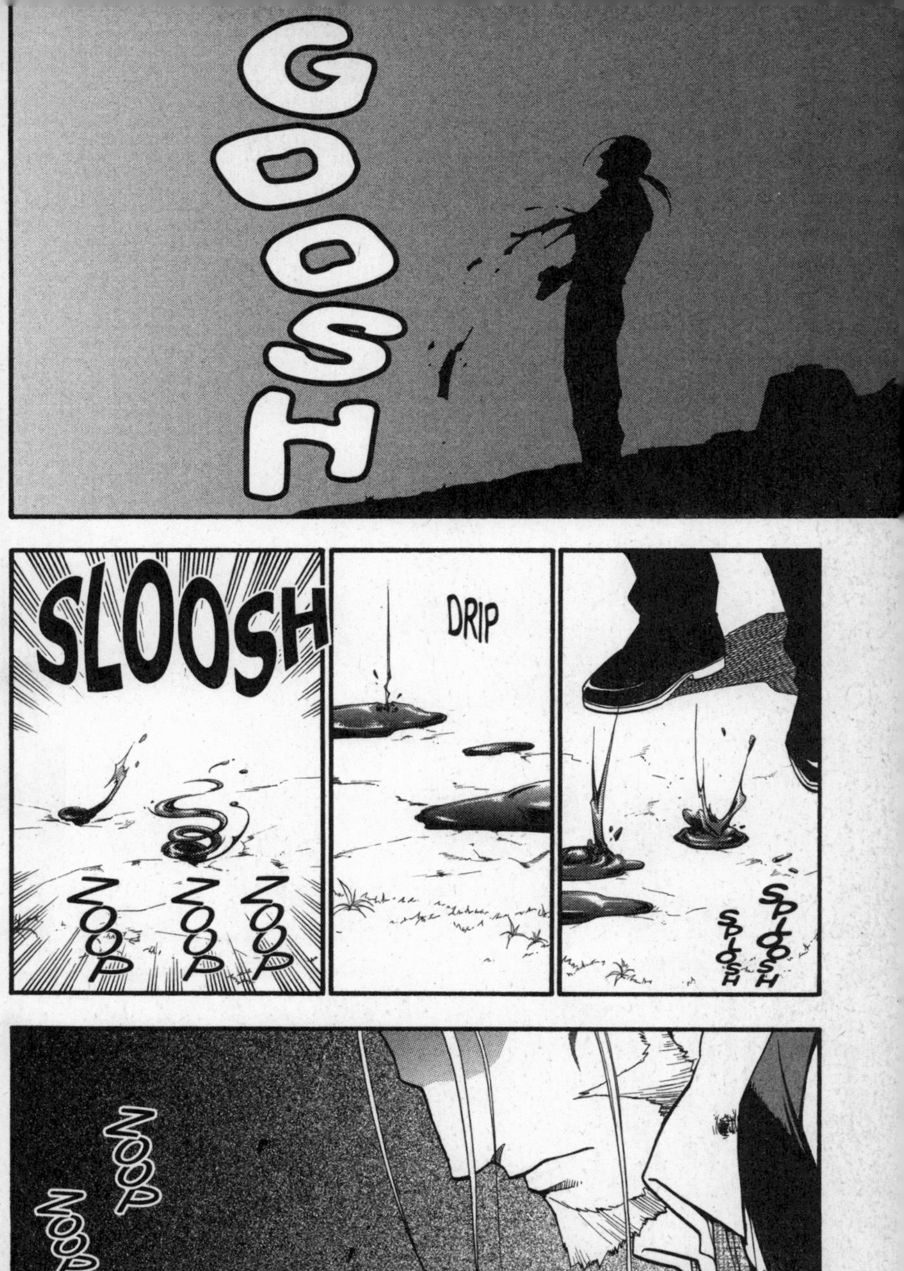
GOOSH
SLOOSH
ZOOP ZOOP ZOOP
DRIP
SPLOOSH SPLOSH
ZOOP ZOOP

FULLMETAL
ALCHEMIST

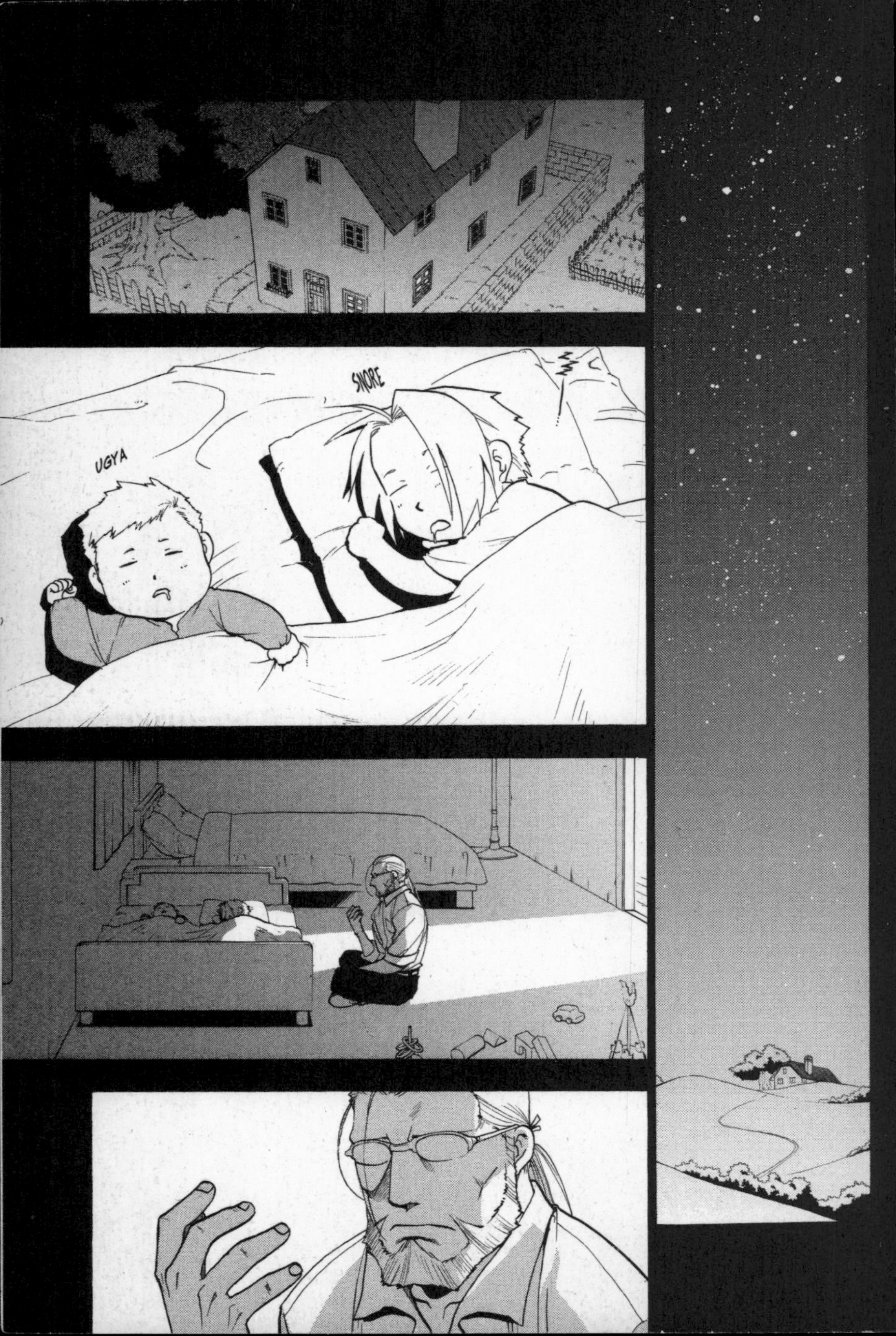

SNORE
UGYA

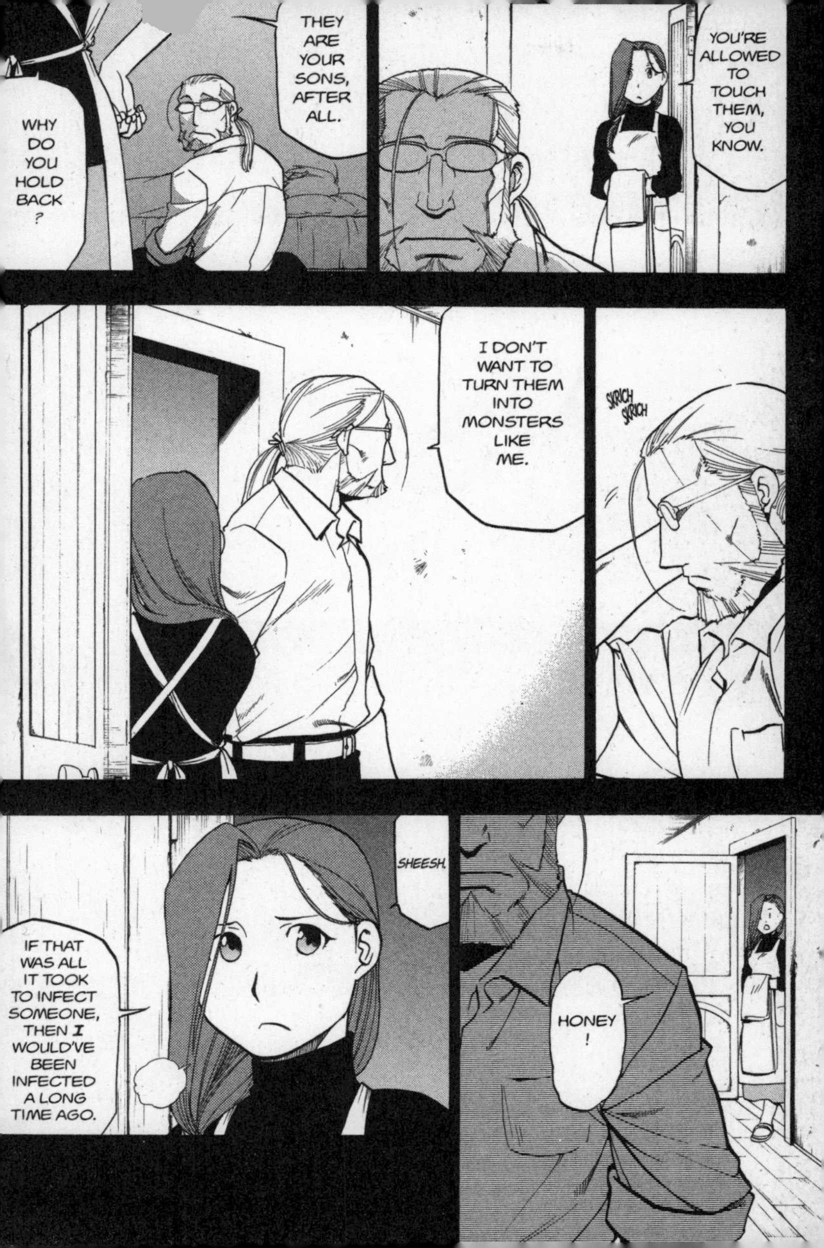
YOU'RE ALLOWED TO TOUCH THEM, YOU KNOW.
THEY ARE YOUR SONS, AFTER ALL.
WHY DO YOU HOLD BACK?
SKRICH SKRICH
I DON'T WANT TO TURN THEM INTO MONSTERS LIKE ME.
HONEY!
SHEESH.
IF THAT WAS ALL IT TOOK TO INFECT SOMEONE, THEN I WOULD'VE BEEN INFECTED A LONG TIME AGO.

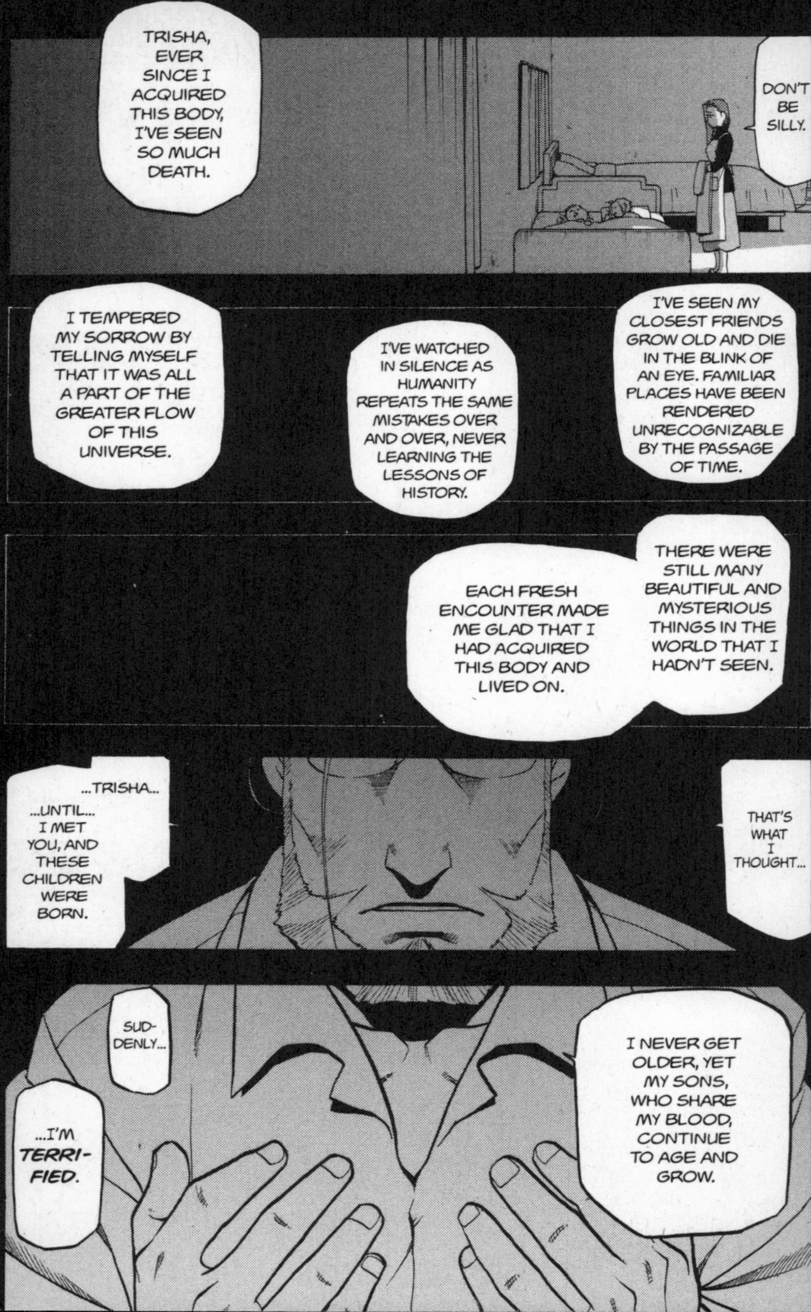
DON'T BE SILLY.
TRISHA, EVER SINCE I ACQUIRED THIS BODY, I'VE SEEN SO MUCH DEATH.
I'VE SEEN MY CLOSEST FRIENDS GROW OLD AND DIE IN THE BLINK OF AN EYE. FAMILIAR PLACES HAVE BEEN RENDERED UNRECOGNIZABLE BY THE PASSAGE OF TIME.
I'VE WATCHED IN SILENCE AS HUMANITY REPEATS THE SAME MISTAKES OVER AND OVER, NEVER LEARNING THE LESSONS OF HISTORY.
I TEMPERED MY SORROW BY TELLING MYSELF THAT IT WAS ALL A PART OF THE GREATER FLOW OF THIS UNIVERSE.
THERE WERE STILL MANY BEAUTIFUL AND MYSTERIOUS THINGS IN THE WORLD THAT I HADN'T SEEN.
EACH FRESH ENCOUNTER MADE ME GLAD THAT I HAD ACQUIRED THIS BODY AND LIVED ON.
THAT'S WHAT I THOUGHT...
...TRISHA... ...UNTIL... I MET YOU, AND THESE CHILDREN WERE BORN.
I NEVER GET OLDER, YET MY SONS, WHO SHARE MY BLOOD, CONTINUE TO AGE AND GROW.
SUD-DENLY...
...I'M ***TERRI-FIED***.

Chapter 68: Portrait of a Family

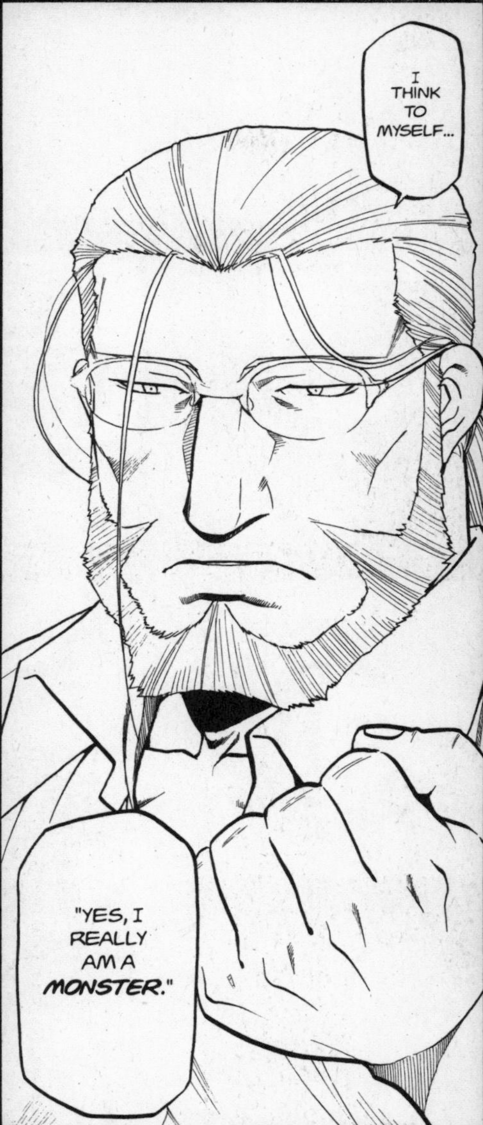
I THINK TO MYSELF...
"YES, I REALLY AM A MONSTER."

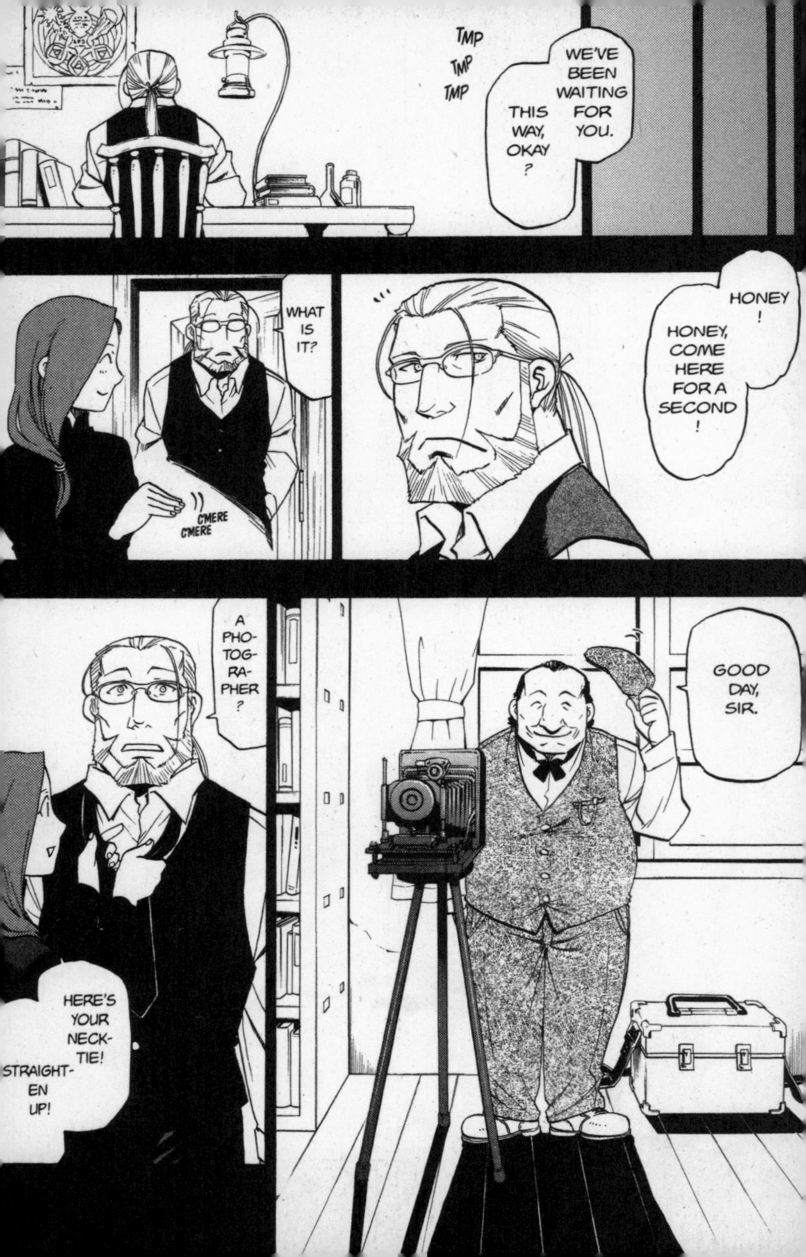
WE'VE BEEN WAITING FOR YOU. THIS WAY, OKAY?
TMP TMP TMP
HONEY!
HONEY, COME HERE FOR A SECOND!
WHAT IS IT?
C'MERE C'MERE
GOOD DAY, SIR.
A PHOTOGRAPHER?
HERE'S YOUR NECKTIE!
STRAIGHTEN UP!

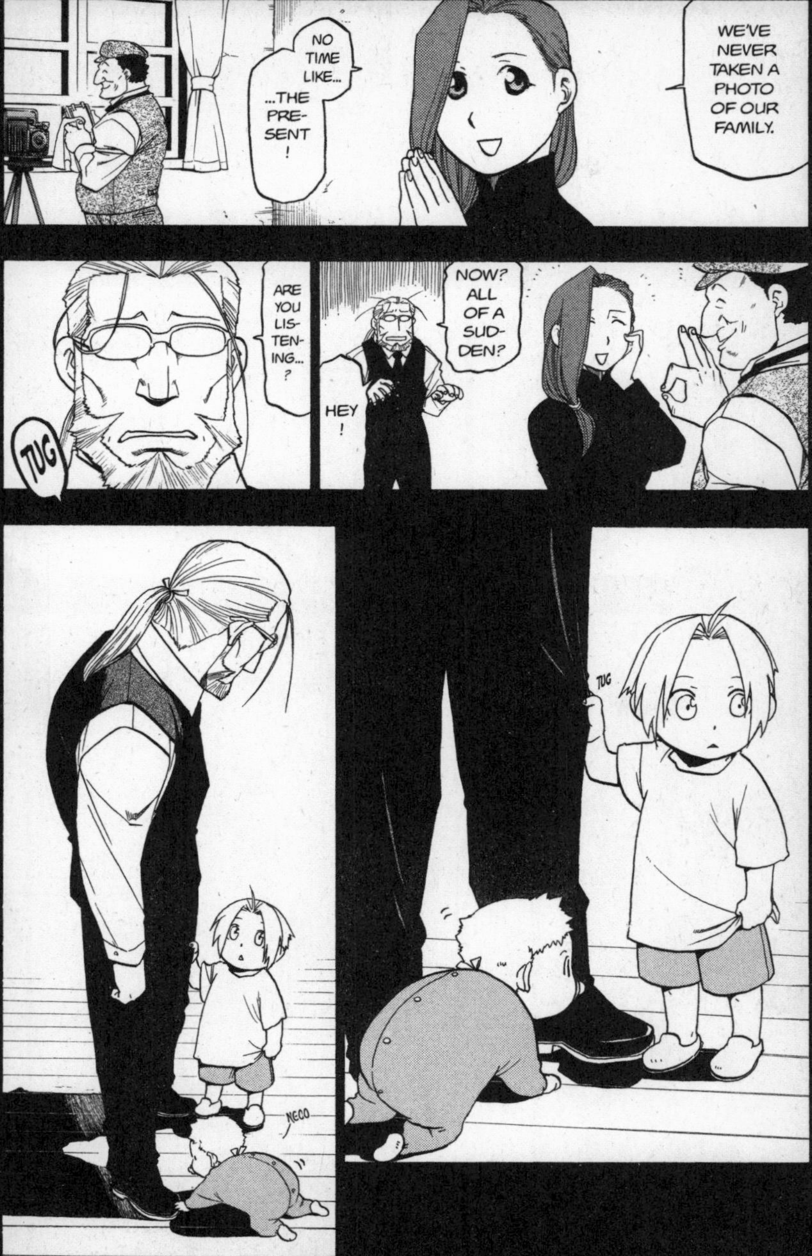
WE'VE NEVER TAKEN A PHOTO OF OUR FAMILY.
NO TIME LIKE...
...THE PRESENT!
NOW? ALL OF A SUDDEN?
HEY!
ARE YOU LISTENING...?
TUG
TUG
NGOO

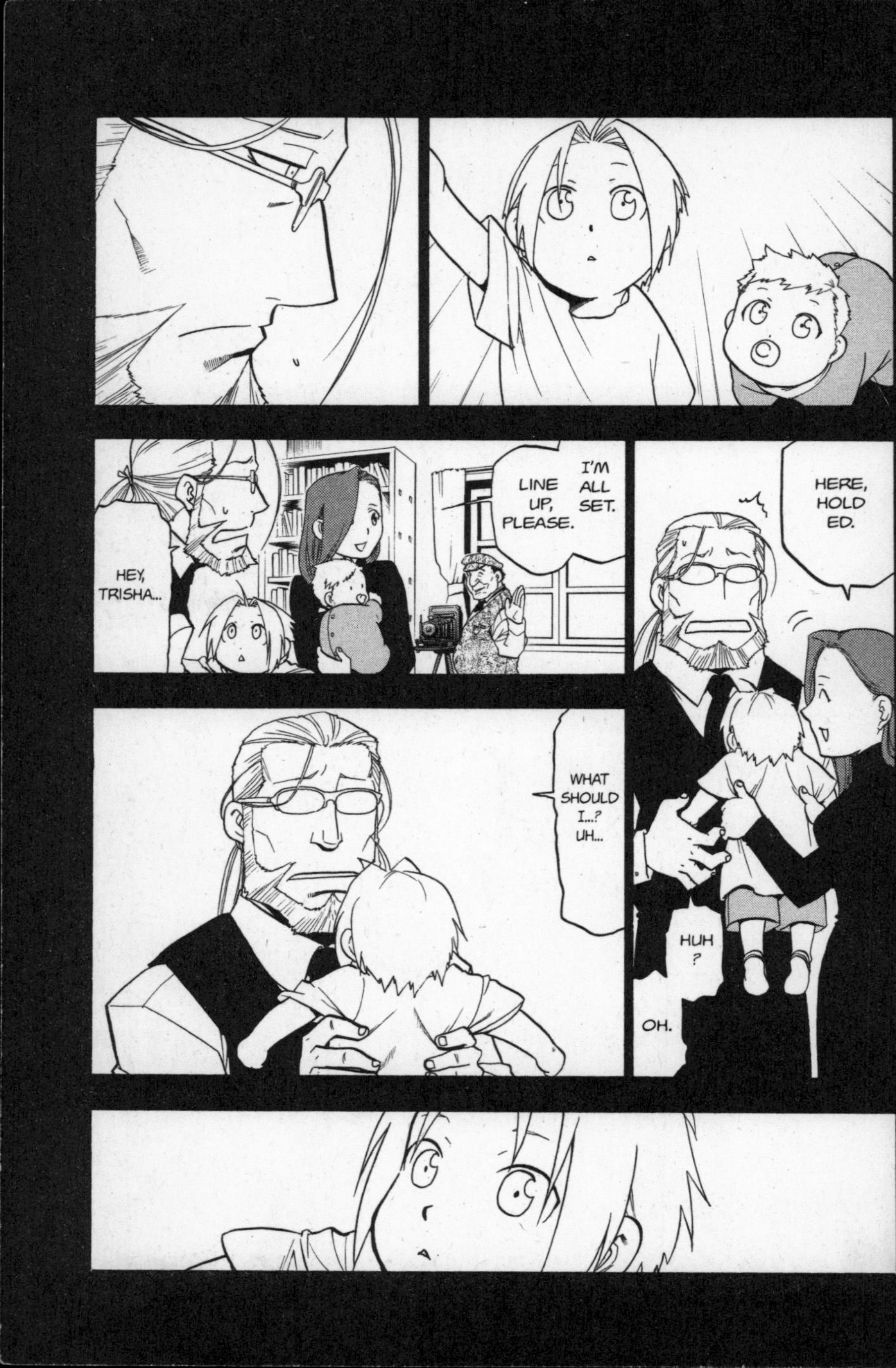
HERE, HOLD ED.
HUH ?
OH.
I'M ALL SET.
LINE UP, PLEASE.
HEY, TRISHA...
WHAT SHOULD I...? UH...

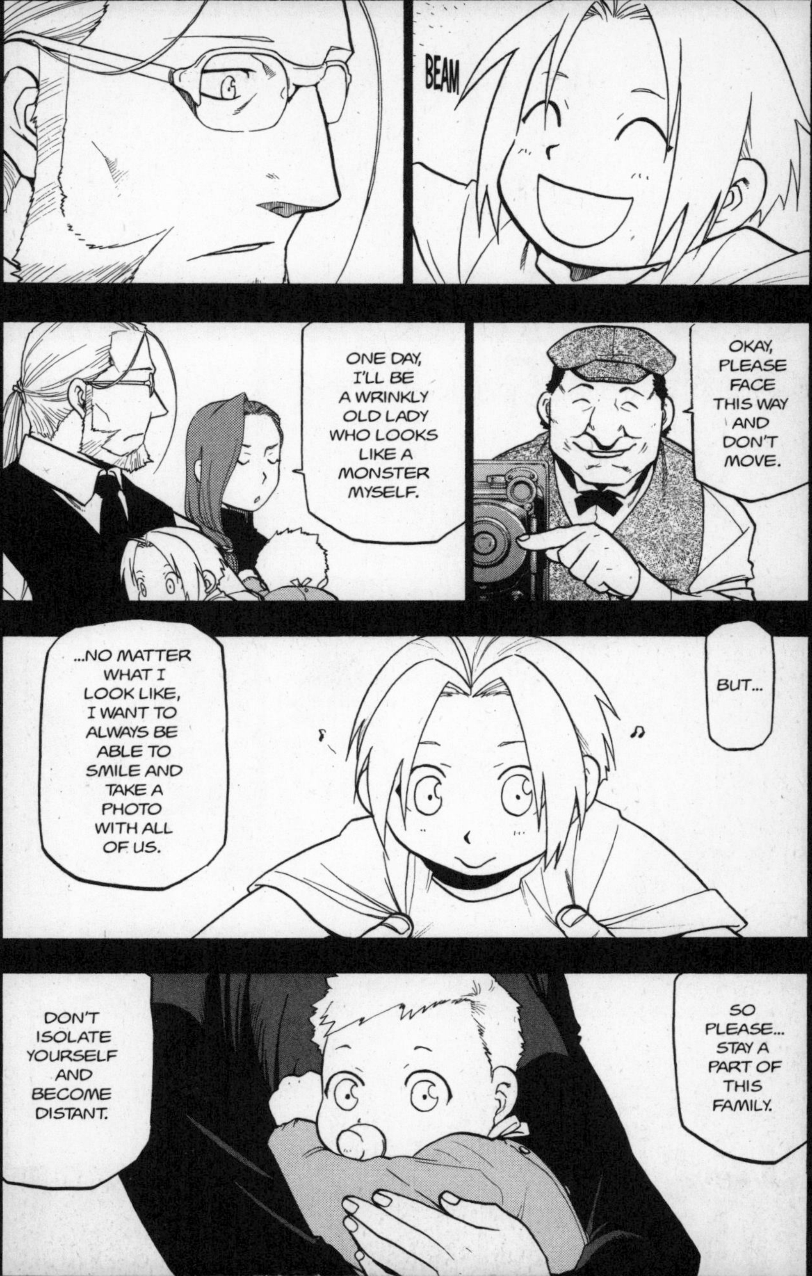
BEAM
OKAY, PLEASE FACE THIS WAY AND DON'T MOVE.
ONE DAY, I'LL BE A WRINKLY OLD LADY WHO LOOKS LIKE A MONSTER MYSELF.
BUT...
...NO MATTER WHAT I LOOK LIKE, I WANT TO ALWAYS BE ABLE TO SMILE AND TAKE A PHOTO WITH ALL OF US.
SO PLEASE... STAY A PART OF THIS FAMILY.
DON'T ISOLATE YOURSELF AND BECOME DISTANT.

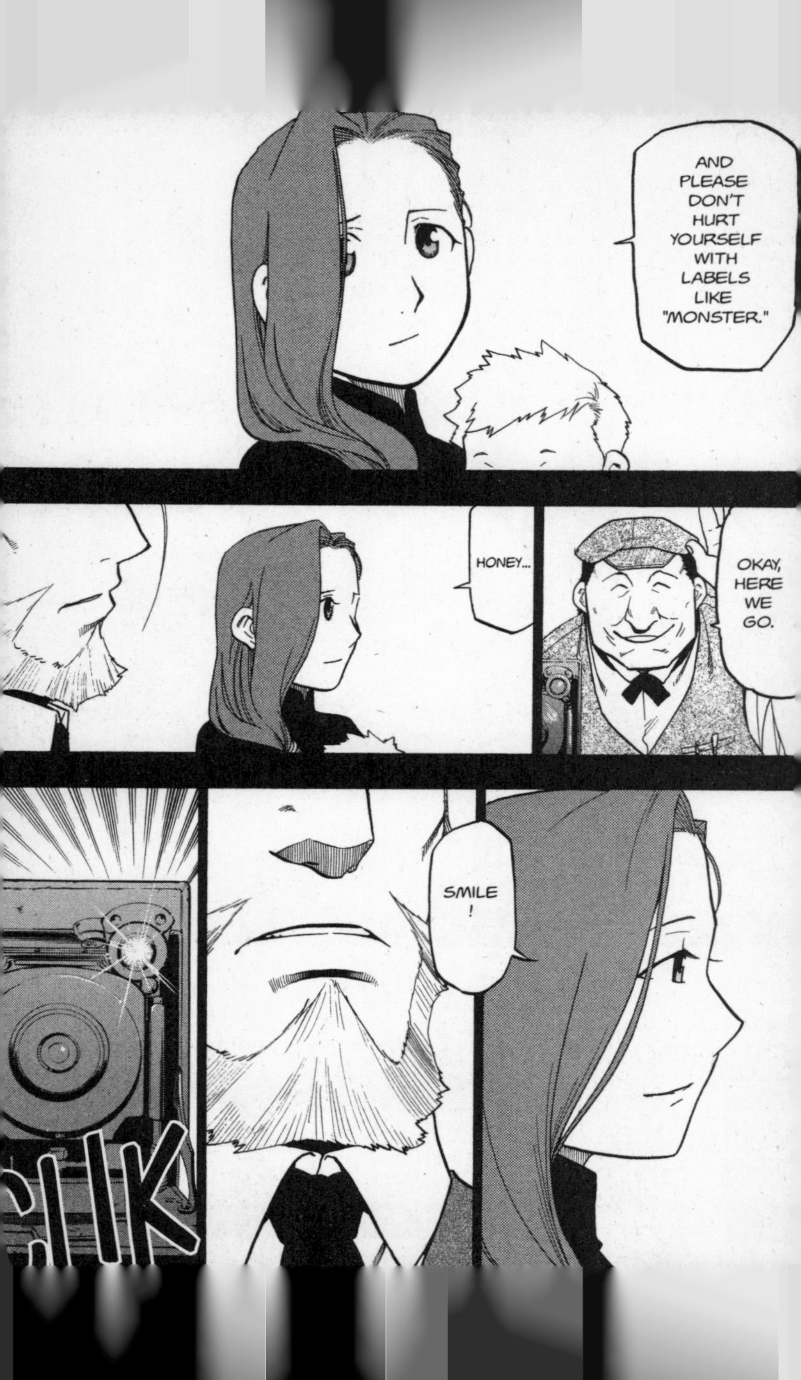
AND PLEASE DON'T HURT YOURSELF WITH LABELS LIKE "MONSTER."
OKAY, HERE WE GO.
HONEY...
SMILE!
CLIK

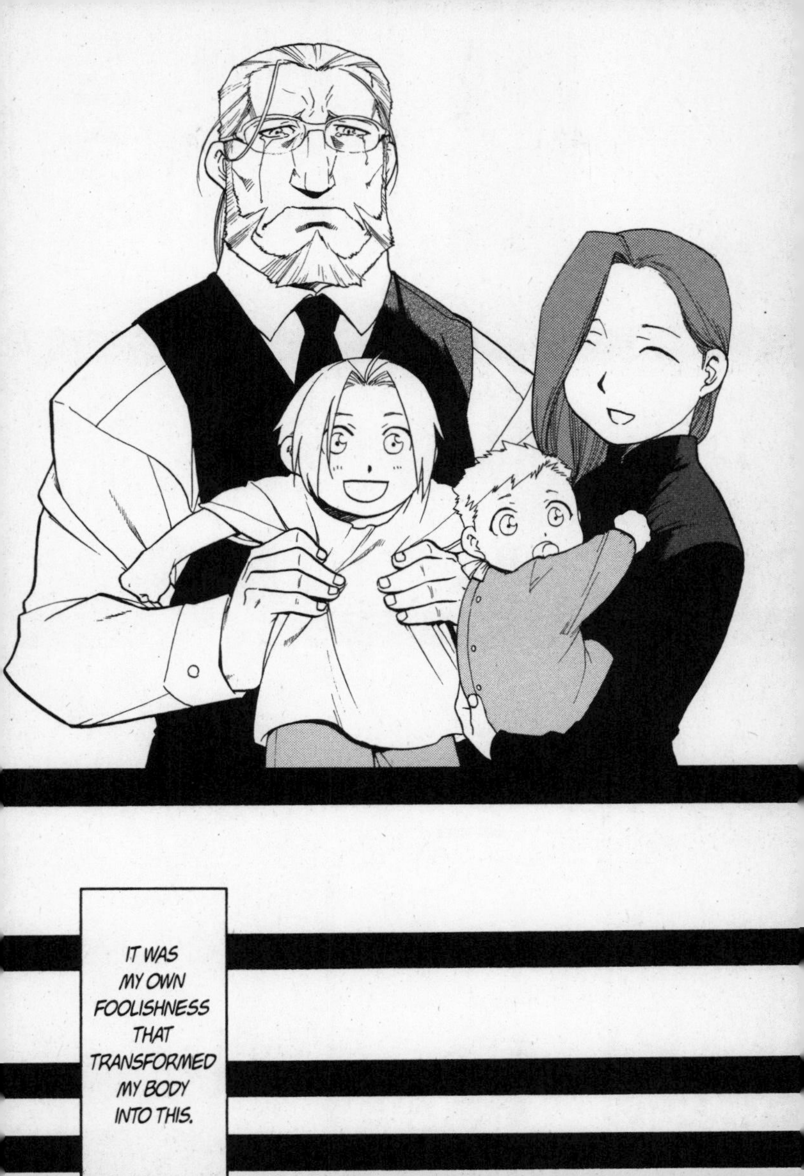
IT WAS MY OWN FOOLISHNESS THAT TRANSFORMED MY BODY INTO THIS.

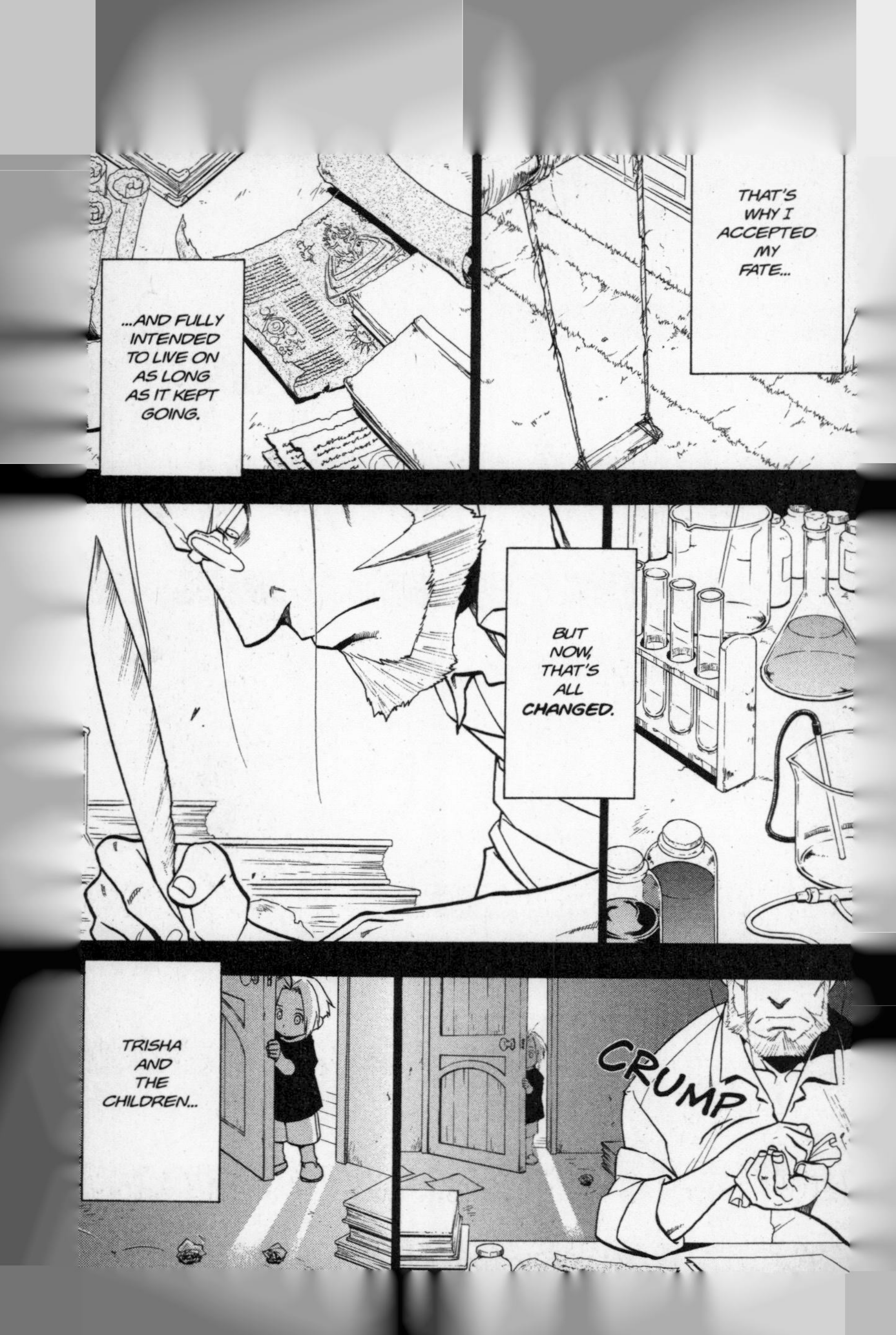
THAT'S WHY I ACCEPTED MY FATE...
...AND FULLY INTENDED TO LIVE ON AS LONG AS IT KEPT GOING.
BUT NOW, THAT'S ALL CHANGED.
CRUMP
TRISHA AND THE CHILDREN...

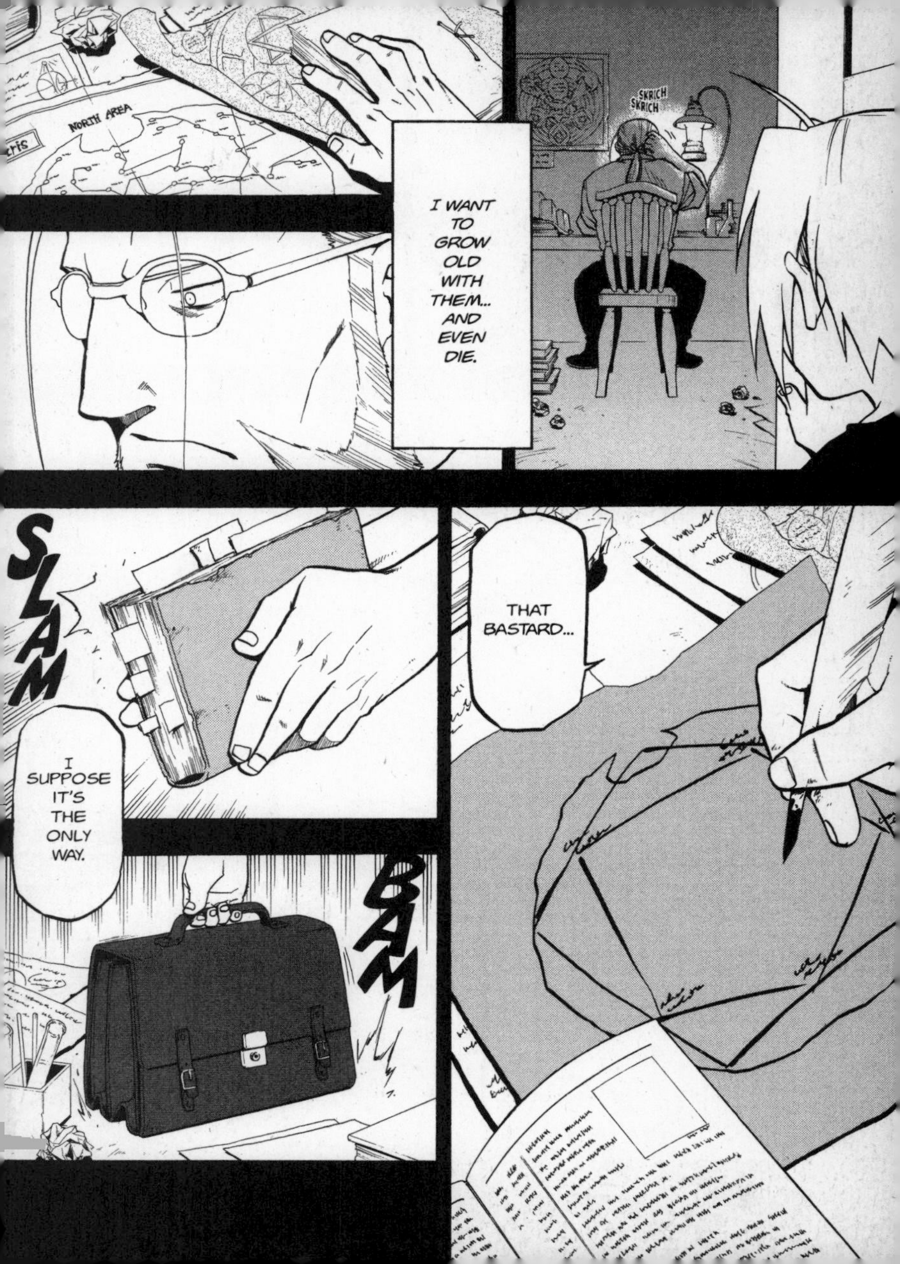
SKRICH
SKRICH
I WANT TO GROW OLD WITH THEM... AND EVEN DIE.
NORTH AREA
THAT BASTARD...
SLAM
I SUPPOSE IT'S THE ONLY WAY.
BAM

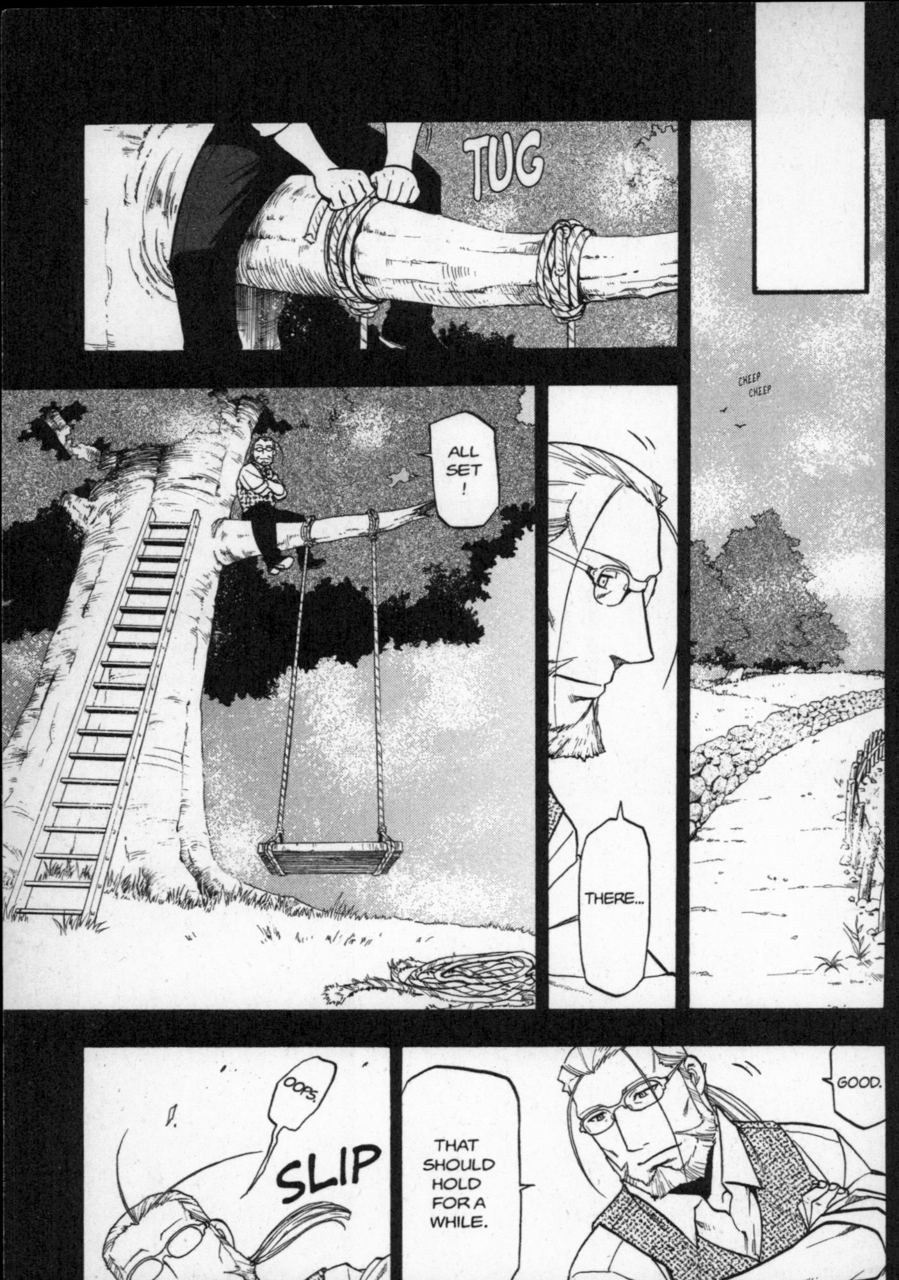
CHEEP CHEEP
TUG
THERE...
ALL SET!
GOOD.
THAT SHOULD HOLD FOR A WHILE.
OOPS.
SLIP

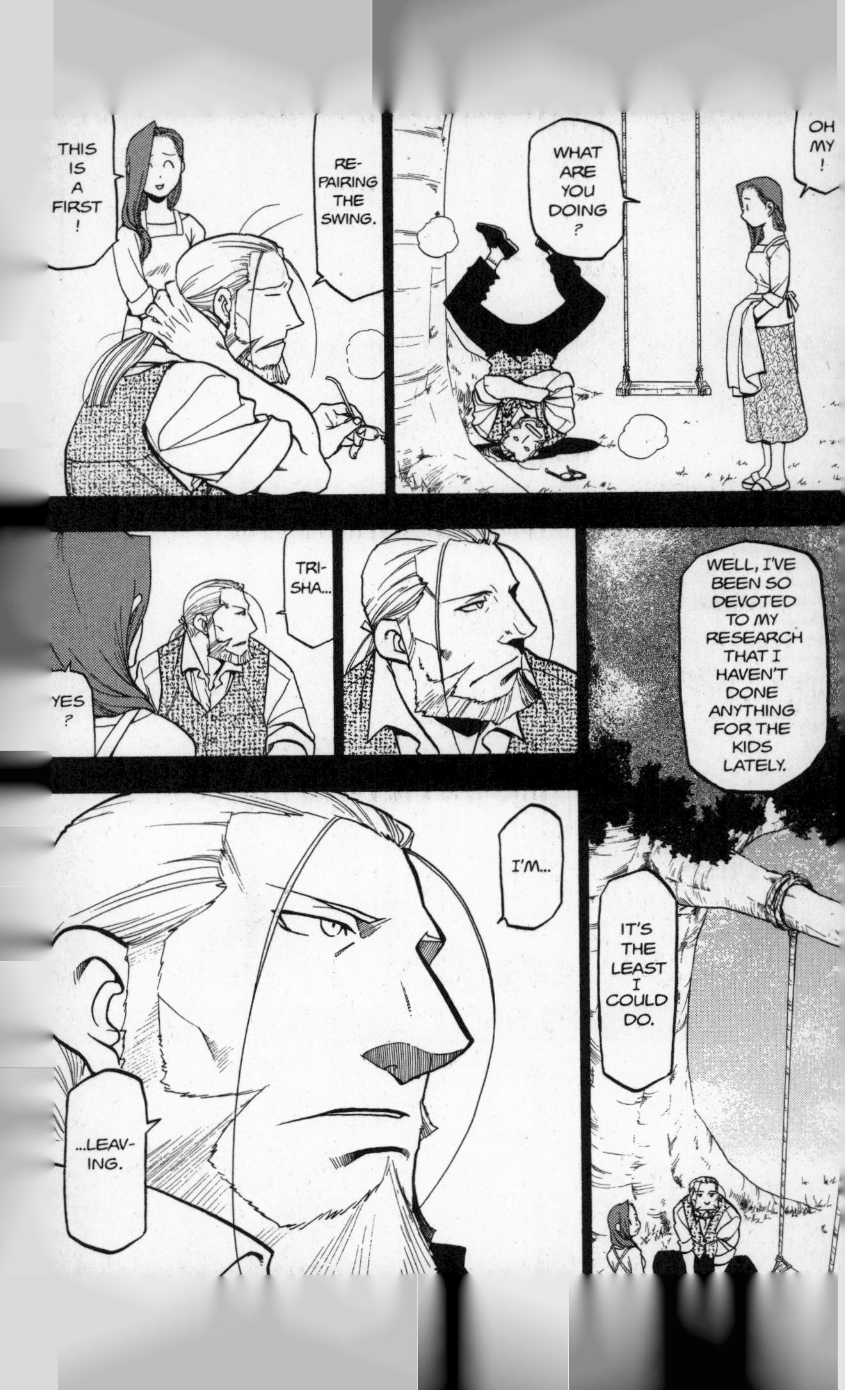
OH MY!
WHAT ARE YOU DOING?
RE-PAIRING THE SWING.
THIS IS A FIRST!
WELL, I'VE BEEN SO DEVOTED TO MY RESEARCH THAT I HAVEN'T DONE ANYTHING FOR THE KIDS LATELY.
IT'S THE LEAST I COULD DO.
TRI-SHA...
YES?
I'M...
...LEAVING.

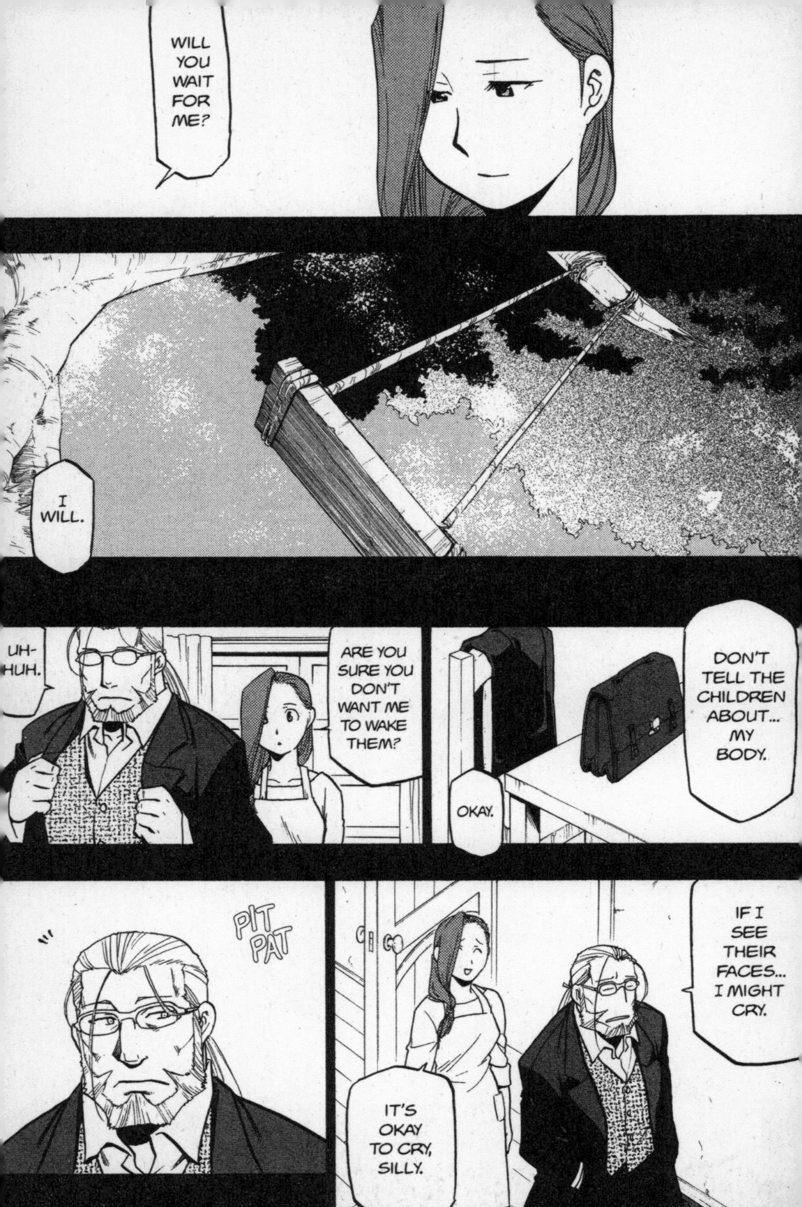
WILL YOU WAIT FOR ME?
I WILL.
DON'T TELL THE CHILDREN ABOUT... MY BODY.
OKAY.
ARE YOU SURE YOU DON'T WANT ME TO WAKE THEM?
UH-HUH.
IF I SEE THEIR FACES... I MIGHT CRY.
IT'S OKAY TO CRY, SILLY.
PIT PAT

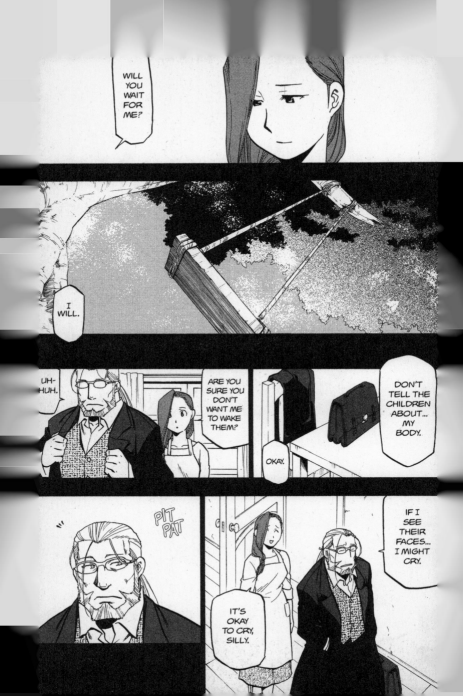

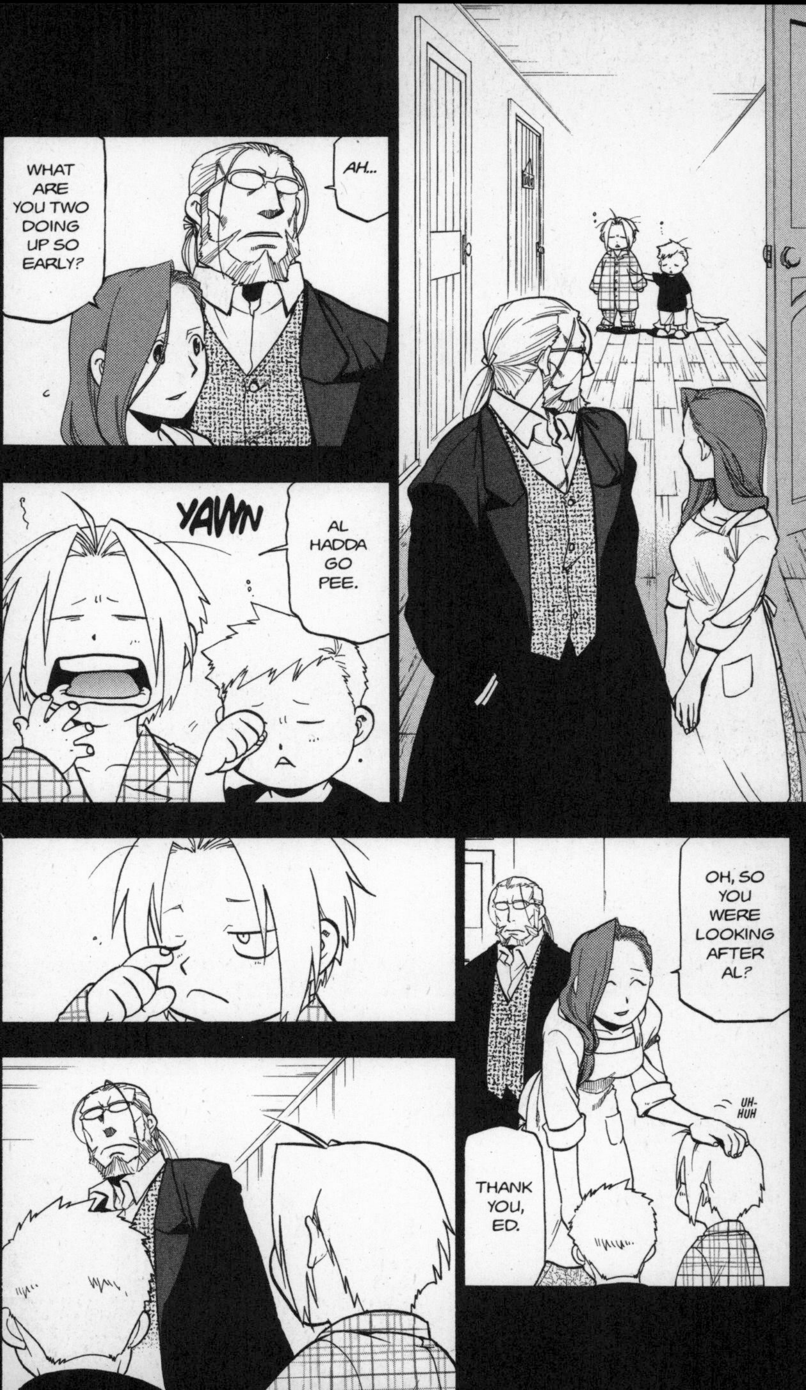
AH...
WHAT ARE YOU TWO DOING UP SO EARLY?
AL HADDA GO PEE.
YAWN
OH, SO YOU WERE LOOKING AFTER AL?
UH-HUH
THANK YOU, ED.

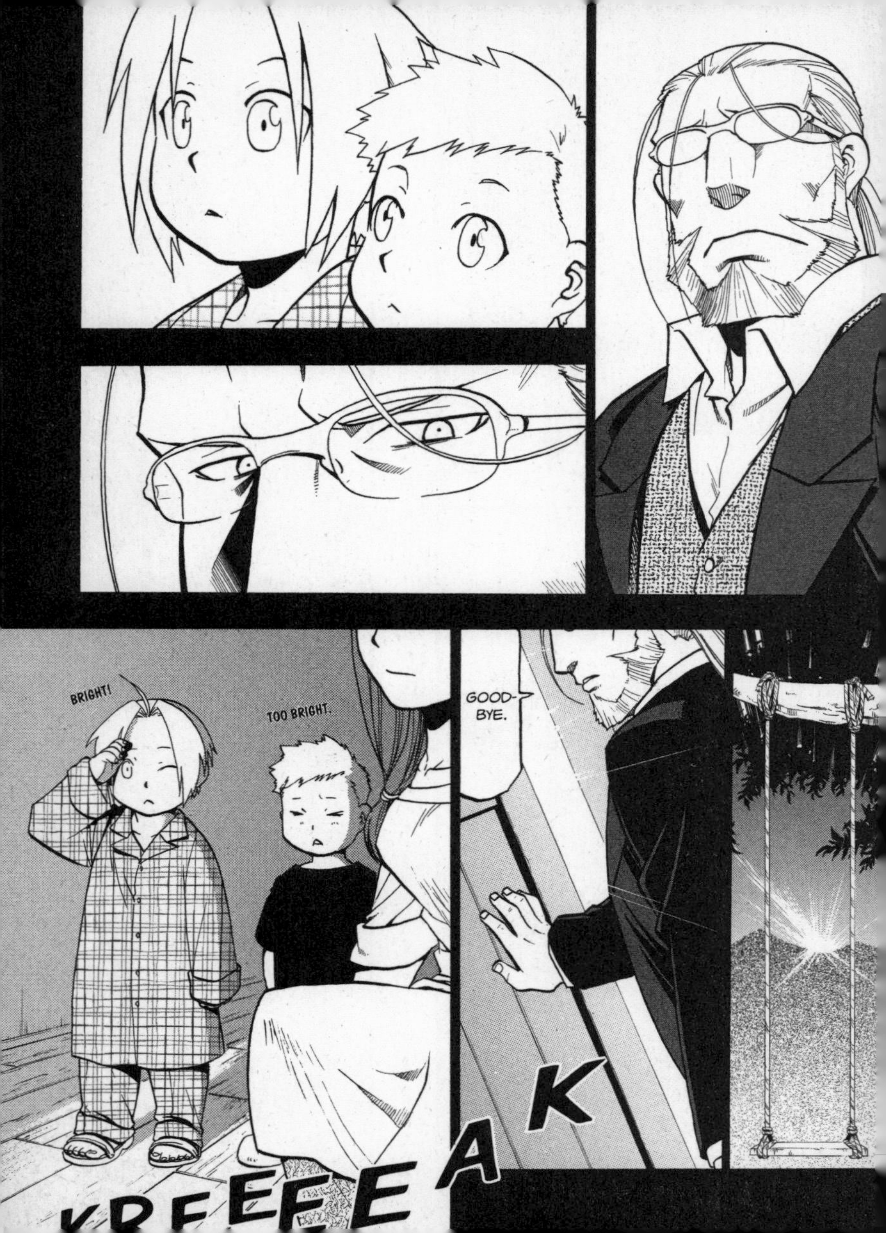
GOOD-BYE.
TOO BRIGHT.
BRIGHT!
KREEEEAK

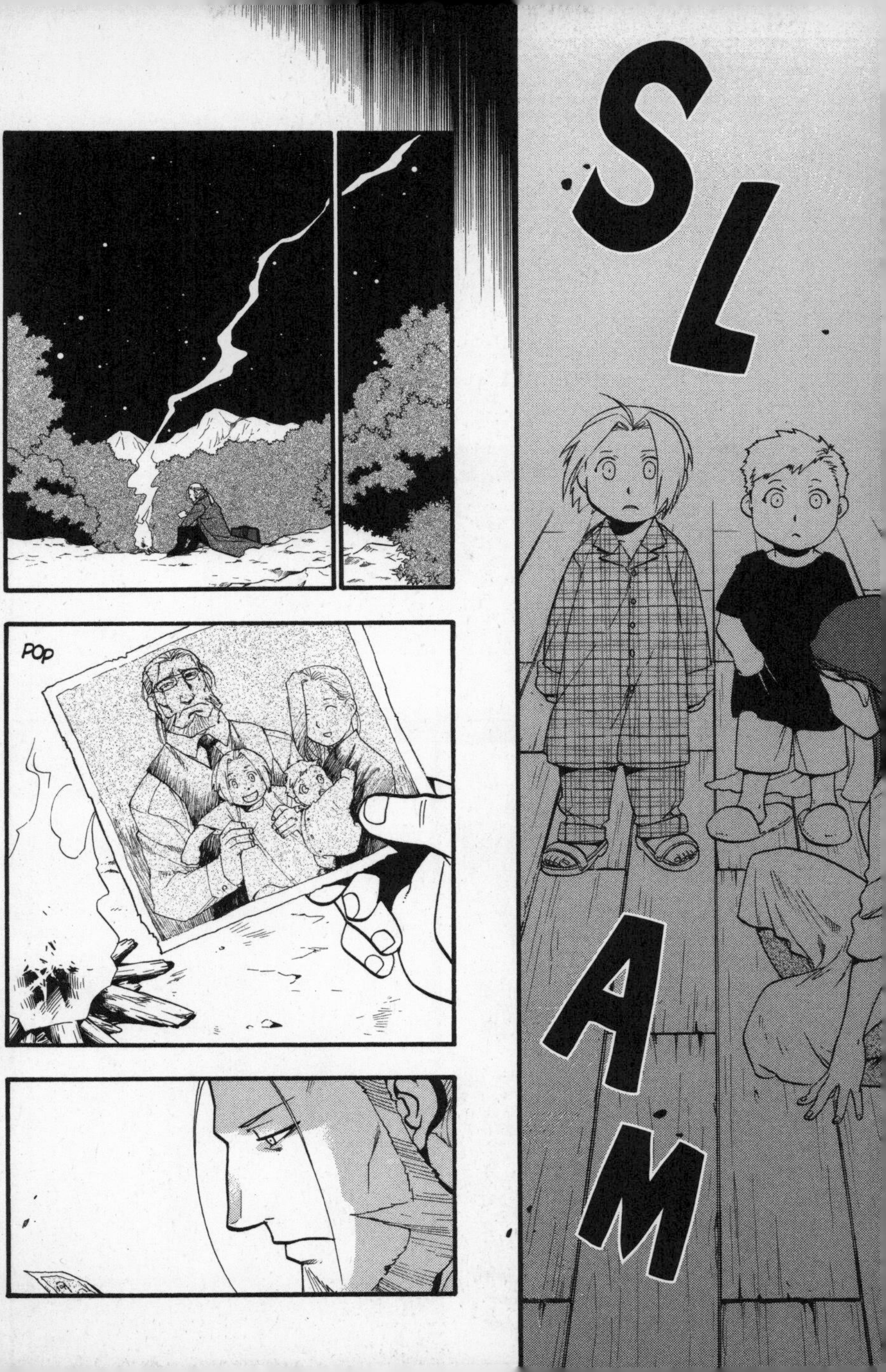
SLAM
POP

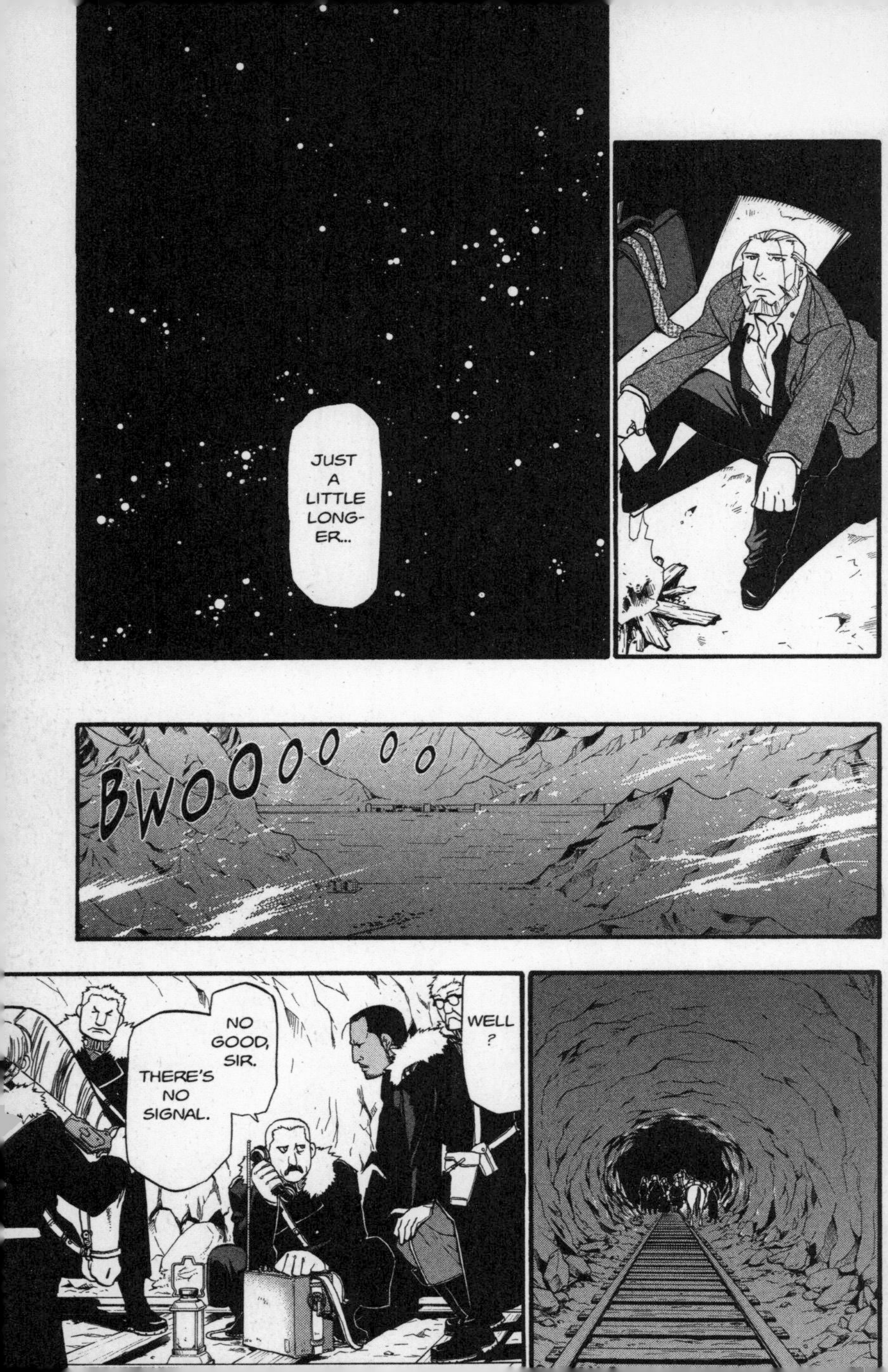
JUST A LITTLE LONG-ER...
BWOOOO OO
WELL?
NO GOOD, SIR. THERE'S NO SIGNAL.

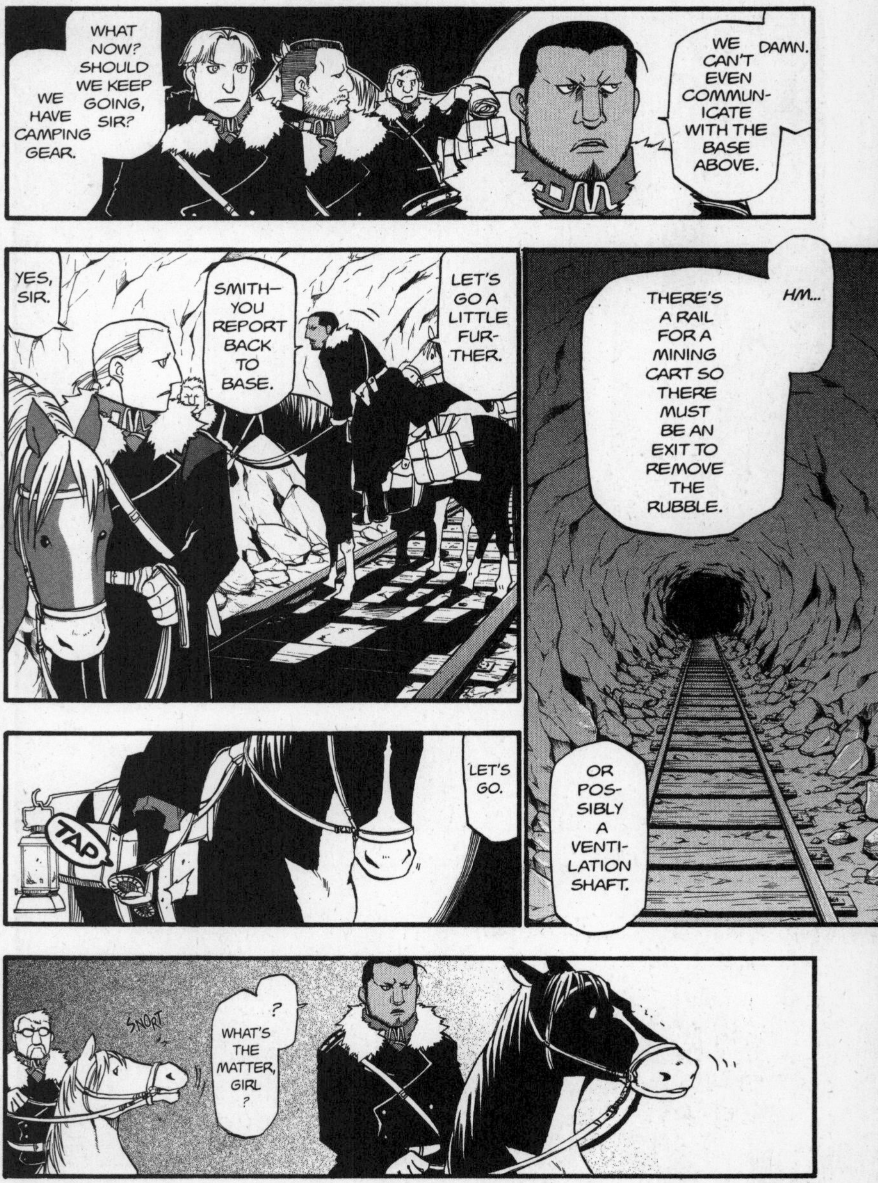
DAMN.
WE CAN'T EVEN COMMUNICATE WITH THE BASE ABOVE.
WHAT NOW? SHOULD WE KEEP GOING, SIR?
WE HAVE CAMPING GEAR.
HM...
THERE'S A RAIL FOR A MINING CART SO THERE MUST BE AN EXIT TO REMOVE THE RUBBLE.
OR POSSIBLY A VENTILATION SHAFT.
LET'S GO A LITTLE FURTHER.
SMITH— YOU REPORT BACK TO BASE.
YES, SIR.
LET'S GO.
TAP
?
WHAT'S THE MATTER, GIRL?
SNORT

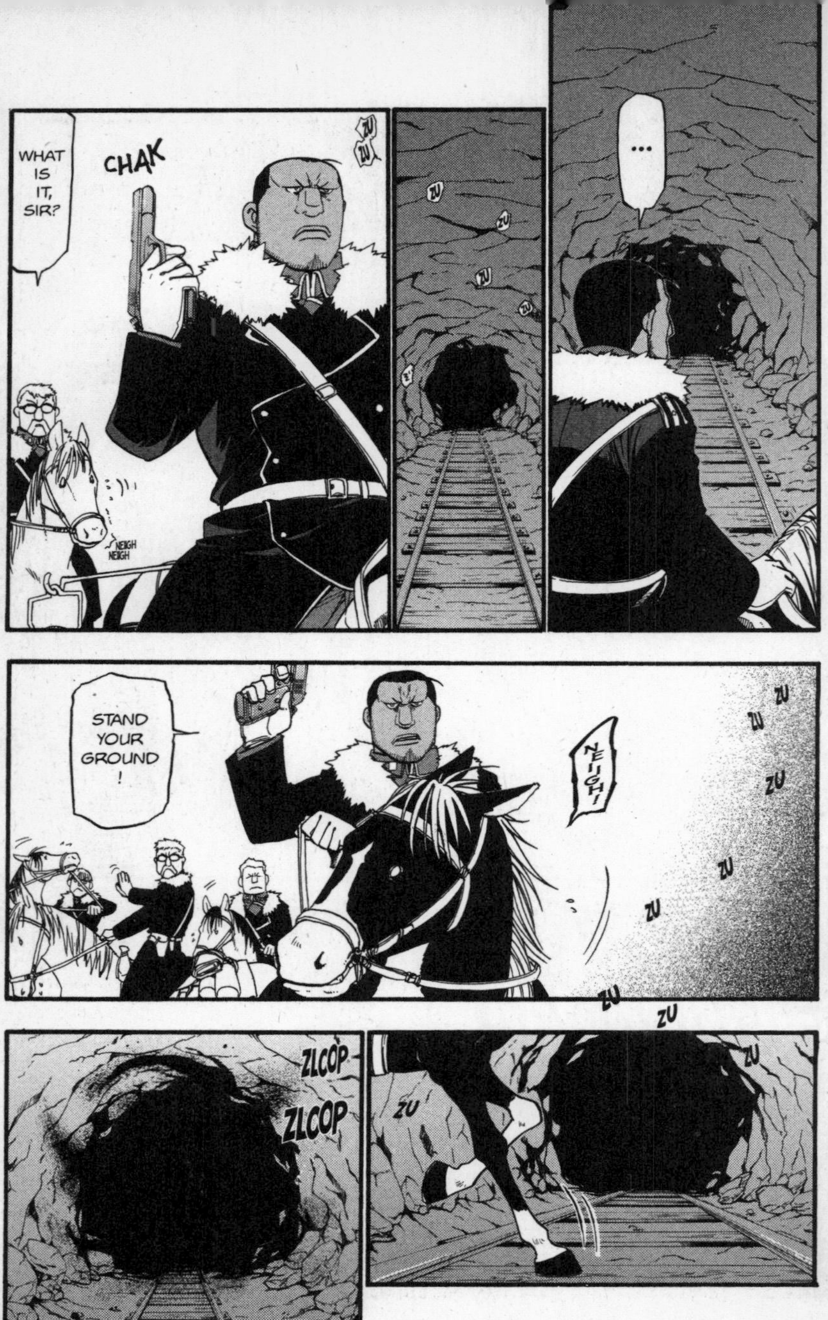
...
ZU
ZU
ZU
ZU
ZU ZU
CHAK
WHAT IS IT, SIR?
NEIGH NEIGH
ZU ZU
ZU
NEIGH!
STAND YOUR GROUND!
ZU
ZU
ZU
ZU
ZU
ZU
ZU
ZLCOP
ZLCOP

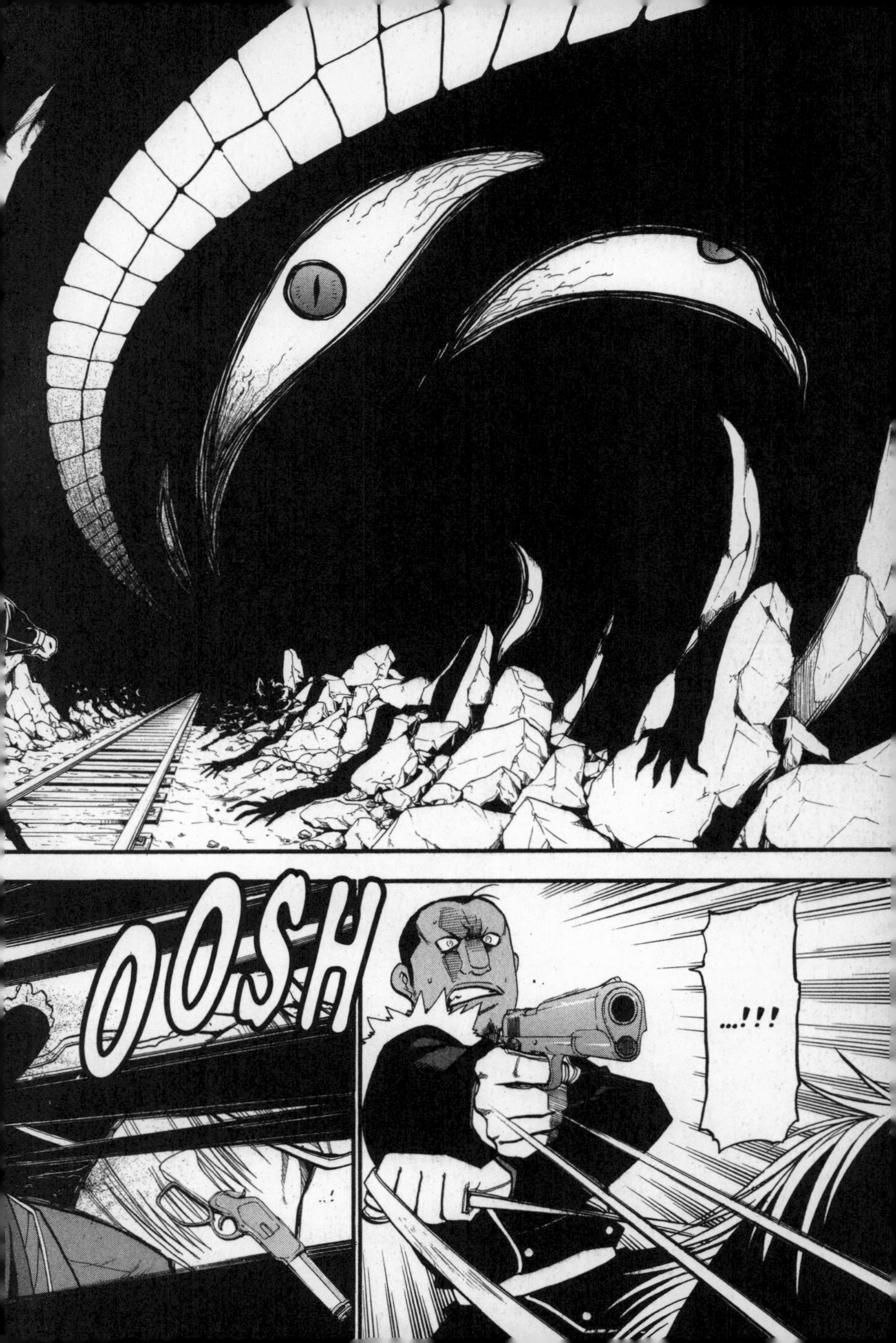
...!!!
..!
OOSH

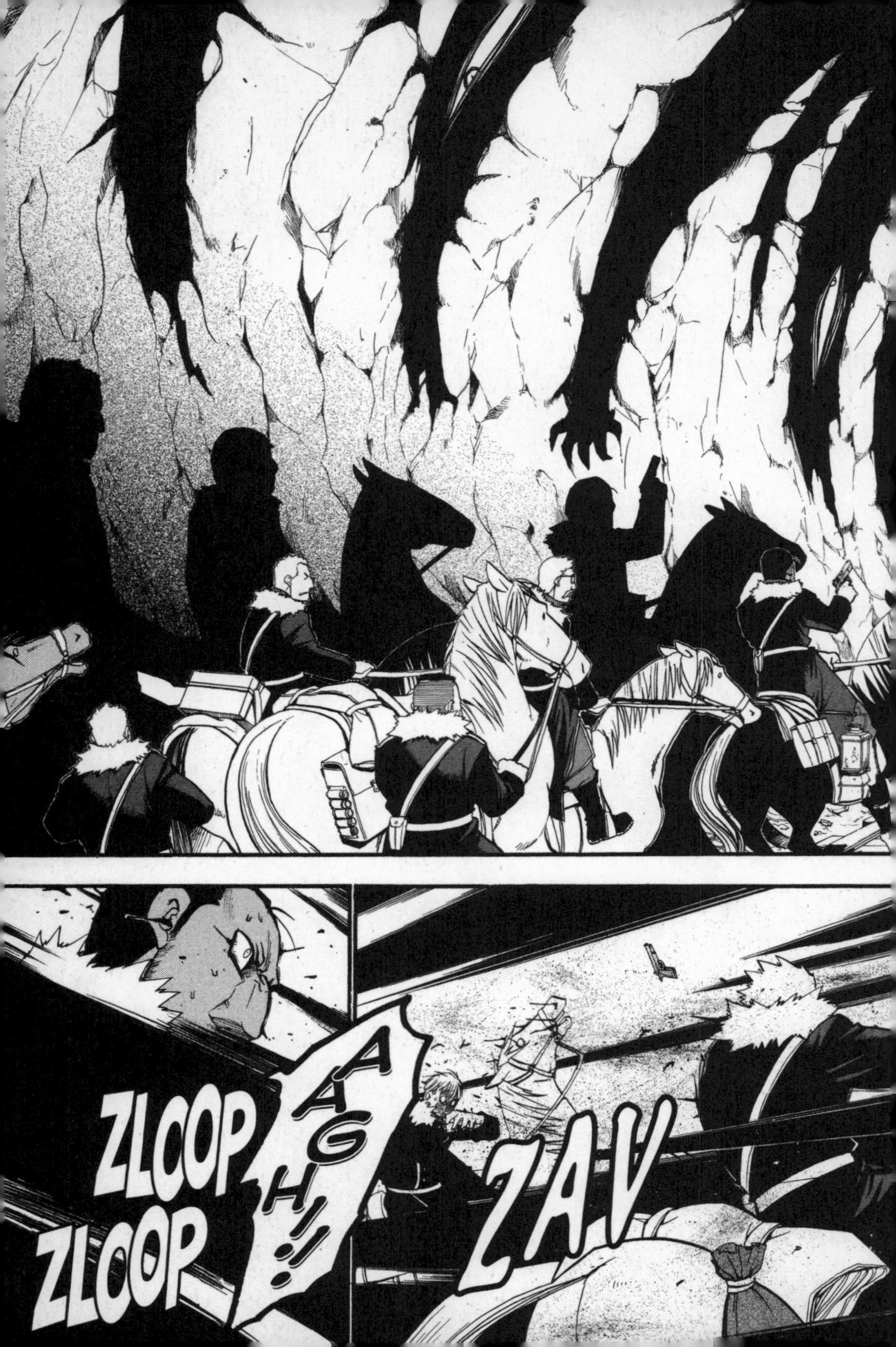
ZAV
AAGH!!!
ZLOOP
ZLOOP

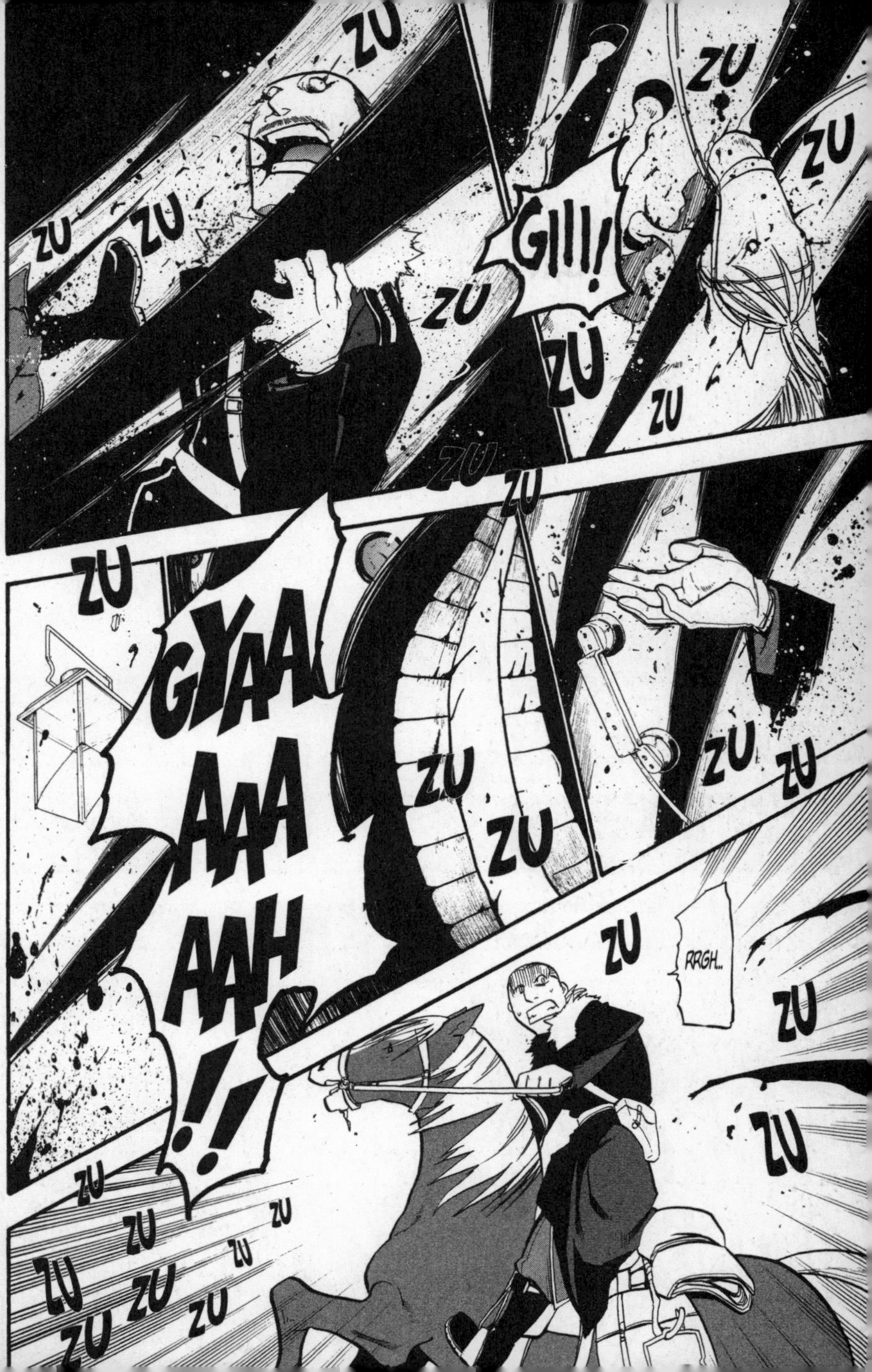
ZU
ZU
GIII!
ZU
ZU
ZU
ZU
ZU
ZU
ZU
ZU
ZU
ZU
GYAAAAAAAAH!!
ZU
ZU
ZU
ZU
RRGH...
ZU
ZU
ZU
ZU
ZU
ZU
ZU
ZU
ZU
ZU
ZU

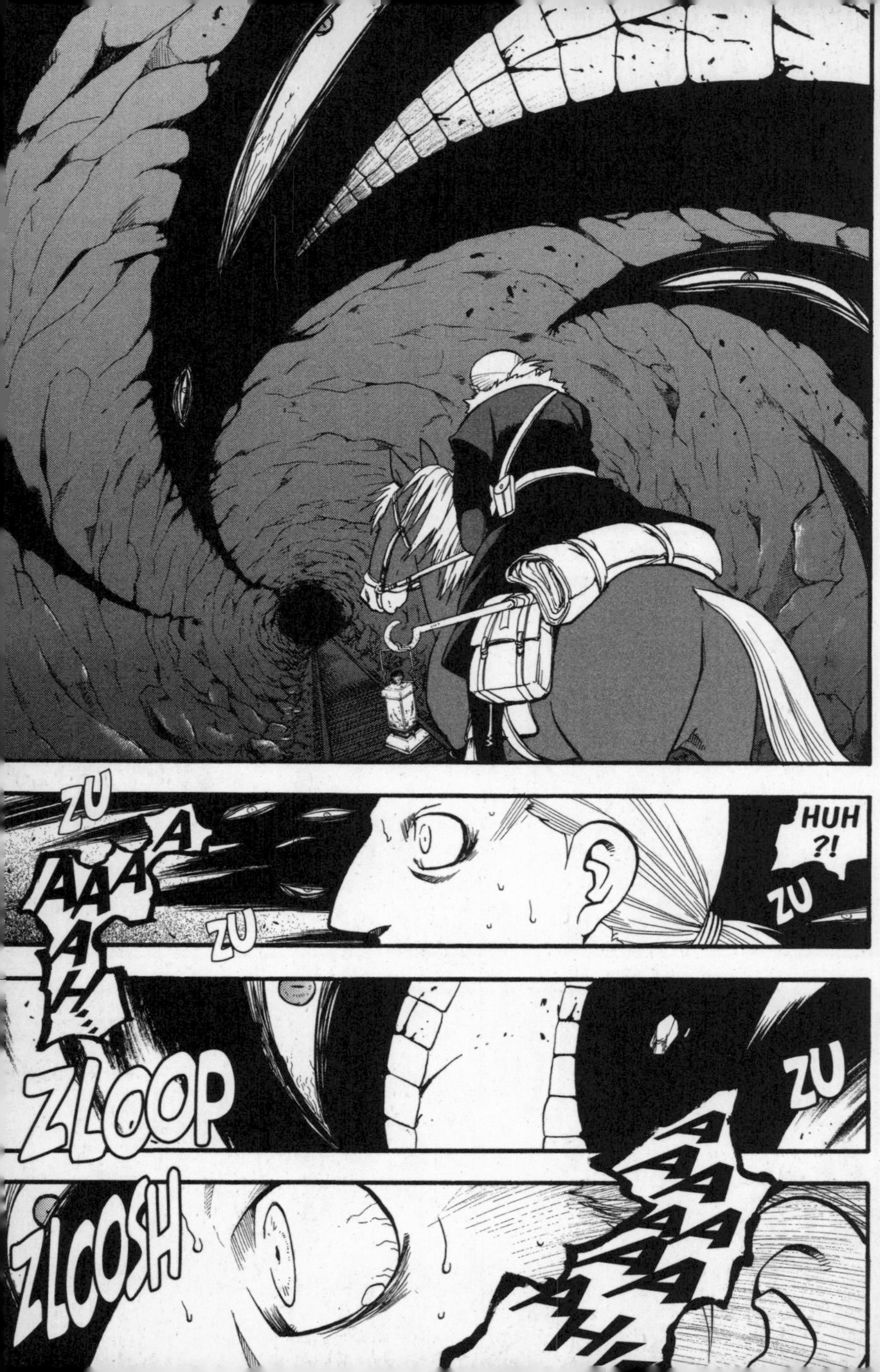
HUH ?!
ZU
ZU
AAAAAH...
ZU
ZU
ZLOOP
AAAAAAAH
ZLCOSH

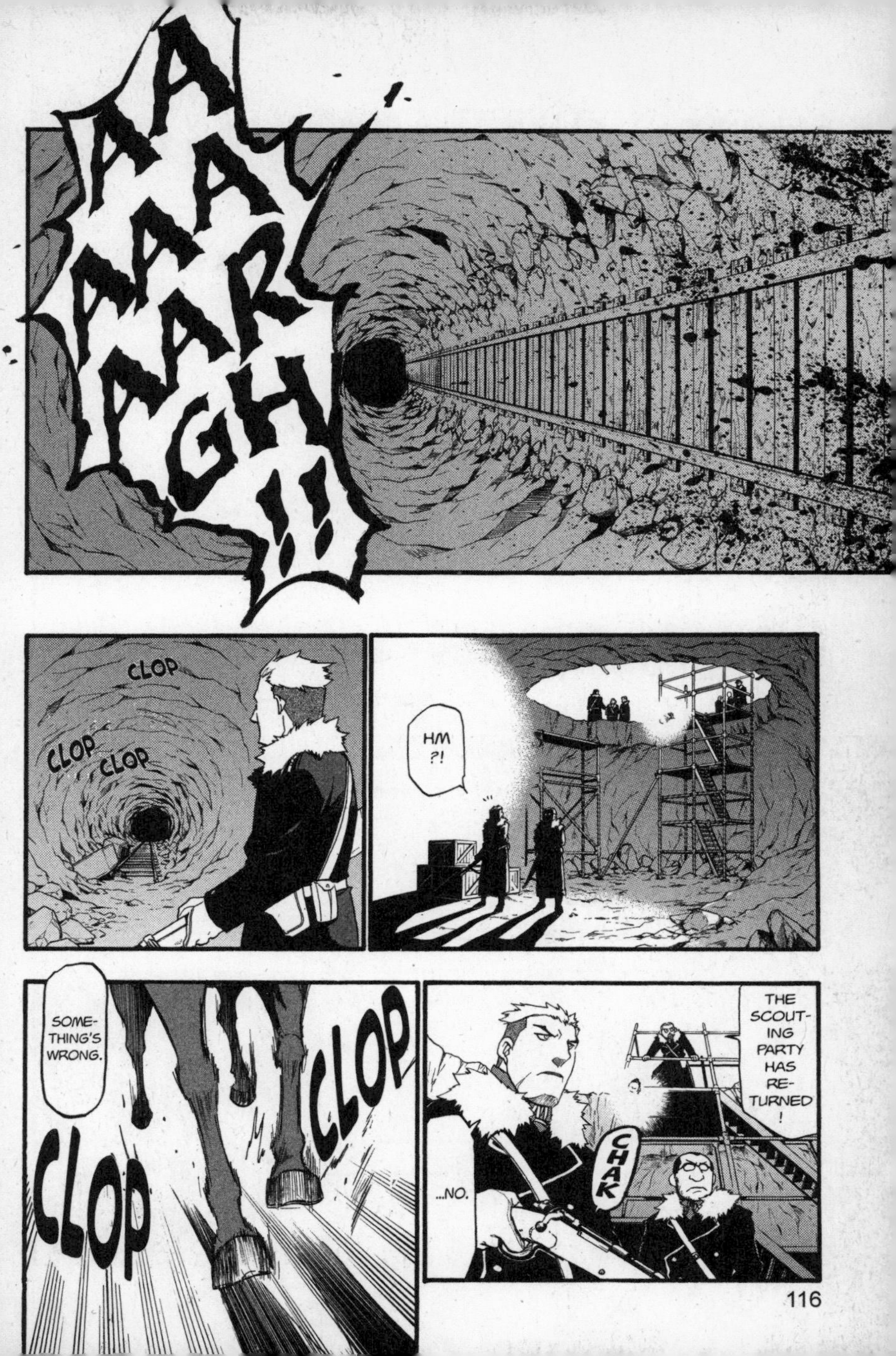
AAAAAAARGH!!!
HM ?!
CLOP
CLOP CLOP
THE SCOUTING PARTY HAS RETURNED!
CHAK
...NO.
SOMETHING'S WRONG.
CLOP
CLOP

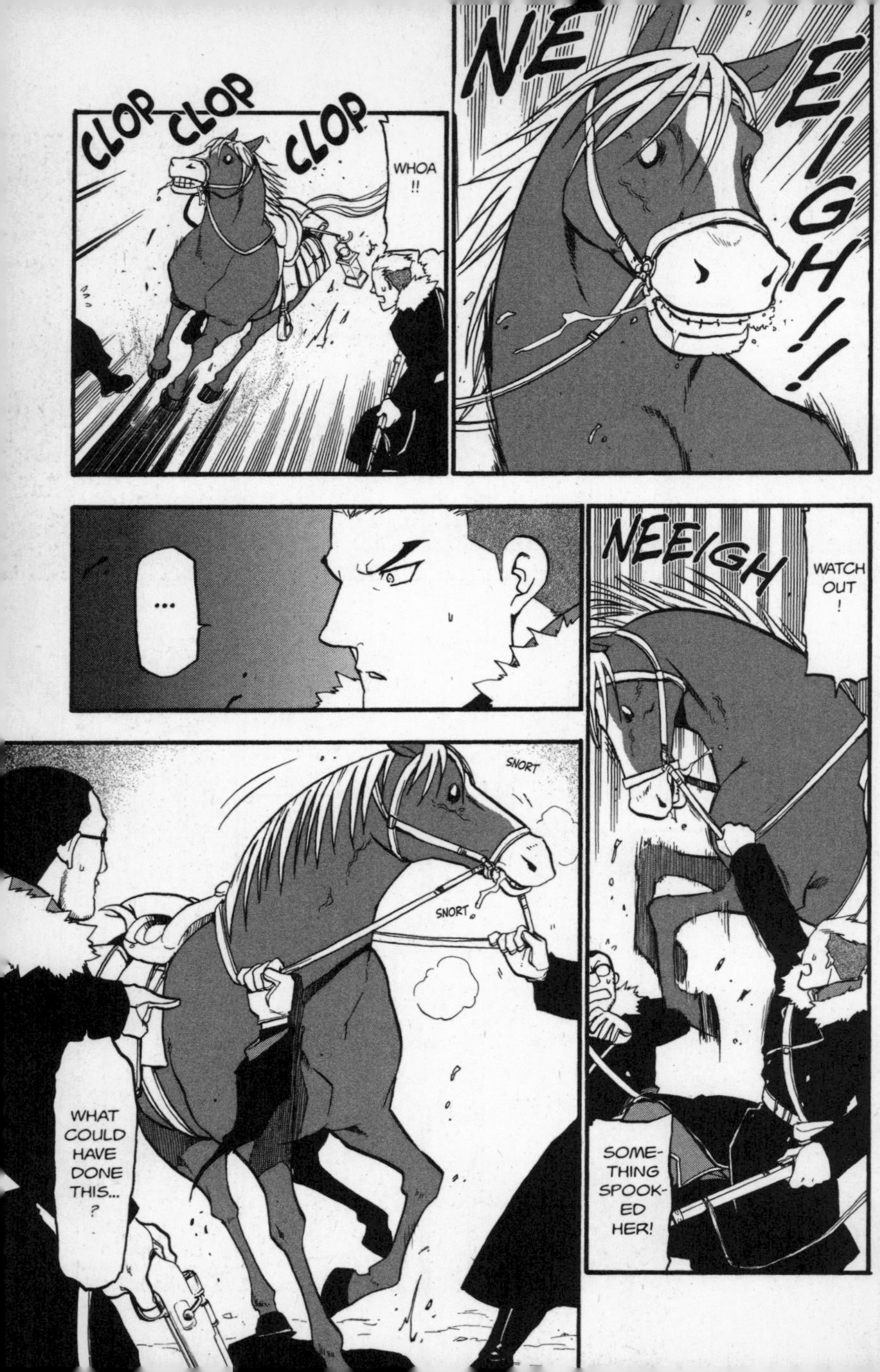
NEEIGH!!
CLOP CLOP CLOP
WHOA!!
NEEIGH
WATCH OUT!
SOMETHING SPOOKED HER!
...
SNORT
SNORT
WHAT COULD HAVE DONE THIS...?

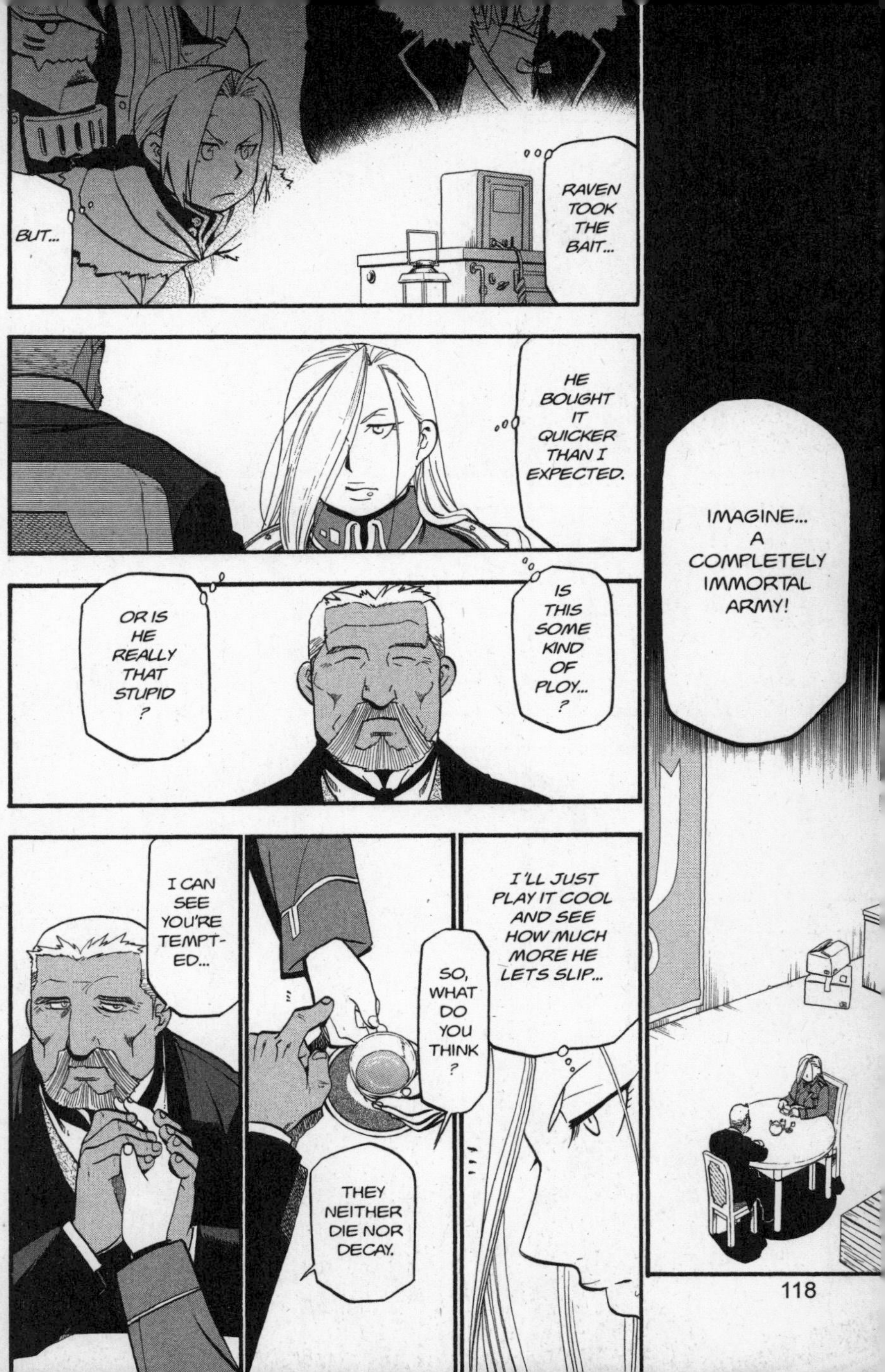
IMAGINE... A COMPLETELY IMMORTAL ARMY!
RAVEN TOOK THE BAIT...
BUT...
HE BOUGHT IT QUICKER THAN I EXPECTED.
IS THIS SOME KIND OF PLOY...?
OR IS HE REALLY THAT STUPID?
I'LL JUST PLAY IT COOL AND SEE HOW MUCH MORE HE LETS SLIP...
SO, WHAT DO YOU THINK?
THEY NEITHER DIE NOR DECAY.
I CAN SEE YOU'RE TEMPTED...

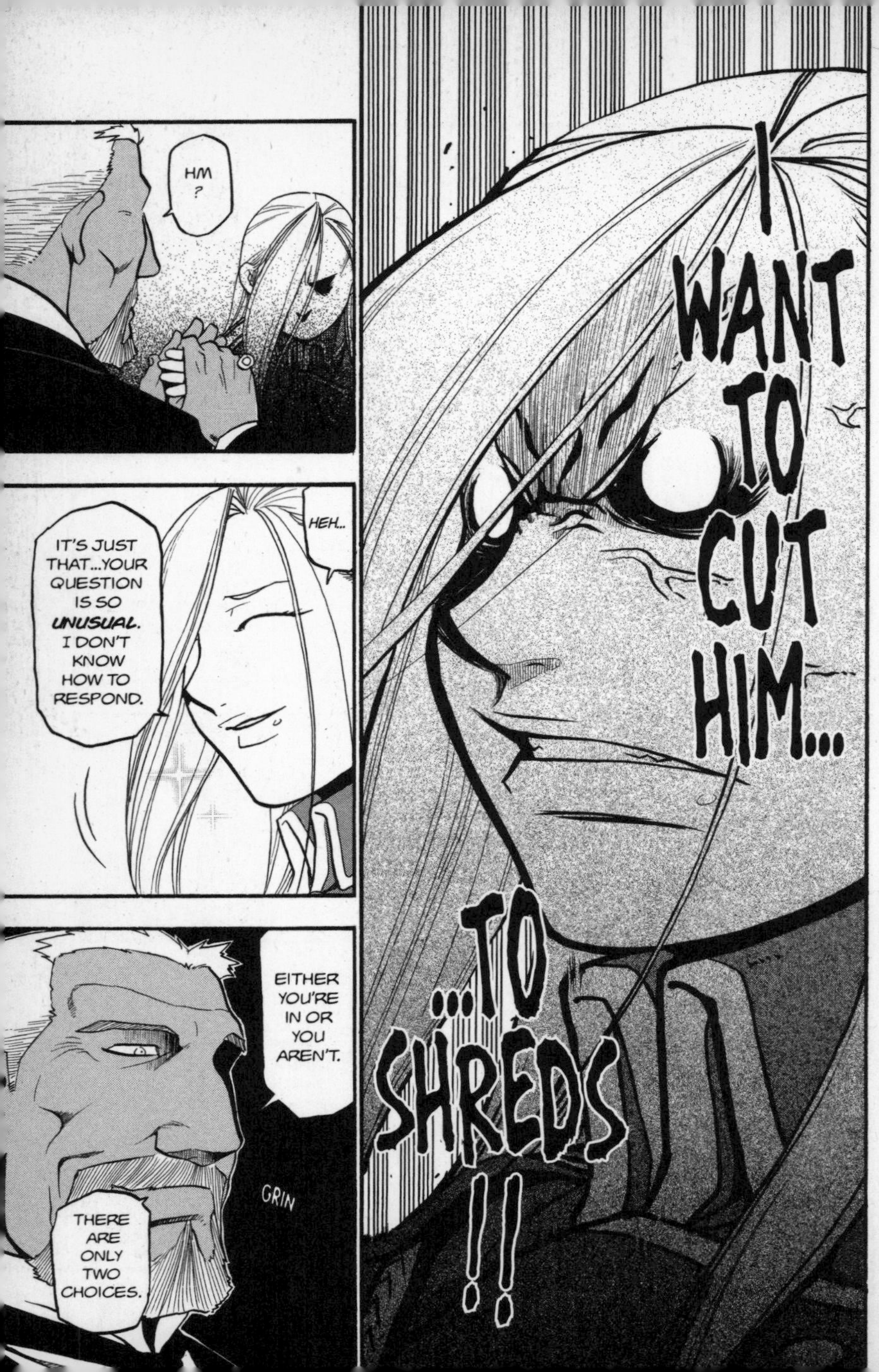
I WANT TO CUT HIM...
...TO SHREDS!!
HM?
HEH...
IT'S JUST THAT...YOUR QUESTION IS SO ***UNUSUAL***. I DON'T KNOW HOW TO RESPOND.
EITHER YOU'RE IN OR YOU AREN'T.
GRIN
THERE ARE ONLY TWO CHOICES.

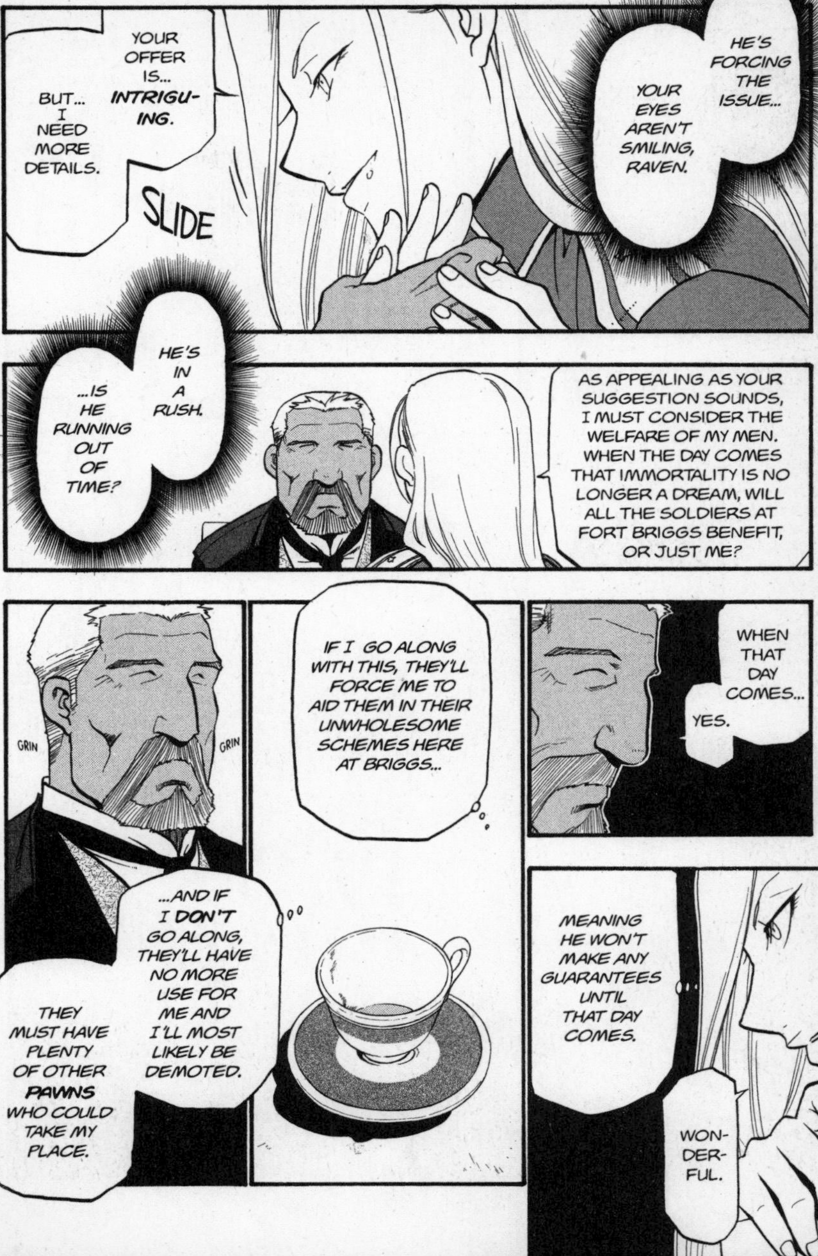
HE'S FORCING THE ISSUE...
YOUR EYES AREN'T SMILING, RAVEN.
YOUR OFFER IS... **INTRIGUING**.
BUT... I NEED MORE DETAILS.
SLIDE
AS APPEALING AS YOUR SUGGESTION SOUNDS, I MUST CONSIDER THE WELFARE OF MY MEN. WHEN THE DAY COMES THAT IMMORTALITY IS NO LONGER A DREAM, WILL ALL THE SOLDIERS AT FORT BRIGGS BENEFIT, OR JUST ME?
HE'S IN A RUSH.
...IS HE RUNNING OUT OF TIME?
WHEN THAT DAY COMES...
YES.
MEANING HE WON'T MAKE ANY GUARANTEES UNTIL THAT DAY COMES.
WONDERFUL.
IF I GO ALONG WITH THIS, THEY'LL FORCE ME TO AID THEM IN THEIR UNWHOLESOME SCHEMES HERE AT BRIGGS...
GRIN
GRIN
...AND IF I **DON'T** GO ALONG, THEY'LL HAVE NO MORE USE FOR ME AND I'LL MOST LIKELY BE DEMOTED.
THEY MUST HAVE PLENTY OF OTHER **PAWNS** WHO COULD TAKE MY PLACE.

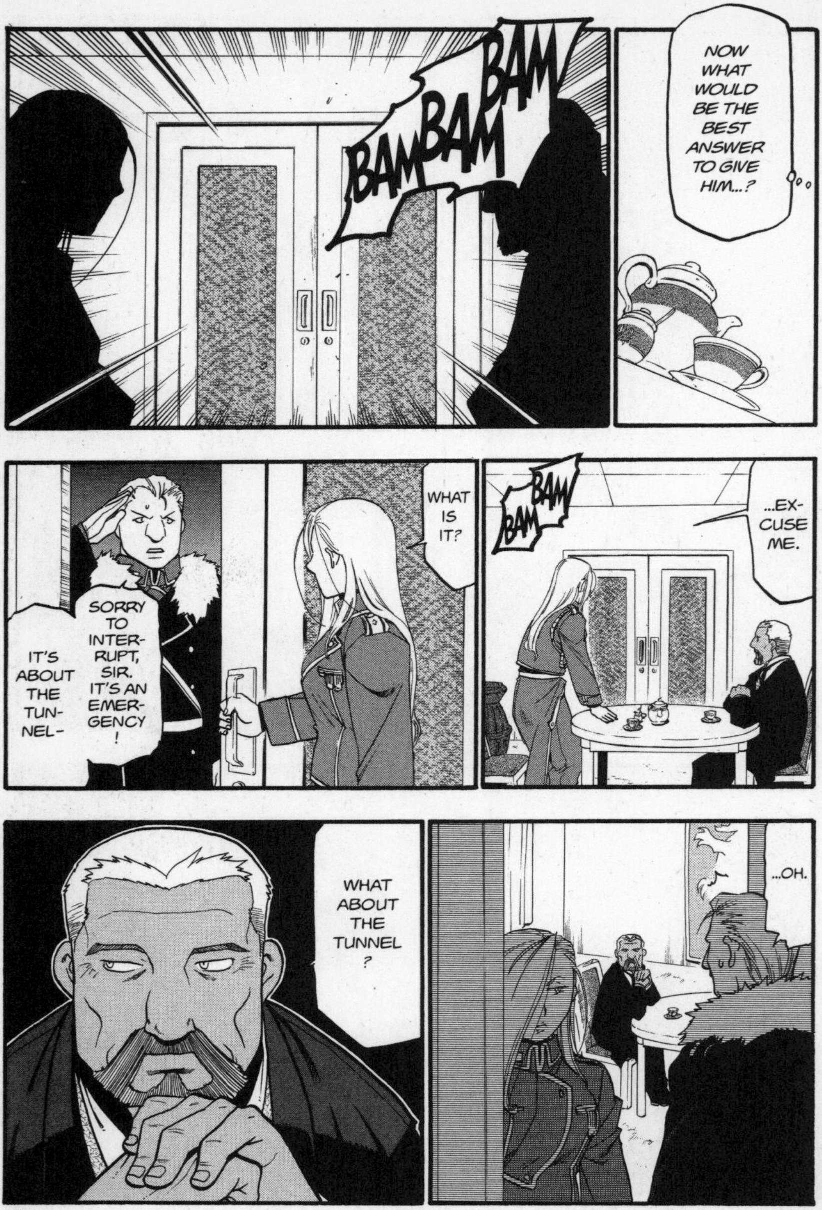
NOW WHAT WOULD BE THE BEST ANSWER TO GIVE HIM...?
BAM BAM BAM
BAM BAM
...EXCUSE ME.
WHAT IS IT?
SORRY TO INTERRUPT, SIR. IT'S AN EMERGENCY!
IT'S ABOUT THE TUNNEL-
...OH.
WHAT ABOUT THE TUNNEL?

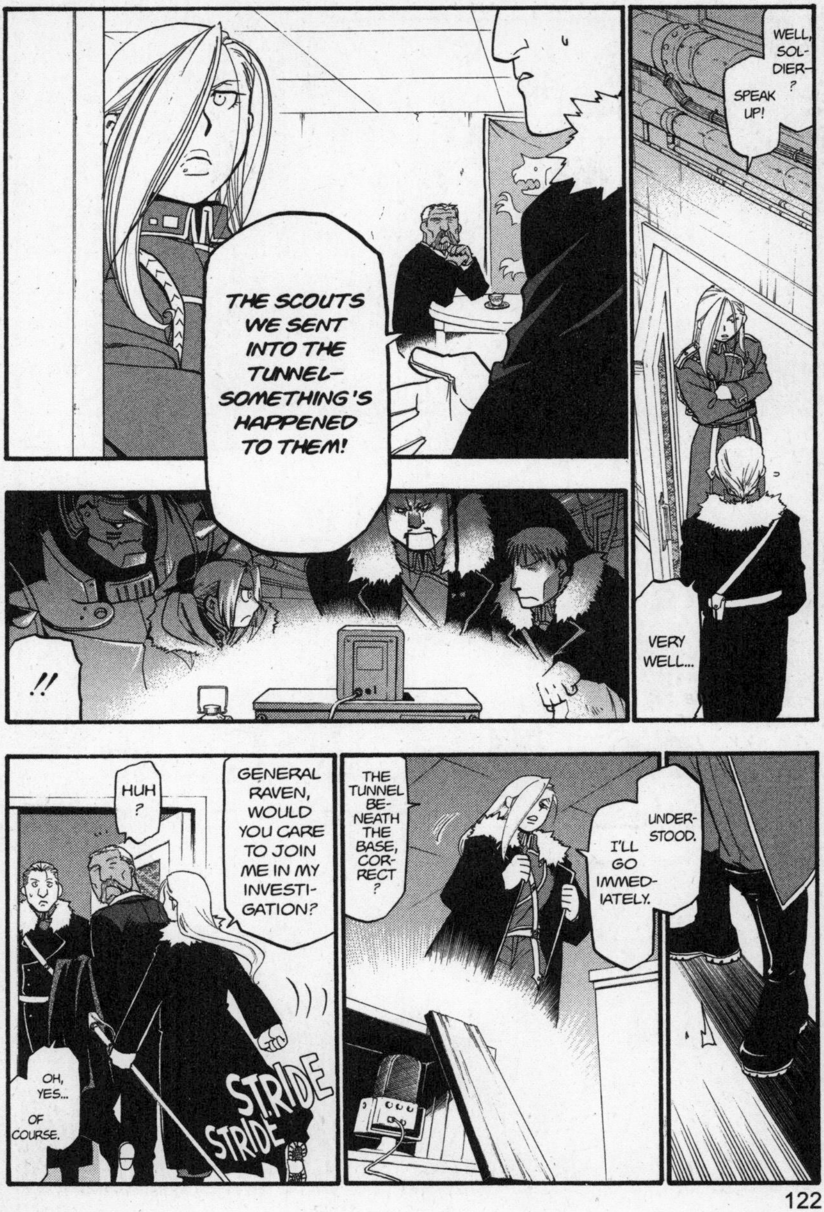
WELL, SOL-DIER-?
SPEAK UP!
VERY WELL...
THE SCOUTS WE SENT INTO THE TUNNEL— SOMETHING'S HAPPENED TO THEM!
!!
UNDER-STOOD.
I'LL GO IMMED-IATELY.
THE TUNNEL BE-NEATH THE BASE, COR-RECT?
GENERAL RAVEN, WOULD YOU CARE TO JOIN ME IN MY INVESTI-GATION?
HUH?
OH, YES...
OF COURSE.
STRIDE
STRIDE

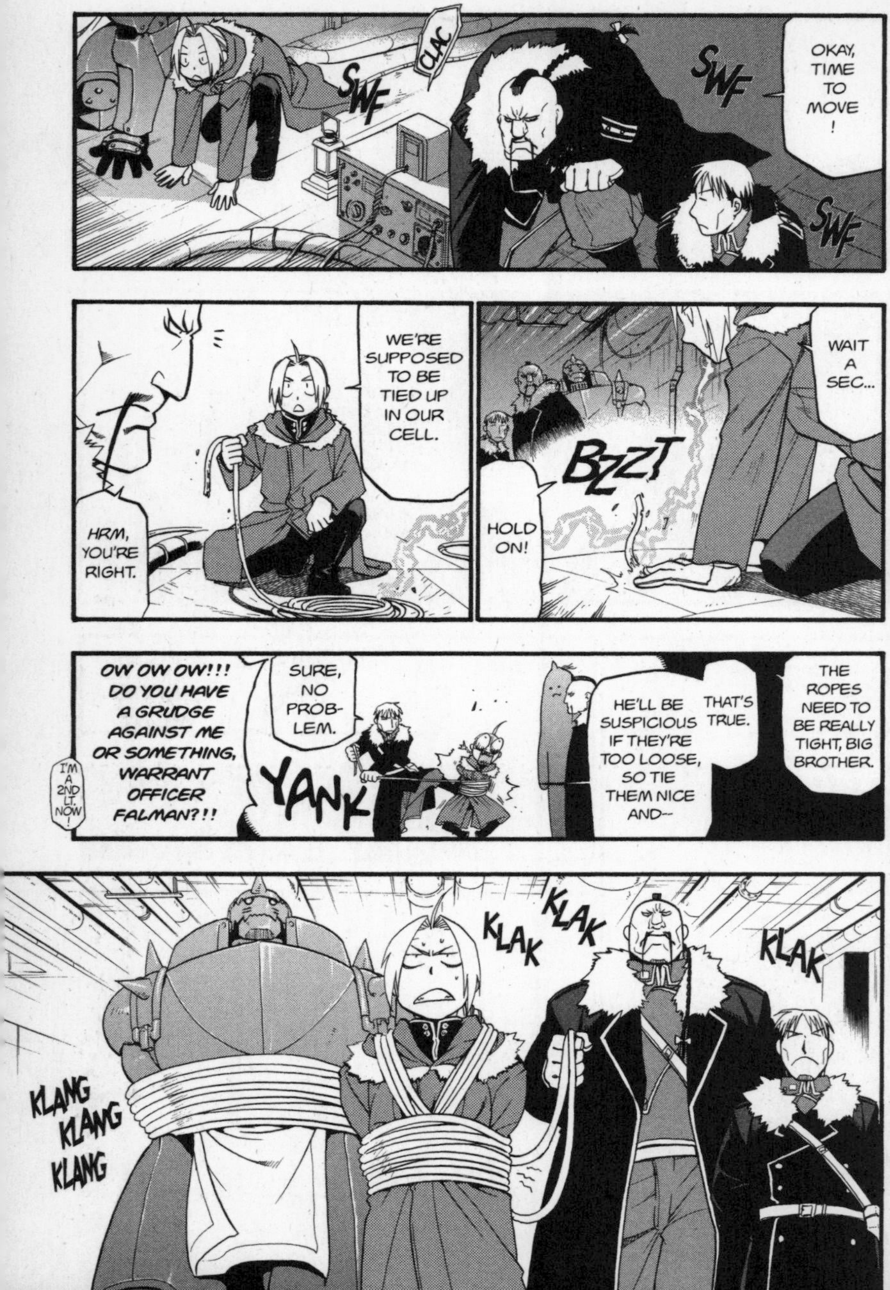
OKAY, TIME TO MOVE!
SWF
SWF
CLAC
SWF
WAIT A SEC...
BZZZT
HOLD ON!
WE'RE SUPPOSED TO BE TIED UP IN OUR CELL.
HRM, YOU'RE RIGHT.
THE ROPES NEED TO BE REALLY TIGHT, BIG BROTHER.
THAT'S TRUE.
HE'LL BE SUSPICIOUS IF THEY'RE TOO LOOSE, SO TIE THEM NICE AND--
SURE, NO PROB-LEM.
YANK
OW OW OW!!! DO YOU HAVE A GRUDGE AGAINST ME OR SOMETHING, WARRANT OFFICER FALMAN?!!
I'M A 2ND LT. NOW!
KLAK
KLAK
KLAK
KLANG KLANG KLANG

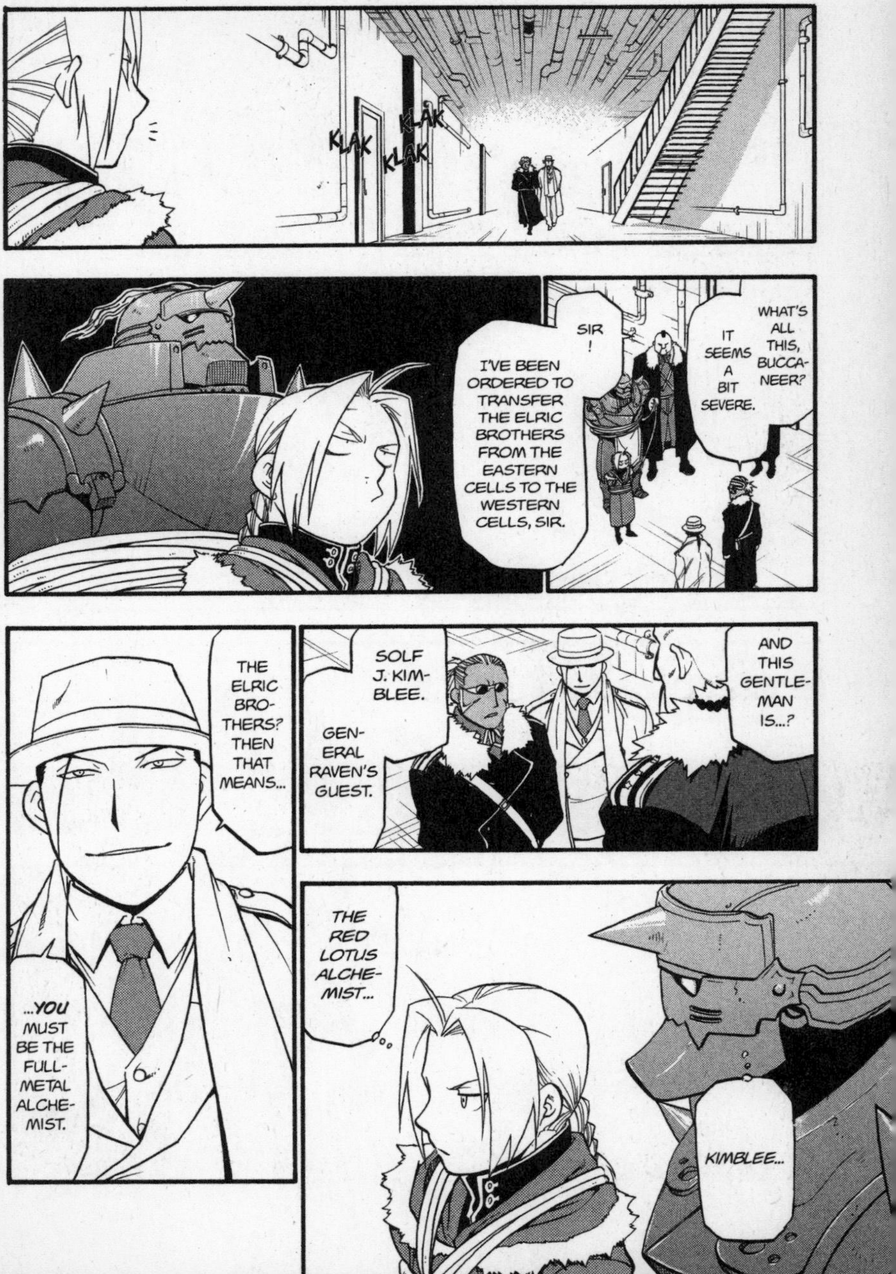
KLAK
KLAK
KLAK
WHAT'S ALL THIS, BUCCANEER?
IT SEEMS A BIT SEVERE.
SIR!
I'VE BEEN ORDERED TO TRANSFER THE ELRIC BROTHERS FROM THE EASTERN CELLS TO THE WESTERN CELLS, SIR.
AND THIS GENTLEMAN IS...?
SOLF J. KIMBLEE.
GENERAL RAVEN'S GUEST.
KIMBLEE...
THE RED LOTUS ALCHEMIST...
THE ELRIC BROTHERS? THEN THAT MEANS...
...YOU MUST BE THE FULLMETAL ALCHEMIST.

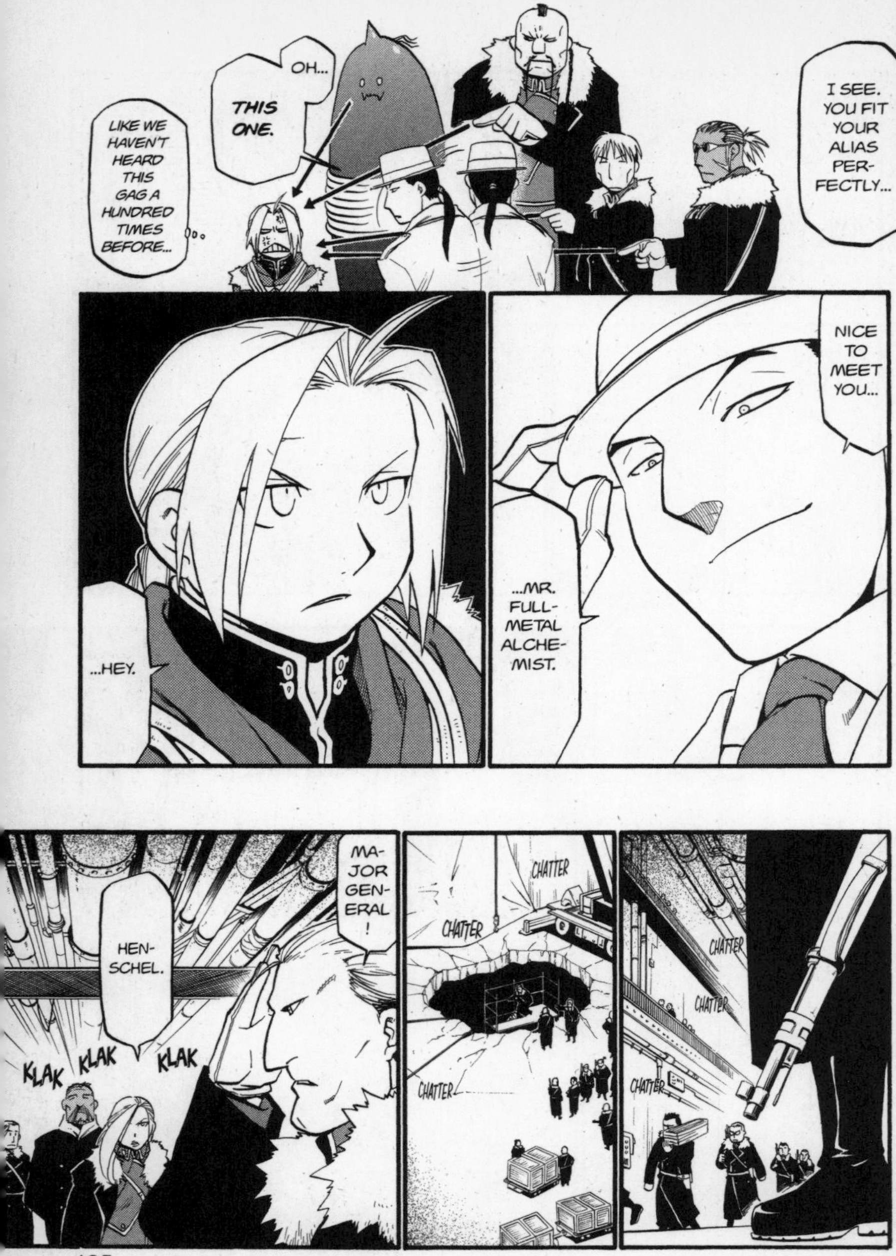
I SEE. YOU FIT YOUR ALIAS PER-FECTLY...
OH...
THIS ONE.
LIKE WE HAVEN'T HEARD THIS GAG A HUNDRED TIMES BEFORE...
NICE TO MEET YOU...
...MR. FULL-METAL ALCHE-MIST.
...HEY.
CHATTER
CHATTER
CHATTER
CHATTER
CHATTER
CHATTER
MA-JOR GEN-ERAL!
HEN-SCHEL.
KLAK
KLAK
KLAK

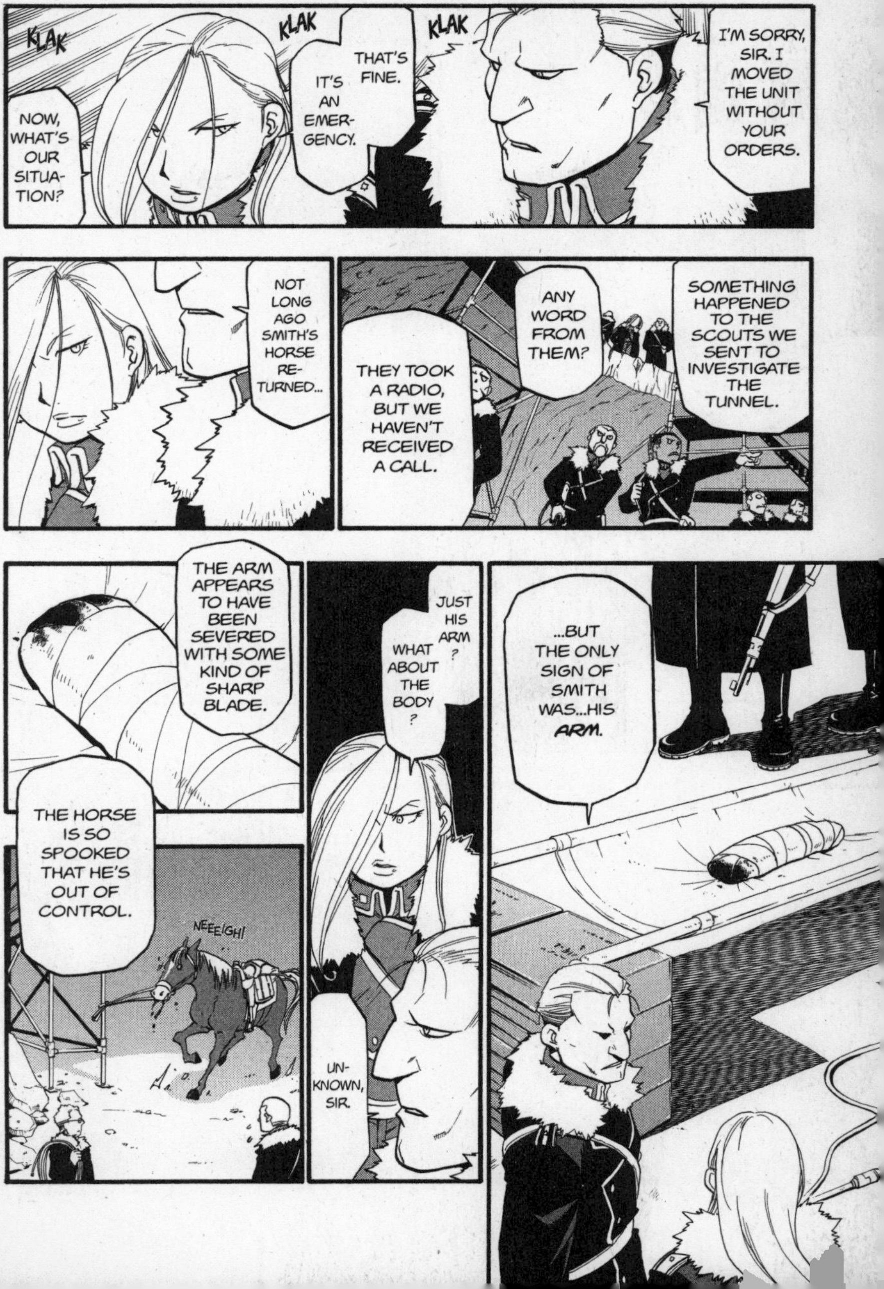
I'M SORRY, SIR. I MOVED THE UNIT WITHOUT YOUR ORDERS.
KLAK
THAT'S FINE.
IT'S AN EMERGENCY.
KLAK
KLAK
NOW, WHAT'S OUR SITUATION?
SOMETHING HAPPENED TO THE SCOUTS WE SENT TO INVESTIGATE THE TUNNEL.
ANY WORD FROM THEM?
THEY TOOK A RADIO, BUT WE HAVEN'T RECEIVED A CALL.
NOT LONG AGO SMITH'S HORSE RE-TURNED...
...BUT THE ONLY SIGN OF SMITH WAS...HIS ARM.
JUST HIS ARM?
WHAT ABOUT THE BODY?
UN-KNOWN, SIR.
THE ARM APPEARS TO HAVE BEEN SEVERED WITH SOME KIND OF SHARP BLADE.
THE HORSE IS SO SPOOKED THAT HE'S OUT OF CONTROL.
NEEEIGH!

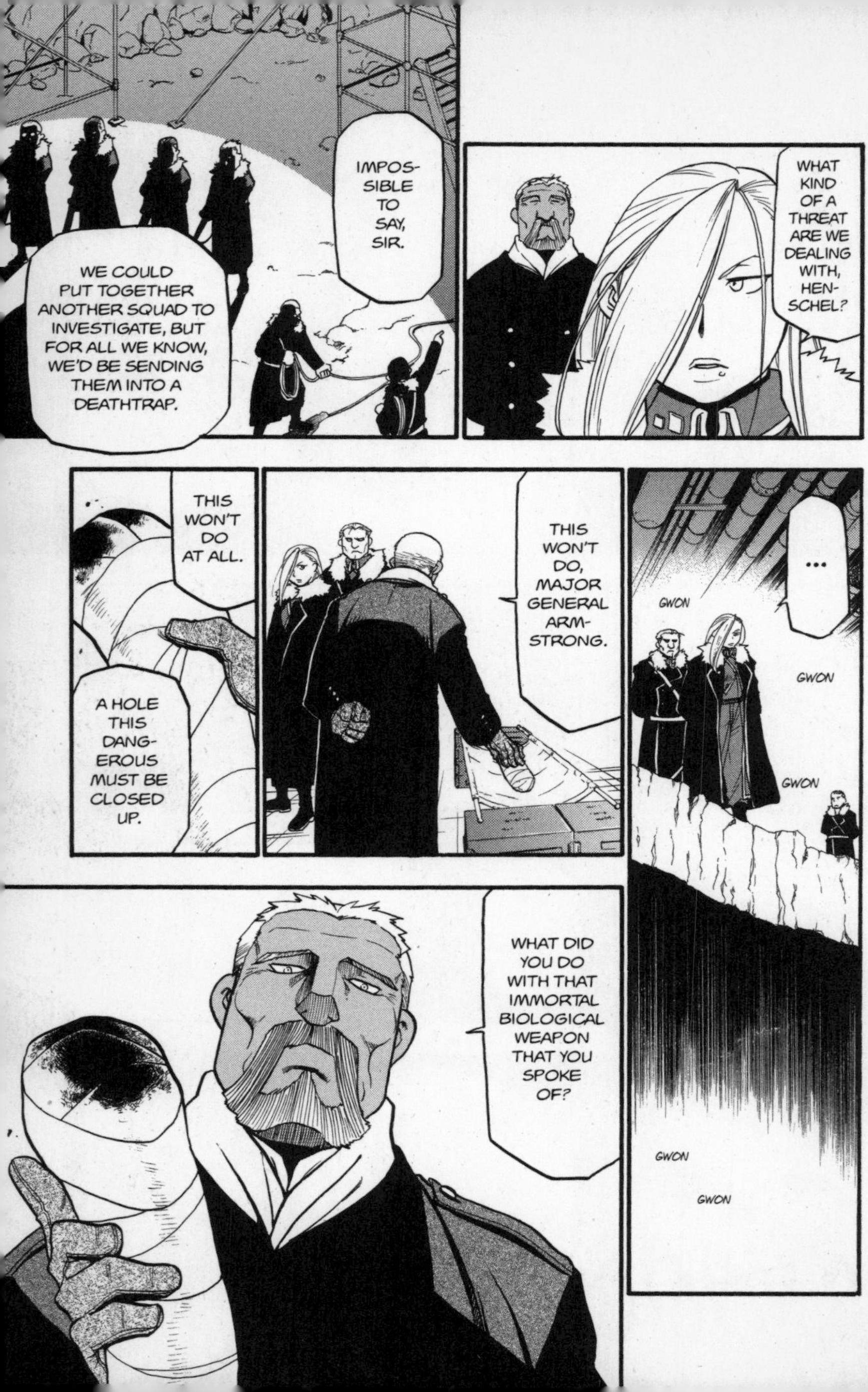
WHAT KIND OF A THREAT ARE WE DEALING WITH, HENSCHEL?
IMPOSSIBLE TO SAY, SIR.
WE COULD PUT TOGETHER ANOTHER SQUAD TO INVESTIGATE, BUT FOR ALL WE KNOW, WE'D BE SENDING THEM INTO A DEATHTRAP.
...
GWON
GWON
GWON
GWON
GWON
THIS WON'T DO, MAJOR GENERAL ARMSTRONG.
THIS WON'T DO AT ALL.
A HOLE THIS DANGEROUS MUST BE CLOSED UP.
WHAT DID YOU DO WITH THAT IMMORTAL BIOLOGICAL WEAPON THAT YOU SPOKE OF?

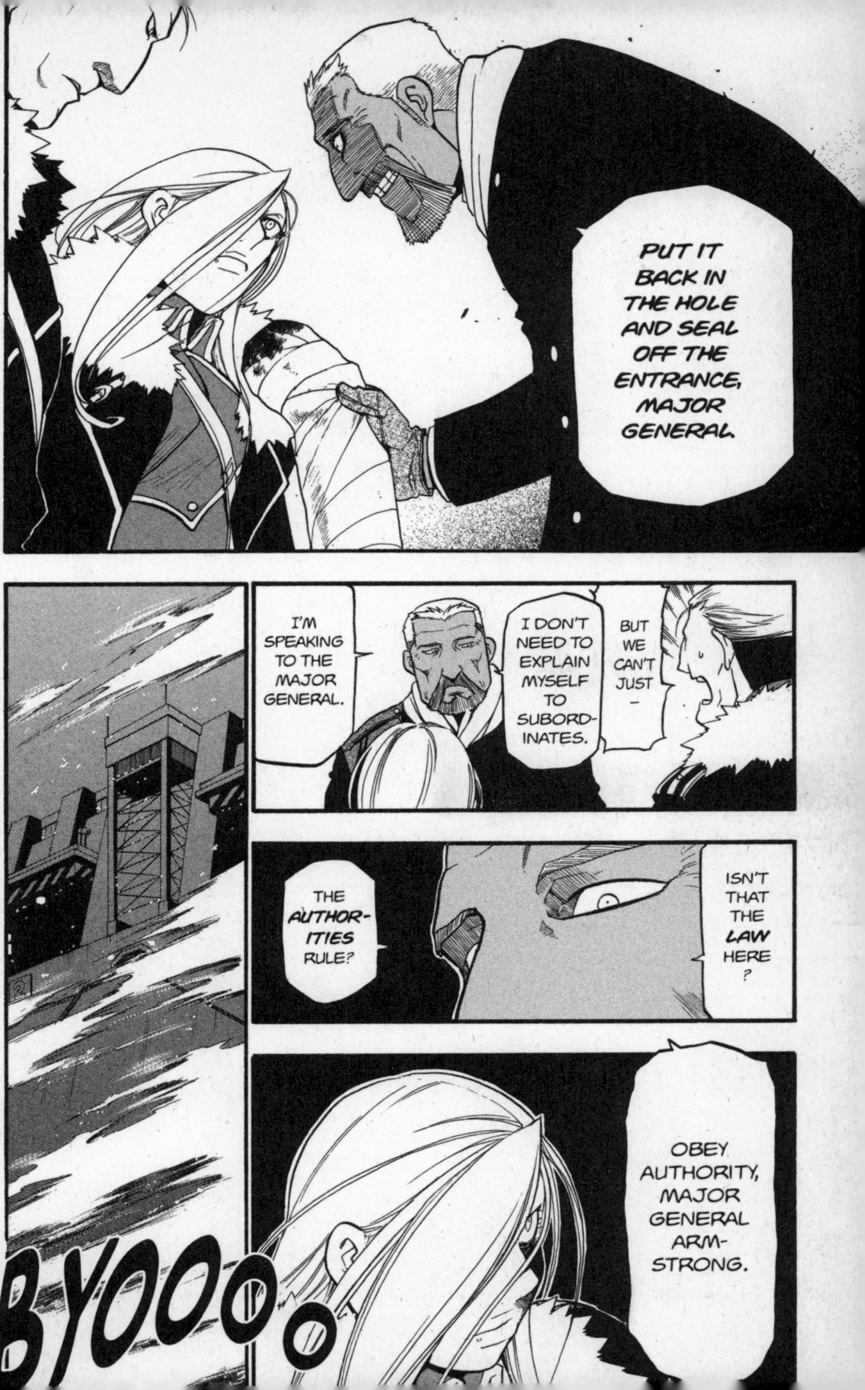
PUT IT BACK IN THE HOLE AND SEAL OFF THE ENTRANCE, MAJOR GENERAL.
BUT WE CAN'T JUST –
I DON'T NEED TO EXPLAIN MYSELF TO SUBORD-INATES.
I'M SPEAKING TO THE MAJOR GENERAL.
ISN'T THAT THE **LAW** HERE?
THE ***AUTHOR-ITIES*** RULE?
OBEY AUTHORITY, MAJOR GENERAL ARM-STRONG.
BYOOO

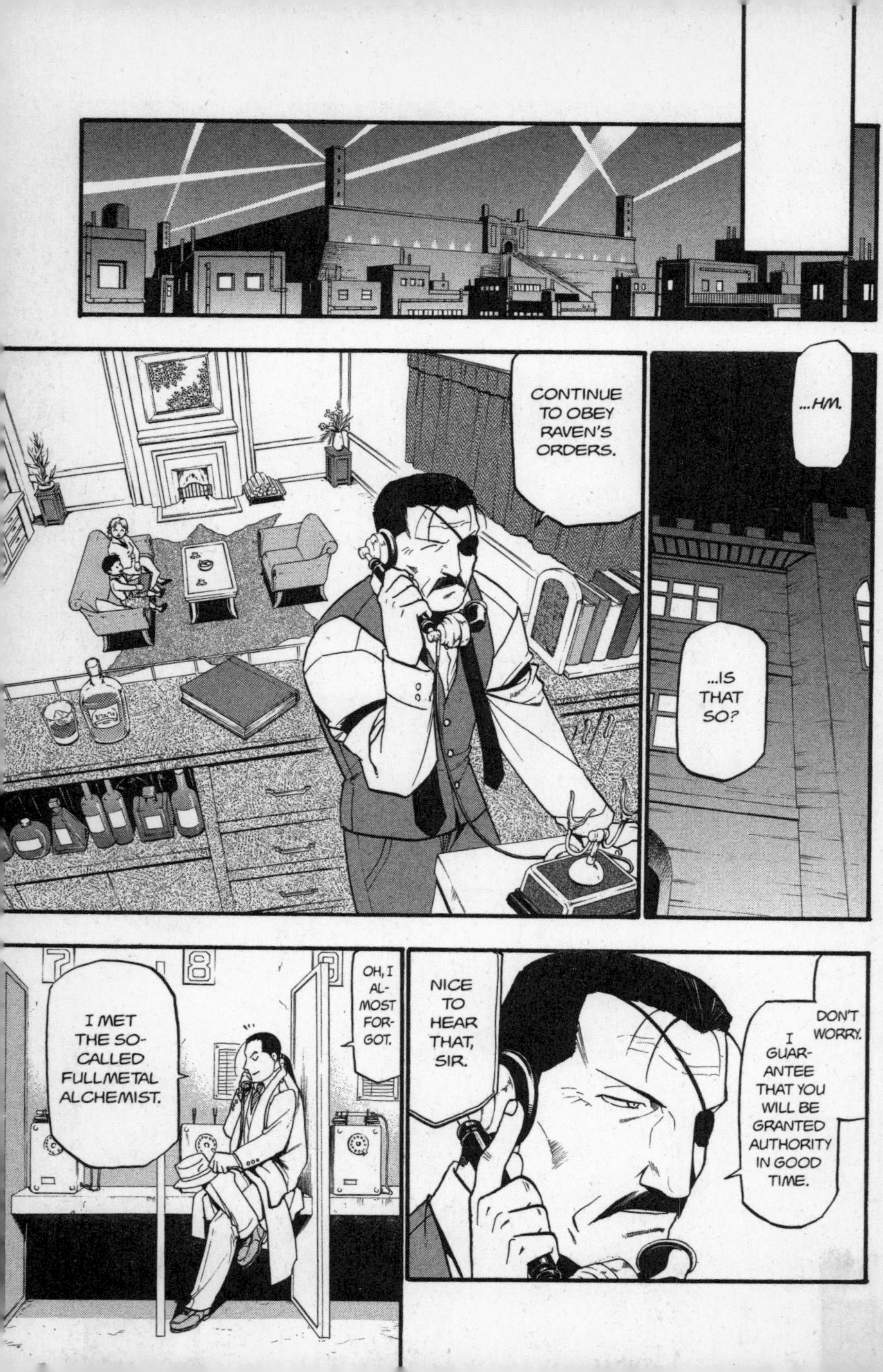
...HM.
...IS THAT SO?
CONTINUE TO OBEY RAVEN'S ORDERS.
DON'T WORRY.
I GUARANTEE THAT YOU WILL BE GRANTED AUTHORITY IN GOOD TIME.
NICE TO HEAR THAT, SIR.
OH, I ALMOST FORGOT.
I MET THE SO-CALLED FULLMETAL ALCHEMIST.

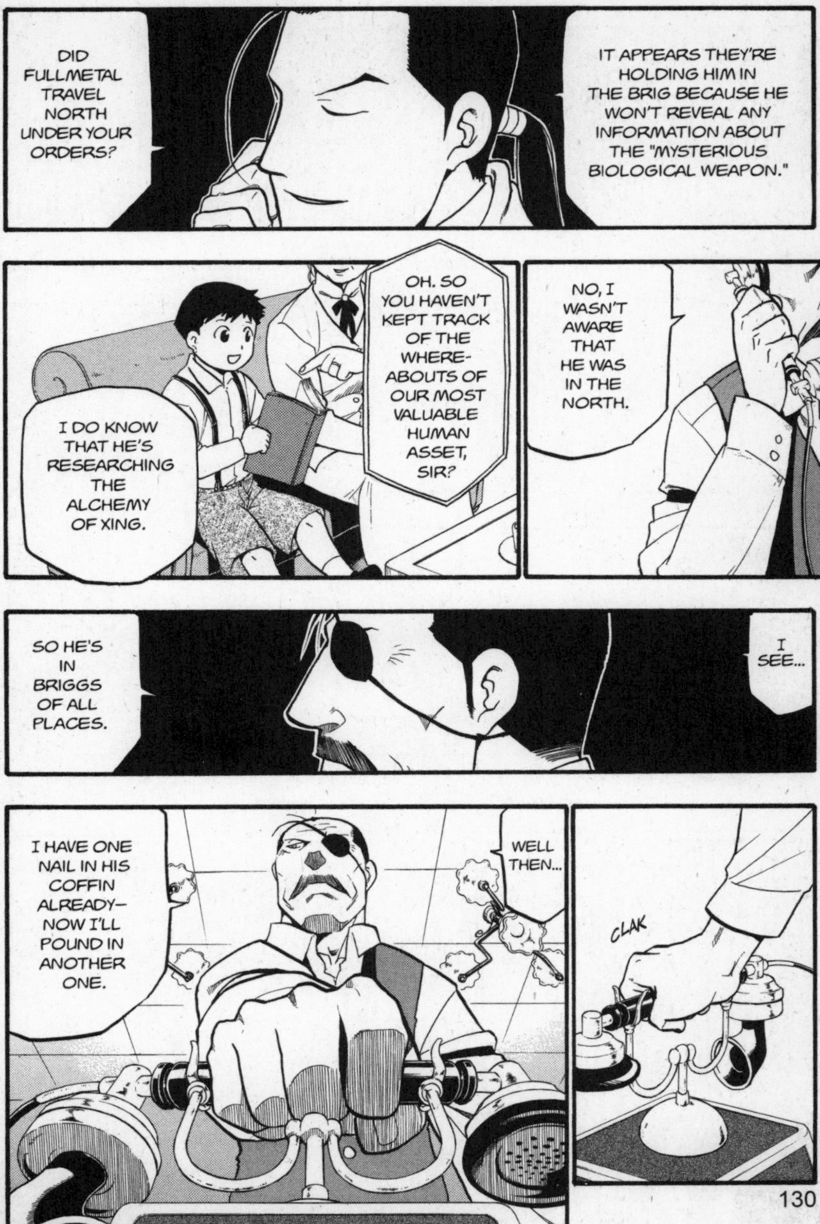
IT APPEARS THEY'RE HOLDING HIM IN THE BRIG BECAUSE HE WON'T REVEAL ANY INFORMATION ABOUT THE "MYSTERIOUS BIOLOGICAL WEAPON."
DID FULLMETAL TRAVEL NORTH UNDER YOUR ORDERS?
NO, I WASN'T AWARE THAT HE WAS IN THE NORTH.
OH. SO YOU HAVEN'T KEPT TRACK OF THE WHERE-ABOUTS OF OUR MOST VALUABLE HUMAN ASSET, SIR?
I DO KNOW THAT HE'S RESEARCHING THE ALCHEMY OF XING.
I SEE...
SO HE'S IN BRIGGS OF ALL PLACES.
CLAK
WELL THEN...
I HAVE ONE NAIL IN HIS COFFIN ALREADY—NOW I'LL POUND IN ANOTHER ONE.

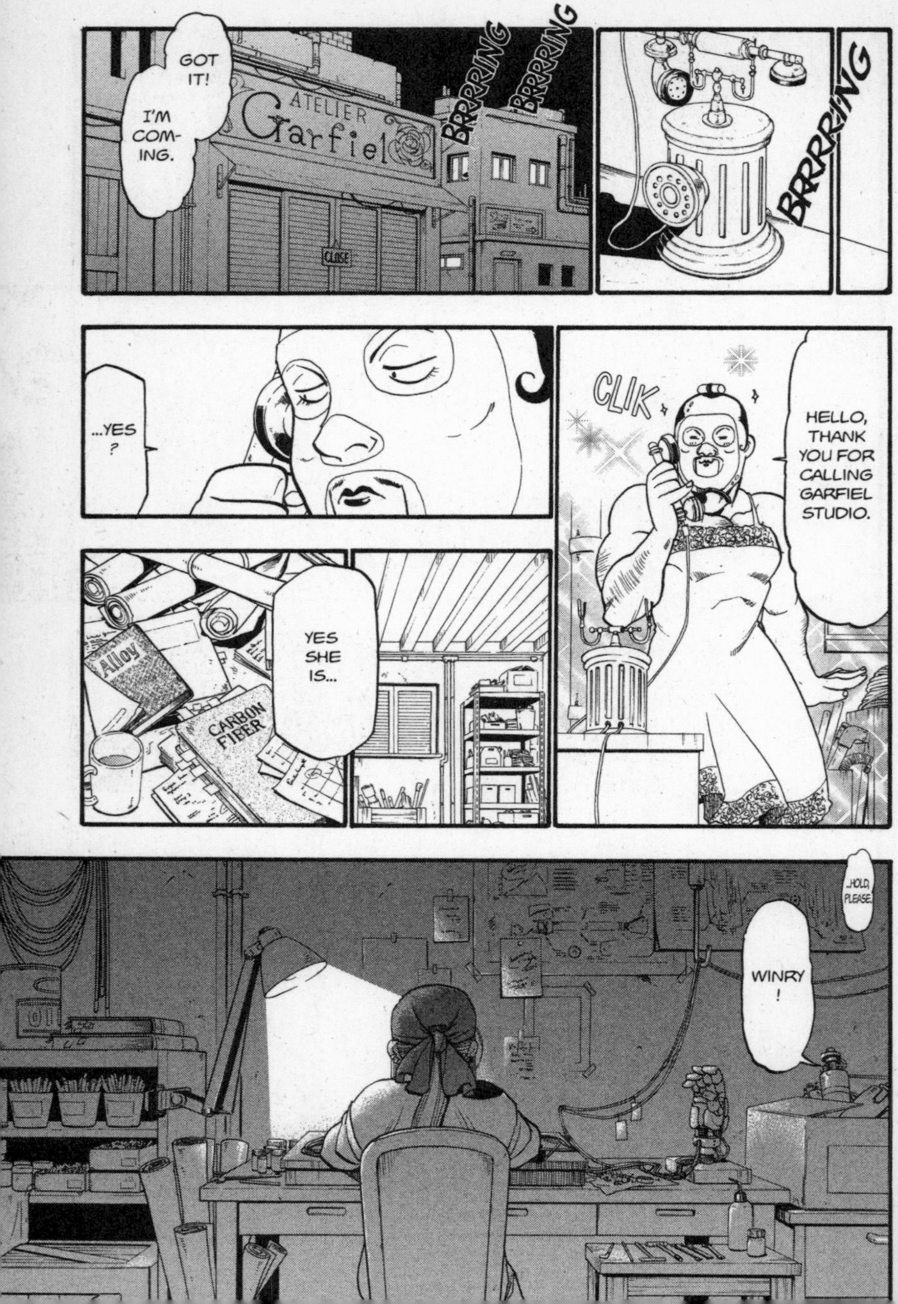
BRRRRING
BRRRRING
BRRRRING
GOT IT! I'M COMING.
ATELIER Garfiel
CLOSE
CLIK
HELLO, THANK YOU FOR CALLING GARFIEL STUDIO.
...YES?
YES SHE IS...
Alloy
CARBON FIBER
...HOLD, PLEASE.
WINRY!

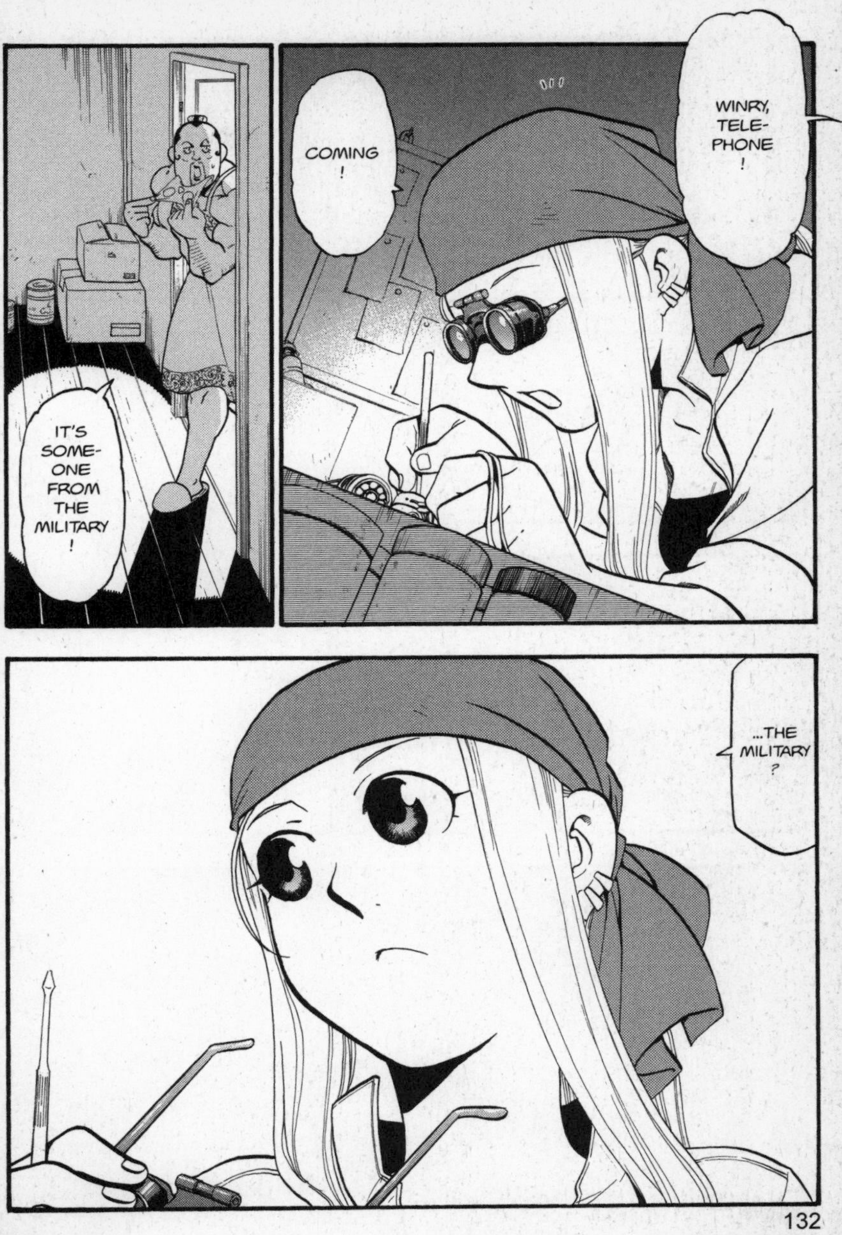
WINRY, TELE- PHONE !
COMING !
IT'S SOME- ONE FROM THE MILITARY !
...THE MILITARY ?

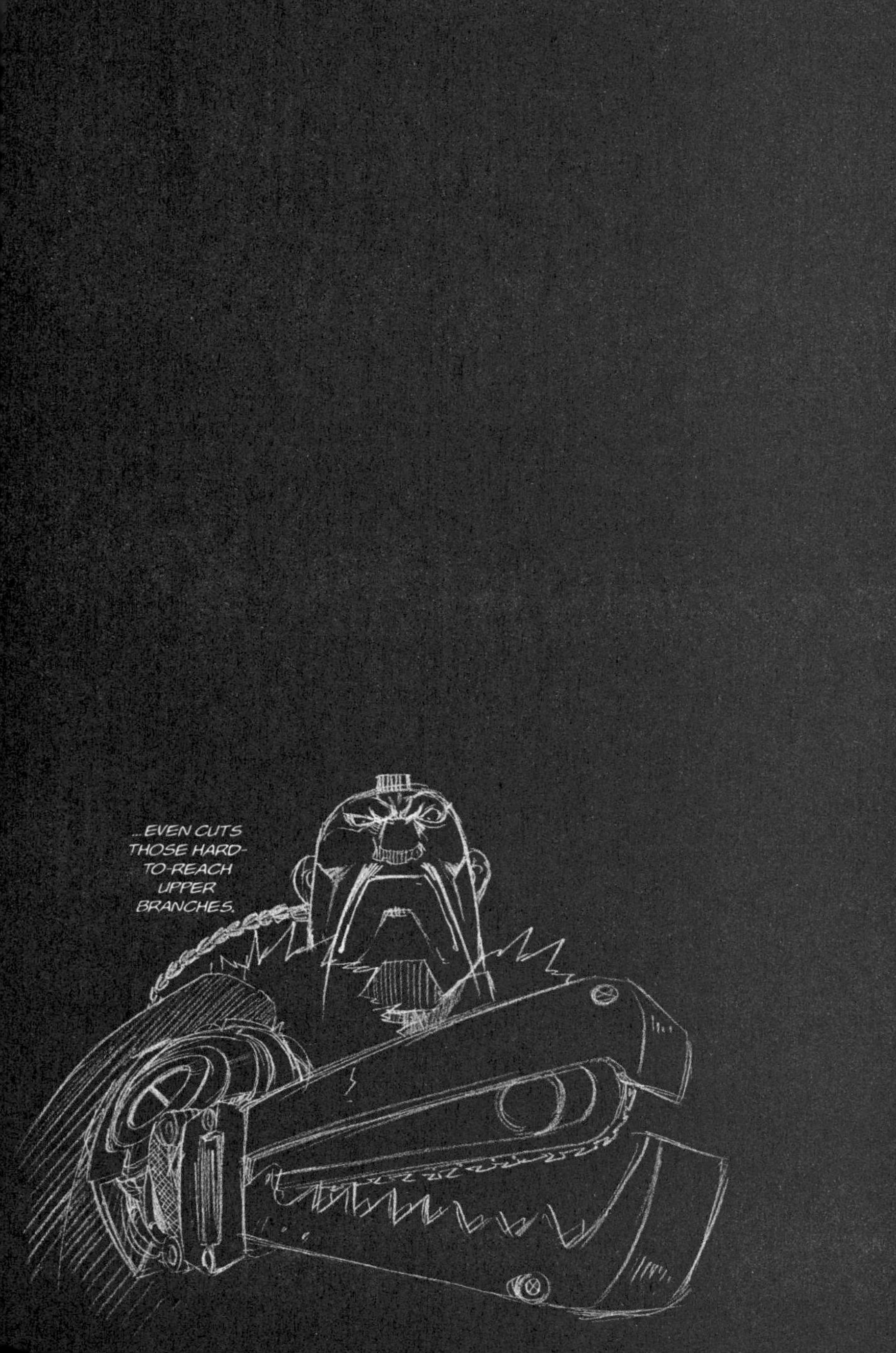
...EVEN CUTS THOSE HARD-TO-REACH UPPER BRANCHES.

FULLMETAL
ALCHEMIST

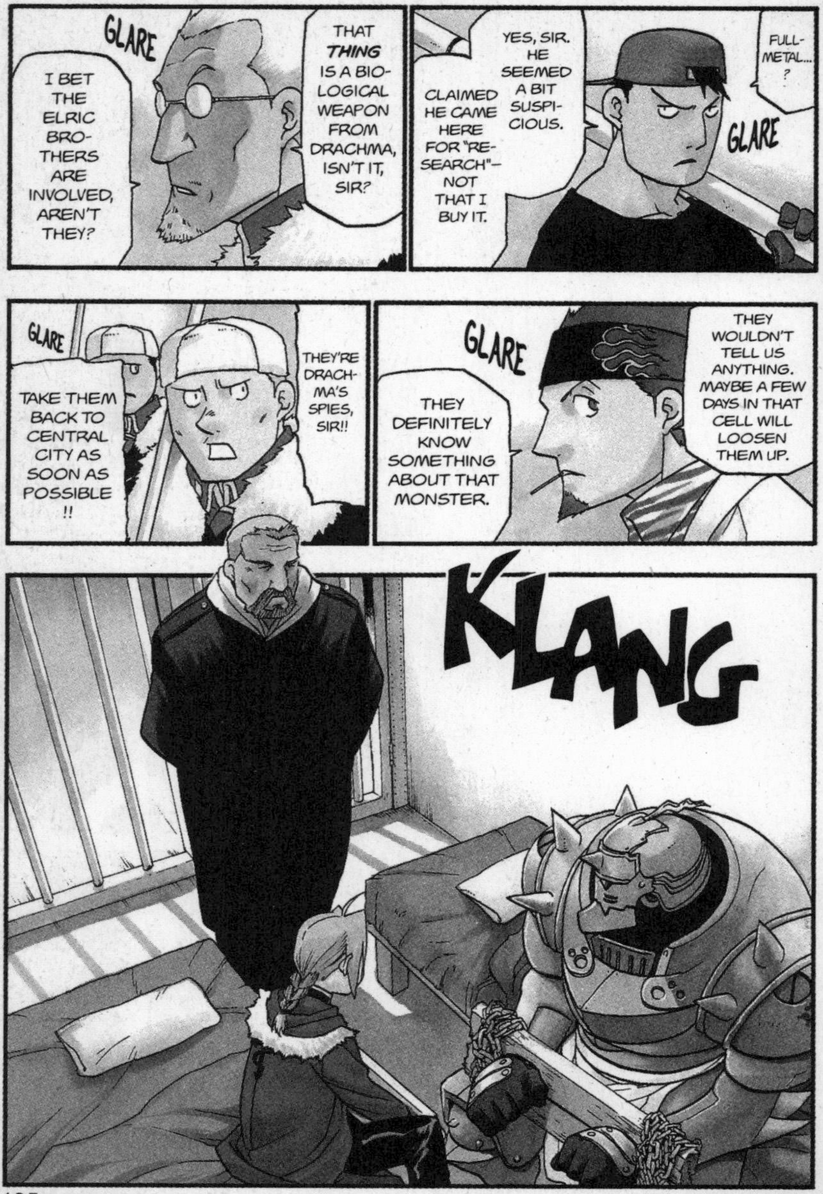
FULL-METAL...?
GLARE
YES, SIR. HE SEEMED A BIT SUSPICIOUS.
CLAIMED HE CAME HERE FOR "RESEARCH"—NOT THAT I BUY IT.
THAT *THING* IS A BIOLOGICAL WEAPON FROM DRACHMA, ISN'T IT, SIR?
GLARE
I BET THE ELRIC BROTHERS ARE INVOLVED, AREN'T THEY?
THEY WOULDN'T TELL US ANYTHING. MAYBE A FEW DAYS IN THAT CELL WILL LOOSEN THEM UP.
GLARE
THEY DEFINITELY KNOW SOMETHING ABOUT THAT MONSTER.
THEY'RE DRACHMA'S SPIES, SIR!!
GLARE
TAKE THEM BACK TO CENTRAL CITY AS SOON AS POSSIBLE!!
KLANG

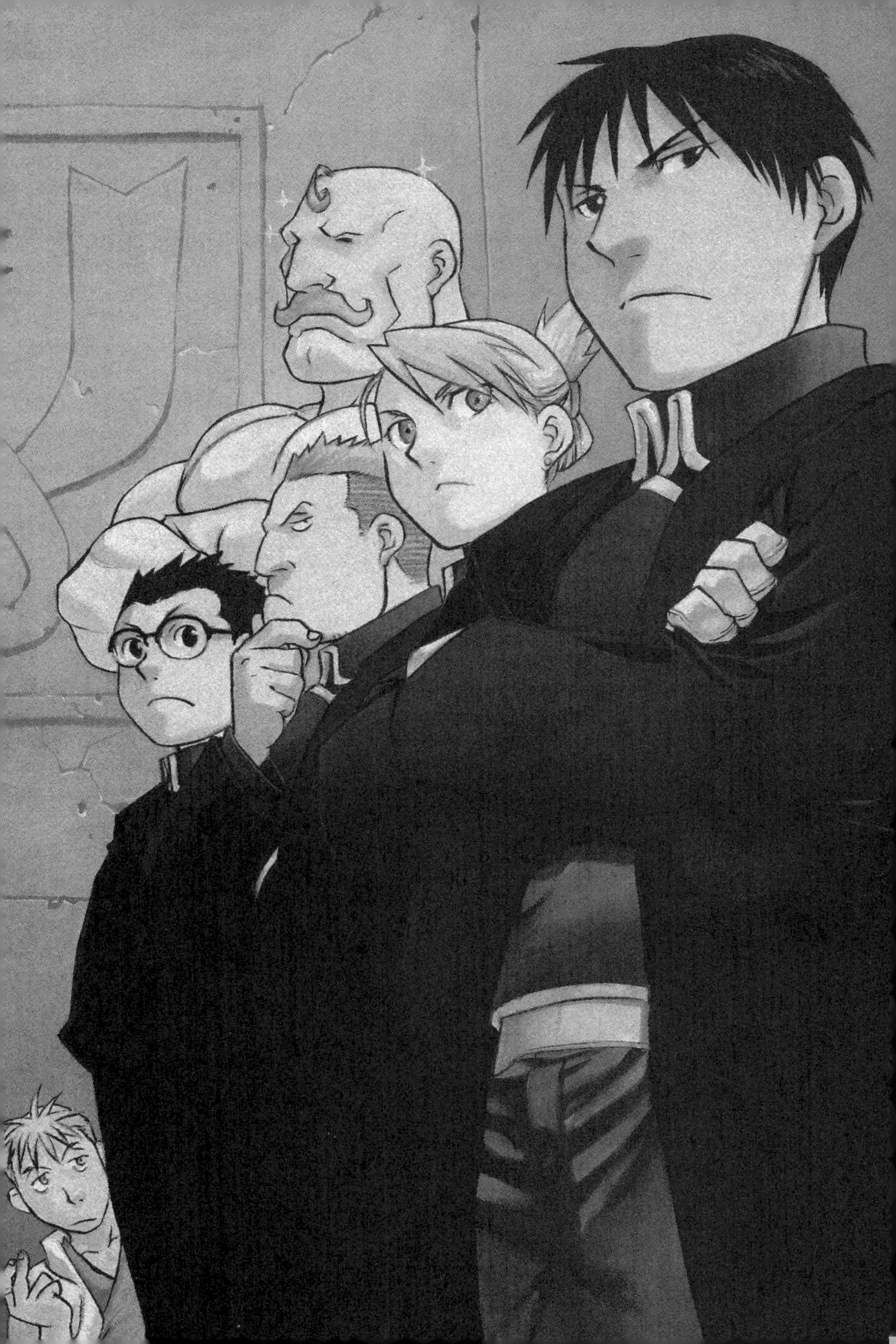

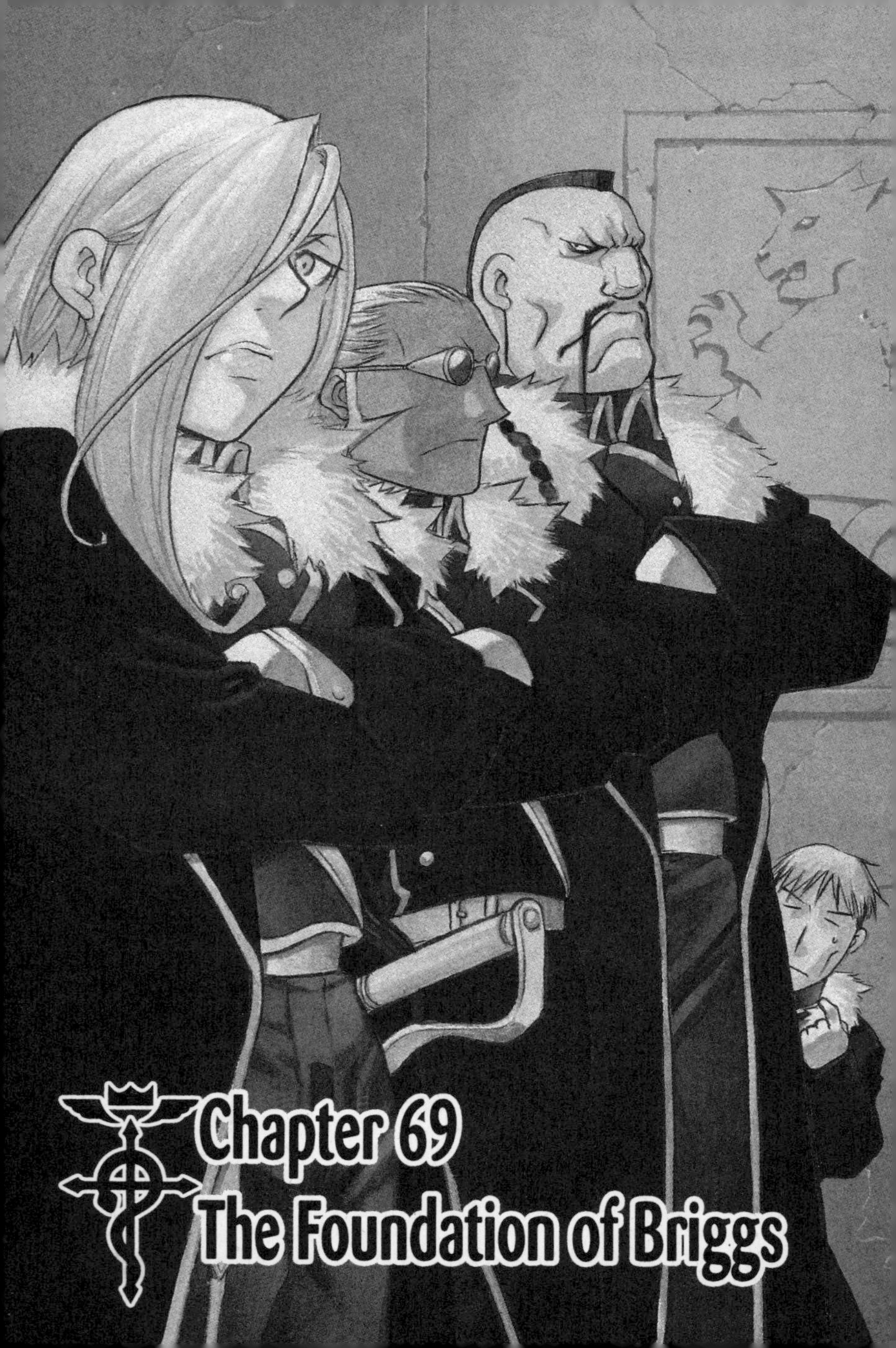
Chapter 69
The Foundation of Briggs

FULLMETAL
ALCHEMIST

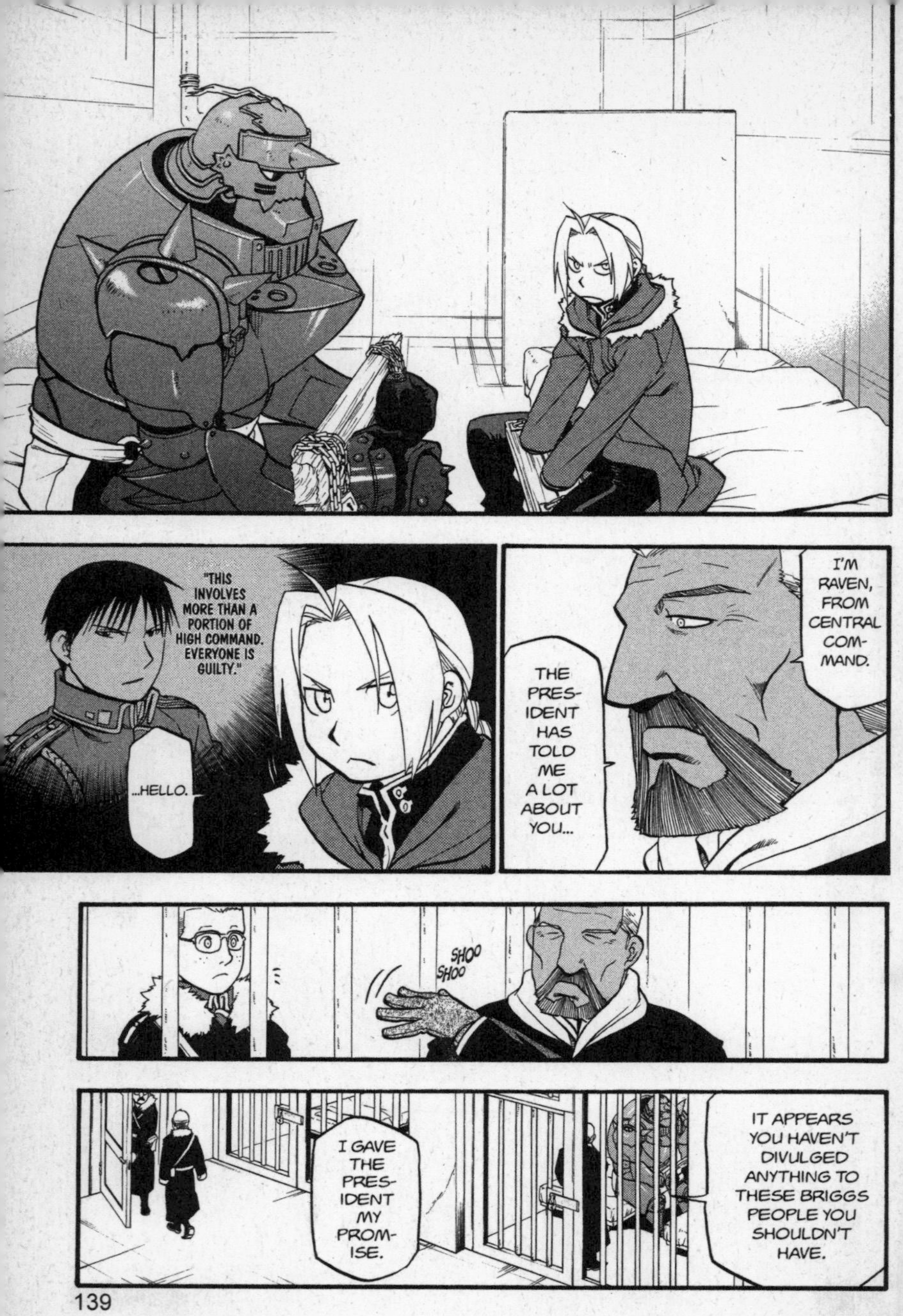
I'M RAVEN, FROM CENTRAL COMMAND.
THE PRESIDENT HAS TOLD ME A LOT ABOUT YOU...
"THIS INVOLVES MORE THAN A PORTION OF HIGH COMMAND. EVERYONE IS GUILTY."
...HELLO.
SHOO SHOO
IT APPEARS YOU HAVEN'T DIVULGED ANYTHING TO THESE BRIGGS PEOPLE YOU SHOULDN'T HAVE.
I GAVE THE PRESIDENT MY PROMISE.

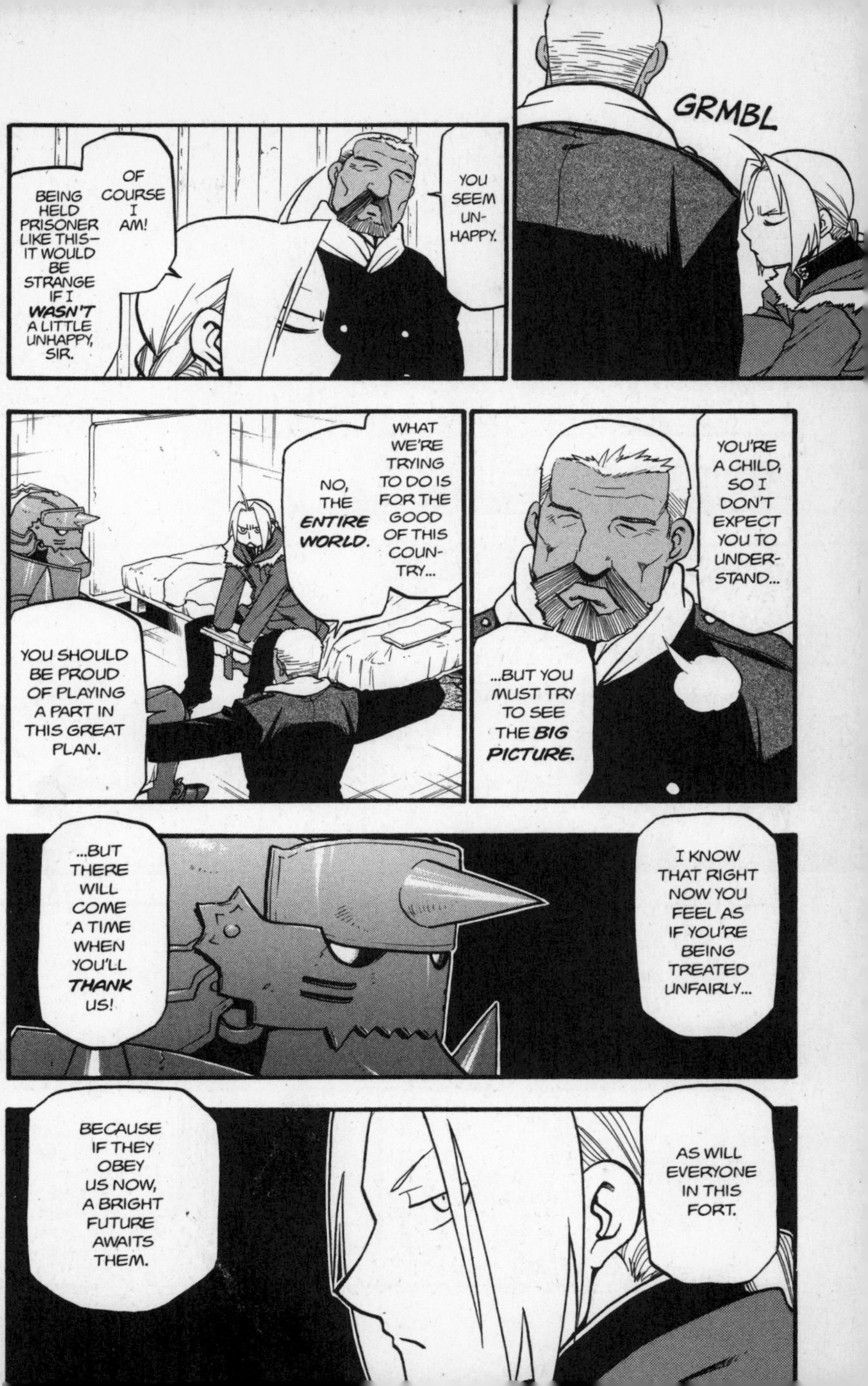
GRMBL
YOU SEEM UN-HAPPY.
OF COURSE I AM!
BEING HELD PRISONER LIKE THIS— IT WOULD BE STRANGE IF I *WASN'T* A LITTLE UNHAPPY, SIR.
YOU'RE A CHILD, SO I DON'T EXPECT YOU TO UNDER-STAND...
...BUT YOU MUST TRY TO SEE THE *BIG PICTURE*.
WHAT WE'RE TRYING TO DO IS FOR THE GOOD OF THIS COUN-TRY...
NO, THE *ENTIRE WORLD*.
YOU SHOULD BE PROUD OF PLAYING A PART IN THIS GREAT PLAN.
I KNOW THAT RIGHT NOW YOU FEEL AS IF YOU'RE BEING TREATED UNFAIRLY...
...BUT THERE WILL COME A TIME WHEN YOU'LL *THANK* US!
AS WILL EVERYONE IN THIS FORT.
BECAUSE IF THEY OBEY US NOW, A BRIGHT FUTURE AWAITS THEM.

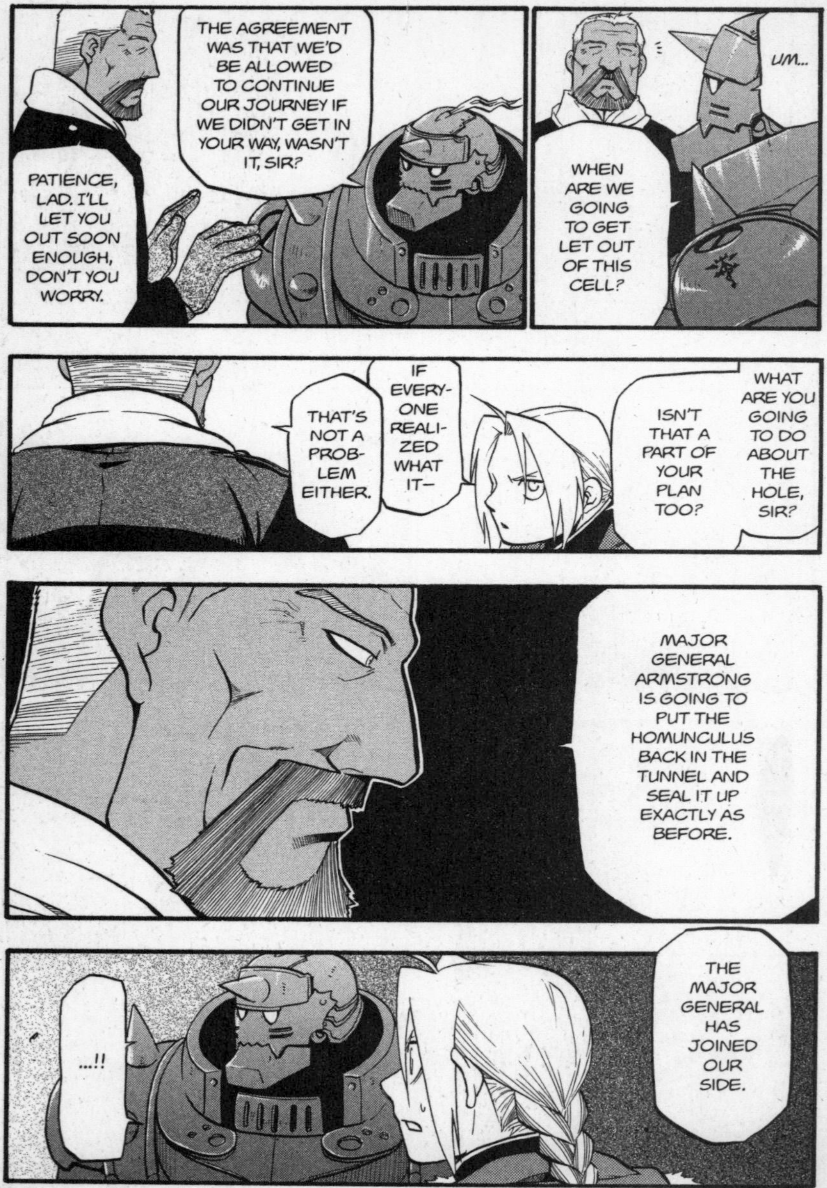
UM...
WHEN ARE WE GOING TO GET LET OUT OF THIS CELL?
THE AGREEMENT WAS THAT WE'D BE ALLOWED TO CONTINUE OUR JOURNEY IF WE DIDN'T GET IN YOUR WAY, WASN'T IT, SIR?
PATIENCE, LAD. I'LL LET YOU OUT SOON ENOUGH, DON'T YOU WORRY.
WHAT ARE YOU GOING TO DO ABOUT THE HOLE, SIR?
ISN'T THAT A PART OF YOUR PLAN TOO?
IF EVERY-ONE REALI-ZED WHAT IT—
THAT'S NOT A PROB-LEM EITHER.
MAJOR GENERAL ARMSTRONG IS GOING TO PUT THE HOMUNCULUS BACK IN THE TUNNEL AND SEAL IT UP EXACTLY AS BEFORE.
THE MAJOR GENERAL HAS JOINED OUR SIDE.
...!!

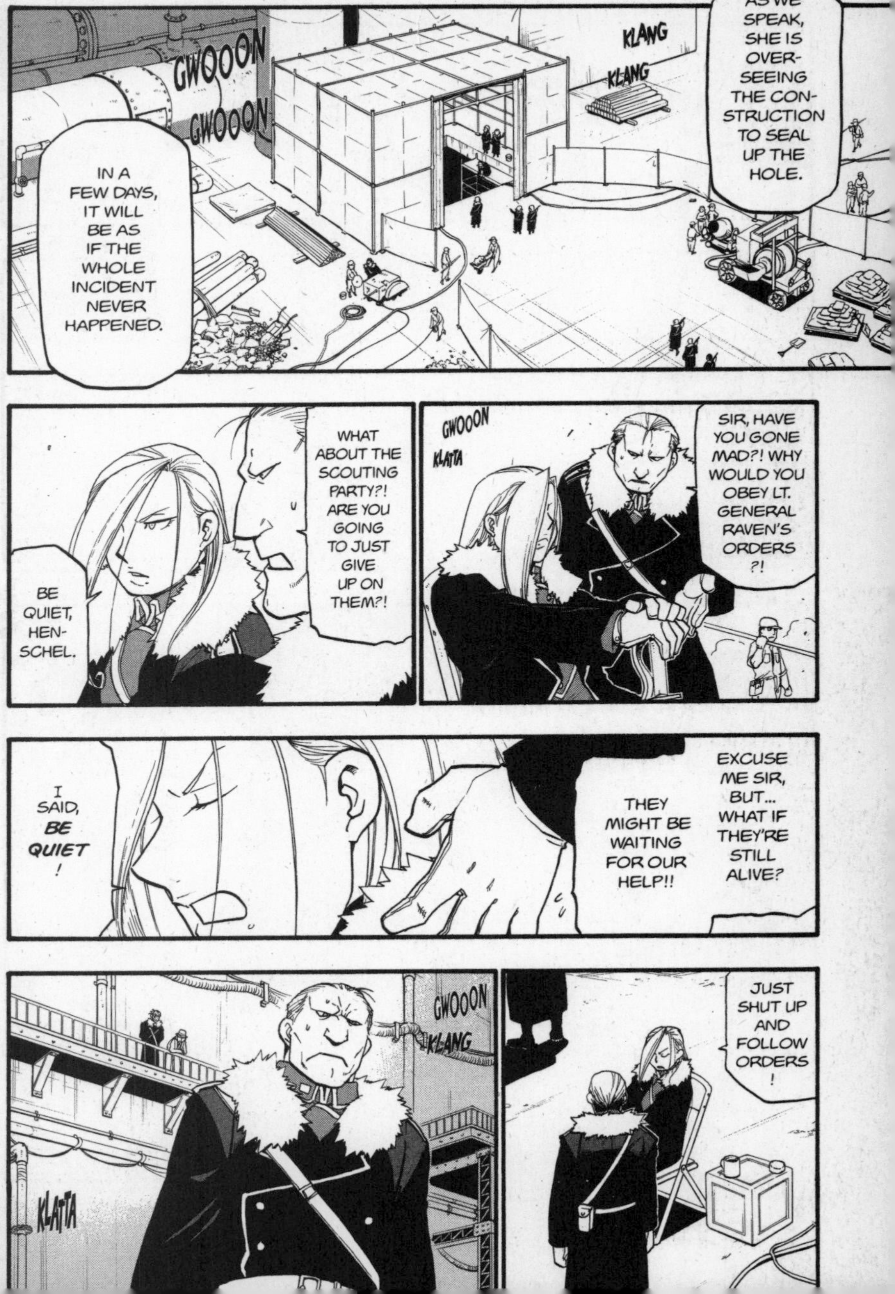
AS WE SPEAK, SHE IS OVER-SEEING THE CON-STRUCTION TO SEAL UP THE HOLE.
KLANG
KLANG
GWOOON
GWOOON
IN A FEW DAYS, IT WILL BE AS IF THE WHOLE INCIDENT NEVER HAPPENED.
GWOOON
KLATTA
SIR, HAVE YOU GONE MAD?! WHY WOULD YOU OBEY LT. GENERAL RAVEN'S ORDERS?!
WHAT ABOUT THE SCOUTING PARTY?! ARE YOU GOING TO JUST GIVE UP ON THEM?!
BE QUIET, HEN-SCHEL.
EXCUSE ME SIR, BUT... WHAT IF THEY'RE STILL ALIVE?
THEY MIGHT BE WAITING FOR OUR HELP!!
I SAID, **BE QUIET**!
JUST SHUT UP AND FOLLOW ORDERS!
GWOOON
KLANG
KLATTA

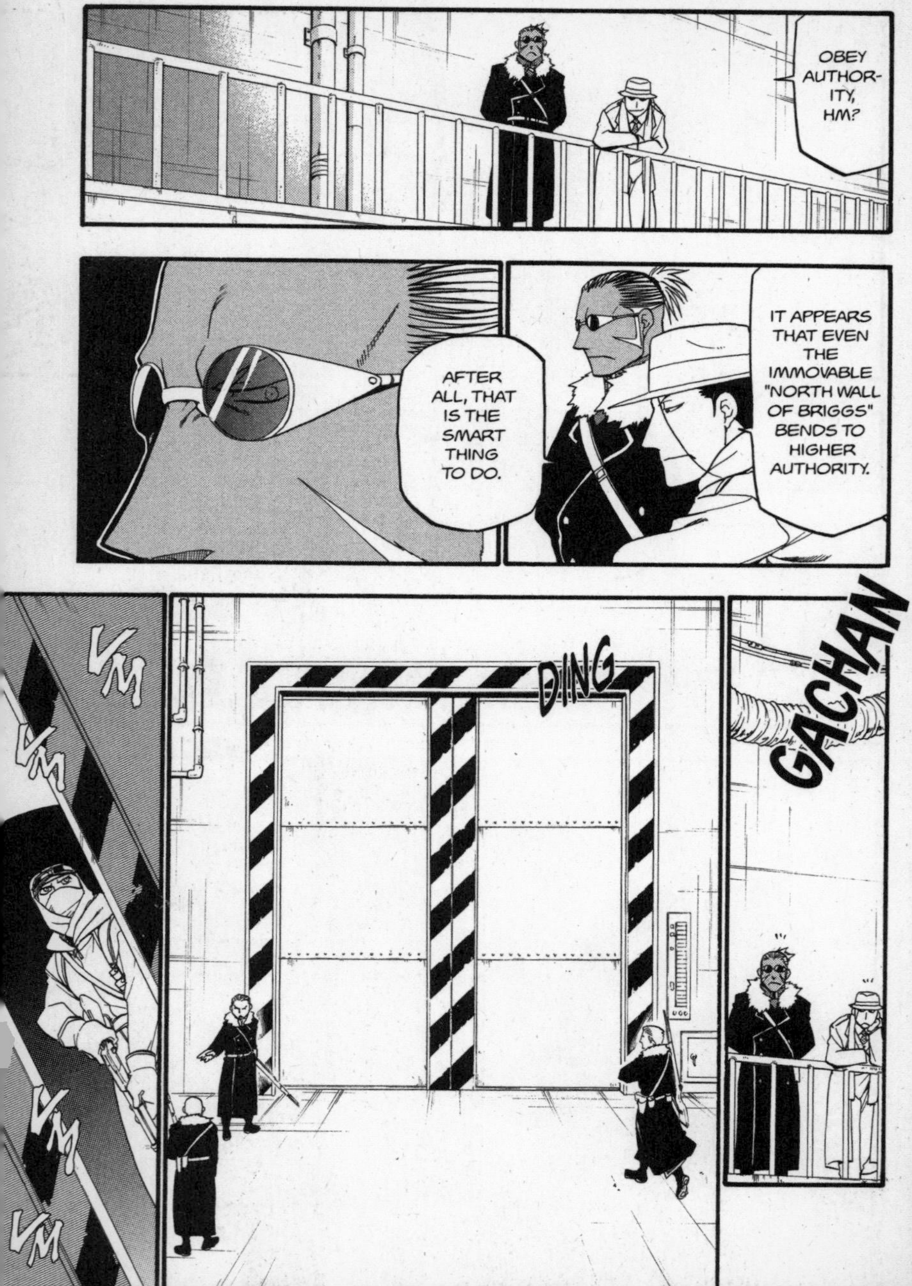
OBEY AUTHORITY, HM?
IT APPEARS THAT EVEN THE IMMOVABLE "NORTH WALL OF BRIGGS" BENDS TO HIGHER AUTHORITY.
AFTER ALL, THAT IS THE SMART THING TO DO.
GACHAN
DING
VM
VM
VM
VM

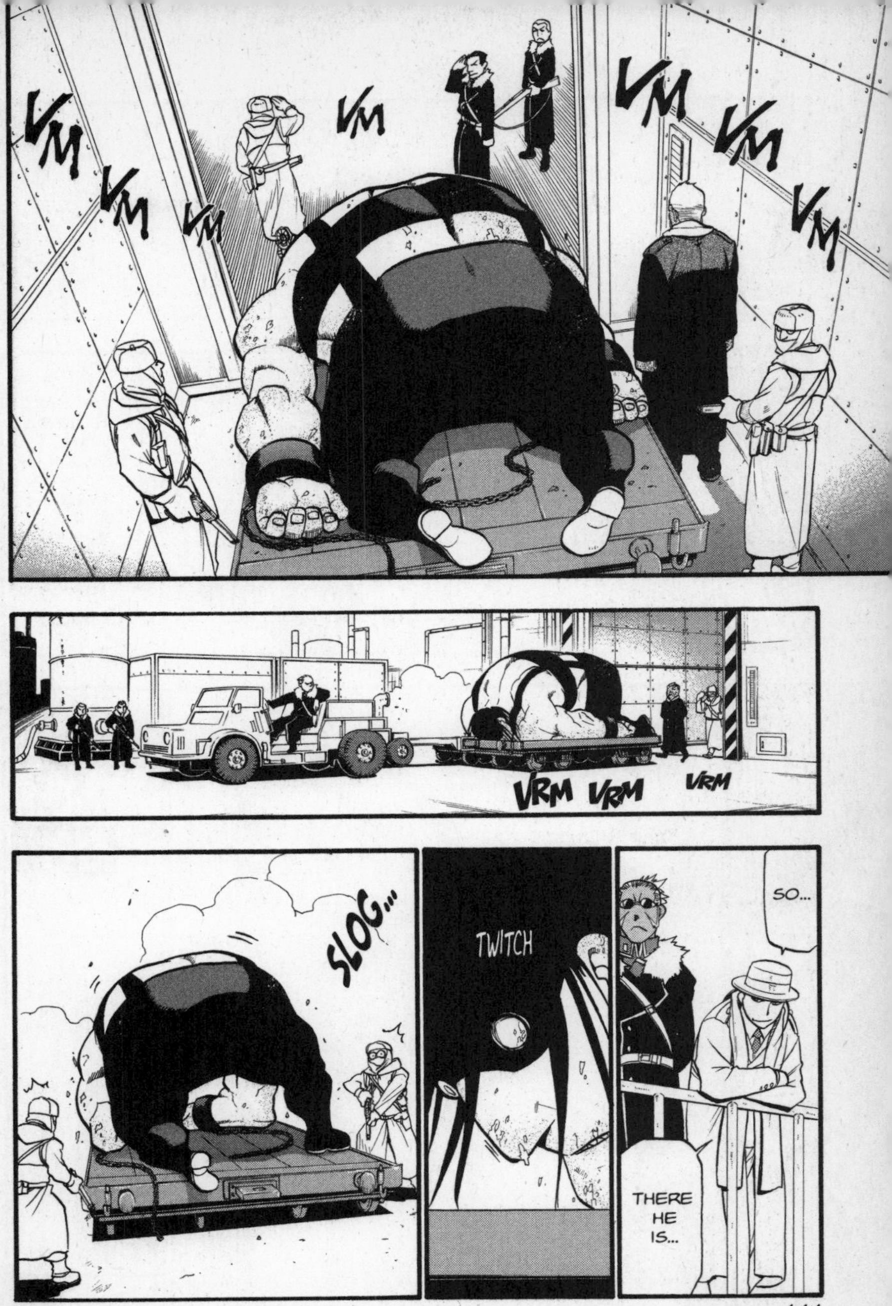
VM VM VM VM
VM VM VM VM VM
VRM VRM VRM
SO...
THERE HE IS...
TWITCH
SLOG...

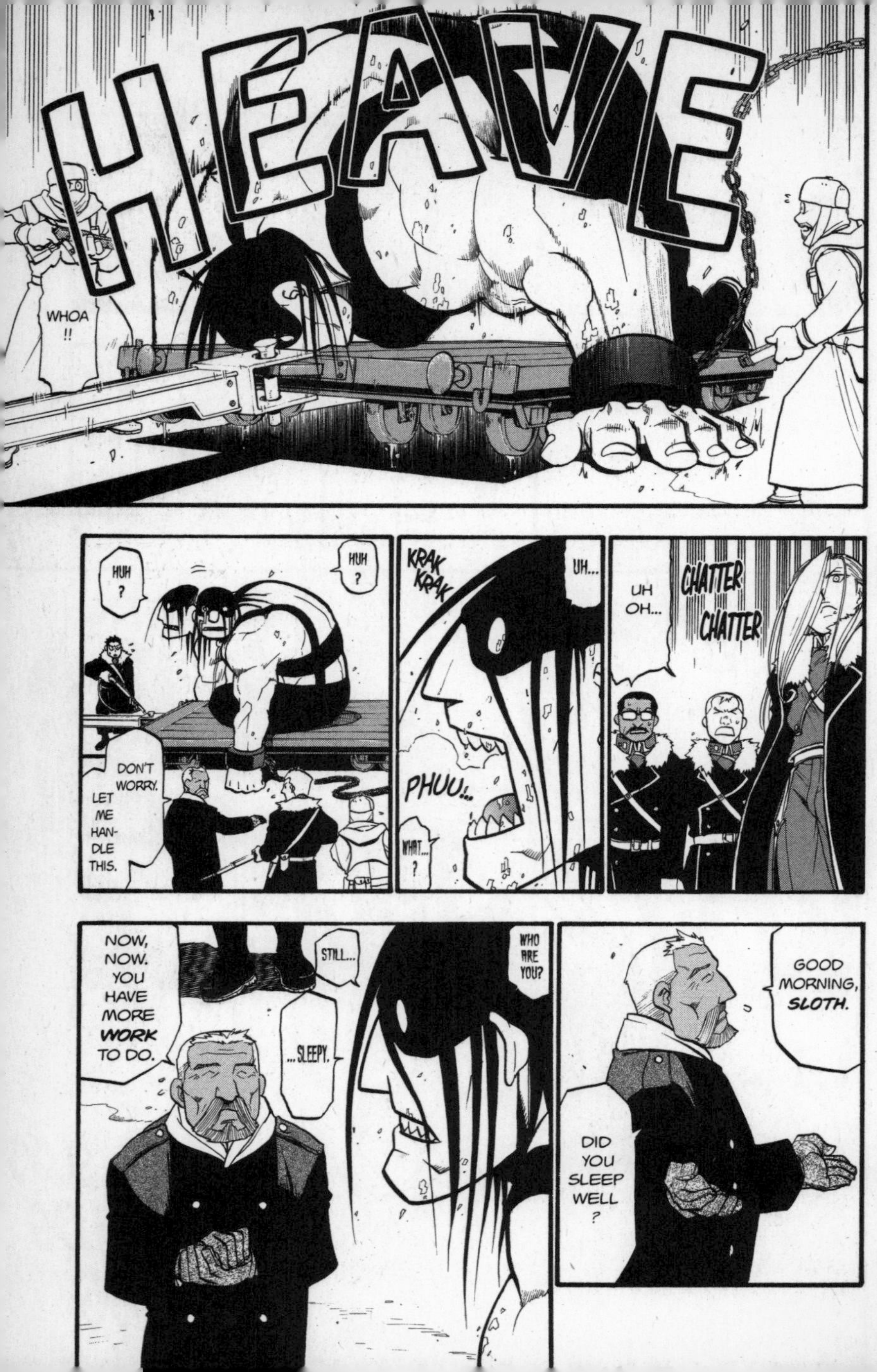
HEAVE
WHOA !!
UH OH...
CHATTER CHATTER
UH...
KRAK KRAK
PHUU!..
WHAT... ?
HUH ?
HUH ?
DON'T WORRY. LET ME HANDLE THIS.
GOOD MORNING, SLOTH.
DID YOU SLEEP WELL ?
WHO ARE YOU?
STILL...
...SLEEPY.
NOW, NOW. YOU HAVE MORE WORK TO DO.

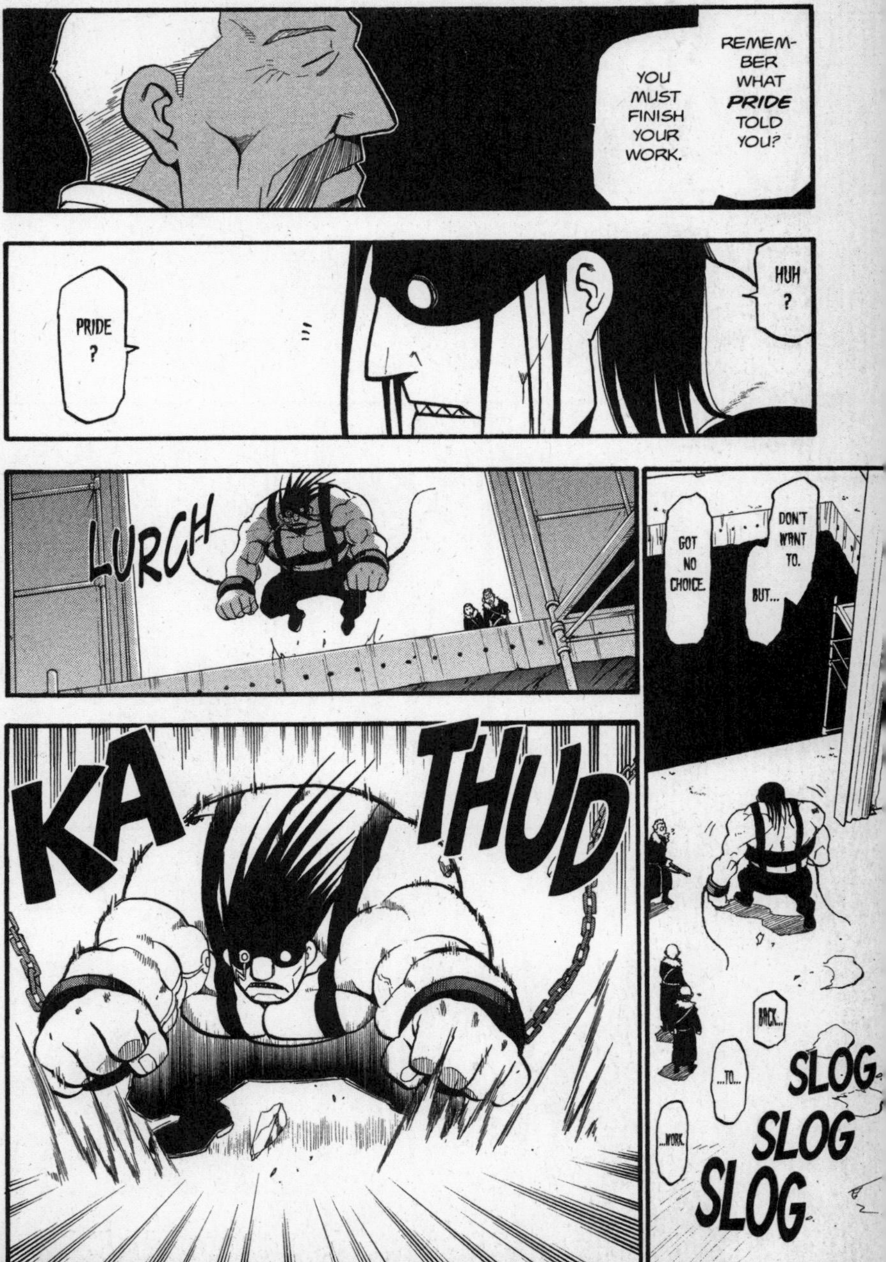
REMEMBER WHAT PRIDE TOLD YOU?
YOU MUST FINISH YOUR WORK.
HUH?
PRIDE?
DON'T WANT TO. BUT...
GOT NO CHOICE.
BACK...
...TO...
...WORK.
SLOG
SLOG
SLOG
LURCH
KA THUD

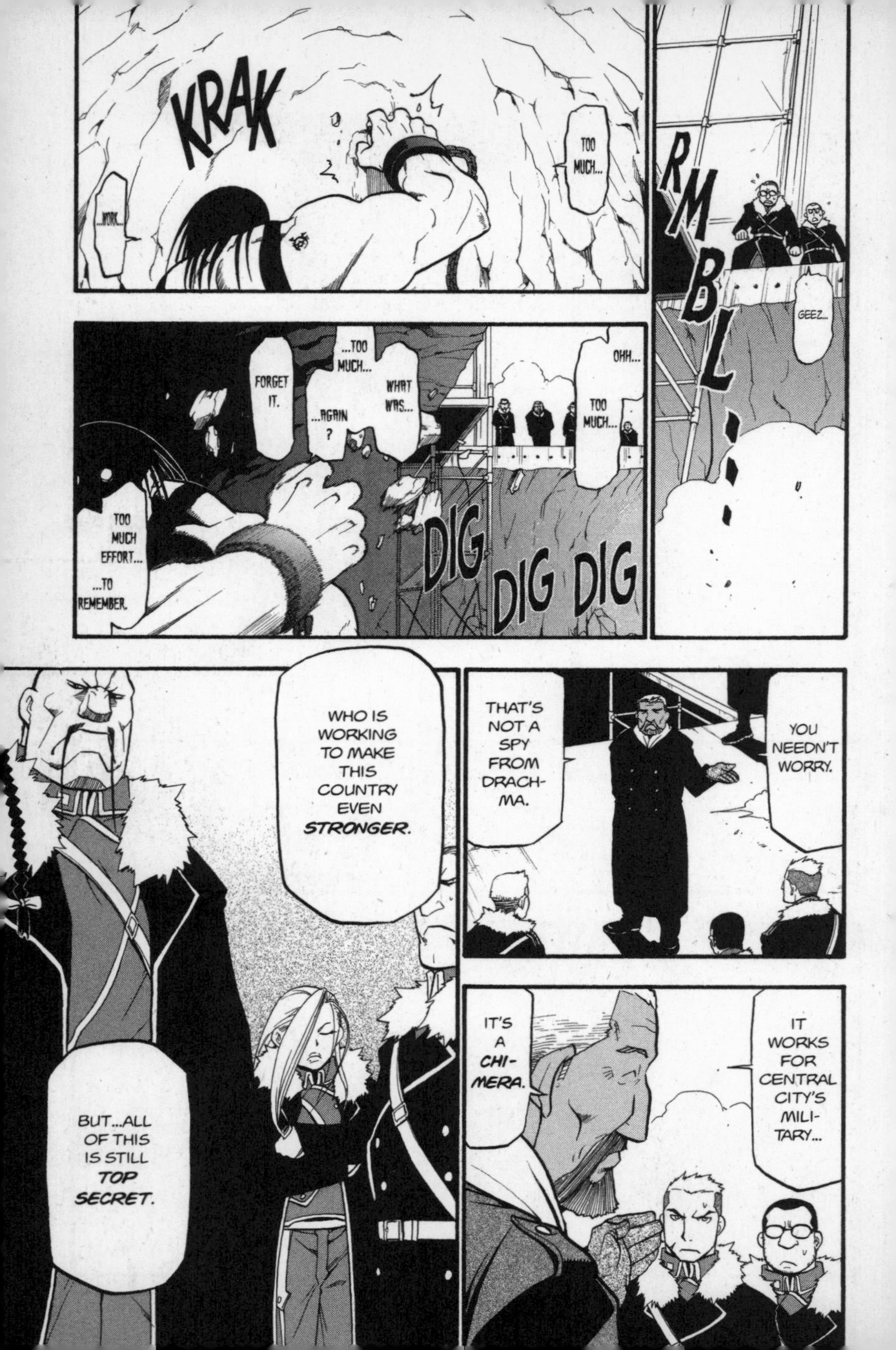
RMBL...
GEEZ...
TOO MUCH...
KRAK
...WORK...
OHH...
TOO MUCH...
WHAT WAS...
...TOO MUCH...
...AGAIN?
FORGET IT.
DIG DIG DIG
TOO MUCH EFFORT...
...TO REMEMBER.
YOU NEEDN'T WORRY.
THAT'S NOT A SPY FROM DRACHMA.
IT WORKS FOR CENTRAL CITY'S MILITARY...
IT'S A CHIMERA.
WHO IS WORKING TO MAKE THIS COUNTRY EVEN STRONGER.
BUT...ALL OF THIS IS STILL TOP SECRET.

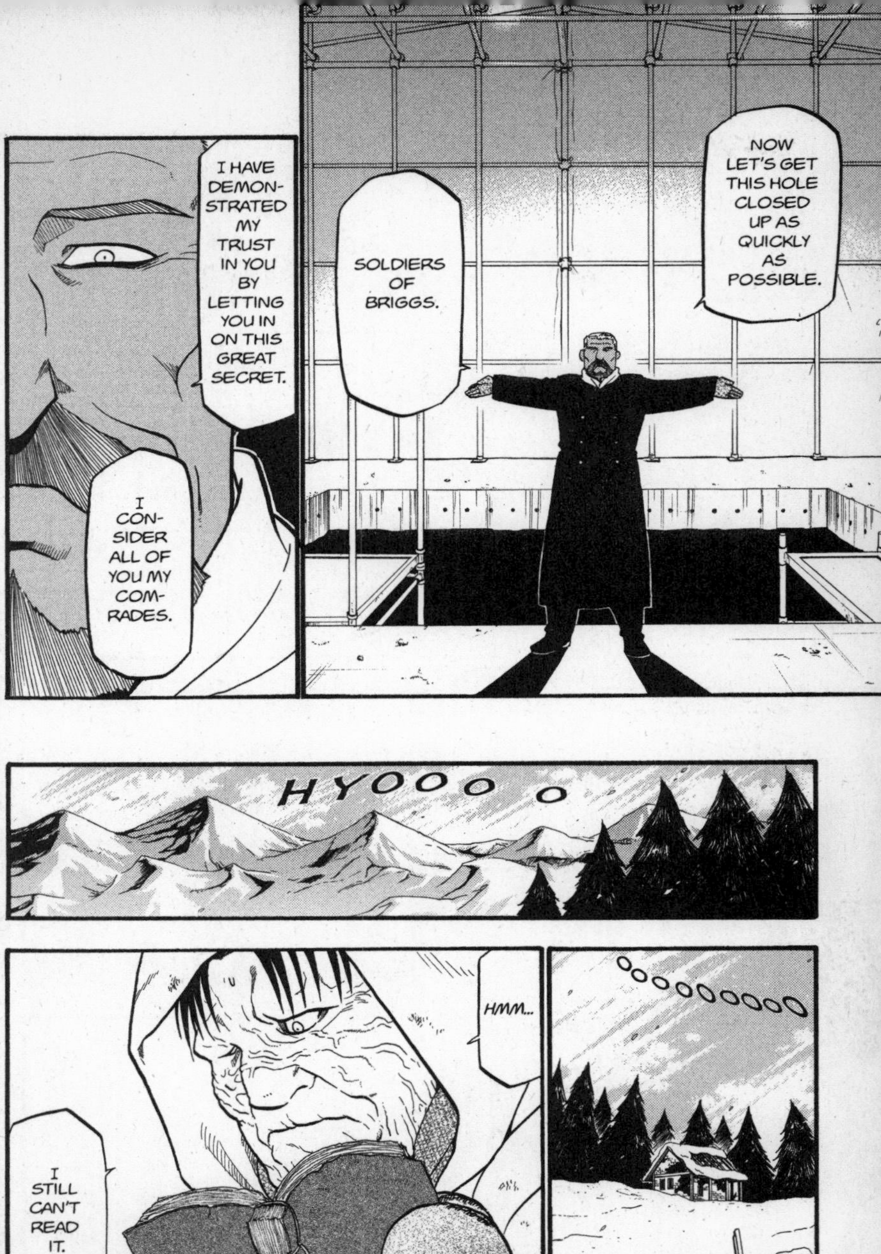
NOW LET'S GET THIS HOLE CLOSED UP AS QUICKLY AS POSSIBLE.
SOLDIERS OF BRIGGS.
I HAVE DEMONSTRATED MY TRUST IN YOU BY LETTING YOU IN ON THIS GREAT SECRET.
I CONSIDER ALL OF YOU MY COMRADES.
HYOOO O
OOOOOOOOO
HMM...
I STILL CAN'T READ IT.

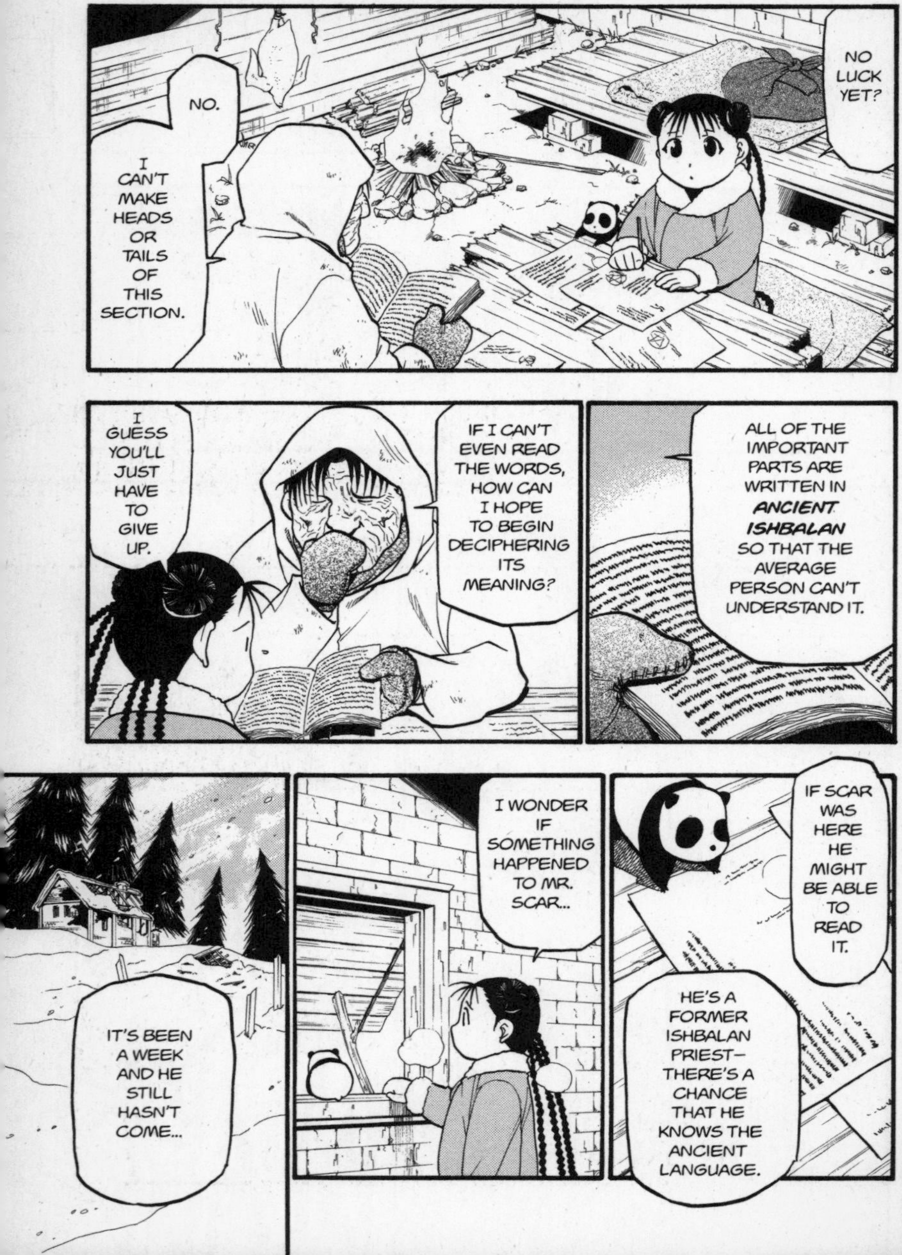
NO LUCK YET?
NO.
I CAN'T MAKE HEADS OR TAILS OF THIS SECTION.
ALL OF THE IMPORTANT PARTS ARE WRITTEN IN ANCIENT ISHBALAN SO THAT THE AVERAGE PERSON CAN'T UNDERSTAND IT.
IF I CAN'T EVEN READ THE WORDS, HOW CAN I HOPE TO BEGIN DECIPHERING ITS MEANING?
I GUESS YOU'LL JUST HAVE TO GIVE UP.
IF SCAR WAS HERE HE MIGHT BE ABLE TO READ IT.
HE'S A FORMER ISHBALAN PRIEST—THERE'S A CHANCE THAT HE KNOWS THE ANCIENT LANGUAGE.
I WONDER IF SOMETHING HAPPENED TO MR. SCAR...
IT'S BEEN A WEEK AND HE STILL HASN'T COME...

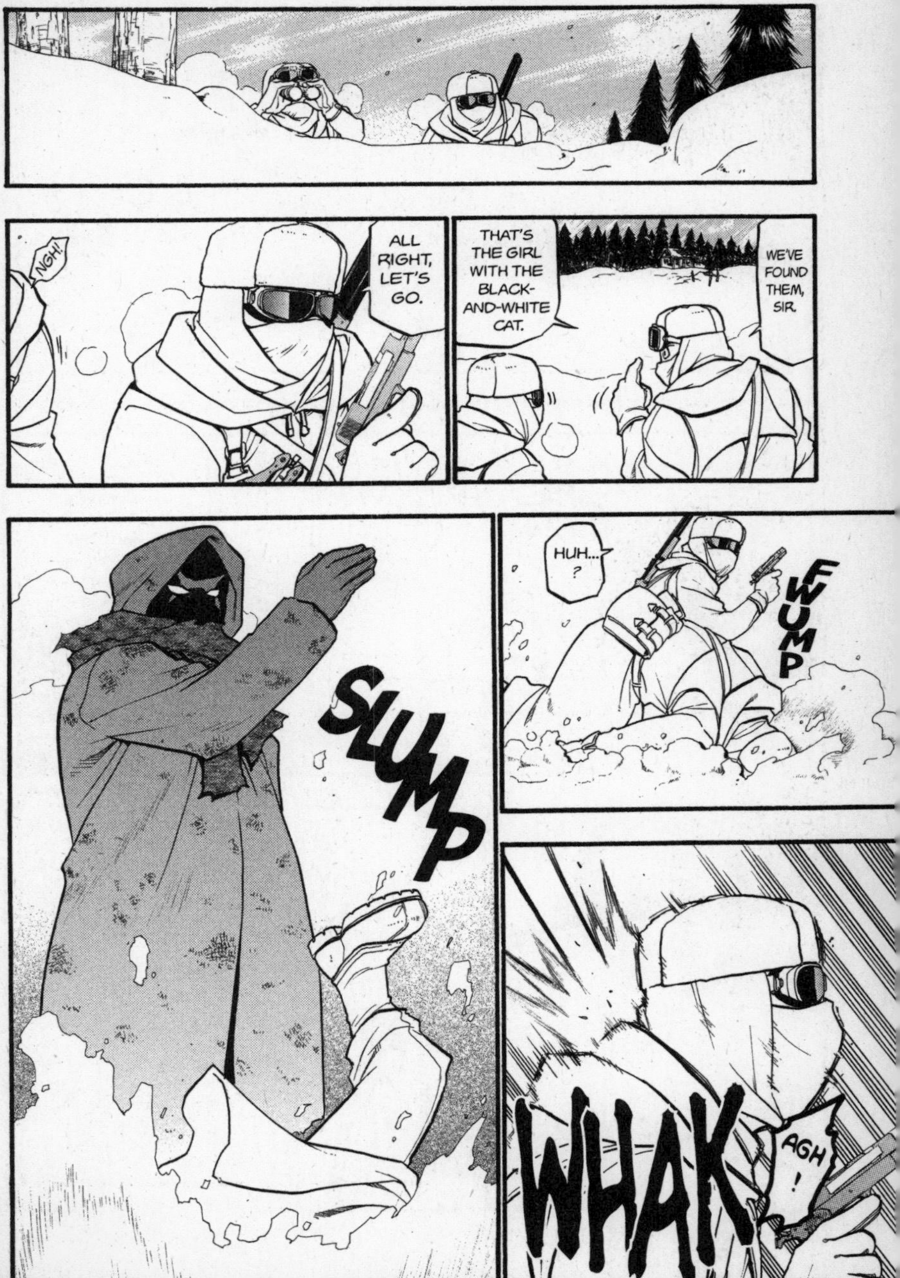
WE'VE FOUND THEM, SIR.
THAT'S THE GIRL WITH THE BLACK-AND-WHITE CAT.
ALL RIGHT, LET'S GO.
NGH!
HUH... ?
FWUMP
WHAK
AGH !
SLUMP

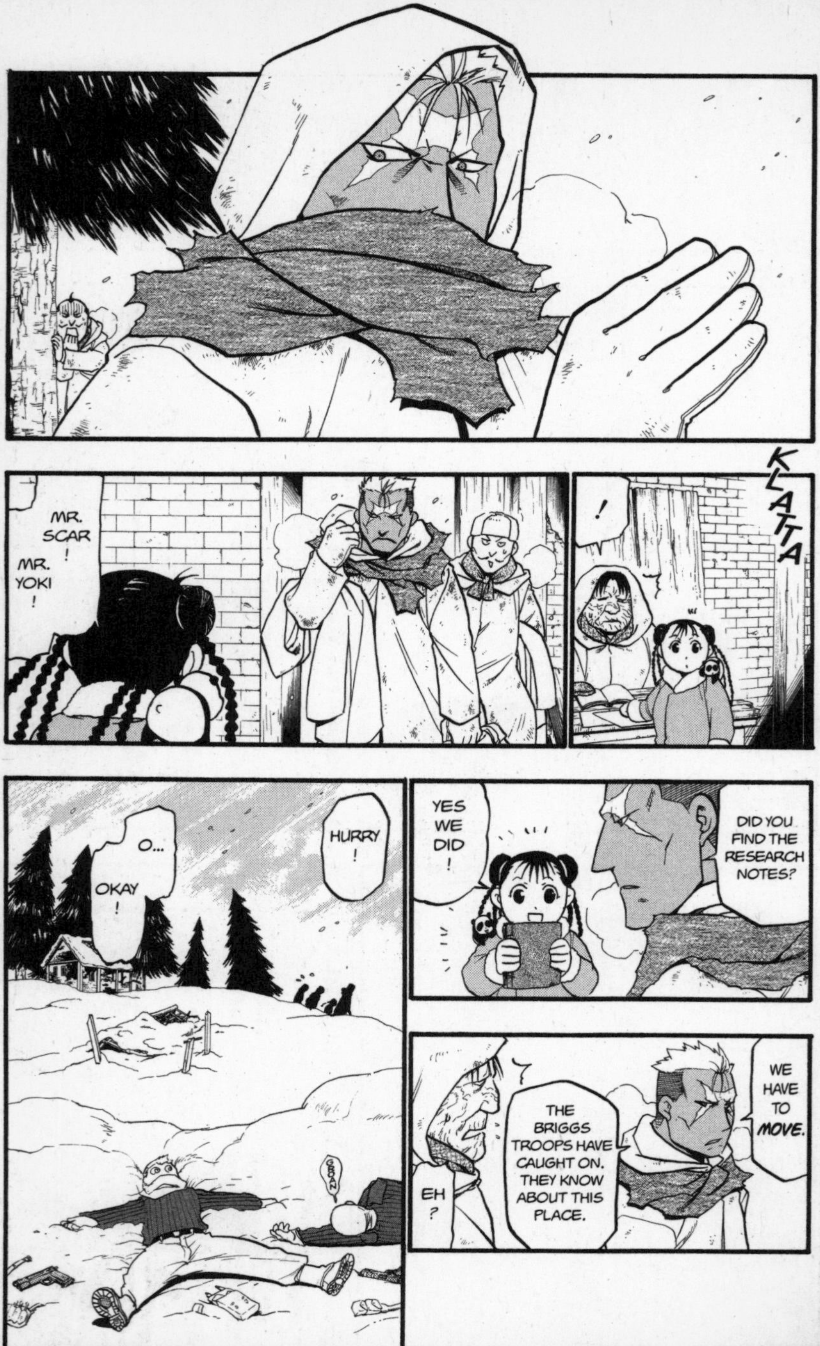
KLATTA
!
MR. SCAR!
MR. YOKI!
DID YOU FIND THE RESEARCH NOTES?
YES WE DID!
WE HAVE TO *MOVE*.
THE BRIGGS TROOPS HAVE CAUGHT ON. THEY KNOW ABOUT THIS PLACE.
EH?
HURRY!
O... OKAY!

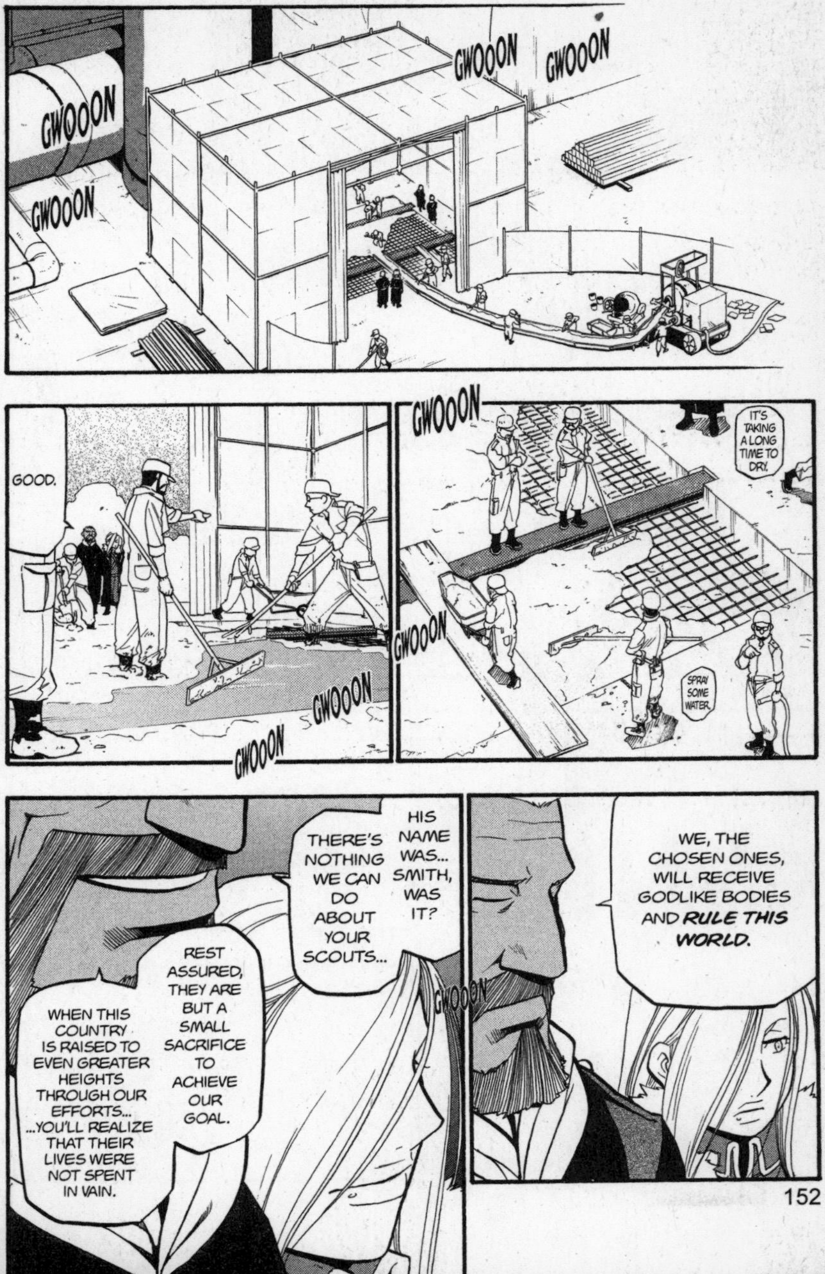
GWOOON
GWOOON
GWOOON
GWOOON
GWOOON
IT'S TAKING A LONG TIME TO DRY.
SPRAY SOME WATER.
GWOOON
GOOD.
GWOOON
GWOOON
WE, THE CHOSEN ONES, WILL RECEIVE GODLIKE BODIES AND **RULE THIS WORLD.**
GWOOON
HIS NAME WAS... SMITH, WAS IT?
THERE'S NOTHING WE CAN DO ABOUT YOUR SCOUTS...
REST ASSURED, THEY ARE BUT A SMALL SACRIFICE TO ACHIEVE OUR GOAL.
WHEN THIS COUNTRY IS RAISED TO EVEN GREATER HEIGHTS THROUGH OUR EFFORTS... ...YOU'LL REALIZE THAT THEIR LIVES WERE NOT SPENT IN VAIN.

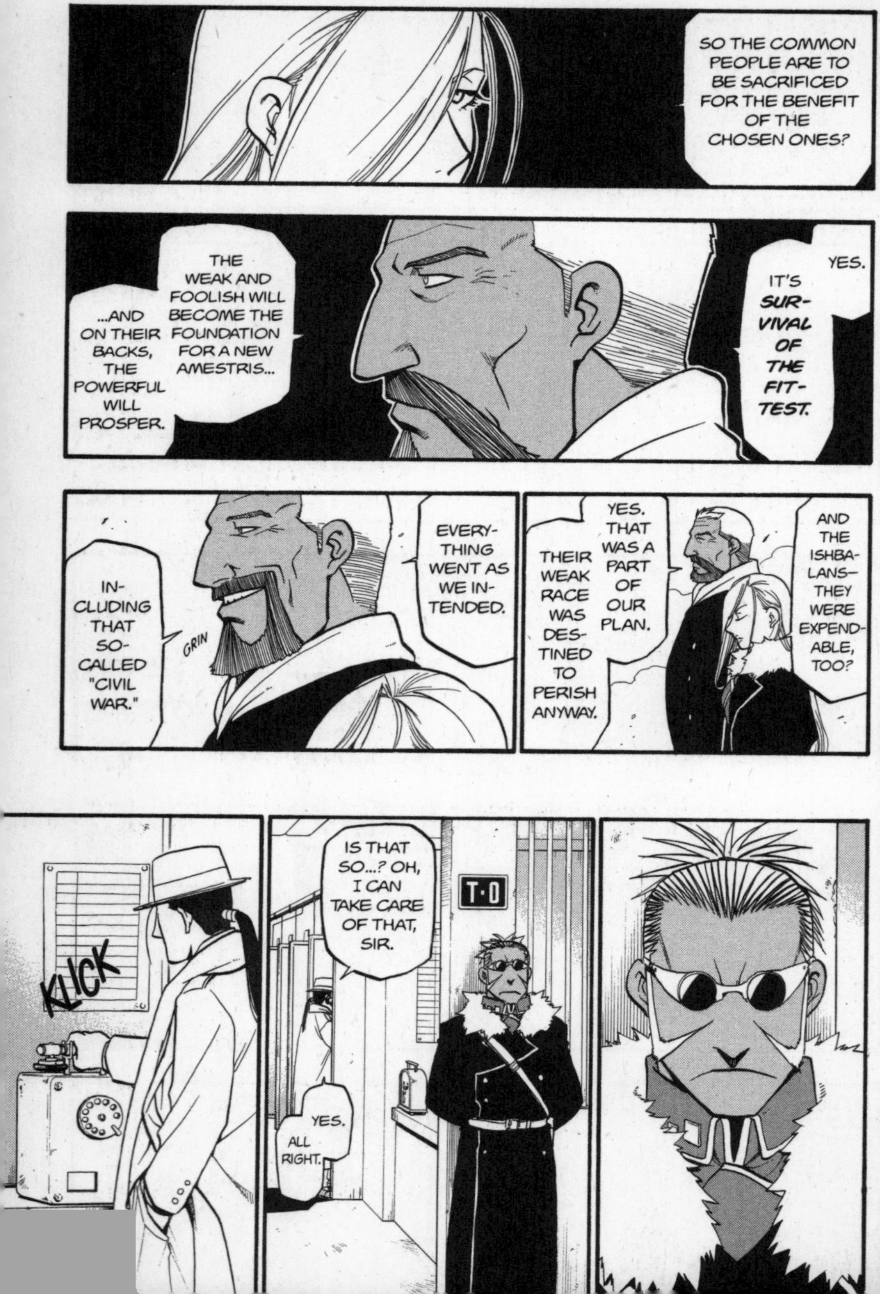
SO THE COMMON PEOPLE ARE TO BE SACRIFICED FOR THE BENEFIT OF THE CHOSEN ONES?
YES.
IT'S *SURVIVAL OF THE FITTEST.*
THE WEAK AND FOOLISH WILL BECOME THE FOUNDATION FOR A NEW AMESTRIS...
...AND ON THEIR BACKS, THE POWERFUL WILL PROSPER.
AND THE ISHBALANS—THEY WERE EXPENDABLE, TOO?
YES. THAT WAS A PART OF OUR PLAN.
THEIR WEAK RACE WAS DESTINED TO PERISH ANYWAY.
EVERYTHING WENT AS WE INTENDED.
GRIN
INCLUDING THAT SO-CALLED "CIVIL WAR."
IS THAT SO...? OH, I CAN TAKE CARE OF THAT, SIR.
T·O
YES. ALL RIGHT.
KLICK

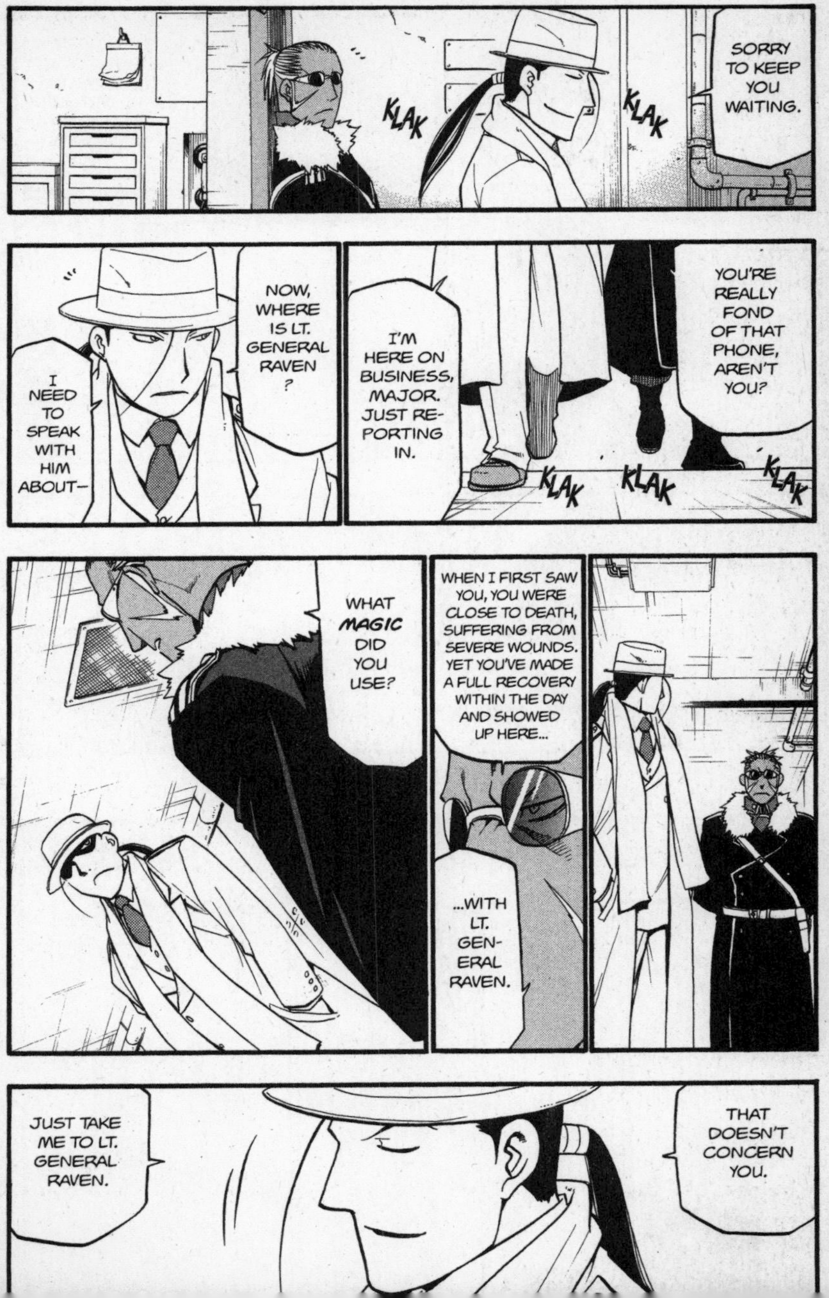
SORRY TO KEEP YOU WAITING.
KLAK
KLAK
YOU'RE REALLY FOND OF THAT PHONE, AREN'T YOU?
I'M HERE ON BUSINESS, MAJOR. JUST RE-PORTING IN.
KLAK
KLAK
KLAK
NOW, WHERE IS LT. GENERAL RAVEN?
I NEED TO SPEAK WITH HIM ABOUT—
WHEN I FIRST SAW YOU, YOU WERE CLOSE TO DEATH, SUFFERING FROM SEVERE WOUNDS. YET YOU'VE MADE A FULL RECOVERY WITHIN THE DAY AND SHOWED UP HERE...
...WITH LT. GEN-ERAL RAVEN.
WHAT MAGIC DID YOU USE?
THAT DOESN'T CONCERN YOU.
JUST TAKE ME TO LT. GENERAL RAVEN.

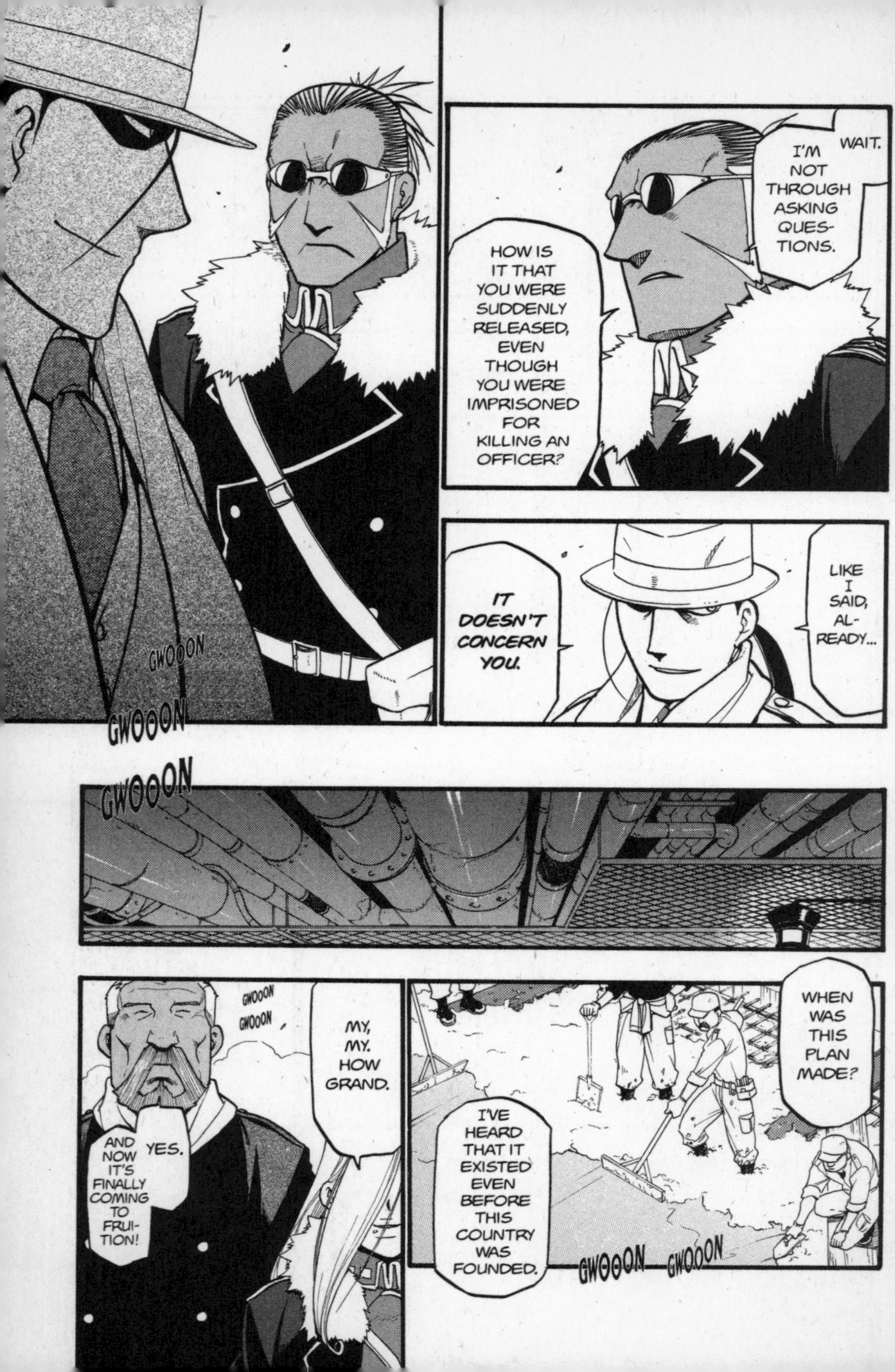
WAIT. I'M NOT THROUGH ASKING QUES-TIONS.
HOW IS IT THAT YOU WERE SUDDENLY RELEASED, EVEN THOUGH YOU WERE IMPRISONED FOR KILLING AN OFFICER?
LIKE I SAID, AL-READY...
IT DOESN'T CONCERN YOU.
GWOOON
GWOOON
GWOOON
WHEN WAS THIS PLAN MADE?
I'VE HEARD THAT IT EXISTED EVEN BEFORE THIS COUNTRY WAS FOUNDED.
GWOOON
GWOOON
GWOOON
GWOOON
MY, MY. HOW GRAND.
YES.
AND NOW IT'S FINALLY COMING TO FRUI-TION!

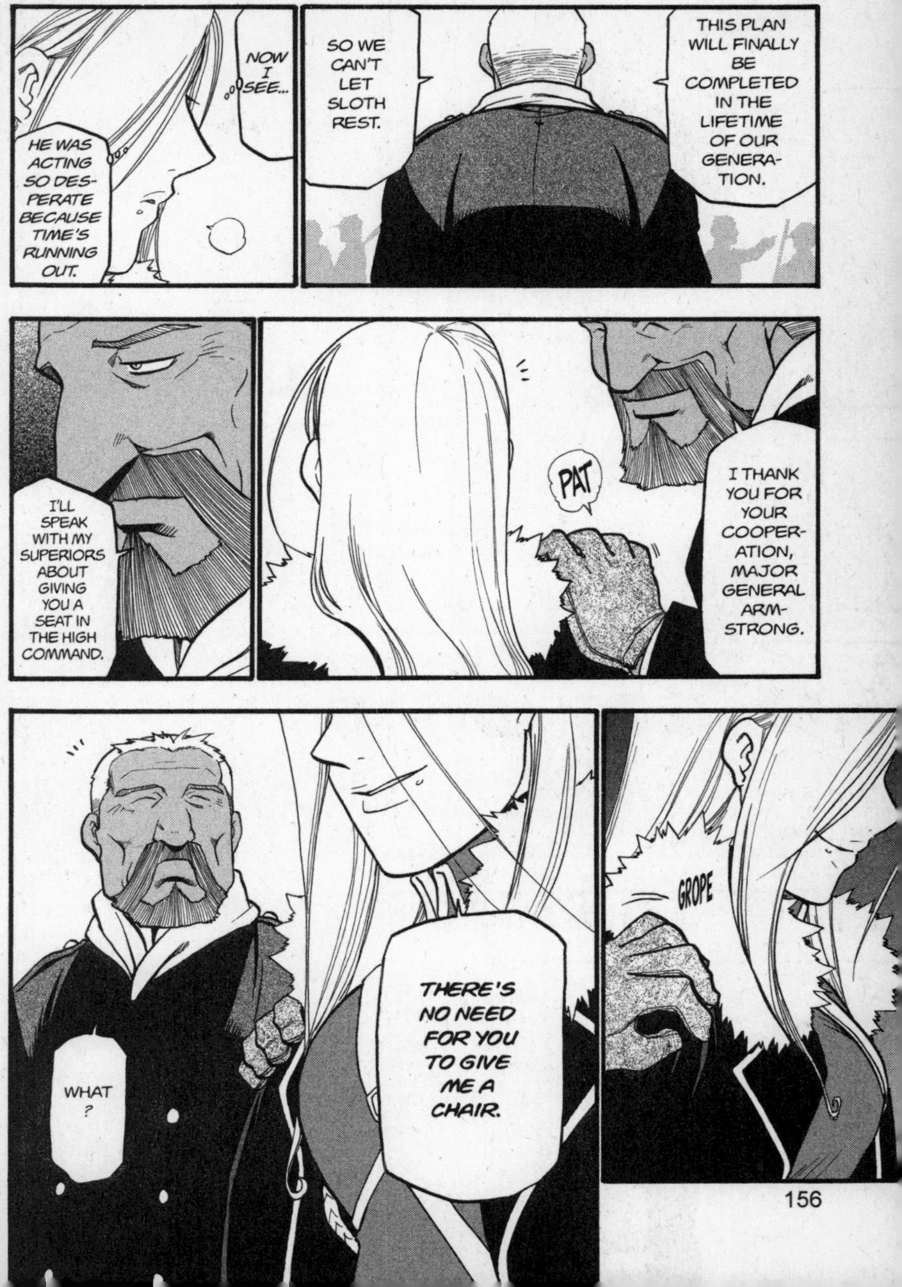
THIS PLAN WILL FINALLY BE COMPLETED IN THE LIFETIME OF OUR GENERATION.
SO WE CAN'T LET SLOTH REST.
NOW I SEE...
HE WAS ACTING SO DESPERATE BECAUSE TIME'S RUNNING OUT.
I THANK YOU FOR YOUR COOPERATION, MAJOR GENERAL ARMSTRONG.
PAT
I'LL SPEAK WITH MY SUPERIORS ABOUT GIVING YOU A SEAT IN THE HIGH COMMAND.
GROPE
THERE'S NO NEED FOR YOU TO GIVE ME A CHAIR.
WHAT?

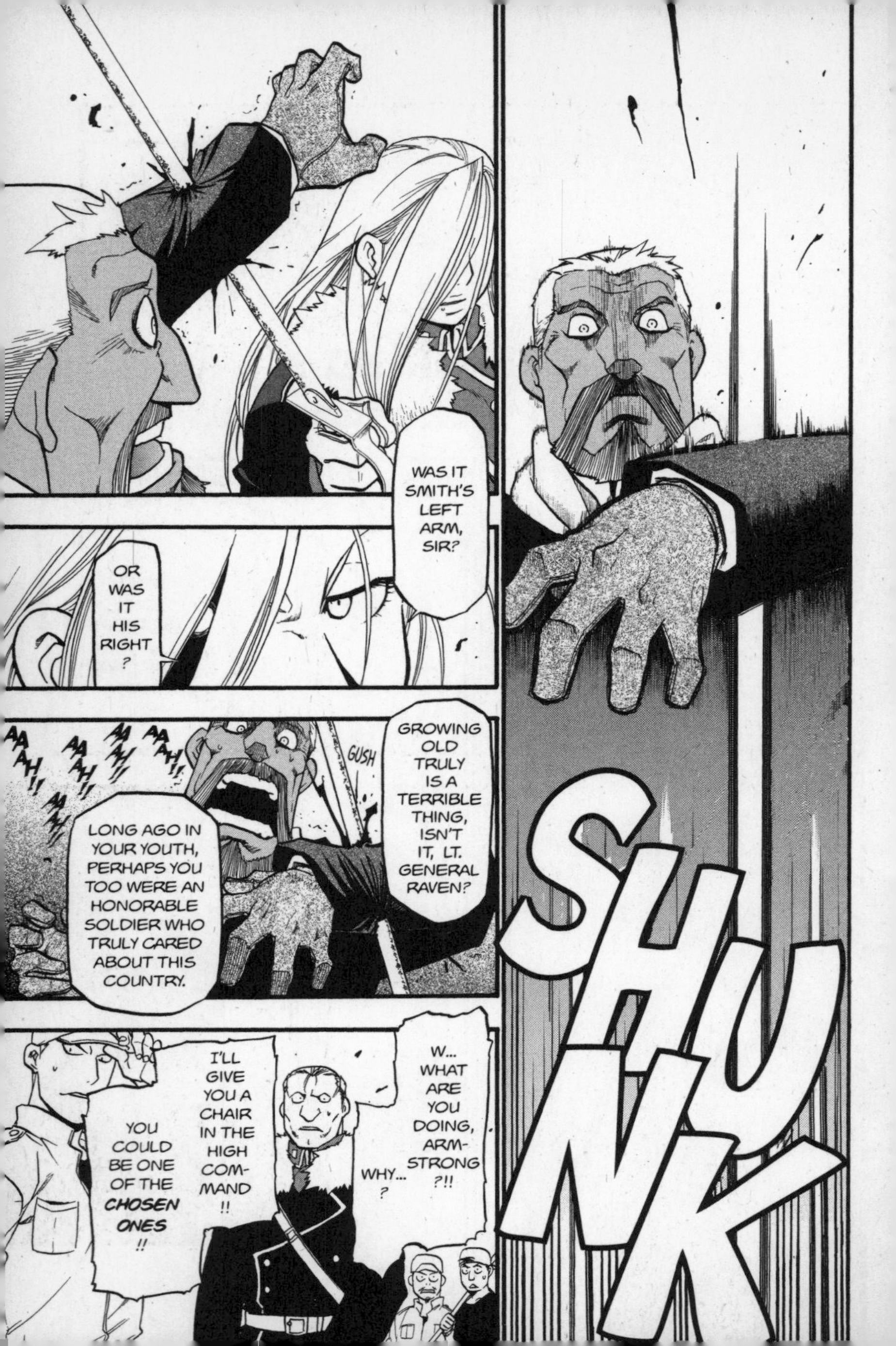
SHUNK
WAS IT SMITH'S LEFT ARM, SIR?
OR WAS IT HIS RIGHT?
GUSH
AAAH!! AAAH!! AAAH!! AAAH!!
GROWING OLD TRULY IS A TERRIBLE THING, ISN'T IT, LT. GENERAL RAVEN?
LONG AGO IN YOUR YOUTH, PERHAPS YOU TOO WERE AN HONORABLE SOLDIER WHO TRULY CARED ABOUT THIS COUNTRY.
W... WHAT ARE YOU DOING, ARM-STRONG?!!
WHY...?
I'LL GIVE YOU A CHAIR IN THE HIGH COM-MAND!!
YOU COULD BE ONE OF THE **CHOSEN ONES**!!

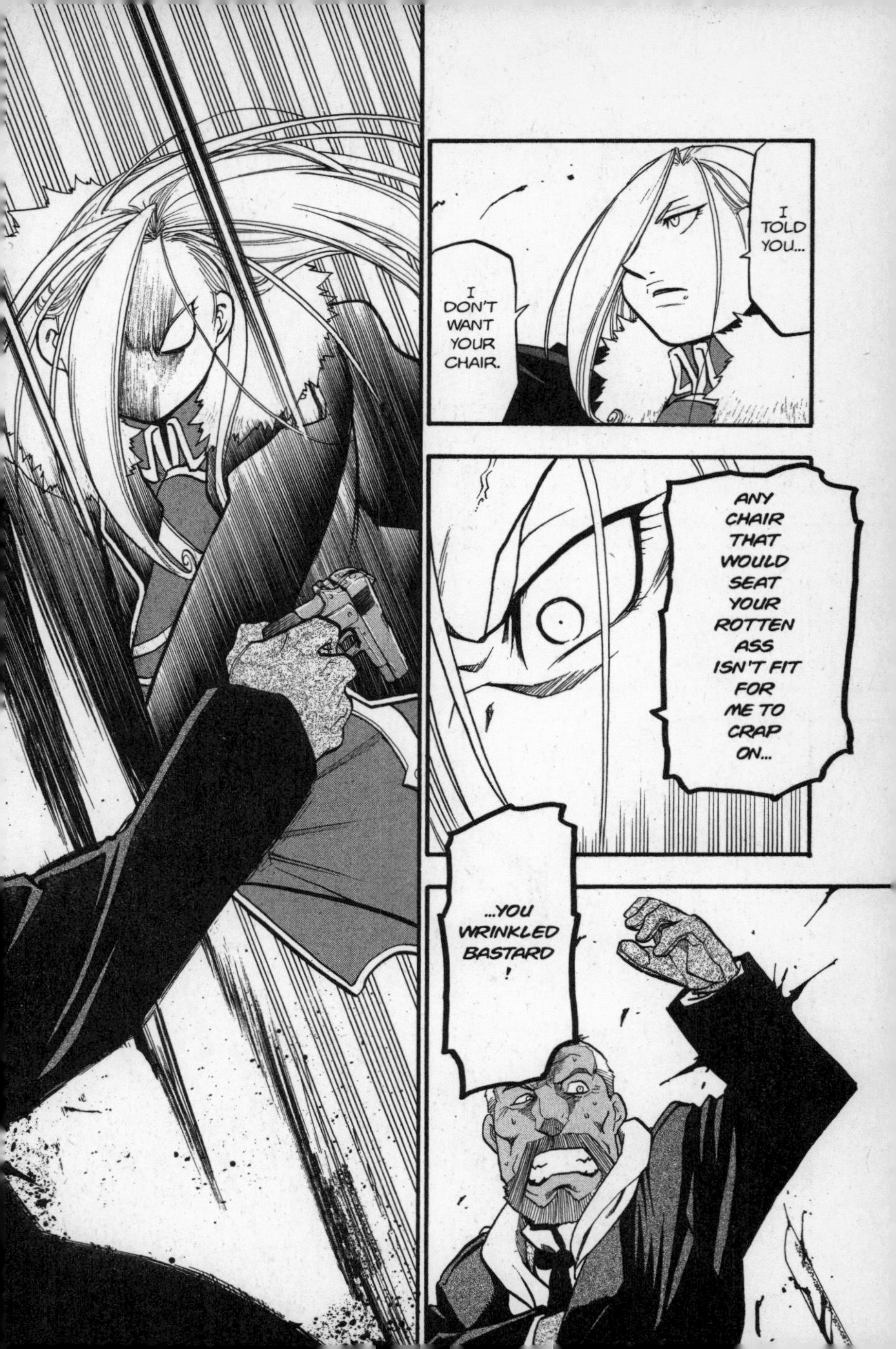
I TOLD YOU...
I DON'T WANT YOUR CHAIR.
ANY CHAIR THAT WOULD SEAT YOUR ROTTEN ASS ISN'T FIT FOR ME TO CRAP ON...
...YOU WRINKLED BASTARD!

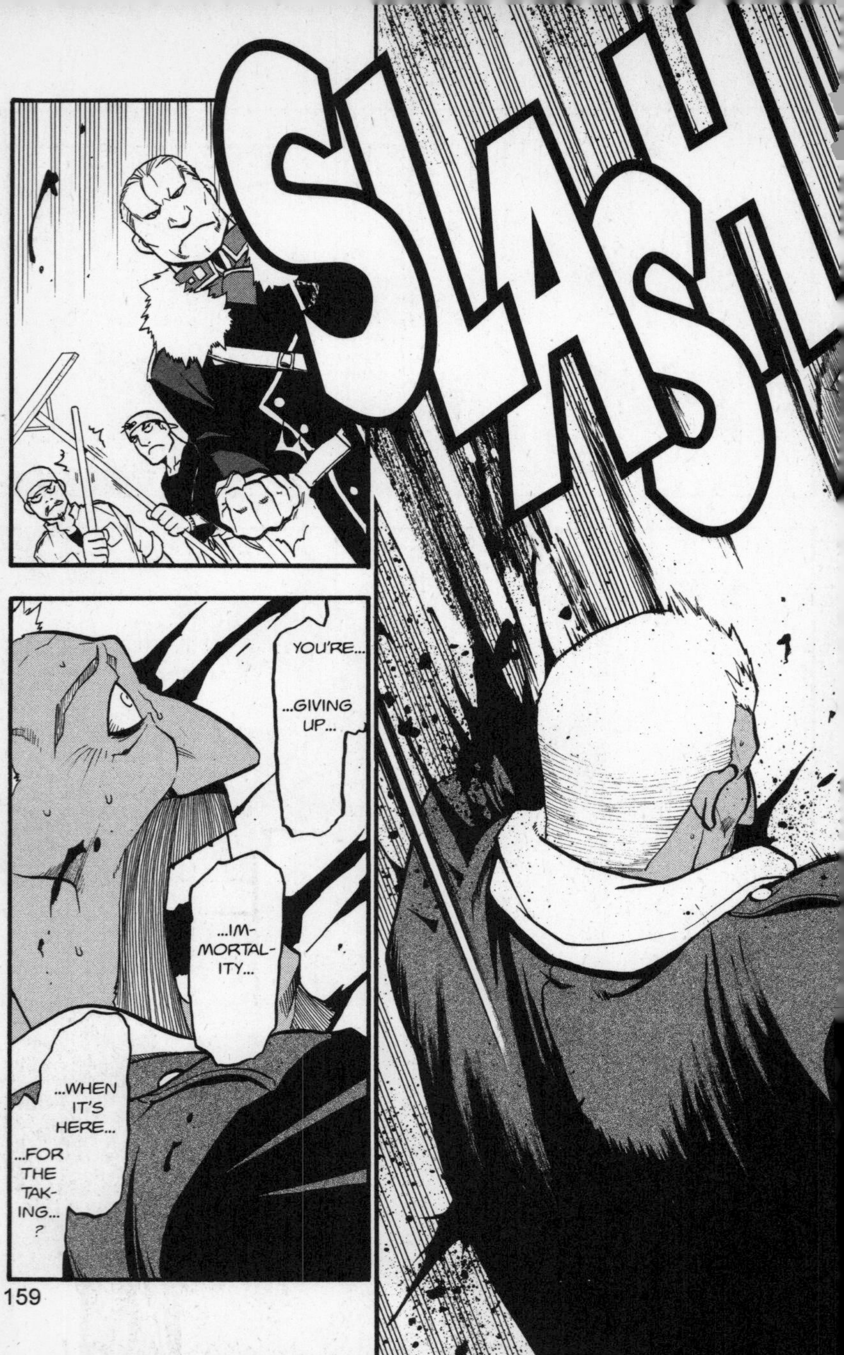
SLASH!
YOU'RE...
...GIVING UP...
...IM-MORTAL-ITY...
...WHEN IT'S HERE...
...FOR THE TAK-ING...?

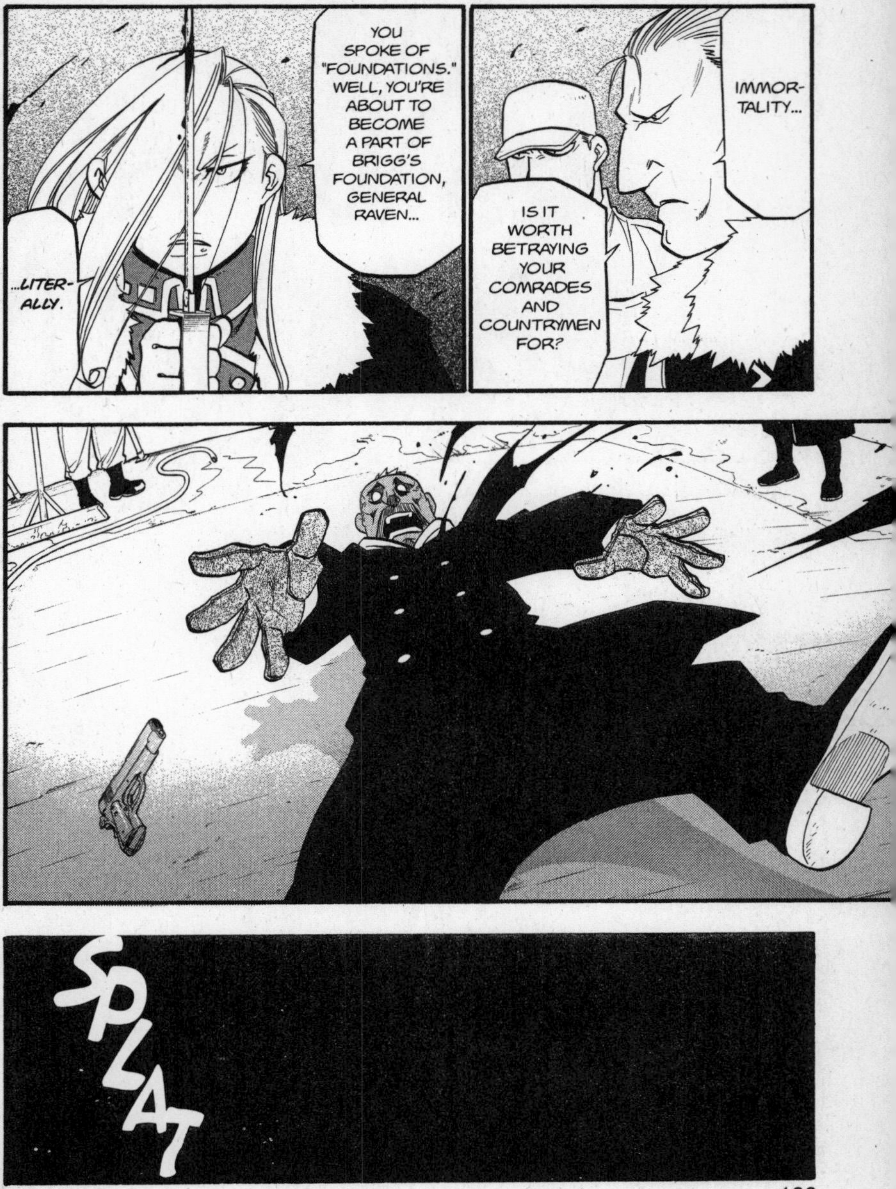
IMMOR-TALITY...
IS IT WORTH BETRAYING YOUR COMRADES AND COUNTRYMEN FOR?
YOU SPOKE OF "FOUNDATIONS." WELL, YOU'RE ABOUT TO BECOME A PART OF BRIGG'S FOUNDATION, GENERAL RAVEN...
...LITER-ALLY.
SPLAT

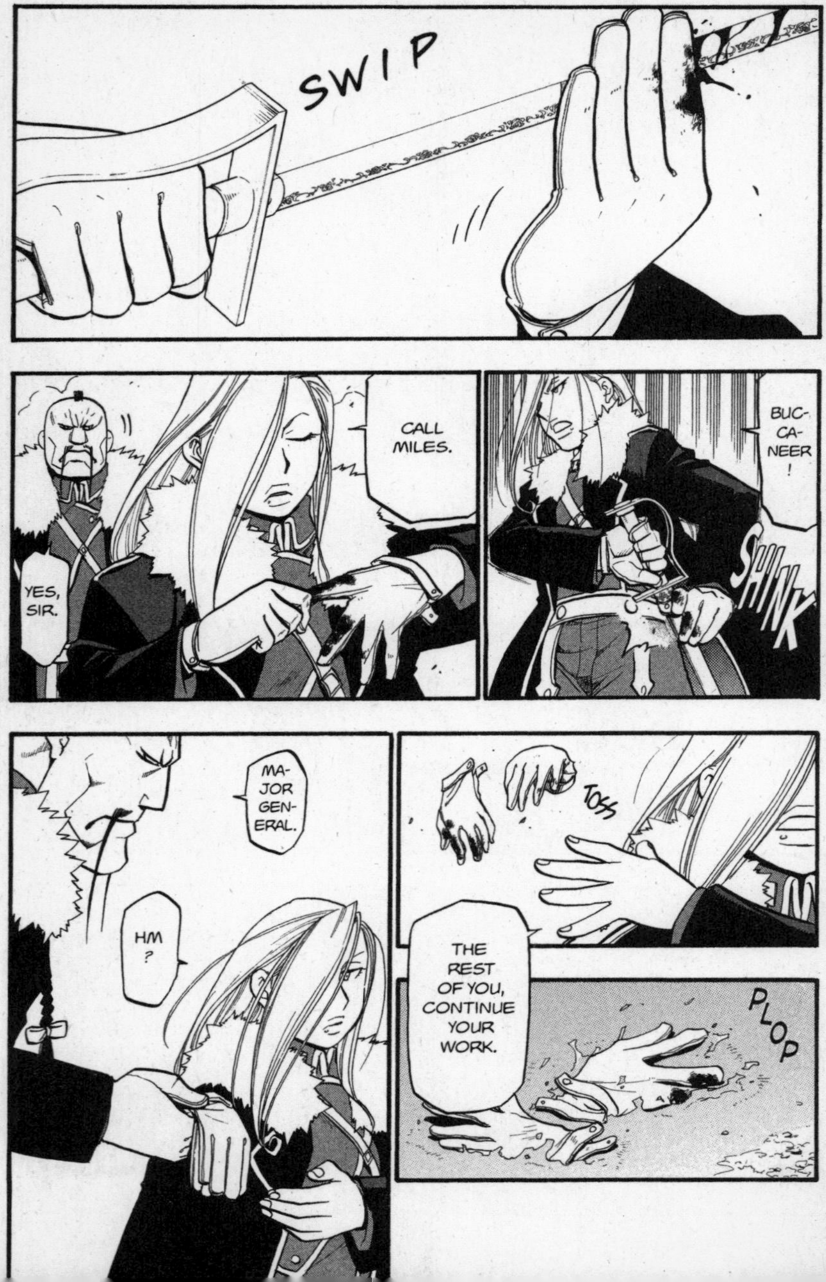
SWIP
BUC-CANEER!
SHINK
CALL MILES.
YES, SIR.
TOSS
THE REST OF YOU, CONTINUE YOUR WORK.
PLOP
MAJOR GENERAL.
HM?

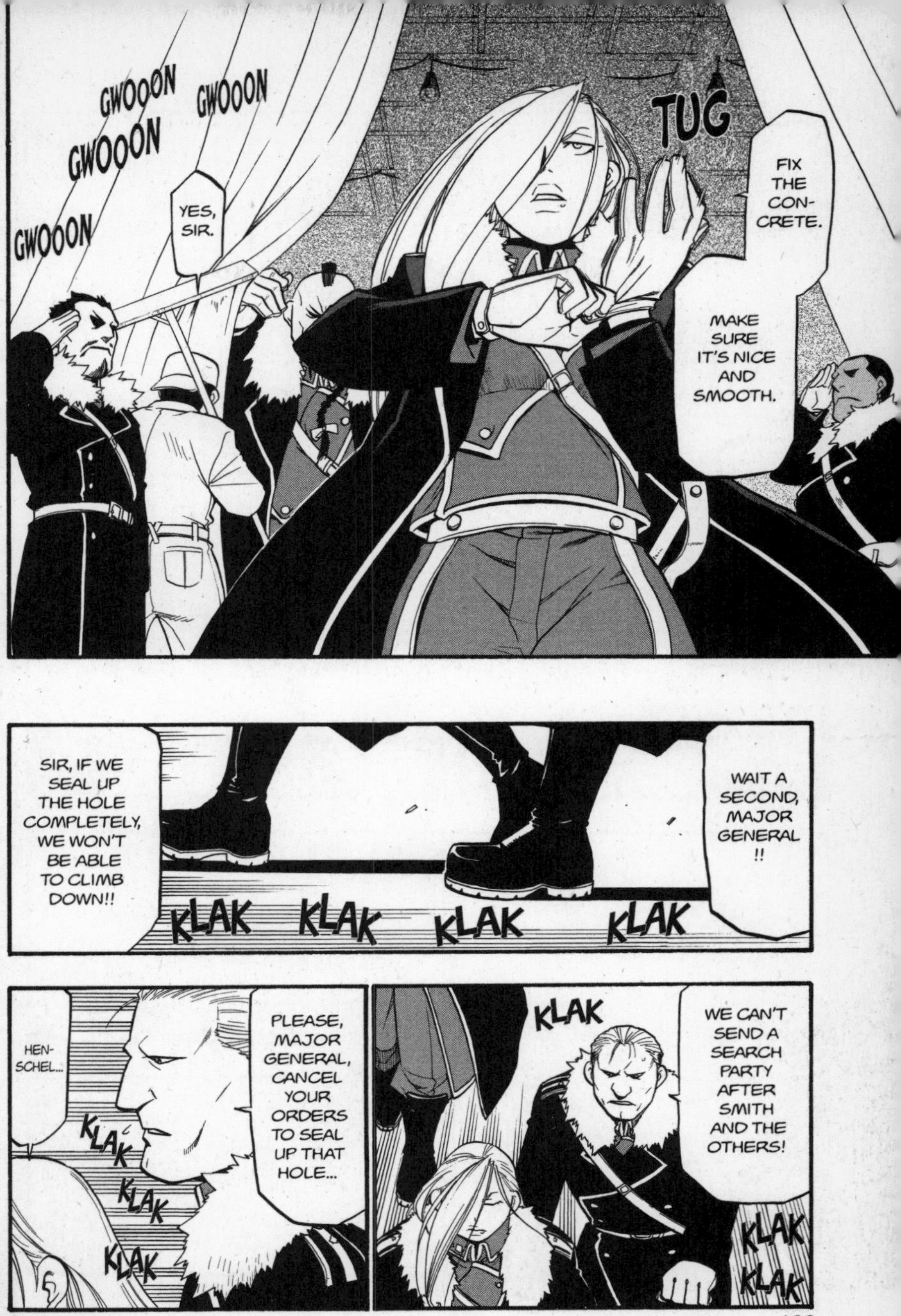
FIX THE CON-CRETE.
TUG
MAKE SURE IT'S NICE AND SMOOTH.
GWOOON
GWOOON
GWOOON
YES, SIR.
GWOOON
WAIT A SECOND, MAJOR GENERAL !!
KLAK
KLAK
KLAK
KLAK
SIR, IF WE SEAL UP THE HOLE COMPLETELY, WE WON'T BE ABLE TO CLIMB DOWN!!
WE CAN'T SEND A SEARCH PARTY AFTER SMITH AND THE OTHERS!
KLAK
KLAK
KLAK
PLEASE, MAJOR GENERAL, CANCEL YOUR ORDERS TO SEAL UP THAT HOLE...
KLAK
KLAK
KLAK
HEN-SCHEL...

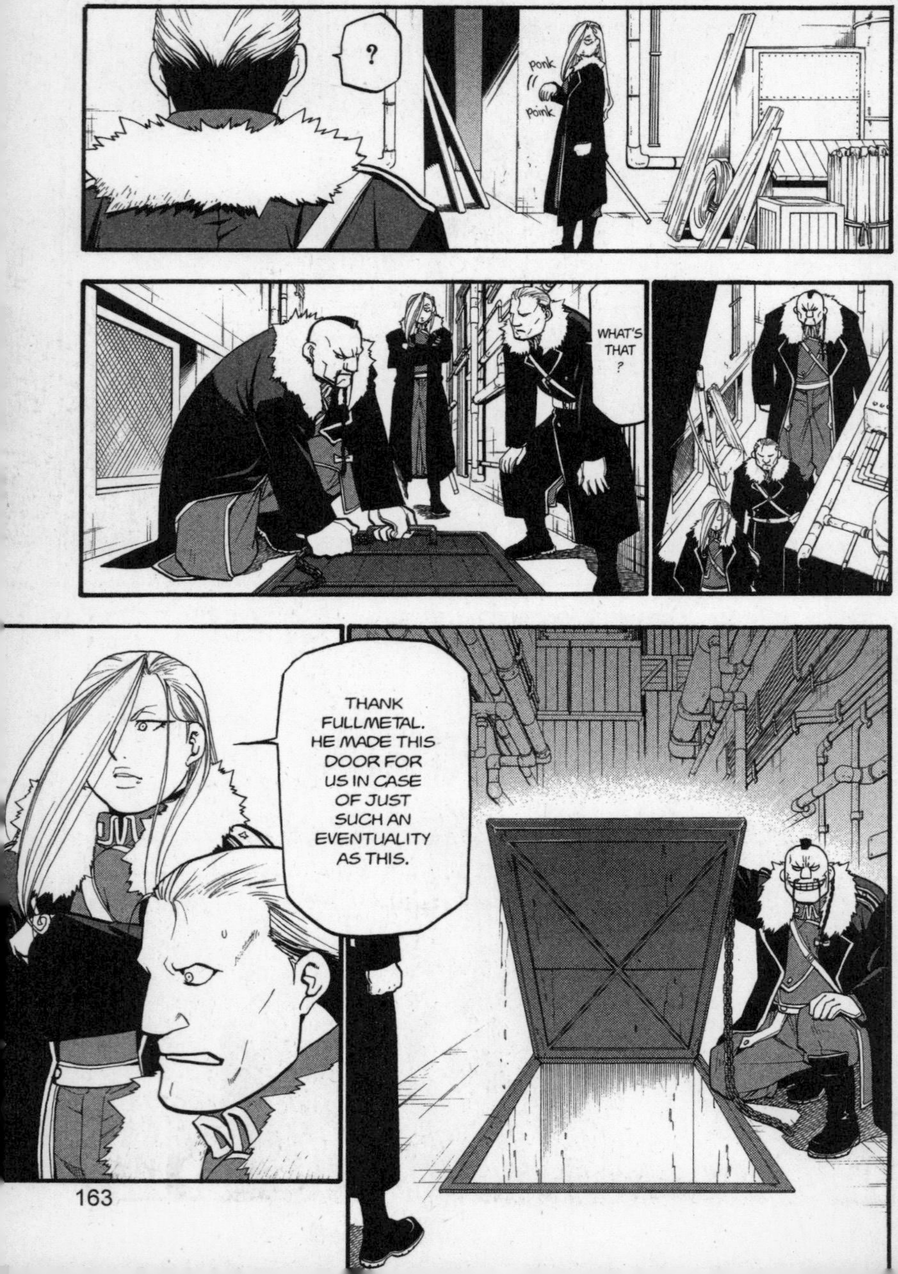
ponk
poink
?
WHAT'S THAT?
THANK FULLMETAL. HE MADE THIS DOOR FOR US IN CASE OF JUST SUCH AN EVENTUALITY AS THIS.

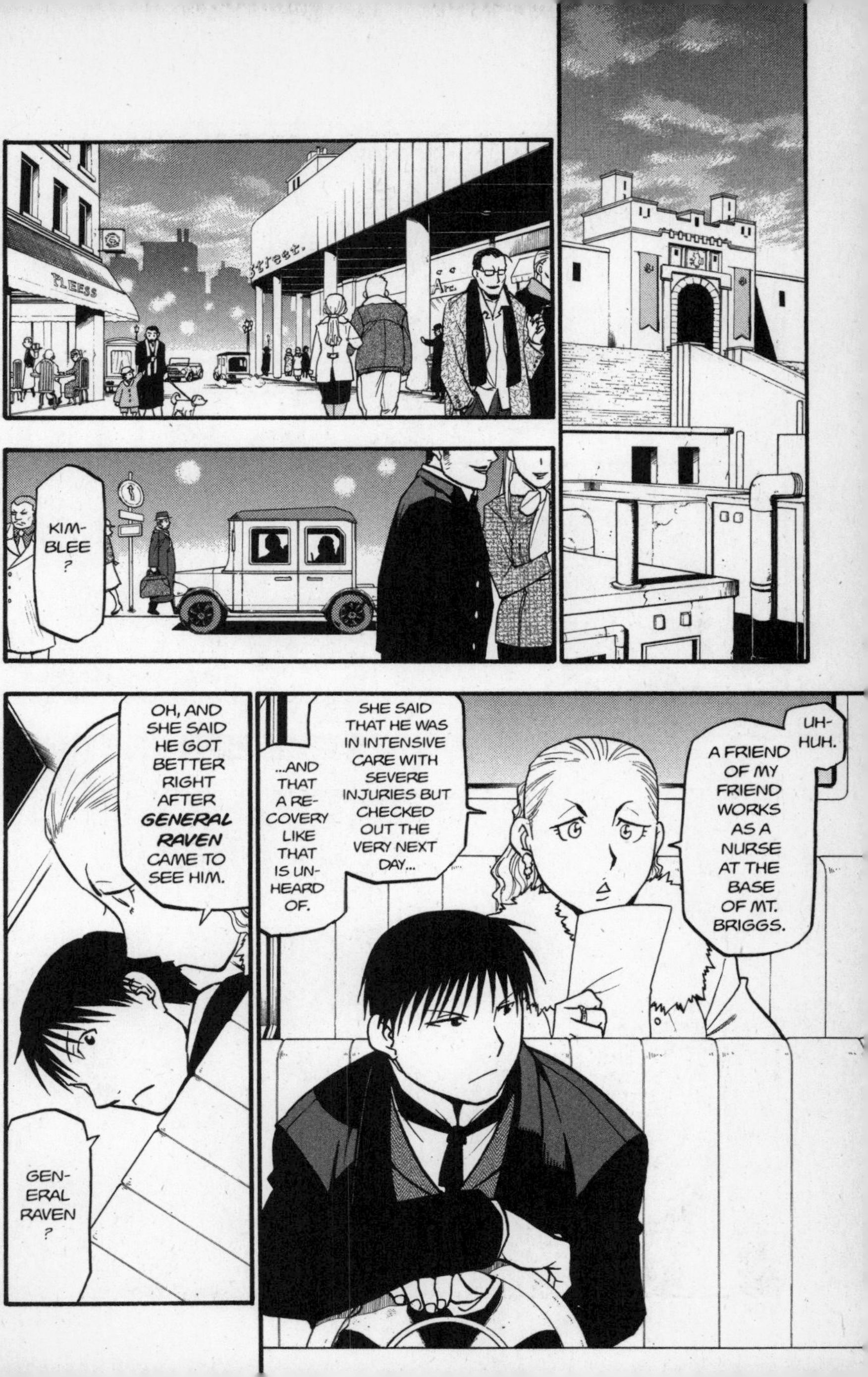

street.
PLEESS
KIM-BLEE?
UH-HUH.
A FRIEND OF MY FRIEND WORKS AS A NURSE AT THE BASE OF MT. BRIGGS.
SHE SAID THAT HE WAS IN INTENSIVE CARE WITH SEVERE INJURIES BUT CHECKED OUT THE VERY NEXT DAY...
...AND THAT A RE-COVERY LIKE THAT IS UN-HEARD OF.
OH, AND SHE SAID HE GOT BETTER RIGHT AFTER **GENERAL RAVEN** CAME TO SEE HIM.
GEN-ERAL RAVEN?

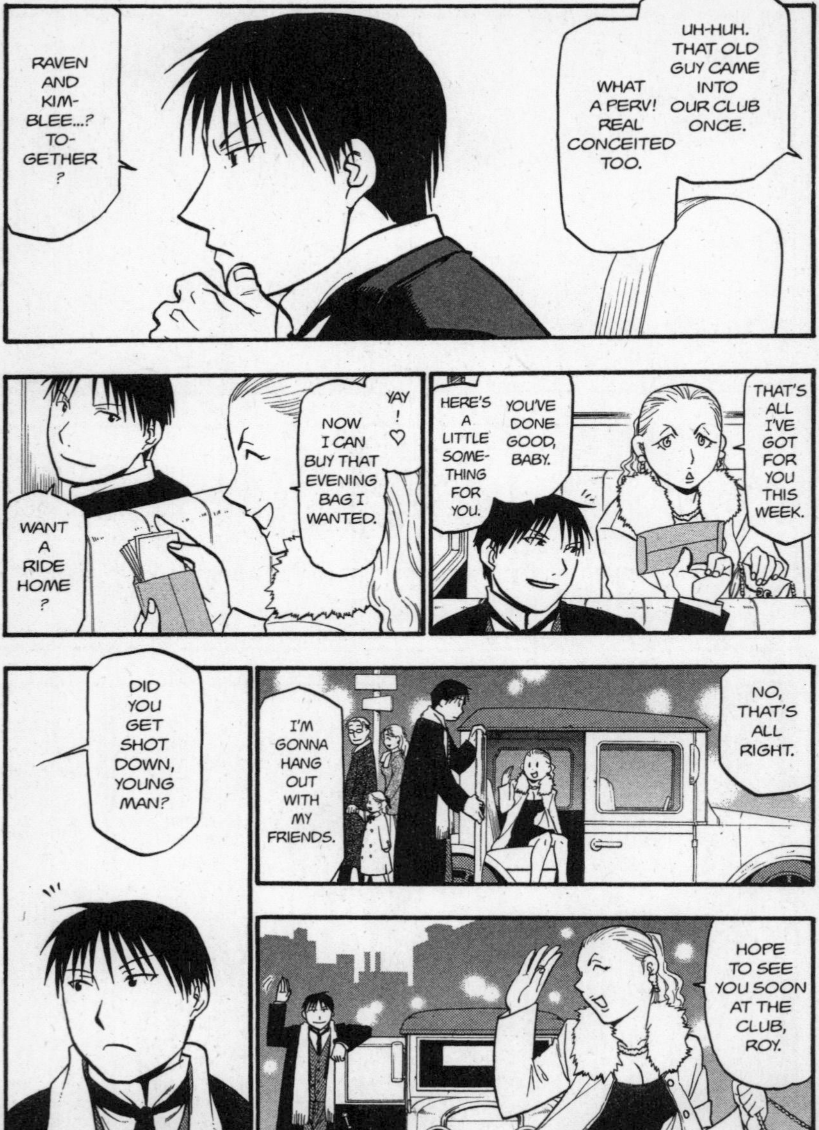
UH-HUH. THAT OLD GUY CAME INTO OUR CLUB ONCE.
WHAT A PERV! REAL CONCEITED TOO.
RAVEN AND KIM-BLEE...? TO-GETHER?
THAT'S ALL I'VE GOT FOR YOU THIS WEEK.
YOU'VE DONE GOOD, BABY.
HERE'S A LITTLE SOME-THING FOR YOU.
YAY! ♥
NOW I CAN BUY THAT EVENING BAG I WANTED.
WANT A RIDE HOME?
NO, THAT'S ALL RIGHT.
I'M GONNA HANG OUT WITH MY FRIENDS.
HOPE TO SEE YOU SOON AT THE CLUB, ROY.
DID YOU GET SHOT DOWN, YOUNG MAN?

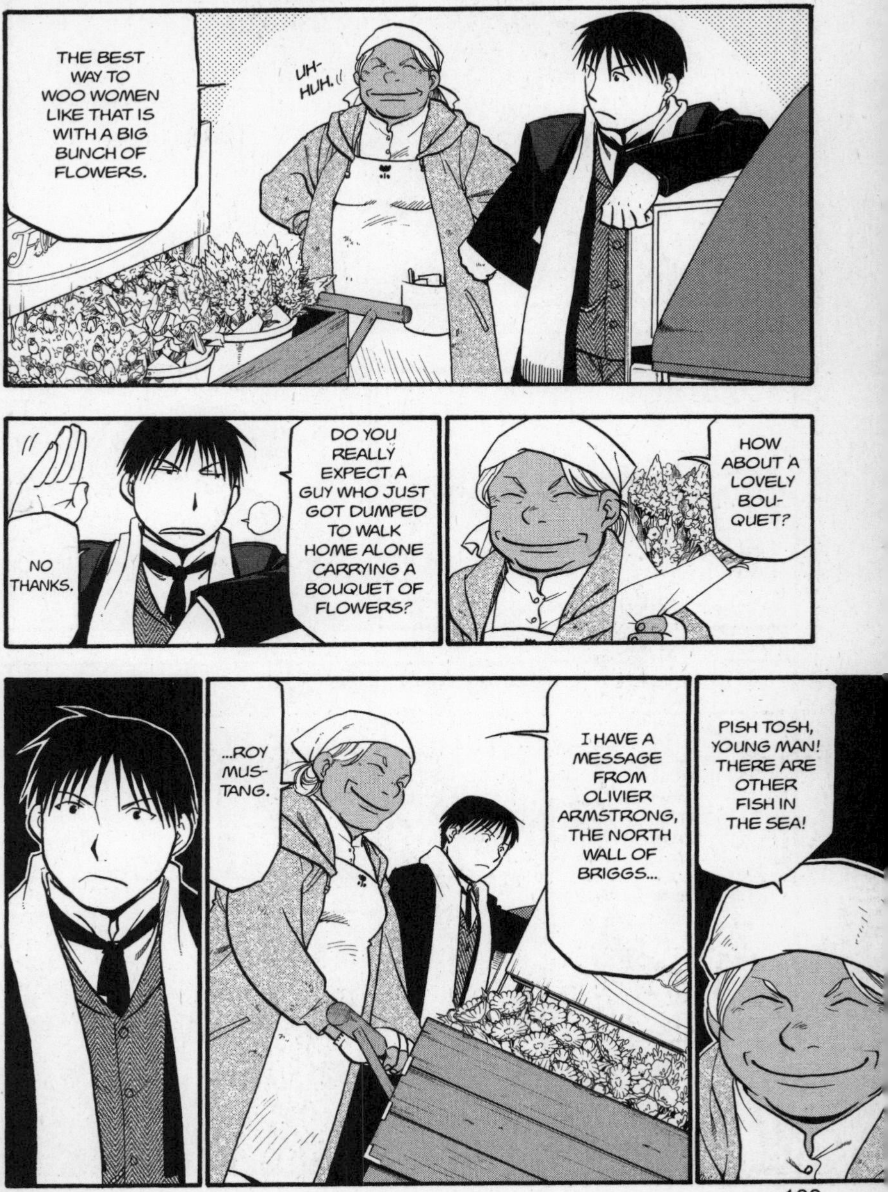
UH-HUH.
THE BEST WAY TO WOO WOMEN LIKE THAT IS WITH A BIG BUNCH OF FLOWERS.
HOW ABOUT A LOVELY BOU-QUET?
DO YOU REALLY EXPECT A GUY WHO JUST GOT DUMPED TO WALK HOME ALONE CARRYING A BOUQUET OF FLOWERS?
NO THANKS.
PISH TOSH, YOUNG MAN! THERE ARE OTHER FISH IN THE SEA!
I HAVE A MESSAGE FROM OLIVIER ARMSTRONG, THE NORTH WALL OF BRIGGS...
...ROY MUS-TANG.

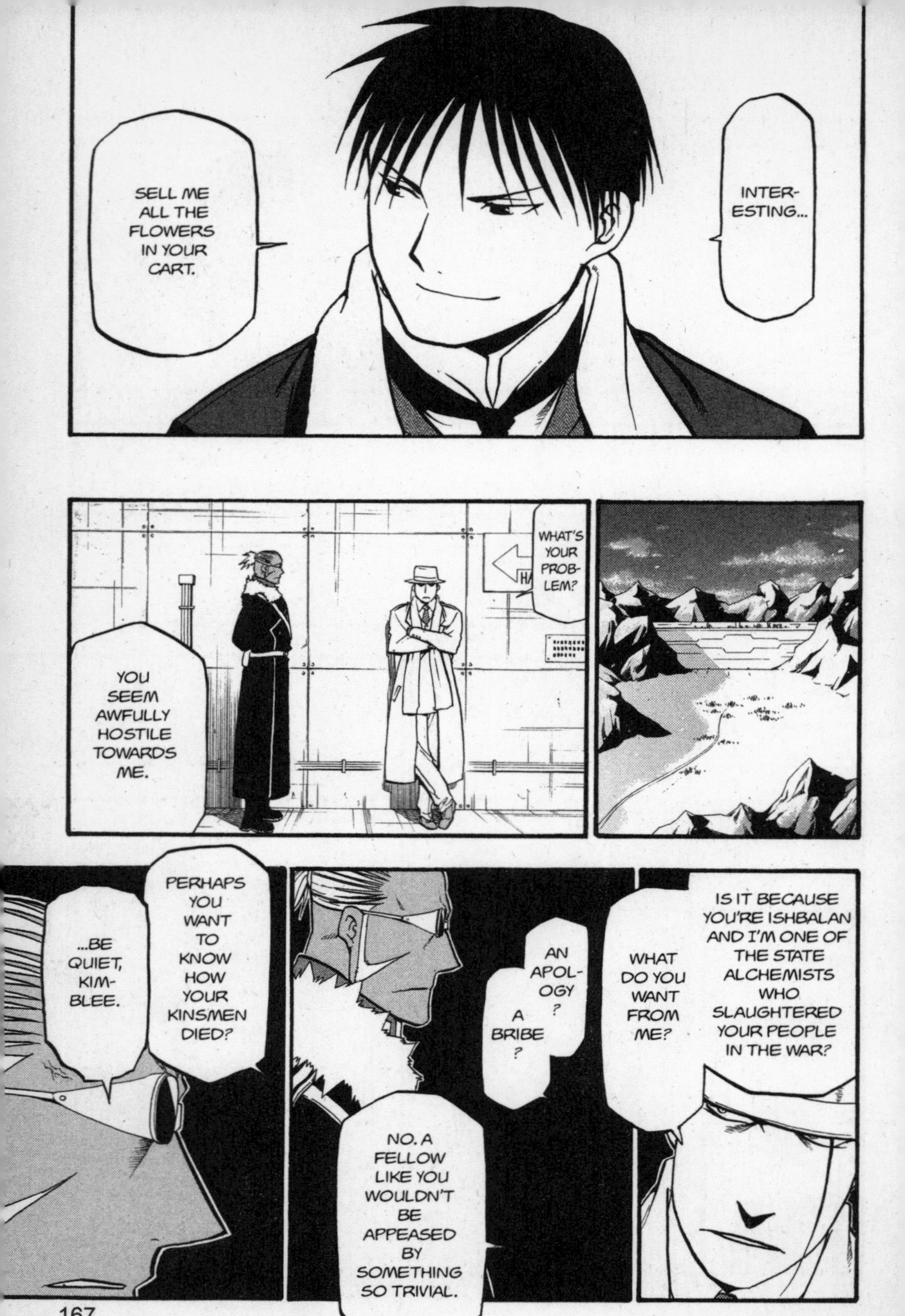
INTER-ESTING...
SELL ME ALL THE FLOWERS IN YOUR CART.
WHAT'S YOUR PROB-LEM?
YOU SEEM AWFULLY HOSTILE TOWARDS ME.
IS IT BECAUSE YOU'RE ISHBALAN AND I'M ONE OF THE STATE ALCHEMISTS WHO SLAUGHTERED YOUR PEOPLE IN THE WAR?
WHAT DO YOU WANT FROM ME?
AN APOL-OGY?
A BRIBE?
NO. A FELLOW LIKE YOU WOULDN'T BE APPEASED BY SOMETHING SO TRIVIAL.
PERHAPS YOU WANT TO KNOW HOW YOUR KINSMEN DIED?
...BE QUIET, KIM-BLEE.

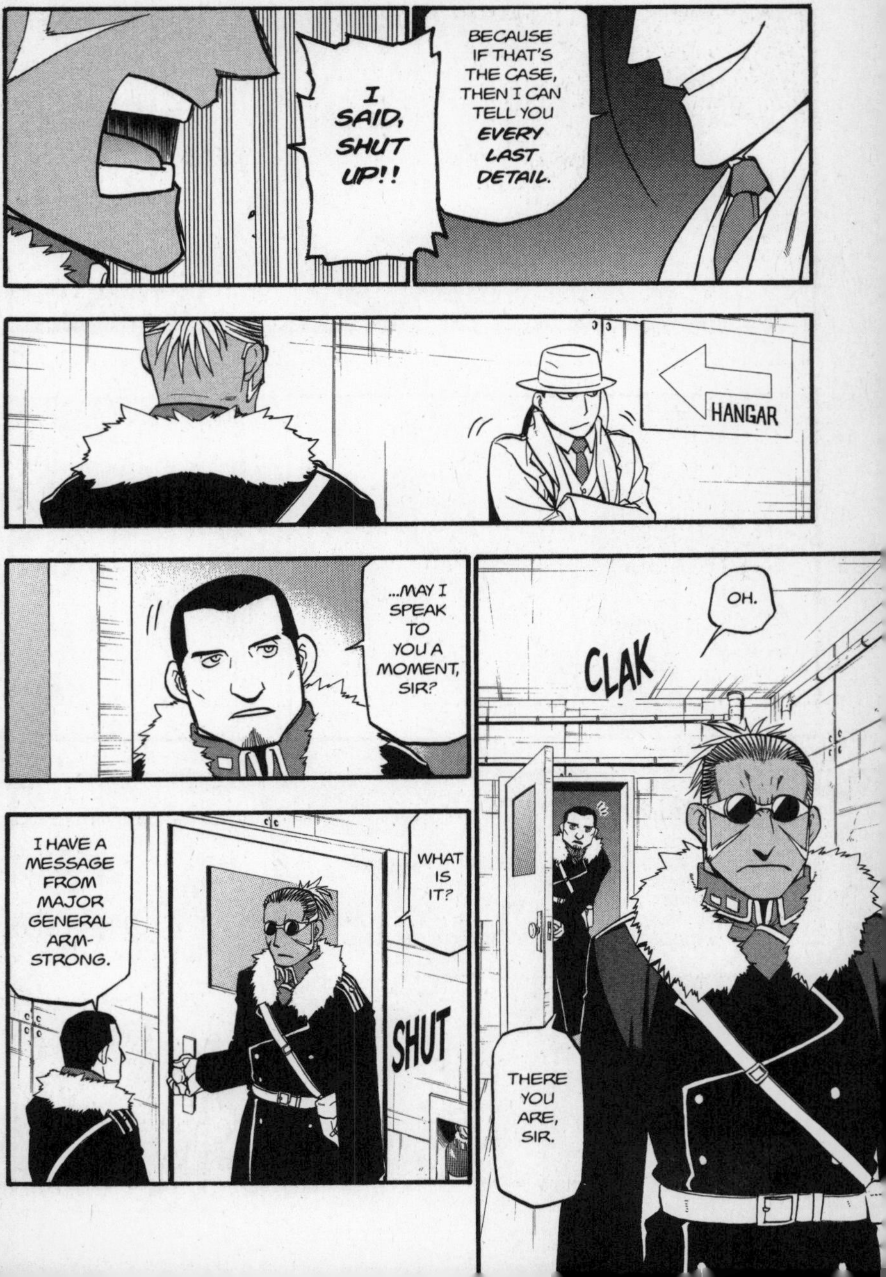
BECAUSE IF THAT'S THE CASE, THEN I CAN TELL YOU *EVERY LAST DETAIL.*
I SAID, SHUT UP!!
HANGAR
OH.
CLAK
THERE YOU ARE, SIR.
...MAY I SPEAK TO YOU A MOMENT, SIR?
WHAT IS IT?
SHUT
I HAVE A MESSAGE FROM MAJOR GENERAL ARM-STRONG.

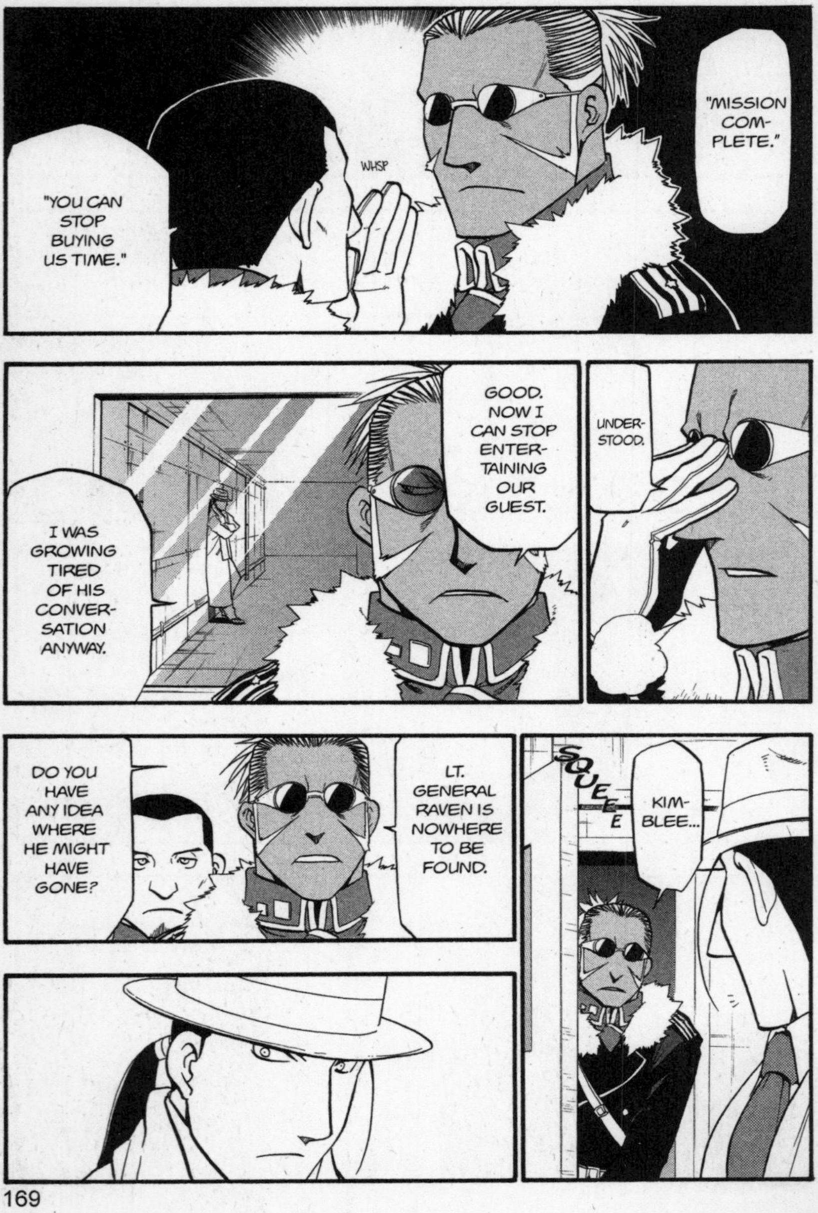
"MISSION COM-PLETE."
WHSP
"YOU CAN STOP BUYING US TIME."
UNDER-STOOD.
GOOD. NOW I CAN STOP ENTER-TAINING OUR GUEST.
I WAS GROWING TIRED OF HIS CONVER-SATION ANYWAY.
SQUEEEE
KIM-BLEE...
LT. GENERAL RAVEN IS NOWHERE TO BE FOUND.
DO YOU HAVE ANY IDEA WHERE HE MIGHT HAVE GONE?

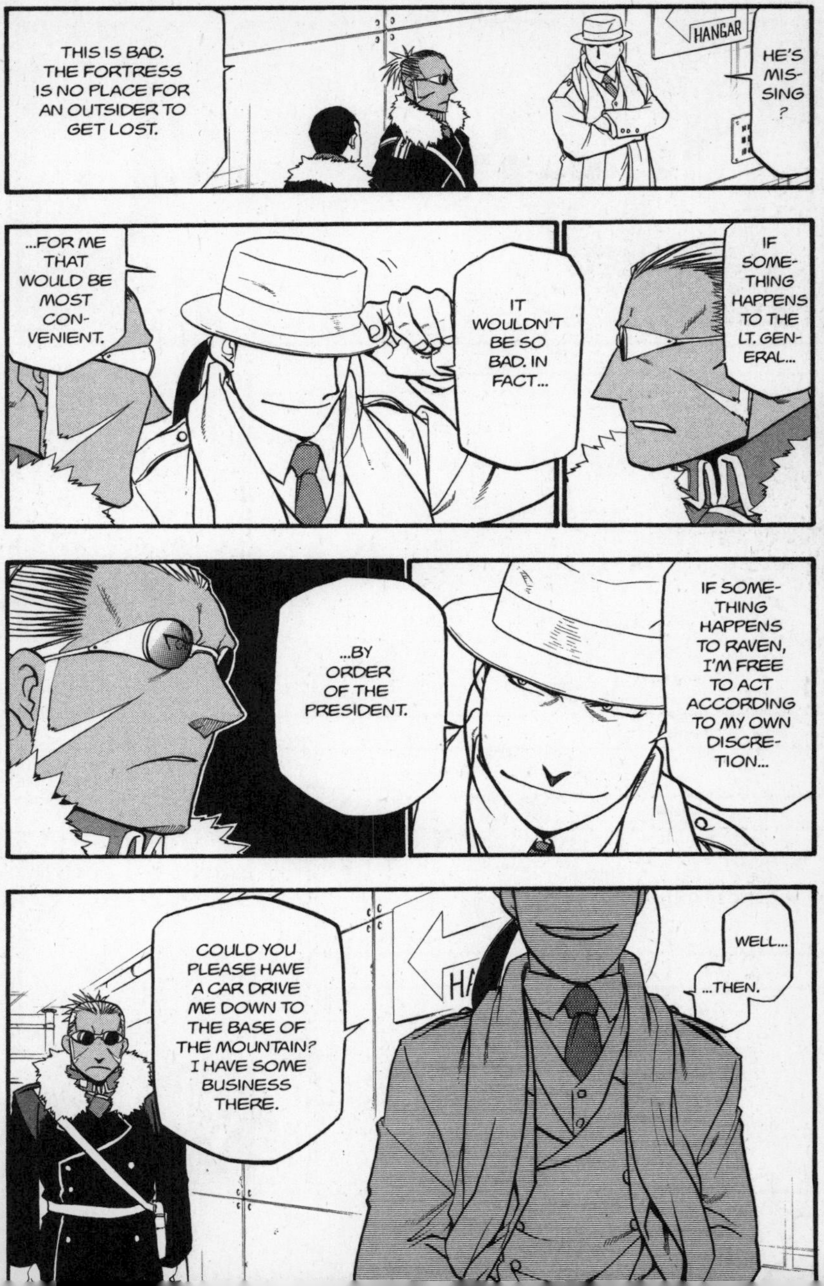
HANGAR
HE'S MISSING?
THIS IS BAD. THE FORTRESS IS NO PLACE FOR AN OUTSIDER TO GET LOST.
IF SOMETHING HAPPENS TO THE LT. GENERAL...
IT WOULDN'T BE SO BAD. IN FACT...
...FOR ME THAT WOULD BE MOST CONVENIENT.
IF SOMETHING HAPPENS TO RAVEN, I'M FREE TO ACT ACCORDING TO MY OWN DISCRETION...
...BY ORDER OF THE PRESIDENT.
WELL...
...THEN.
COULD YOU PLEASE HAVE A CAR DRIVE ME DOWN TO THE BASE OF THE MOUNTAIN? I HAVE SOME BUSINESS THERE.

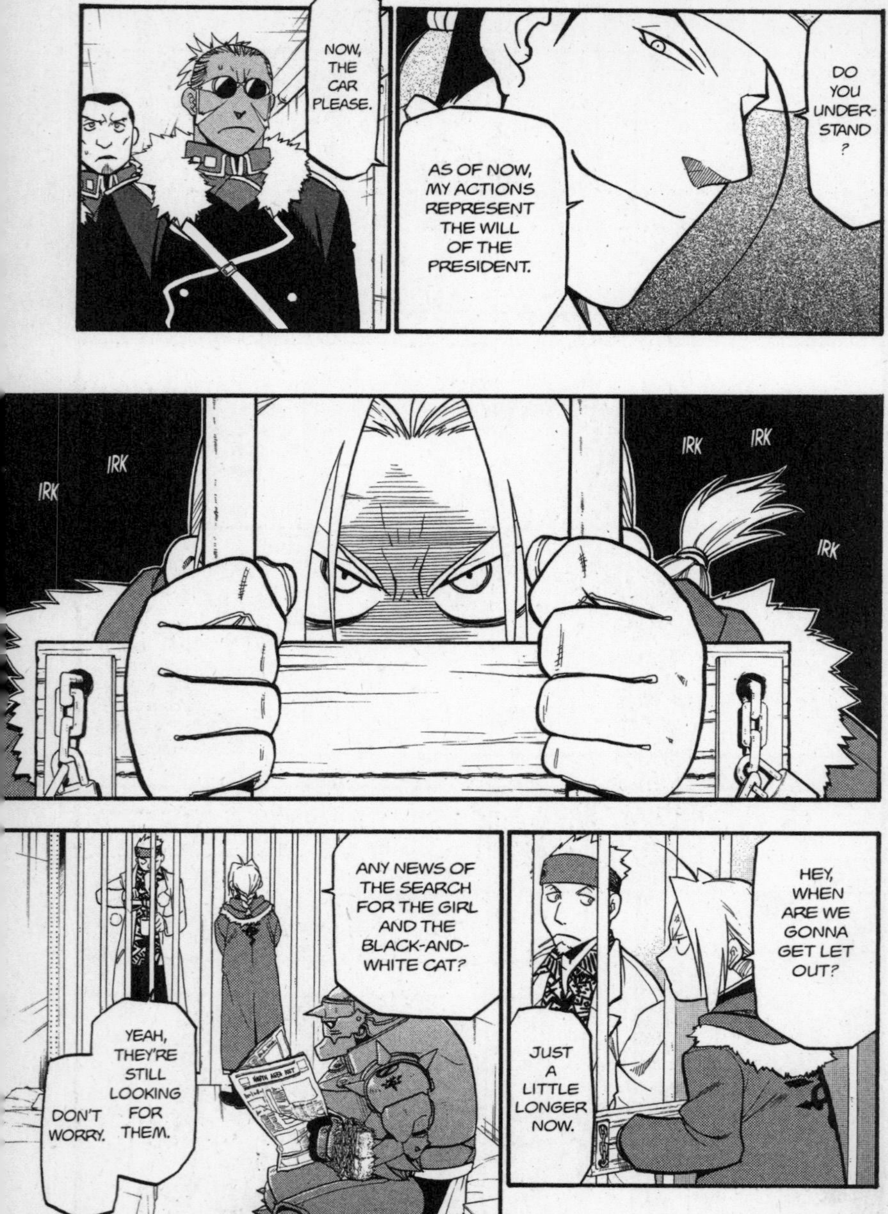
DO YOU UNDERSTAND?
AS OF NOW, MY ACTIONS REPRESENT THE WILL OF THE PRESIDENT.
NOW, THE CAR PLEASE.
IRK
IRK
IRK
IRK
IRK
HEY, WHEN ARE WE GONNA GET LET OUT?
JUST A LITTLE LONGER NOW.
ANY NEWS OF THE SEARCH FOR THE GIRL AND THE BLACK-AND-WHITE CAT?
YEAH, THEY'RE STILL LOOKING FOR THEM.
DON'T WORRY.

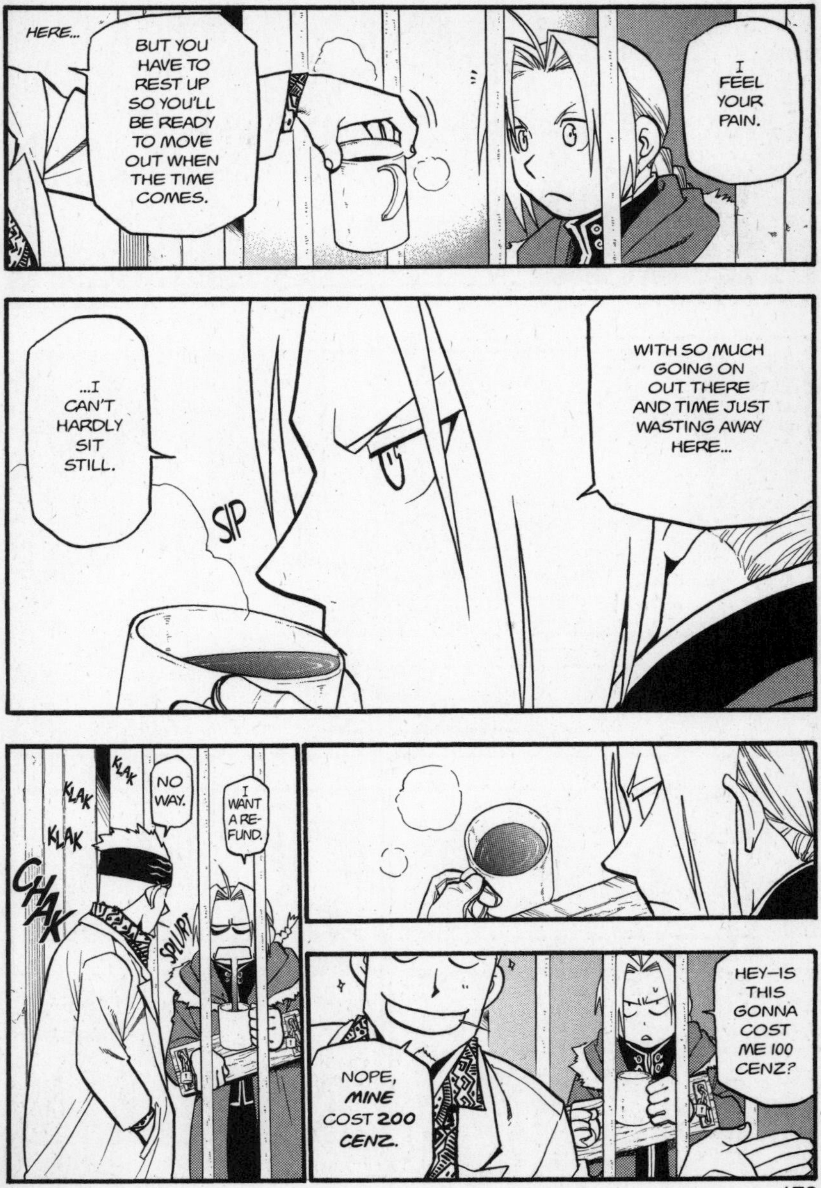
I FEEL YOUR PAIN.
HERE...
BUT YOU HAVE TO REST UP SO YOU'LL BE READY TO MOVE OUT WHEN THE TIME COMES.
WITH SO MUCH GOING ON OUT THERE AND TIME JUST WASTING AWAY HERE...
...I CAN'T HARDLY SIT STILL.
SIP
HEY—IS THIS GONNA COST ME 100 CENZ?
NOPE, *MINE* COST 200 CENZ.
KLAK
NO WAY.
I WANT A RE-FUND.
KLAK
KLAK
CHAK
SPLURT

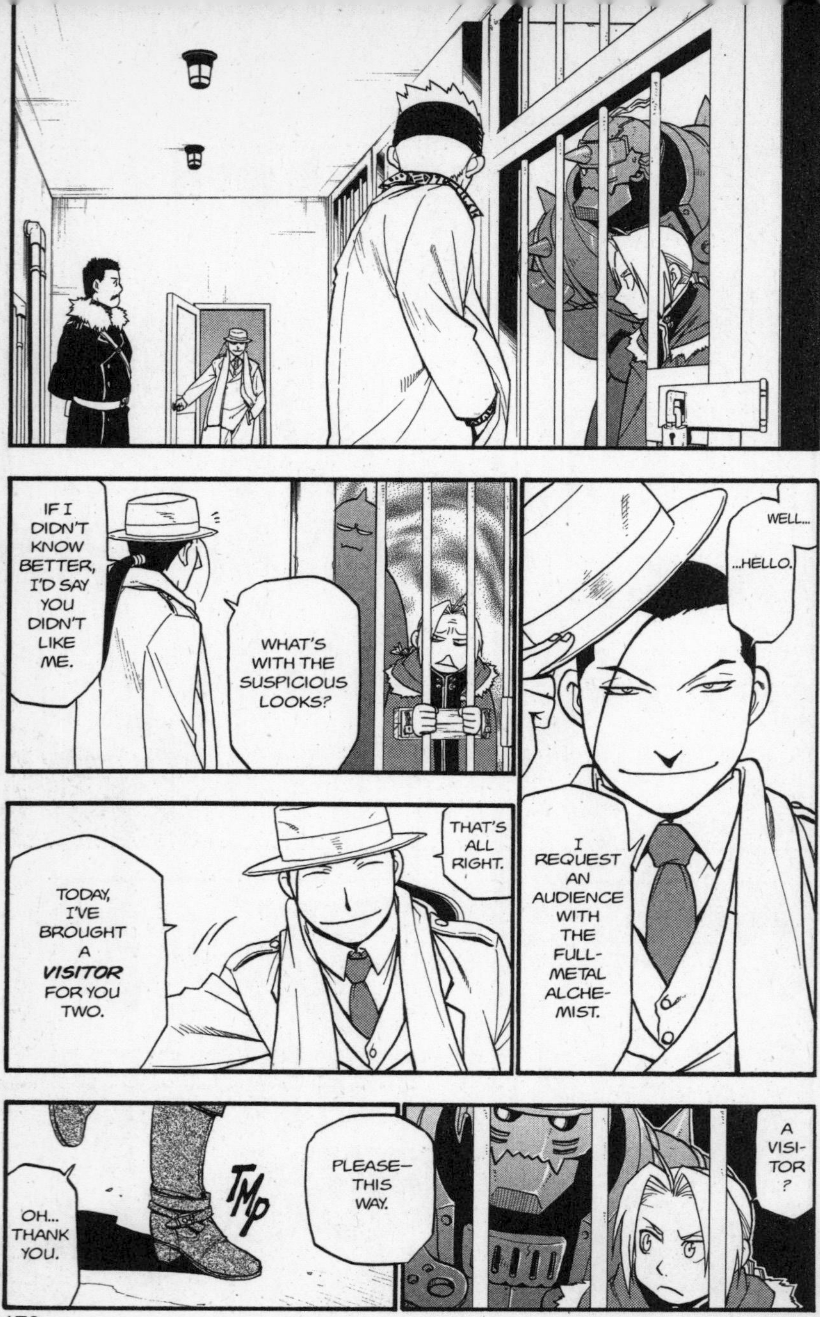
WELL...
...HELLO.
I REQUEST AN AUDIENCE WITH THE FULL-METAL ALCHEMIST.
WHAT'S WITH THE SUSPICIOUS LOOKS?
IF I DIDN'T KNOW BETTER, I'D SAY YOU DIDN'T LIKE ME.
THAT'S ALL RIGHT.
TODAY, I'VE BROUGHT A **VISITOR** FOR YOU TWO.
A VISI-TOR?
PLEASE— THIS WAY.
TMP
OH... THANK YOU.

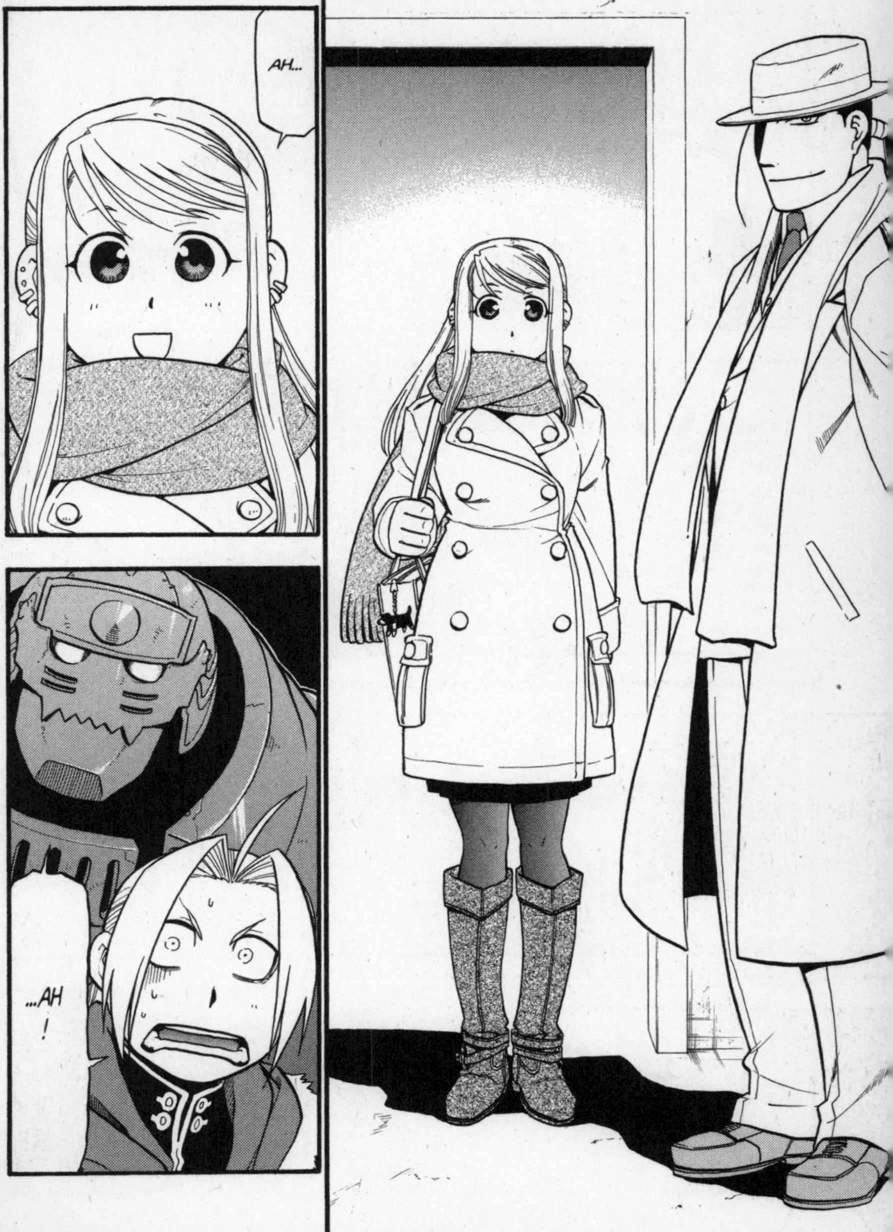
AH...
...AH !

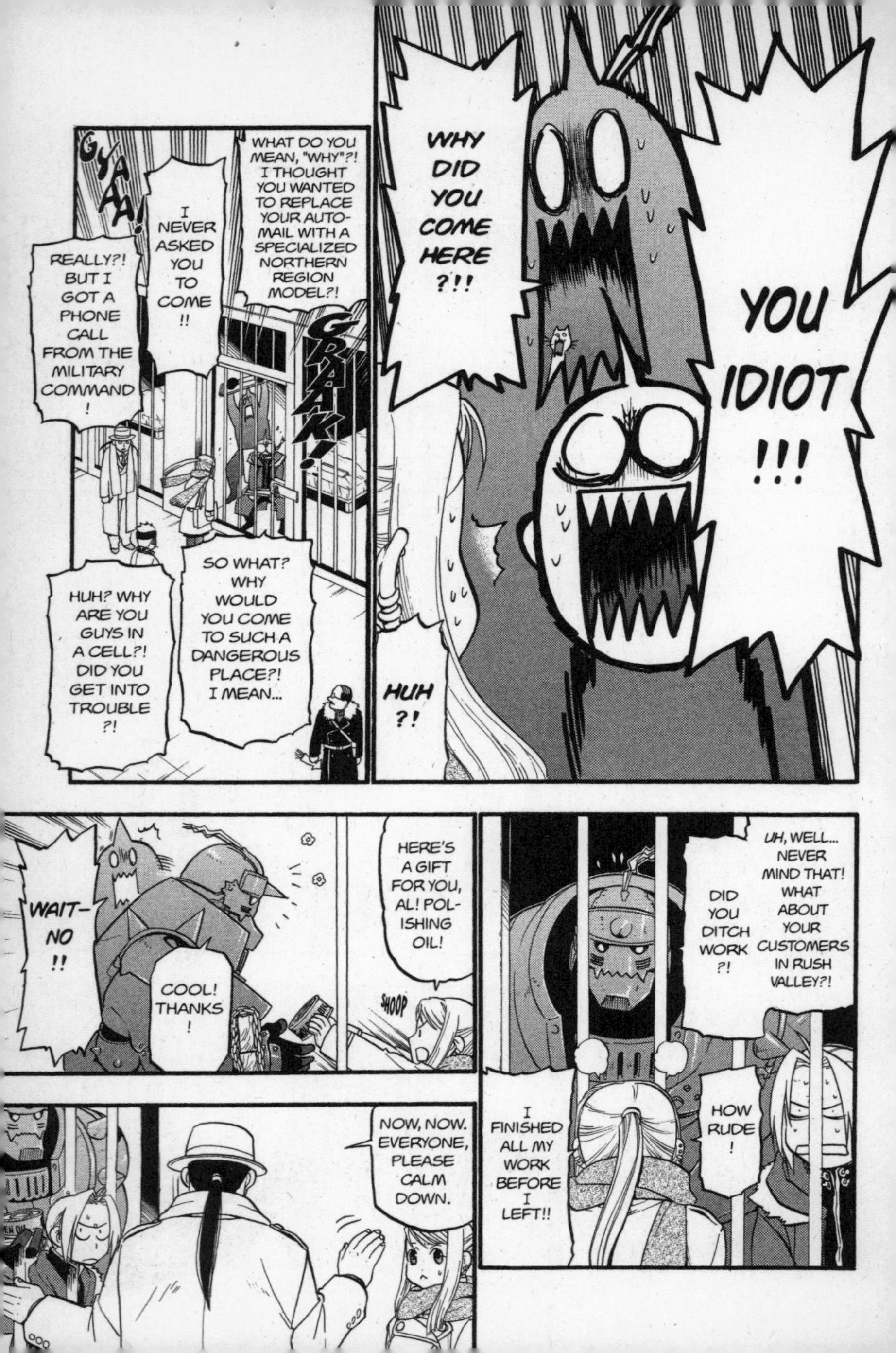
WHY DID YOU COME HERE?!!
YOU IDIOT!!!
HUH?!
WHAT DO YOU MEAN, "WHY"?! I THOUGHT YOU WANTED TO REPLACE YOUR AUTO-MAIL WITH A SPECIALIZED NORTHERN REGION MODEL?!
I NEVER ASKED YOU TO COME!!
GYAAA!
REALLY?! BUT I GOT A PHONE CALL FROM THE MILITARY COMMAND!
GRABAK!
SO WHAT? WHY WOULD YOU COME TO SUCH A DANGEROUS PLACE?! I MEAN...
HUH? WHY ARE YOU GUYS IN A CELL?! DID YOU GET INTO TROUBLE?!
UH, WELL... NEVER MIND THAT! WHAT ABOUT YOUR CUSTOMERS IN RUSH VALLEY?!
DID YOU DITCH WORK?!
HOW RUDE!
I FINISHED ALL MY WORK BEFORE I LEFT!!
HERE'S A GIFT FOR YOU, AL! POL-ISHING OIL!
SHOOP
WAIT—NO!!
COOL! THANKS!
NOW, NOW. EVERYONE, PLEASE CALM DOWN.

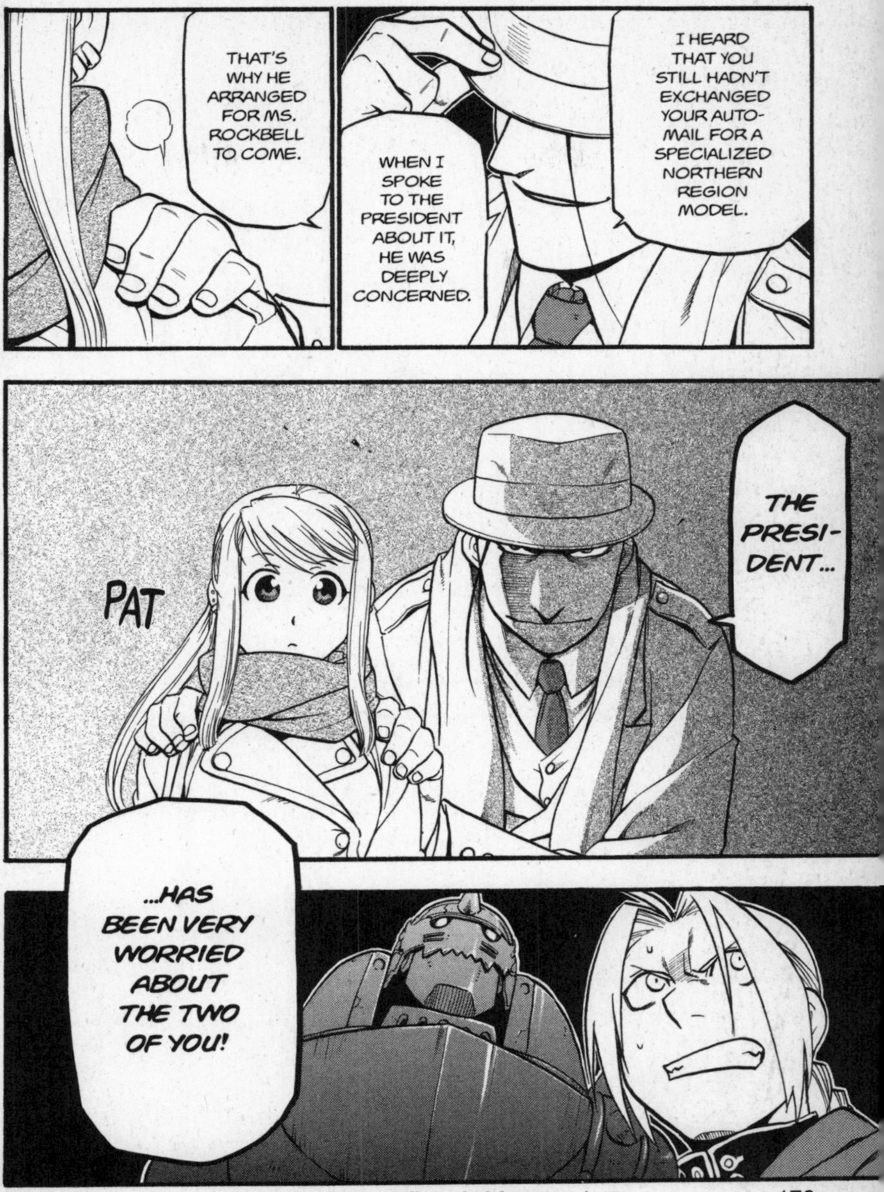
I HEARD THAT YOU STILL HADN'T EXCHANGED YOUR AUTO-MAIL FOR A SPECIALIZED NORTHERN REGION MODEL.
WHEN I SPOKE TO THE PRESIDENT ABOUT IT, HE WAS DEEPLY CONCERNED.
THAT'S WHY HE ARRANGED FOR MS. ROCKBELL TO COME.
THE PRESI-DENT...
PAT
...HAS BEEN VERY WORRIED ABOUT THE TWO OF YOU!

To be continued in **Fullmetal Alchemist** Vol. 17

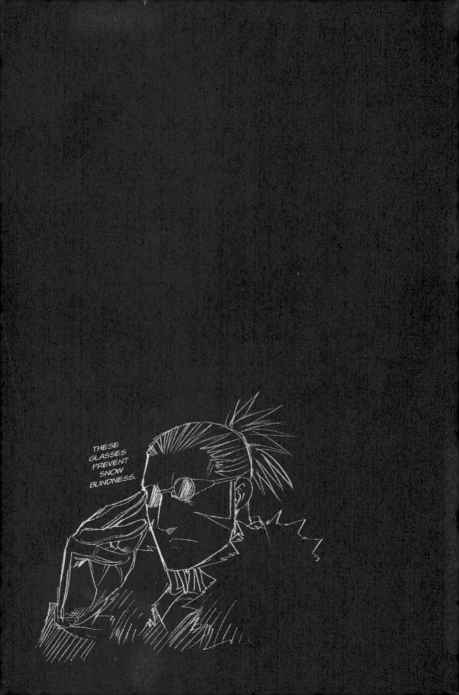

THESE
GLASSES
PREVENT
SNOW
BLINDNESS.

FULLMETAL
ALCHEMIST

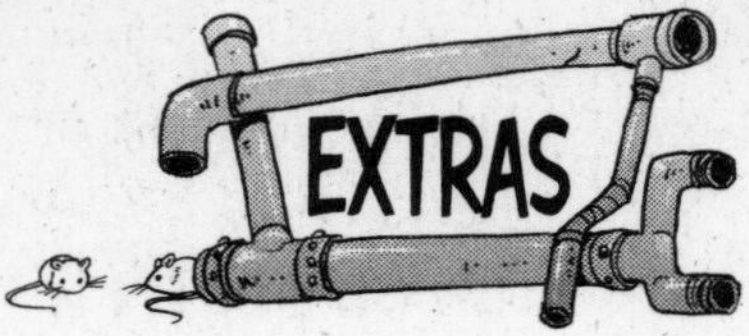
EXTRAS

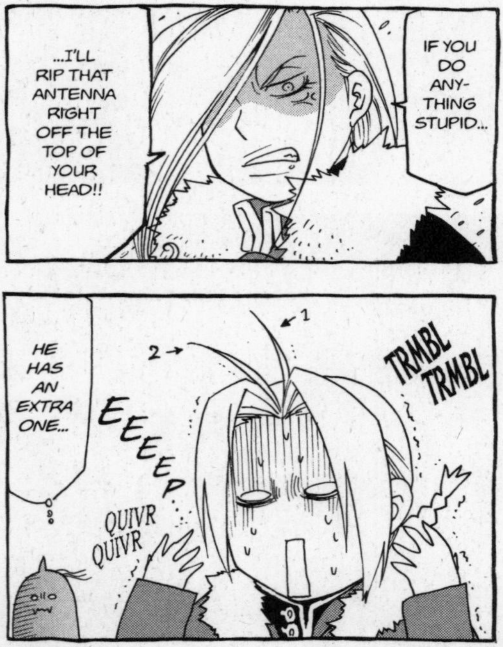
IF YOU DO ANY-THING STUPID...
...I'LL RIP THAT ANTENNA RIGHT OFF THE TOP OF YOUR HEAD!!
TRMBL TRMBL
1
2
EEEEP
HE HAS AN EXTRA ONE...
QUIVR QUIVR

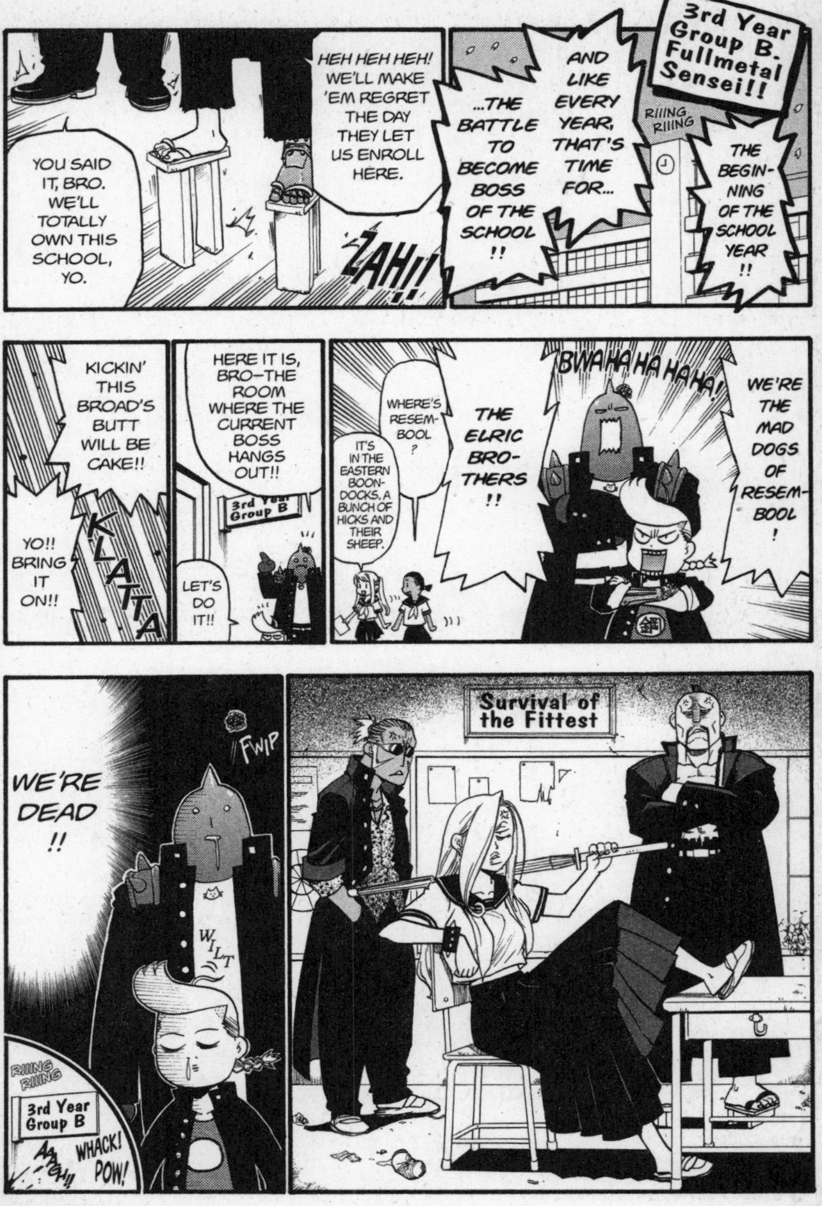
3rd Year Group B. Fullmetal Sensei!!
RIIING RIIING
THE BEGIN-NING OF THE SCHOOL YEAR !!
AND LIKE EVERY YEAR, THAT'S TIME FOR...
...THE BATTLE TO BECOME BOSS OF THE SCHOOL !!
HEH HEH HEH! WE'LL MAKE 'EM REGRET THE DAY THEY LET US ENROLL HERE.
ZAH!!
YOU SAID IT, BRO. WE'LL TOTALLY OWN THIS SCHOOL, YO.
WE'RE THE MAD DOGS OF RESEM-BOOL !
BWAHAHAHAHA!
THE ELRIC BRO-THERS !!
WHERE'S RESEM-BOOL ?
IT'S IN THE EASTERN BOON-DOCKS. A BUNCH OF HICKS AND THEIR SHEEP.
HERE IT IS, BRO—THE ROOM WHERE THE CURRENT BOSS HANGS OUT!!
3rd Year Group B
LET'S DO IT!!
KICKIN' THIS BROAD'S BUTT WILL BE CAKE!!
KLATTA
YO!! BRING IT ON!!
Survival of the Fittest
FWIP
WE'RE DEAD !!
WILT
RIIING RIIING
3rd Year Group B
WHACK! POW!
AAAGH!!

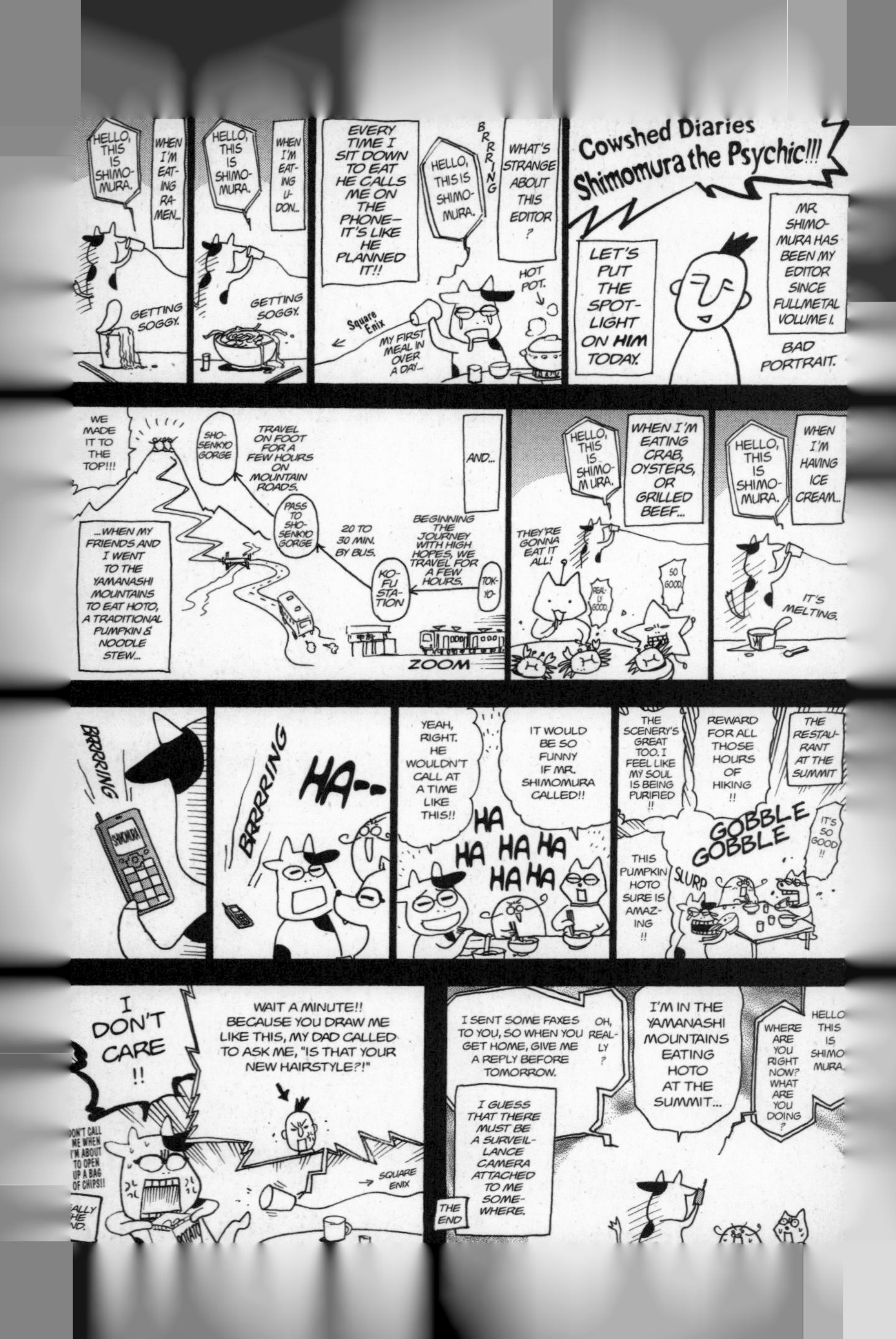
Cowshed Diaries
Shimomura the Psychic!!!
MR. SHIMOMURA HAS BEEN MY EDITOR SINCE FULLMETAL VOLUME 1.
LET'S PUT THE SPOTLIGHT ON HIM TODAY.
BAD PORTRAIT.
WHAT'S STRANGE ABOUT THIS EDITOR?
BRRRRING
HELLO, THIS IS SHIMOMURA.
EVERY TIME I SIT DOWN TO EAT HE CALLS ME ON THE PHONE— IT'S LIKE HE PLANNED IT!!
HOT POT.
Square Enix
MY FIRST MEAL IN OVER A DAY...
WHEN I'M EATING UDON...
HELLO, THIS IS SHIMOMURA.
GETTING SOGGY.
WHEN I'M EATING RAMEN...
HELLO, THIS IS SHIMOMURA.
GETTING SOGGY.
WHEN I'M HAVING ICE CREAM...
HELLO, THIS IS SHIMOMURA.
IT'S MELTING.
WHEN I'M EATING CRAB, OYSTERS, OR GRILLED BEEF...
HELLO, THIS IS SHIMOMURA.
THEY'RE GONNA EAT IT ALL!
SO GOOD.
REALLY GOOD.
AND...
...WHEN MY FRIENDS AND I WENT TO THE YAMANASHI MOUNTAINS TO EAT HOTO, A TRADITIONAL PUMPKIN & NOODLE STEW...
TOKYO
BEGINNING THE JOURNEY WITH HIGH HOPES, WE TRAVEL FOR A FEW HOURS.
KOFU STATION
20 TO 30 MIN. BY BUS.
PASS TO SHOSENKYO GORGE
TRAVEL ON FOOT FOR A FEW HOURS ON MOUNTAIN ROADS.
SHOSENKYO GORGE
WE MADE IT TO THE TOP!!!
ZOOM
THE RESTAURANT AT THE SUMMIT
REWARD FOR ALL THOSE HOURS OF HIKING!!
THE SCENERY'S GREAT TOO. I FEEL LIKE MY SOUL IS BEING PURIFIED!!
GOBBLE GOBBLE
IT'S SO GOOD!!
THIS PUMPKIN HOTO SURE IS AMAZING!!
SLURP
IT WOULD BE SO FUNNY IF MR. SHIMOMURA CALLED!!
YEAH, RIGHT. HE WOULDN'T CALL AT A TIME LIKE THIS!!
HA HA HA HA HA HA
HA--
BRRRRING
BRRRRING
SHIMOMURA
HELLO THIS IS SHIMOMURA.
WHERE ARE YOU RIGHT NOW? WHAT ARE YOU DOING?
I'M IN THE YAMANASHI MOUNTAINS EATING HOTO AT THE SUMMIT...
OH, REALLY?
I SENT SOME FAXES TO YOU, SO WHEN YOU GET HOME, GIVE ME A REPLY BEFORE TOMORROW.
I GUESS THAT THERE MUST BE A SURVEILLANCE CAMERA ATTACHED TO ME SOMEWHERE.
THE END
WAIT A MINUTE!! BECAUSE YOU DRAW ME LIKE THIS, MY DAD CALLED TO ASK ME, "IS THAT YOUR NEW HAIRSTYLE?!"
SQUARE ENIX
I DON'T CARE!!
ON'T CALL ME WHEN 'M ABOUT TO OPEN UP A BAG OF CHIPS!!

Edward & The Magic Lamp 3

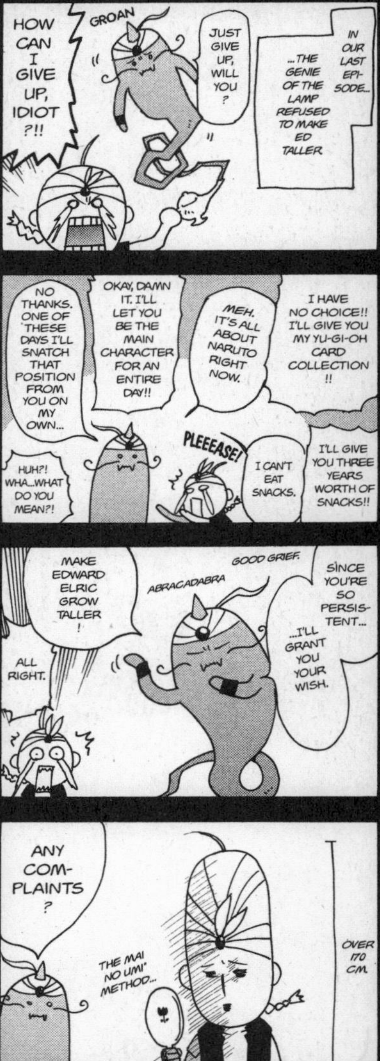
IN OUR LAST EPI-SODE...
...THE GENIE OF THE LAMP REFUSED TO MAKE ED TALLER
JUST GIVE UP, WILL YOU?
GROAN
HOW CAN I GIVE UP, IDIOT?!!
I HAVE NO CHOICE!! I'LL GIVE YOU MY YU-GI-OH CARD COLLECTION!!
MEH. IT'S ALL ABOUT NARUTO RIGHT NOW.
OKAY, DAMN IT. I'LL LET YOU BE THE MAIN CHARACTER FOR AN ENTIRE DAY!!
NO THANKS. ONE OF THESE DAYS I'LL SNATCH THAT POSITION FROM YOU ON MY OWN...
I'LL GIVE YOU THREE YEARS WORTH OF SNACKS!!
I CAN'T EAT SNACKS.
PLEEEASE!
HUH?! WHA...WHAT DO YOU MEAN?!
SINCE YOU'RE SO PERSIS-TENT...
...I'LL GRANT YOU YOUR WISH.
GOOD GRIEF.
ABRACADABRA
MAKE EDWARD ELRIC GROW TALLER!
ALL RIGHT.
OVER 170 CM.
ANY COM-PLAINTS?
THE MAI NO UMI* METHOD...

*MAI NO UMI IS A SUMO WRESTLER WHO IMPLANTED SILICONE IN HIS HEAD TO MEET SUMO HEIGHT REQUIREMENTS.

Havoc & The Magic Books

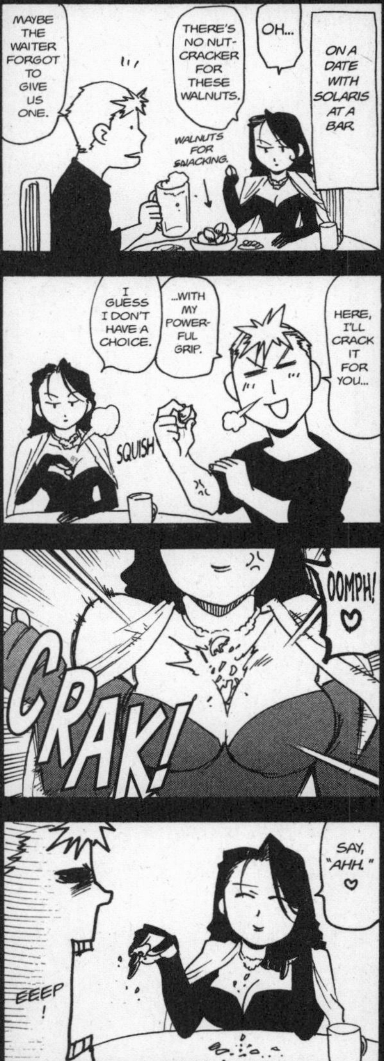
ON A DATE WITH SOLARIS AT A BAR
OH...
THERE'S NO NUT-CRACKER FOR THESE WALNUTS.
MAYBE THE WAITER FORGOT TO GIVE US ONE.
WALNUTS FOR SNACKING.
HERE, I'LL CRACK IT FOR YOU...
...WITH MY POWER-FUL GRIP.
I GUESS I DON'T HAVE A CHOICE.
SQUISH
OOMPH! ♡
CRAK!
SAY, "AHH." ♡
EEEP!
SHELL FRAGMENTS

A Day in the Life of Father

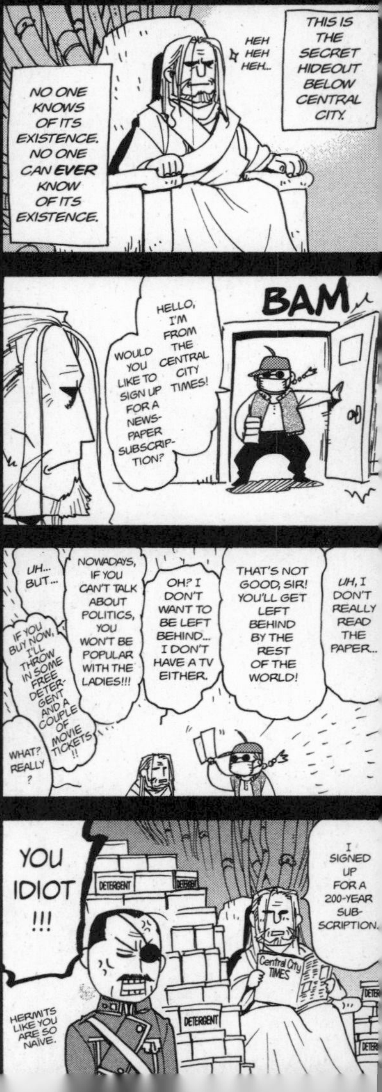
THIS IS THE SECRET HIDEOUT BELOW CENTRAL CITY.
HEH HEH HEH...
NO ONE KNOWS OF ITS EXISTENCE. NO ONE CAN EVER KNOW OF ITS EXISTENCE.
BAM
HELLO, I'M FROM THE CENTRAL CITY TIMES!
WOULD YOU LIKE TO SIGN UP FOR A NEWS-PAPER SUBSCRIP-TION?
UH, I DON'T REALLY READ THE PAPER...
THAT'S NOT GOOD, SIR! YOU'LL GET LEFT BEHIND BY THE REST OF THE WORLD!
OH? I DON'T WANT TO BE LEFT BEHIND... I DON'T HAVE A TV EITHER.
NOWADAYS, IF YOU CAN'T TALK ABOUT POLITICS, YOU WON'T BE POPULAR WITH THE LADIES!!!
UH... BUT...
IF YOU BUY NOW, I'LL THROW IN SOME FREE DETER-GENT AND A COUPLE OF MOVIE TICKETS!!
WHAT? REALLY?
I SIGNED UP FOR A 200-YEAR SUB-SCRIPTION.
Central City TIMES
DETERGENT
YOU IDIOT!!!
HERMITS LIKE YOU ARE SO NAIVE.

FULLMETAL ALCHEMIST 17

SPECIAL THANKS to:

SANKICHI HINODEYA
JUN TOHKO
AIYABALL
NONO
Big bro YOICHI KAMITONO
MASASHI MIZUTANI
SAKAMAKI
COUPON
NORIKO TSUBOTA
HARUHI NAKAMU
JUNSHI BABA sensei
MASANARI YUZUKA sensei
ICHTYS sensei
My Editor YOICHI SHIMOMURA

AND...YOU!!

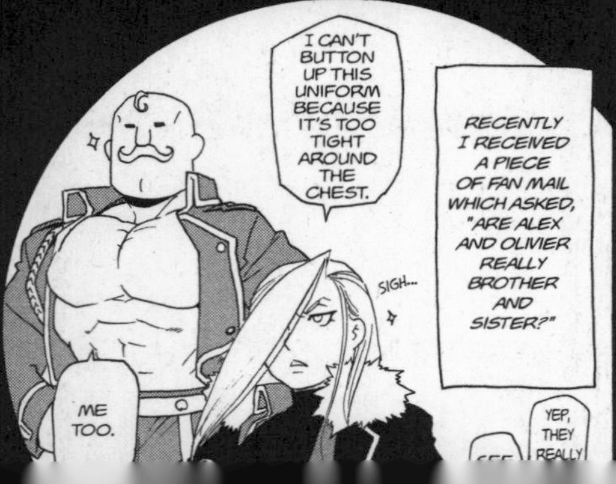
RECENTLY I RECEIVED A PIECE OF FAN MAIL WHICH ASKED, "ARE ALEX AND OLIVIER REALLY BROTHER AND SISTER?"
I CAN'T BUTTON UP THIS UNIFORM BECAUSE IT'S TOO TIGHT AROUND THE CHEST.
SIGH...
YEP, THEY REALLY
ME TOO.

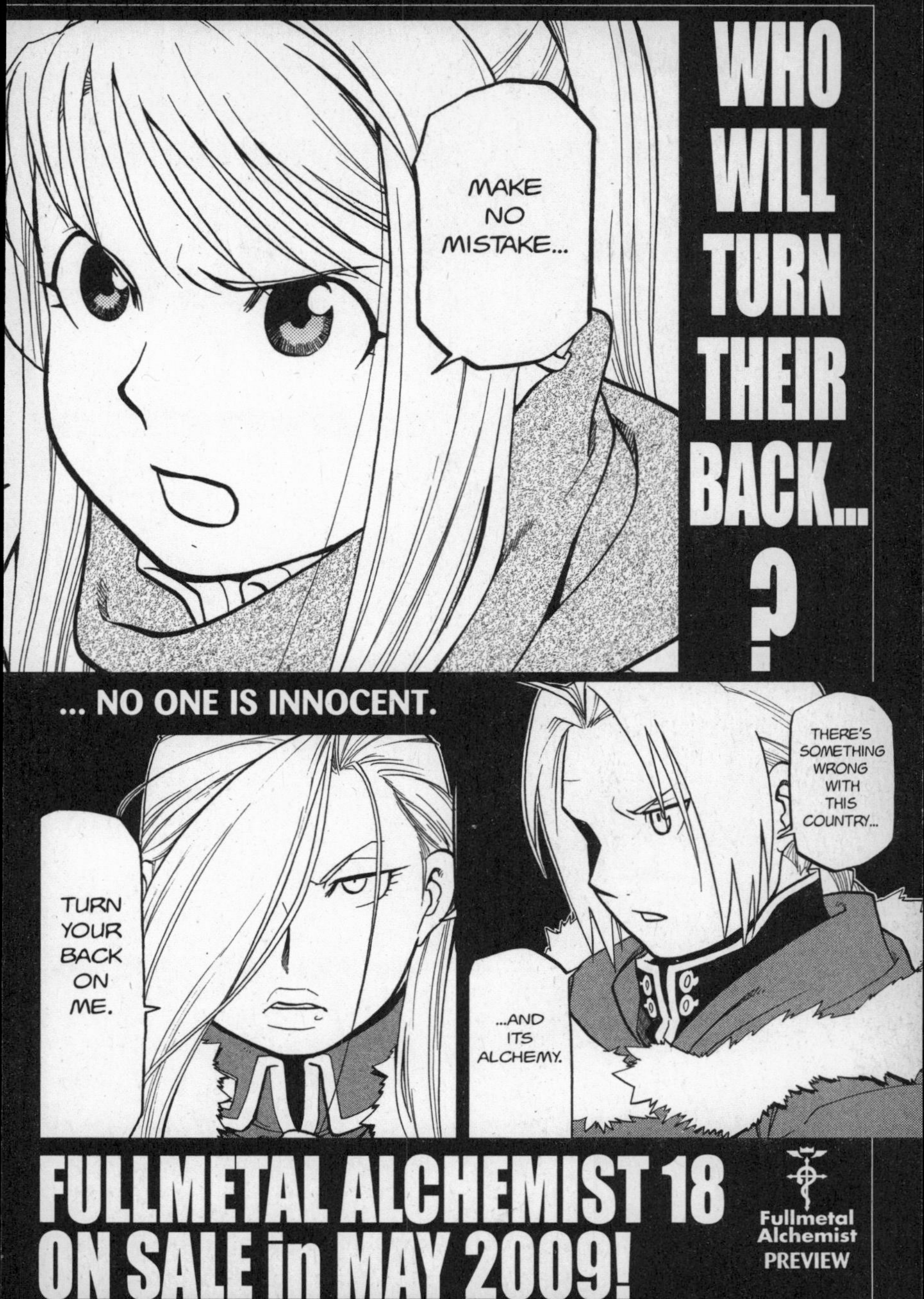
WHO WILL TURN THEIR BACK...?
MAKE NO MISTAKE...
... NO ONE IS INNOCENT.
THERE'S SOMETHING WRONG WITH THIS COUNTRY...
...AND ITS ALCHEMY.
TURN YOUR BACK ON ME.
FULLMETAL ALCHEMIST 18
ON SALE in MAY 2009!
Fullmetal Alchemist
PREVIEW

SECOND DAUGHTER
ELDEST DAUGHTER
THIRD DAUGHTER
ELDEST SON
THE ARMSTRONG FAMILY'S FIVE SIBLINGS
FOURTH DAUGHTER
CATHERINE
ALEX
STRONGINE
AMUE
OLIVIER

AWW...

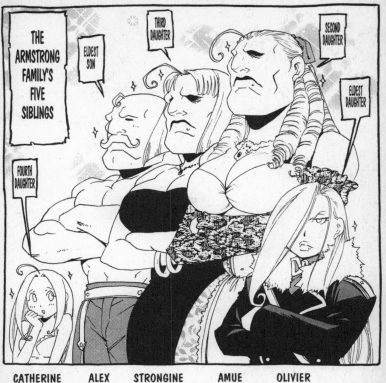

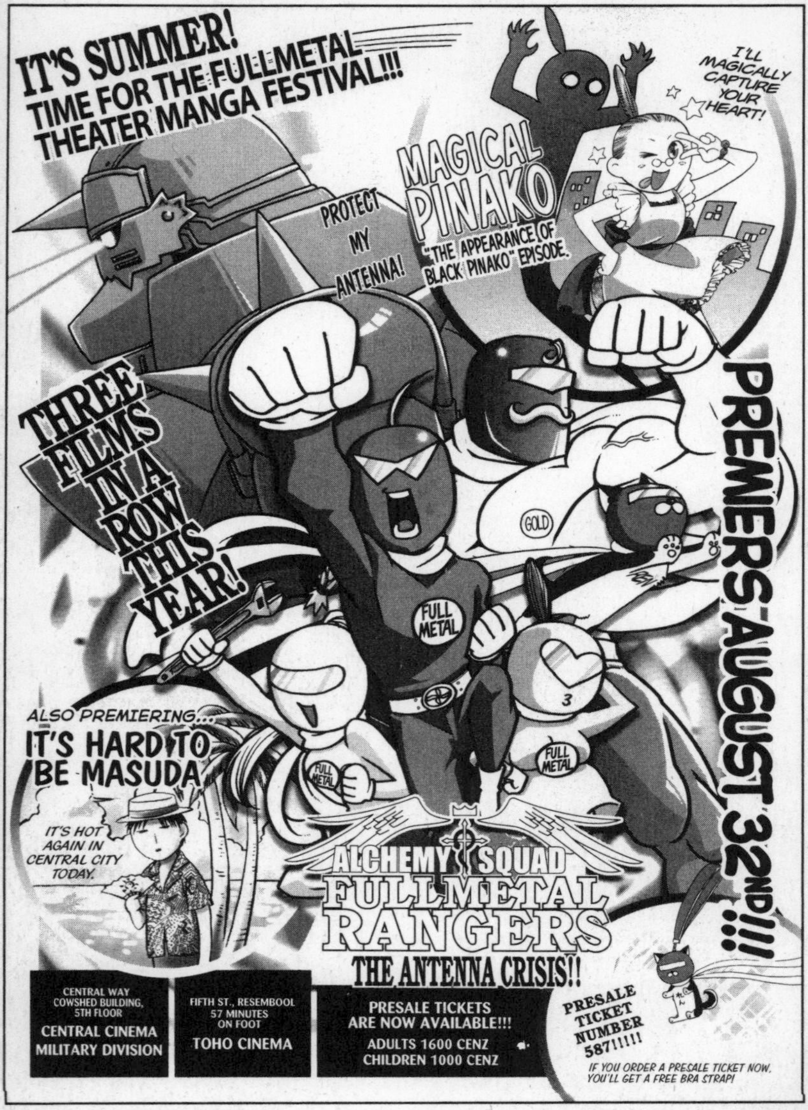
IT'S SUMMER!
TIME FOR THE FULLMETAL THEATER MANGA FESTIVAL!!!
I'LL MAGICALLY CAPTURE YOUR HEART!
MAGICAL PINAKO
"THE APPEARANCE OF BLACK PINAKO" EPISODE.
PROTECT MY ANTENNA!
THREE FILMS IN A ROW THIS YEAR!
PREMIERS AUGUST 32ND!!!!
GOLD
FULL METAL
FULL METAL
FULL METAL
3
ALSO PREMIERING...
IT'S HARD TO BE MASUDA
IT'S HOT AGAIN IN CENTRAL CITY TODAY.
ALCHEMY SQUAD
FULLMETAL RANGERS
THE ANTENNA CRISIS!!
CENTRAL WAY COWSHED BUILDING, 5TH FLOOR
CENTRAL CINEMA MILITARY DIVISION
FIFTH ST., RESEMBOOL 57 MINUTES ON FOOT
TOHO CINEMA
PRESALE TICKETS ARE NOW AVAILABLE!!!
ADULTS 1600 CENZ
CHILDREN 1000 CENZ
PRESALE TICKET NUMBER 587!!!!!
IF YOU ORDER A PRESALE TICKET NOW, YOU'LL GET A FREE BRA STRAP!

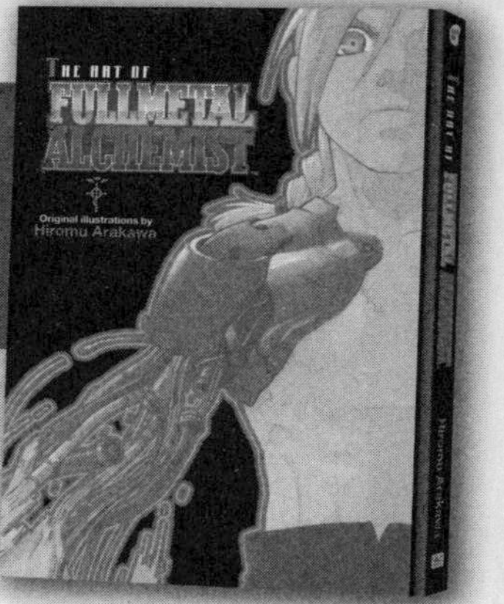
The Art of
Fullmetal
Alchemist
Original illustrations by
Hiromu Arakawa

The Art of Fullmetal Alchemist

- Manga artwork and illustrations from 2001 to 2003
- Color title pages, Japanese tankobon and promotional artwork
- Main character portraits & character designs from the video games
- Special two-page message from series creator Hiromu Arakawa

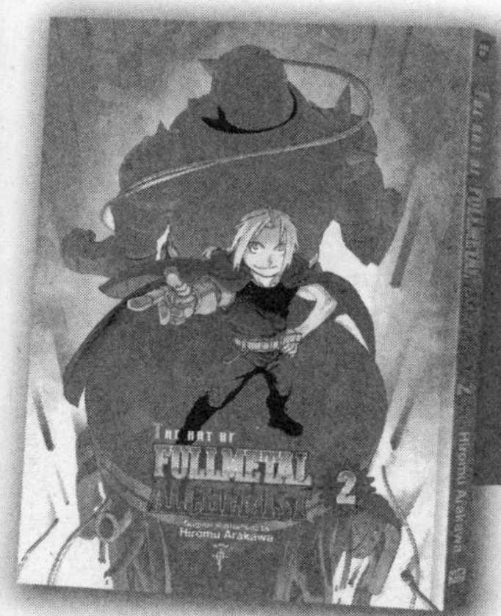
The Art of
Fullmetal
Alchemist
2
Hiromu Arakawa

The Art of Fullmetal Alchemist 2

- Original color manga artwork
- Illustrations presented in sequential order with commentary from creator from Hiromu Arakawa
- Character designs for the FMA PS2 video game
- Brand new manga pages

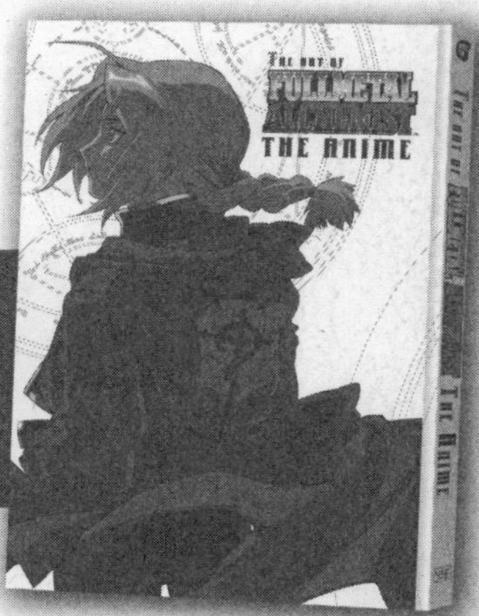
The Art of
Fullmetal
Alchemist
The Anime

The Art of Fullmetal Alchemist: The Anime

- Initial character designs and artwork
- Cel art
- Production notes
- Interview with Yoshiyuki Itoh, character designer for the anime

FULLMETAL ALCHEMIST™

ART OF

viz media™

www.viz.com
store.viz.com

An Artful Science

Complete your *Fullmetal Alchemist* collection with these art books—buy yours today at store.viz.com!

Fullmetal Alchemist Profiles

Get the background story and world history of the manga, plus:

- Character bios
- New, original artwork
- Interview with creator Hiromu Arakawa
- Bonus manga episode only available in this book

Fullmetal Alchemist Anime Profiles

Stay on top of your favorite episodes and characters with:

- Actual cel artwork from the TV series
- Summaries of all 51 TV episodes
- Definitive cast biographies
- Exclusive poster for your wall

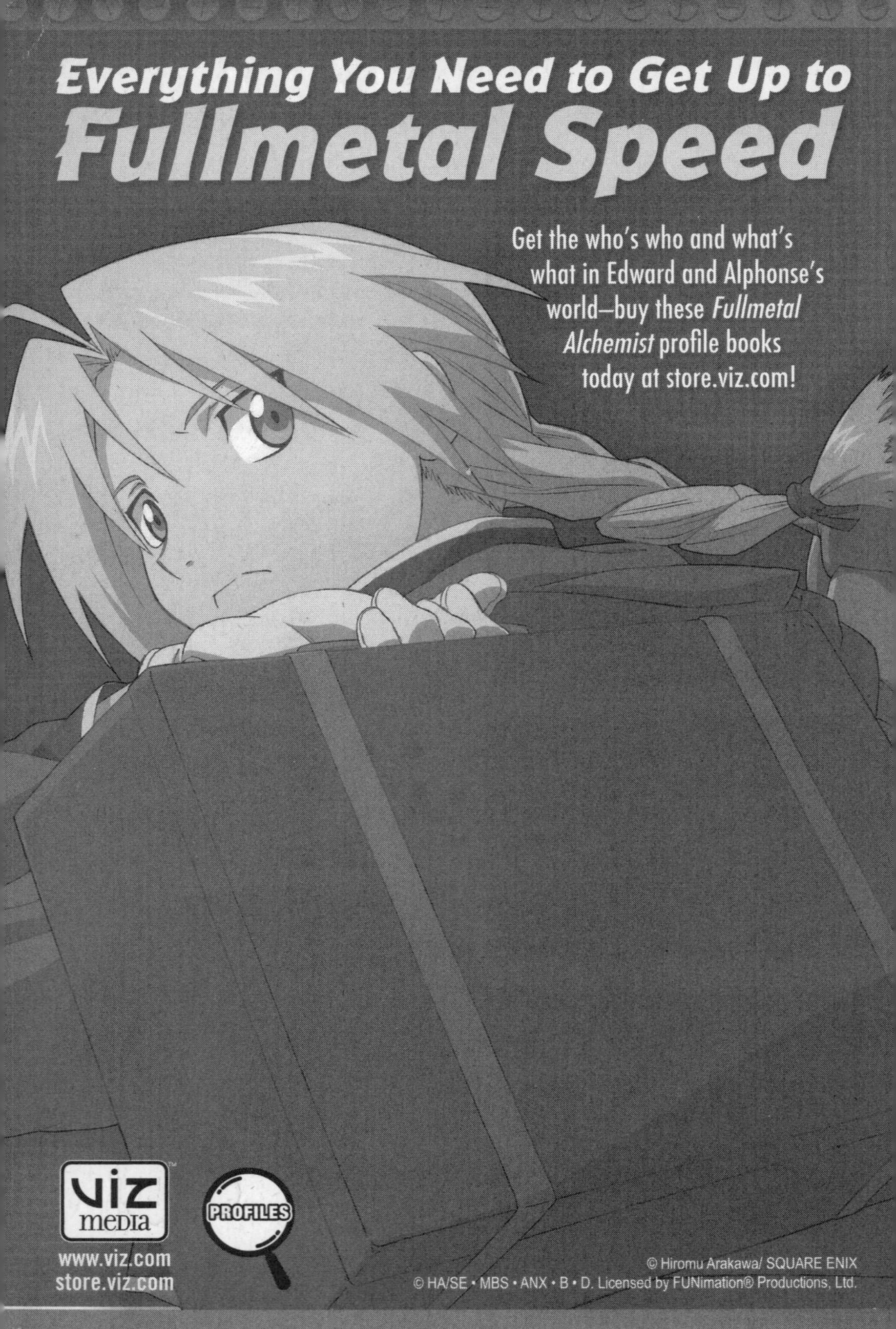
Everything You Need to Get Up to
Fullmetal Speed
Get the who's who and what's what in Edward and Alphonse's world—buy these *Fullmetal Alchemist* profile books today at store.viz.com!
VIZ media
PROFILES
www.viz.com
store.viz.com
© Hiromu Arakawa/ SQUARE ENIX
© HA/SE • MBS • ANX • B • D. Licensed by FUNimation® Productions, Ltd.

LOVE MANGA?
LET US KNOW WHAT YOU THINK!

OUR MANGA SURVEY IS NOW
AVAILABLE ONLINE. PLEASE VISIT:
VIZ.COM/MANGASURVEY

P9-DDM-410

CHASE BRANCH LIBRARY
17731 W. SEVEN MILE
DETROIT, MI 48235
578-8002

HELP US MAKE THE MANGA
YOU LOVE BETTER!

FULLMETAL ALCHEMIST © Hiromu Arakawa/SQUARE ENIX INUYASHA © 1997 Rumiko TAKAHASHI/Shogakukan Inc.
NAOKI URASAWA'S MONSTER © 1995 Naoki URASAWA Studio Nuts/Shogakukan Inc. ZATCH BELL! © 2001 Makoto RAIKU/Shogakukan Inc.